CW00340045

Sir Robert Brooke's New Cases With March's Translation

Robert Brooke

SIR ROBERT BROOKE'S NEW CASES

WITH

MARCH'S TRANSLATION.

ADVERTISEMENT.

IN purſuance of our plan to reprint, in a handſome form, a Series of the Early Reports, that, by reaſon of antiquity or ſome other cauſe, have become rare, and in many inſtances impoſſible to procure, we now produce Bellewe's Collection of Brooke's New Caſes, temp. Henry VIII., Edward VI., and Queen Mary, firſt publiſhed in 1578, ſeven years prior to Bellewe's Caſes, temp. Richard II.

Though compiled by Bellewe, there is no indication in the volume known and cited as " Brooke's New Caſes" that he was the author, but in the very quaint and intereſting epiſtle prefixed to the "Caſes temp. Richard II." Bellewe ſtates that the favour extended to his Collection of Brooke's New Caſes prevailed with him to publiſh another volume.

For reaſons given by Bellewe in the above

Advertisement.

mentioned Epiftle, he compiled the two collections upon different fyftems, one under years, and the other under titles; but it would feem that the chronological arrangement was not fo ufeful as the other, for MARCH, in his *tranfla-tion* of Brooke's New Cafes, has reduced them alphabetically under their proper heads and titles. Both the original and the tranflation having long been very fcarce, and the mif-paging and other errors in March's book making a new and corrected edition peculiarly defirable, we here reprint the two books in one volume, uniform with the preceding volumes of our feries.

We have to acknowledge the valuable aid afforded us by Mr. Alfred Kingfton, of the Public Record Office, and Honorary Secretary of the Camden Society, in reading the proof-fheets and fuperintending the progrefs of this work through the prefs.

Our warmeft thanks are alfo due to RALPH D. M. LITTLER, Efq. Q.C., for kind per-miffion to make ufe of any volumes we might require out of his valuable and moft complete law library.

THE PUBLISHERS.

February, 1873.

¶ASCVNS
Nouell cases de
les ans et temps le Roy,
H.8. Ed.6. et la Roygne Mary,
Escrie ex la graund Abridgement,
compose per Sir Robert
Brooke Chiualer &c.
la disperse en les
Titles. Mes icy
collect sub
ans.
(.·.)

ANNO DO. 1578.

¶ *In aedibus Richardi*
Tottelli.

☞ Cum priuilegio.

ASCVNS NOUELL CASES.

Anno fexto Henrici octaui in banco Regis Rotulo. 22.

Conc 2. M. 1.
B. Judgmēt
147. in fine.

OME recouer per def. vers inf. & linf. port br̄e derrour, & reuerfe ceo pur ſo nonage. Et econtra, ſil vſt appeare & perde per plea, ou per voucher, il ne ceo reuerſera per nonage. *Brooke, Sauer del defaut* 50.

Nonage ſaue
defaut.
Recouery vers
enfant per def.
& per acc trie
diuerſitie.

¶ *Anno* 14. *Henrici octaui.*

Vide 13. H. 8.
Fo. 13. p. Newd
& fo. 14. p Brud
33. H. 6. 12.

39. H. 6. 21.
p Prifot.

2 ¶ Nota quant eſt nul patron come ou le prior eſt prieſt, & ē admit a ceo benefice demeſn̄. Ou lou mon aduowſon eſt alien en mortmayne, & approper a vn meaſon de religion, Et ſimilia : in ceux caſes ieo poy auer Quare impedit, & la plenartie p vj. mois neſt plee. *B. Plenerty.* 10.

Ou plenertie
neſt plee.
Mortmaine.
Perſon en
perſon.

¶ *Anno* 15. *Henrici octaui.*

Conc. M. 26.
H. 8. in Eſſex,
et Fitzh. in ca-
mera Ducat

3 ¶ Nota q̄ dictum fuit pro lege, que taile poit eſtre de copy holde, & q̄ formedon poit giſer de ceo in diſcēd per proteſtac̄, in nature de

Formedon en
deſcender per
copyholder.

B briefe

briefe de formed in difcend al commen ley, et
bone per omnes Juftic̃, car cõt q̃ formedon in
difcend ne fuit done nifi per ſtatute, vnc̃ ore
ceſt bře gyſt al commen ley, et ſerra entende
que ceo ad eſte vn cuſtõe la de tēpore &c. et
le dďt recouera p aduiſe de toutes les Juſtices.
B. Tenant per copie 24.

Intendement (margin)

Lanc. (margin)
Litt. 16. (margin)
4 El. Com 233 (margin)
Weſt 2. ca. 1. (margin)
Raſt. Taile. 1. (margin)

Ann̄ 17. *Henrici octaui.*

Difcont ou non-
fuit in feconde
deliuerance. (margin)

4 ¶ Nota per opinionē curie, q̃ ſi hõe
ſoit nõſue in repleuine, et reť eſt agard, et le
pł port briefe de ſeconde deliueraunce, et ſuffeř
ceo deſtre diſcontinue, reť irreplegiable ſerra
ag. ſibien cõe ſi le pł vſt eſtre nonſue en le bře
de ſecond deliueraunce, *B. Ret. de auers* 37.
Second deliuerance 15.

19. H. 8. 11. (margin)
6. & 7. E. 6. (margin)
Com. 82. (margin)

Ann̄ 18. *Henrici octaui.*

Cafus ſir T.
Louel heredib'
maſcul' Patent
le roy, & en
graunt dun
comen perſon
diuerſitie. (margin)

5 ¶ Roy done ťř a I. S. et heredibus
maſcuł ſuis. Et fuit adiuge p touts les Juſt.
in Camera Scaccař q̃ le graũt eſt void, eo q̃ le
roy eſt deceiue en ſon graunt, car ceo founde in
fee ſimple, ou vt videtur le roy ne intend niſi
eſtate taile, quel neſt iſſint expreſſe, et ideo ore
nē que tenant a volunt. Et econtra in caſu
cõmunis pſone. *B. Patents* 104. *Eſtates.* 84.

Raſt. 60. (margin)
M. 9. & 10. El. (margin)
Com. 335. (margin)

Litt 6. (margin)
Raſt. 60. (margin)
27. H. 8. 27. (margin)

Ann̄ 19. *Henrici octaui.*

Home plede
non culp, et puis
pled pardon. (margin)

6 ¶ Nota ſi felon ad pardon de pleder, et
plede non culp̃, il pdra laduantage de ſon
pardon, & ne c̄ pledra apres. *B. Corone* 199.

M. 3. M. 1. (margin)
contra 11. H. 4. (margin)
41. per Huls et (margin)
Tirwith accord. (margin)

Court baron al
maner incident.
Graunts. (margin)

7 ¶ Court baron eſt incident al manner.
Et court de pipowders al faire. Et fuit dit
arguend, quod ideo le ſeignior del maner ou
faire,

33 H. 8. 210. (margin)
D. S. 11. (margin)
8. H. 7. 4. P. (margin)
Vaviſour. (margin)

faire, ne poet graunt oufter le court baron, ne le court de pipowders, Ou fils grāt le manor oue le faīr, ils ne poient referue tielz courts, car font incidēt &c. *B. Incidents* 34.

8 ¶ Ou home eſt barre per faux verdiĉt, et port attaint ꝑs le prīm ī, nontenure neſt plee, car il eſt priuye, Contr̄ dun eſtranger, come ou le tenaunt enfeoffe eſtranger puis. *B. Non-tenure* 6.

Nontenure bone
plee en attaint
pur eſtrange.
Contr pur priuy.

Anñ 20. *Henrici octaui.*

9 ¶ Det fur obligaē oue conditiō de per-forme touts couenaunts conteine in certein in-dentures, le def. ne poit plede le condīĉt et reherfe les couenants, et dire generalment que il ad performe touts les couenaunts, mes monſtre comt, per Prenotar. *B. Conditions* 2.

Special monſtrās
del performance
de condic cōtein
in indentures.

10 ¶ Si Labbe et couēt dōe toutz lour terres et poſſeſſiōs a auī in fee, vncore le cor-poration remayne, per *Fitzh.* Juſtice *B. Extinguiſhment* 35.

Corporation.
Ou nontenure
ferra bone plee
en attaint, et
ou nemy.

11 ¶ En attaynt nontenure neſt plee pur priuie al primer accion, contra pur eſtraunger al primer action. (*B. Nontenure* 16) Et Dicitur q̄ neſt plee en attaint, adīr̄ q̄ le pl'en le attaint ad enter puis le darrayne continuance. *B. Nontenure* 22.

Entre en attaint
puis le darr cōt.

13 ¶ Nota per Juſtīc, q̄ ſi home graunt, ꝓximā prefentationem al A. et puis deuāt auoydāce graunt ꝓximam prefentationem eiuſ-dem ecclefie a B. le fecōd graunt eſt void, car ceo fuit graunt oufter ꝑ le graūtour deuant. Et il nauera le feconde prefentment, car le graūt ne import ceo. *B. Prefentation* 52.

Deux graunts de
prox. prefentac'.

¶ Anno

❡ *Anno* 21. *Henrici octaui.*

Eſtate in fee durant vie I. S.

14 ❡ Dicitur p lege, q̃ ſi feoffem̃t ſoit fait a W. N. durant le vie J. S. hec v̄ba (durãt le vie J. S.) &c. ſerront voides, car ſont cõtrariants al fee. Contrarium de feſſement en fee cy longe que Paules ſteeple eſtoiera. *B. Eſtates* 50.

27. H. 8. 29.
contra.
Vide 24. H. 8. 56.

Poſterioritie.

15 ❡ Home ad terre in vſe, dount part eſt tenus de A. per prioritie, et le reſt del roy p poſteriority in chiualrie, et deuy, le roy auera le garde del corps per ſon Prerogatiue, et per leſtatute de 4. H. 7. que done le garde de ceſty que vſe, ou nul volunt eſt declare, et p Prerogatiuam regis. Tamē aliter dicitur de terre en vſu tenus del comen perſon, car le tenant en vſe ne deuie ſeiſie, et ideo extra caſ. Prerogatiue pur le terre. *B. Prerogatiue.* 29.

Terre in vſe.

Vide 3. EL. Com. 240.
4 H. 7. ca. 17.
Pre. Re. cap. 2.
Stp. 9. & 4. E. 6 Com. 59. per Mountegue econtra.
Pre. Re. ca. 1.

❡ *Anno* 22. *Henrici octaui.*

Leaſe de tenaunt pur vie eſt void per ſon mort. Voyd & voidable leaſe diũſity.

16 ❡ Nota per *Fitziames* et *Engleſilde* Juſtices, ſi tenant in dower leſſa pur ans rend rent et deuye, le leaſe eſt voide, & acceptãce per lheire del rent ne voit faire le leaſe bone, car fuit void deuãt. Contra de voidable leaſes. *B. Acceptance* 14.

24. H. 8. 54.

Coſtes in Quare impedit.

17 ❡ Nota per *Spilman* Juſtice que al commen ley, home recouer coſtes en Quare imped̃. Mes econtra puis leſtatut Weſt. 2 cap. 5. pur ceo q̃ leſtat̃ done graund damages en Quare imp̄. *B. Coſtes* 25.

9. H. 6. 32.
per Newton.
27. H. 6. 10.
Weſt. 2. cap. 5.

Præmunire per bille.

18 ❡ Dicebatur que Premunire ſerra maintenable per byll in banco Regis, coment que le partie ne ſoyt in cuſtod̃ mareſcalli. (*B. Byll* 1.) Et fuit comen que plur̃ clarkes fueront arctes

27. H. 6. 5.
econtra.

de

de reſponder al billes la, que ne fueront in cuſtođ mareſcalli, *B. Præmunire* 1.

19 ¶ Nota que nul poet faire proclamation, mes per aucthoritye del Roy, ou Maiors, et huiuſmodi, que oũt priuiledge in Cities et burroughes de ceo faire, ou ount vſe ceo p cuſtome. Et ſir Edmõd Knightly executor a ſir Williã Spencer fiſt proclamations in certein market villes q̃ les creditors veignera per certeine iour, et claima et prouera lour dets &c. due p le teſtator, et pur ceo q̃ il ceo fiſt ſans aucthoritie, il fuit cõmit al Fleete, et miſe a vn fine. *B. Proclamation*. 10. — Pena pur feiser d'pclamation sans aucthoritie.

19. E. 4. 9. Vide 21. H. 7. 9. — 20 ¶ Home ne pledra record, niſi fuerit in eađ curia vbi recordum illud remanet, ſauns monſtre le recorde exemplifie ſub magno ſigillo Anglie, ſil ſoit denie, car doit vener in Canc. per Cerciorare, et la deſte exemplifie ſub magno ſigillo, Car ſi ſoit exemplifie ſub ſigillo de communi banco, Scaccario, vel hm̃di, ceux ne ſount niſi euidence al iurie. *B. Recorde*. 65. — Exemplification, et sub quo sigillo

Vide 11. H. 7. 2. p Fairefax.

3. H. 7. 3. per Keble. Stp. 63. 21. E. 4. 2. per Noting. — 21 ¶ Dictur pro lege que nul poit trauerſe niſi il fait title a meſme le terre in les premiſſes, ou parcloſe de ſon trauerſe. *B. Trauerſe doſfice* 48. — Title fait sur trauerse tende.

St. 34. C. Vide 9. E. 4. 28. p Neele. — 23 ¶ Nota q̃ al ſeſſions a Newgate home fuit iudge deſte pende, et liuer al vic̃ a faire execution, et puis eſcape & ſua al eſgliſe. Et auoit le priuiledge de ceo. *B. Corone* 110. *in fine*. — Felon puis iudgmẽt auoit le priuiledge desgl'.

Ann 23. Henrici octaui.

Vide 24. H. 8. 47. — 23 ¶ En action ſur leſtatute de Anno H. 8 6 de forcible entrie. Ou in trñs ſur 5. R. 2. — Son frankt nul plees en acc sur

vbi

vbi ingreſſus nõ datur per legem. Non ingreſſus eſt contra formam ſtatuti, eſt bone plee,
Mes ſon franketenement neſt plee. Vt dicitur
per *Sherwood* & alios. *B. Accion ſur leſtatut* 40.

24. ❡ Fuit dit que ſeignior de manour ne
poit tener court, ne faire iuſtice ſãs deux ſutors,
et ſils deuie, ou q̃ ne ſoit niſi vn ſutor, le
manour eſt determine, car neſt manor ſãs
ſutors. *B. Court baron* 22 *in fine.*

25. ❡ Home recoũ rent & arrerages p aſſiſe,
Ou ſil recoũ annuitie et arrerages de ceo en
briefe dannuitie, le def. deuie, le pleintiſe port
ſcire faċ Ꝑſus lheire, il nauera ſon age del
arrerages, car ceux ſont reals, et parcel del rent,
ou annuitie. Mes ſi le iudgement ſoit del
arrerages et damages, la il aũa. s. age (*B. Age.*
50) Et ou il recouer en briefe dannuitie ou
aſſiſe come deuant, Ou ad auowe pur rent que
eſt franketenement, et recouer les arrerages
ſauns coſtes & dammages, il nauera action
de det de ceo, mes ſcīr facias, car eſt real.
Mes ou il ad iudgement de ceo oue coſtes &
damages queux va enſemble iſſint q̃ ſoit mixt
oue le perſonaltie, donques gyſt briefe de dette
vers lheire del arrerages et damages (*Et hoc*
B. penſe in default del execuc') per Curiam. *B.*
Det 212. & *Age* 50.

26 ❡ Per *Fitzh.* & *Curiam,* ou briefe
derrour fuit ſue de remouer record extra communem bancum in bancum regis, enter vn
Abbe & I. N. le garrantie dattourney vary en
le rolle en le noſme Labbe, & fuit amend puis
iudgement. Et ſils ne vſſent ceo amende, ils
diſount que ceux del banke le roy voyent ceo
amender. *B. Amendment* 85. en fine.

27 ❡ Dictum

leitat de 8. H.
6. ou 5. R. 2

Neſt manour
ſans ſutors.

Arr de rent ou
dannuitie, &
dam. diūſitie.

Scire facias
vers lheire.
Choſe real, et
choſe perſonal
diuerſitie.

Auowrie.

Coſtes.

Lou det gift, &
ou Scire facias,
diuerſitie.

Variance amend
puis iudgment.

27. H. 8. 26.

33. H. 8. 210.

Conc. Kirton
43. E. 3. 2.

24. H. 8. 43.

Conc. T. 25.
H. 8.

27 ¶ Diⁿum fuit pro lege, Si A. leſſa le terre de I. N. a moy pur ans, rend rent, le leſſee ent, & paya le rent al leſſor, le leſſour eſt diſſeiſour, car ceo counteruault vn commaundement dentre. Et ceſty que commaund eſt diſſeiſour, quod nota per ſon voide leaſe. *B. Diſſeiſ.* 77.

Fitzh. 179. G.

11. H. 4. 34.
p. Thirning.

Leaſe de terre dauter home.

Commaunder eſt diſſeiſor.

28 ¶ Nota per *Fitſh.* et *Curiam,* ſi home recouer en briefe dannuitie, il auera fieri facias del arrerages encurre deins lan, et ſcire facias puis, cy toſt que lannuity eſt arrere, & nunquam briefe dannuity arrere, car eſt executorye. Et eadem lex de acc̄, & iudgement ſur compoſition que eſt executorie de tempore in tēpus, et huiuſmodi. Et in cheſcun ſcire facias, en q̄ il recouer puis le primer iudgement, il auera execution de arrerages deins lan per fieri facias, car cheſcun eſt foundue ſur le iudgement. *B. Executions.* 119. *Scire facias.* 213.

6. E. 6.
Com. 137.

2. H. 6. 9. caſ. 6.

De choſe executorie home aver execuc̄ imppetuum per ſcire facias.

6. E. 4. 1.

7. E. 4. 9.
per Choke.

29 ¶ Fuit notiue per *Fitzher.* et auters, que en aⁿion de det vers execut An. 34. H. 6. ſur obligatiō lour teſtatour, que plede nient ſon fait, et troue encounter eux, le iudgement per le recorde ſoit, que le pl' rec̄ des biens le mort ſil ad, & pur ceo que le liuer alarge, fol. 24. eſt report vltra in hec verba, & ſil nad, donques de bonis propriis, queux parolx ne ſont en le recorde, fuyt commaunde per eux damend le liuer, car eſt contrary al record, et iſſint miſreported. *B. Executours,* 22.

Exec' deder le fait lour teſtatour.

30 ¶ Nota per *Fitzh.* pur clere ley, que en briefe de faux iudgement in nullo eſt erratum neſt plee, car ils ioynder iſſue ſur aſcun matter en fait certaine all' per le partie, et ſerra

In nullo eſt erratum.

Trial in faux iudgment, &

ſerra trie per pais, car neſt recorde, Contra in error. *B. Faux iudg.* 17.

31 ℭ Home fait feffement dun meaſon cum pertineñ, riens paſſa per hec verba cum pertineñ, mes le gardein, le curtilage, & cloſe adioinãt al meaſon, et ſur que le meaſon eſt edifie, et nul auter terre, coment que auter īre ad eē occupie oue le meaſ. *B. Feoffements* 53.

32 ℭ Ceſty que ad eē ſeiſi peaceablement per 3. ans poit reteyner oue force. Mes ſi diſſeiſour ad continue ſon poſſeſſion 3. ans peaceablement, et puis le diſſeiſie reentre (come il poet loyalment) et puis le diſſeiſor reentre, il ne poet deteine oue force, pur ceo que ceo primer diſſeiſine eſt determyne per lentrie del diſſeiſie, et le diſſeiſie per ceo remitte, et ceo entrie eſt vn nouel dyſſeiſin. Mes ſi home ad eē ſeiſie per bon et iuſt title per 3. ans, et puys eſt diſſeiſie per tort, et puis il reenter, il poet reteine oue force, car il eſt remitte et eins per ſon primer title, per que il primes couñt peaceablement per 3. ans, per quoſdam : car videtur illis per le prouiſo in le fine del ſtatute que ceſt bone ley en ceo darrain caſe, et ſtat bene cum ſtatuto, tamen per aliquos ceo neſt ley, ideo quere. *B. Forcible entrie,* 22.

33 ℭ Si ieo ay title per Formedon, ou Cui in vita, & enter, & lauter recouer enuers moy, ieo ſue remitte a mon primer aɛtion. Mes ſi home recouer enuers moy per faux tytle per aɛtyon trie, ou ieo ſue eins per bone title, ieo auera tunc error ou attaint, ou briefe de droyt. *B. Iudgement* 111.

34 ℭ Nota pro lege, ſi paine ſoit miſe ſur home

Margin left:
en bre derrour diuerſitie,
Feoffement dun meaſon cū ptin.
Ou home poet ten oue force, & ou nemy.
Remitter.
Quære.
Lou home ſerra reſtore al primer acc, & lou auer Errour, Attaint, ou bre de droit.
Paine en le leete

Margin right:
9. E. 4. 32.
31. H. 8. 160.
Vide 6. & 7. E. 6. Com. 36. per Hales iuſtice.
4. M. 1. Com. 171.
6. & 7. E. 6. Com 85.
3. M. 1. Com. 168.
27. H. 6. 2.
22. H. 6. 18.
Poſt. 40.

home en leete pur redreſſer noiſance per vn
iour ſub pena 1 0. li. et puis eſt preſent que il
ne ceo fiſt, et forfeitera le payne, ceſt bone
preſentment et le paine ne ſerra auterment

10. H. 7. 4.
per Keble.
Conc. Vauiſor
13. H. 7. 19.

affere. Et le ſeignior auera action de det
cleremēt. Mes il ne poit diſtreine, et faire
auowrie Niſi p p̄ſcripc. duſage de diſtreine et
faire auowrie. *B. Leete*, 37.

Vide Stp. 31.

35 ¶ Si le roy licence ſon tenant daliener
ſon manner de Dale, & il alien ceo except vn
acre, le lycence ne ſeruera ceo, car la le roy neſt
aſcerten de ſ. tenaunt de tout. Et ſi iay licence
denparker 200. acres, et ceo fait accorde, et
puis encreaſe per aut 10. acres, la ceo neſt
parke. *B. Patents.* 76.

36 ¶ Dictum fuit que home auera briefe de
Electione cuſtodie dun rent, et hoc deuaunt
ſeiſine de ceo, car ſeiſine in ley ſerra ent adiudge
ratione que il ne poet reſceue ceo deuaunt le
rent iour. Tamen econtra de terre, car la il
poyt enter. *B. Quare Eiecit infra terminum*, 5.

14. H. 8. 23.
per Brudnel.

Vid 25. H. 8. 87

37 ¶ Recouery vers baron et ſemme per
briefe dentre en le poſt, ou le ſeme eſt tenant in
taile, et ils vouch ouſter, & iſſint le demaūdant
recouer vers le baron et feme, et ils ouſter in
value, ceo liera le tayle et lheire le femme. *B.*
Recouerie in value 27.

38 ¶ Recouery ſur voucher p̄s tenaunt in
taile eſt barre ratione del recompence in value.
Et recouery per briefe dentre in le poſt per
ſingle voucher ne done, mes leſtat que le teñ in
taile ad in poſſ. tempore recuperationis, iſſint
que ſil fuit eyns dauter eſtate que le taile, la le
tayle neſt lye vers lheire. Mes le double
voucher eſt de faire le tenāt in tayle pur diſ-

c   continuer

Marginal notes:

pur redreſſer nuſance forfait per preſentment.

Lou le ſnr auera det ſur paine en leet, Et ou diſtreinera pur ceo.

Licence le Roy nient purſue.

Electione cuſtod' dun rent deuant ſeiſin.
Contra de terre.

Ceſt aſſurance fuit fait per lad uiſe de Brudnel, & auts Juſtices.

Rec' en value pur lier le taile.

Single voucher, & double vouch. diuerſitie.

continuer et de porter le bře dentrie vers le
feoffee, et donques le feoffee vouchera le tenaunt
en tayle, et il vouchera oufter, et fic perdera, et
ceo liera toutes interestes et tayles que le vouche
ad. *B. Taile.* 32.

Rec' de lier cefty
en reuerc' p aid
prier & voucher.

39 ¶ Ou briefe dentre in le post est vers
tenant pur terme de vie de lier le fee fimple, il
doyt prayer ayde de cestuy en reuersion, et
donques ils de voucher fur le ioynder &c.   Et
autiel recouerie oue voucher est vse pur docker
le tayle in auncien demesne fur briefe de droyt,
et voucher ouster: Et cest de franketenement la.
Tamen *B.* dubitat de tiel recouery fur pleint la de
terre de base tenure, car ceo ne poit este garrant,
ideo quere.   *B. Recouerie in value* 27. *in medio.*

Auncien de-
mefn.

Quære.
Garrantie.

24. H. 8. 56.

40 ¶ Si home enter ou son entrie nest congeable, Come lheire in tayle puis difcontinu-
aunce, ou lheire dun feme, ou le feme mefme
puis difcont. Et lauter fur que il enter recouer
vers luy, la ila. s. lheire in taile, ou le femme,
ou son heire, est reftore a lour primer action de
Formedon, ou Cui in vita.   Tamen si tiel que
enter ou son entrie nest congeable, fait feoffement, et lauter fur que il enter recouer, ore le
primer action nest reftore al iffue en taile, ne al
femme, ne a son heire, ratione de le feffement
que extinct droyt et actyon.   Mes si tyel que
iffint enter, fait feoffement fur condition, et pur
le condytion enfreint reenter, deuant que cefty
fur q̃ il enter auoit recouer, et donques il recouer
puis le reentrie fait p le códić, la cefty que fift
le feoffement fur códition est reftore al son primer
action, car lentrie p le condition extinct son
feoffement.   *B. Reftore al primer action.* 5.

Remitter al pri.
mer accion, &
econtra.

Supra 33.

Acc nient reftor
cōe feoff. facti.
cōtr fur feoffemt
fur condic.

Droit extinct.

Conc. Fineux
9. H. 7. 25.
& Thorp 41.
E. 3. 18.

38. E. 3. 16.

41 ¶ Nota que le court de commen banke ne
voet

Cōtr en formd

16. E. 3. Fitzh.
Verdict 21.

3. M. 1. Com.
92. 93.

voet permit verdicte alarge en briefe dentre in
nature daffile, eo que fuit precipe quod reddat.
Tamen *B.* miratur inde, car luy femble que fur
chefcun general iffue verdict alarge poet efte
done. *B. Verdict* 85.

*Verdict alarge.
en bre dentre.*

46. E. 3. 31. V.
Waft 48.

N. B. 38.
Conc. Litt.
10. E. 4. 1.

42 ¶ Fuit dit pur ley, q̃ fi termor fait waft,
et fait executors & deuie, laccion de waft eft
perle, car c̃ ne gift Vs fes executors, mes pur
waft fait p eux m̃s, & nõ pur le waft le teftator,
car eft comen trñs, quod eft actio perfonalis que
moritur cum perfona. *B. VVaft.* 138.

*VVaft falt p ter-
mour q deuy de-
uant acc port.*

Anno 24. *Henrici octaui.*

23. H. 8. 26.

43 ¶ Nota quod ou garrantie de attourney
vary del nofme de corporation del partie, et brief
de errour fuit port a ceux del common banke,
ils ceo amend maintenaunt. Et dixerunt quod
hii de banco regis voile auer fayt fimiliter. *B.*
Amendement, 47.

*Amendemt puis
bre derror, vient
en comen bank.*

44 ¶ Caueatur in chefcun action tryable per
Jurie, del quantitie del terre, come ou home
demaunde 200. acres, ou ils ne font q̃ 100.60.
vel huiufmodi, et le title eft pur le demaund, la
fi le Jurie troue quod diffeifiuit eum del 200.
acres, vel huiufmodi, ceo eft matter de Attaint.

*Faux quantitie
en demaunde.*

1. E. 5. 6. per
Sulyard.
1. R. 3. 3. p.
Huff.

Et fic ou ils luy troue culp en trefpas vel huiufmodi, de plufours trefpaffes que il ne fift. Vel
de exceffiue damage et huiufmodi. *B. Attaint.* 96.

*Attaint de ex-
ceffe dam.*

45 ¶ Seignior et teñ per fealty et 3. d. de
rent, le feignior deuie, fon fẽe eft endowe del
feigniory, el poet diftreine pur i. d. et lheire pur
ii. d. et iffint ore le terre eft charge de 2. diftreffes,
ou il fuit charge nifi de vn deuaunt, Mes ceo
neft inconuenient, car il ne pay pluis rent que il
paye

*Terr charge oue
2. diftr. p. dower
de parte.*

Partitiō eſt cauſe de ij. diſtreſſes.

paye deuaunt. Eadem lex ou ſeygniorie eſt deuyde per partytion enter heyres females, et huiuſmodi. *B. Diſtreſſe.* 59. *Auowrie.* 139.

Molin.
Lou acc ſur le caſe giſt, & lou nemy diuerſitie.

46 ¶ Si iay molin en B. et auter fait auter molin la, per que ieo perd mon tolle per aler de diuers a ceo, vncore aƈtyon ne giſt. Contra ſi le molyn diſturbe lewe de vener a mō molin, La ieo auera aƈtyon ſur mō caſe. *B. Aƈtion ſur le caſe.* 42. in fine.

Conc. Newt.
22. H. 6. 15.
11. H. 4. 47.
per Hank.

Sur ſtatut de 5. R. 2. ſon frankt.

47 ¶ En treſpas ſur 5. R. 2. adire que le lieu &c. eſt le franketenement de J. N. et il per ſon commaundement entre, neſt plee, car laƈtion eſt done per leſtatut, & ideo doit auer ſpecial reſpons, et non vt in generall briefe de treſpas. *B. Aƈtion ſur leſtatute.* 15.

23. H. 8. 22.
Tēp. H. 8. 360.

Quel deuorce poet baſtarder liſſue, & quel nemy.

Deuorce puis mort.

48 ¶ Nota que fuit priſe per communem domum parliamenti, Si home mary ſa coſin infra gradus maritagii, queux ont iſſue & ſont deuorce en lour vies, per ceo leſpouſels ſont auoydes et liſſue eſt baſtarde. Et econtra ſi lun deuie deuaunt deuorce, la devorce ewe puis ne ferra liſſue baſtard, car leſpouſels ſont determines per mort deuaunt, et nemy per l'deuorce. Et mort perſon ne poet ameſne eyns ſon proues, car deuorce poſt mortem partium neſt que ex officio ad inquirendum de peccatis, car mort perſon ne poet eſtre cite ne ſummon a ceo. *B. Baſtardy* 44 *Darraignement* 11.

39. E. 3. 31.
per Thorpe.

Home ſerf noſm heire, ou exec en les premiſſes, & non in le alias diƈt.

49 ¶ Fuit in vre, en det vers J. N. de C. yoman, alias diƈtus J. N. de C. fils et heire U. N. et luy charge come heire, que le bryefe abate, pur ceo que il luy charge cōm heire, et il neſt noſme heire in les premiſſes, mes in le alias diƈtus. Iſſint in det vers J. N. de C. yoman, alias diƈtus J. N. de C. executor teſtamenti W.

30. H. 6. 5.

P. et

P. et declare vers luy come executor. *B.*
Bryefe. 418.

50 ℂ Si home deuiſe xx. li. a W. S. de eſtre
pay in 4. ans puis ſon mort et deuy, et puis le
deuiſee, deuy deins le 4. ans, vncore les executors
del deuiſee aſſa le money, ou le reſt de ceo per
ſuit deuant le ordinary en court ſpiritual, car
eſt vn duitie per le teſtament ou deuiſe. *B.*
Deuiſe. 27. 45. *Conditions.* 187.

51 ℂ Per *Fitzh.* ſi home deuaūt leſtatut de
tenures, vſt ſayt vn done de terꝛ a vn in fee pur
repairer vn pont, Ou pur garder tiel caſtel, Ou
pur marier annuatim vn poore virgin de S. ceo
eſt vn tenure, et nemy condition, et le donour
poet diſtraine et faire auowrie. Mes ſi feme
done terre a vn home pur luy marier, ceo eſt vn
condition in effeꝗ, et nul tenure, quod nemo
negauit. *B. Conditions.* 188. *Tenures.* 53.

52 ℂ Home vend leaſe de terꝛ et certayne
drape pur 10. li. le contraꝗ eſt entier. Et ſi lun
de ceux ſuit p defeiſible title, vncore le vendour
auera lentier ſome, coment que lun parte ſuit
deueſt del vendee, car contraꝗ ne poet eſte
ſeuere. *B. Contraꝗ.* 35.

53 ℂ Nota fuit tenus per omnes in domo
parliamenti, que ſi home tua vn que eſt attaint
per premunire, ceo neſt felony, car il eſt extra
proteꝗionem regis, que eſt ſicome il fuit extra
regnum, & poteſtatem regis. Et econtra de
ceſtuy q̄ eſt attaynt de felonie, et iudge al mort,
le tuer de luy eſt felony. *B. Corone.* 196.

54 ℂ Per *Fitziames* chiefe Juſtyce, *Engle-*
fielde Juſtyce, et plures alios, ſi tenaunt pur vie
leſſa terra pur ans rendaunt rent et deuie, le
leaſe eſt voyde, et donques le rent eſt determine.

Eadem

Conc. Fineux
11. H. 7. 12. &
12. H. 7. 18.

14. H. 8. 10.
per Brudnel.
Fitzh. 205.

30. H. 8. 135.
Vid 12. H. 8. 18.

St. 13. D.

D. S. 134.
35. H. 6. 58.
St. 13. C.

22. H. 8. 16.
14. H. 8. 14.
p Brudnel.
22. E. 4. 27.
per wood.

Limitac' de pay-
ment, & nemy
condic'.

Executors.

Ordinary.

Teſtament.

Tenure et cōdic
diuerſitie.

Auowrie.

Cauſa matrimo-
nii prælocuti.

Contraꝗ ne poet
eſte deuide.

Attainder per
præmunire, &
attaind' de fe-
lony diuerſitie.

Voyd leaſe.

Acceptaunce per ſucceſſour de pſon ſur leaſe pur ans, et ſur leaſe pur vie diuerſity.

Eadem lex dun perſon. Et coment le ſucceſſour reſceiue le rent, le leas neſt bon vers luy, car quaunt ceo eſt voyde per mort le leſſour, ceo ne poet eſte perſited per nul acceptance. (*B. Leaſes.* 19. *Debt.* 122.) Contra *B.* ſemble dun leas pur vie fayt per perſon rendant rent, et le ſucceſſor accept le rēt, c̄ affirme le leaſe pur vie. *B. Leaſes* 19.

4. E. 6. Com 30.
4. & 5. El. Com 264.
32. H. 8. 172.

Vide 1. E. 6. Com. 370.
8. H. 5. 10.

Teſtament per feme couert del aſſent le baron.

Deuiſe per le fēe al baron.

55 ❡ Nota que femme couert, del aſſent et volunt le barron poet faire teſtament, et deuiſe les byens ſon baron, vncore ſi le baron prohibite le probation del teſtament le ſeme puis ſa mort, donques tout eſt voyd, car le baron poſt coūtermaūder ceo. (*B. Deuiſe.* 34. in fine. *Teſtament* 21. in fine.) Et vn deuiſe per baron a ſa feme eſt bone, coment que ils ſount vn meſme perſon in ley, car le deuyſe ne pryſt effeɔ̃ tanque puys le mort le baron, et donques ils ne ſount vn perſon. *B. Deuiſe.* 34.

Meſme le caſe 34. H. 8. a ſaint Albons.

Litt. 37.
N B. 86.

Terre done, Habend' al graūt & hered' pro termino vitæ.

Lou ceſty en reuerſion fauxera rec' ewe vers tenant pur vie, & ou nemy.

Aid prie deſtrāg eſt cauſe de forfeiture.

56 ❡ Tenaunt a terme de vie alien a *B.* habend ſibi et hered ſuis pro termino vite del tenant a terme de vie, ceo neſt forfayture, car tout neſt que le limitation del eſtate. (*B. Forfayture de terres* 87.) Et ſi tenaunt pur terme de vie ſuffer recouerie, ceſtuy in reuerſion ne poet entre, mes eſt miſe a ſon briefe dentre ad terminum qui preteriit, vel briefe de droit, et fauxera le recouerie en ceo, ſil ad cauſe. (Et ſil voet auer ceo ſure, le tenaunt pur vye doyt prier en ayde de ceſty en reuerſion, et ſil ioyne en ayde, et ambydeux voucheront ouſtre, tunc bene ſur recouerie ewe &c. Ut enter Corbet et Clifford in Com̃ Buck. hoc Anno.) Mes ſi tenaunt pur vie ſoyt implede et prie en ayde dun eſtraunger, ceſtuy in
reuerſion

Vid. 21. H. 8. 1.
Conc. Fitzh. & Brooke.
12. H. 8. 7.
N B. 124.
4. H. 7. 2.
& 14. H. 7. 6.

23. H. 8. 39.
30. H. 8. 143.

1. H. 7. 22.
10. H. 7. 20.
per Keble.
25. H. 8. 70.

reuerſion poet enter, car ceſt vn forfayture.
Mes ſil ne enter tanque lauter ad recouer,
donques il ne poet entrer, mes eſt miſe a ſon
briefe dentre ad terminum qui preteriit, vel
ingreſſu ad communem legem, et fauxera le recouerie la. *B. Entre congeable.* 115. *Fauxe-
fier.* 44. *Forfayture de terres* 87. in fine.

Vide Cand.
44. E. 3. 32.
Vide D S. 57.
164.

57 ❡ Prohibition giſt ſepe, ou premunire
ne gyſt, come de groſſe arbres, vel pro decimis
de ſeptima parte, prohibition giſt et non premunire, car le nature del actyon pertinet al
ſpiritual Court, mes nemy le cauſe en ceſt
fourme.

Conc. 44.
E. 3. 36.
Vid. D S. 106.
&8. E. 4. 13. per
Cateſby, q pro-
hibition giſt.

Mes ou eſt de lay choſe que ne vnques apper-
tayne al ſpiritual court, de ceo giſt premunire,
Come de dett vers executourz ſur ſimple contract, Ou pro leſione fidei ſur promiſe de pay
10. li. per tiel iour. *B. Præmunire* 16.

58 ❡ Nota in *Scaccario,* que ſi terre diſcend
al moy, que eſt tenus de J. S. per homage,
et ieo face a luy homage, et puis auter terre
diſcende al moye per auter aunceſter tenus de
luy per homage, ieo fra fealtie mes nemy homage arrere, car ieo ſoy deuenus ſon home
deuaunt. Et ſi ambideux les tenementes ſont
tenus del roy per homage, il ne reſpitera ambideux les homages in *Scaccario,* mes vn homage
tantum. *B. Fealtie.* 8.

Poſt. 60. ppe
finem.

59 ❡ Per *Shelley* Juſtice ou le pier enfeoffe
ſon fits et heire appar al entent defrauder le
ſeignour del gard, ceſt feoffement fuit al vſe
le pier duraunt ſon vie, et il priſt les profittes
duraunt ſon vie, et ſic vide que vſes fuere in
aũcient temps B. *Feoffements al vſis.* 20. in
fine.

33. H. 6. 16.
per Priſot.

60 ❡ Home

Entre cong. &
lou nemy.

Lou prohibition
giſt, & lou pre-
munire diuſitie.

Premunire giſt
pur choſe q ne
vnques apper-
taine al ſpiritual
court.

Home ne fra 2.
hom pur 2. te-
nures a vn home
Ne al Roy.

Roy.

Fitzh. ſeiſi al
vſe le pere.

Tenant en taile ne ferra feifie al auter vfe.

1.
Vfe expreffe.

2
Que ferra feifi al auter vfe, et que non.

Corporation ne poet efte feifi al vie.

Sine affenfu capituli.
En le poft.
Mortmaine.
Efchete.
Perquifite.
Recouery.
Dower.
Curtefie.

3.
Formedon fur difcontinuance.

Vfe en taile.

60 ❡ Home fift feoffement in fee al 4. a fon vfe, et les feoffees fieront done in tayle fans confideratyon al eftraunge que nauoyt conuf. del primer vfe, habendum in taliato ad vfum de ceftuy que vfe et fes heires, Le tenaunt in tayle ne ferra feifie al primer vfe, mes al fon vfe demefne, car leftatut de Weftm̄. 2. cap. primo voet, quod voluntas donatoris in omnibus obferuetur, que home doit referre fon volunt al ley, et non ley al fon volunt. Auxi nul poet eftre feifie al vfe del auter, mes ceftuy que poet execute eftate al cefty que vfe que ferr̄ perfeⅽt en le ley, quel tenaunt en tayle ne poet faire, car fil execute eftate, fon iffu aūa formeⅾ. Et optima opinio q̃ Abbe, Maire et cõminaltie, ne auis corporatiõs ne ferra feifies al vn vfe, car lour capaciť eft tantū de preⅾ al lour vfe demefne. Et auxi fi labbe execute eftate, le fucceffour aūa br̄ denť fine affẽfu capiť. Et ceux q̃ font eyns en le poft, come per efchete, mortmaine, perquifit del villeine, recouery, dower per le curtefie et fimilia, fount feifies al lour vfe demefne, & nemy al auť vfe. Et auxi leftatute de 1. R. 3. eft que toutes dones, feoffementes, et grauntes de cefty que vfe ferra bone vers toutes &c. Sauant al toutes perfons lour droites et interestes en taile, ficome ceft eftatute nuft eftre fayt, et ideo tenaunt en tayle ne ferra feifie al vn vfe. Et fuit agree per *Curiam* que les parols in fine ftatuti de 1. R. 3. Sauaunt tiel droit & intereft al tenaunt en tayle &c. eft pryfe tenaunt en taile en poffeffion, et nemy tenant en tayle en vfe, car cefty que vfe en taile nad droyt ne intereft. Et auxy icy eft tenure enter les donours

Weft. 2. ca. 1.

27. H. 8. 10.
p. Moūtague.

2. M. 1. Com 103.
3. El. Com 238
4. El. Com 241.

Defchete
14. H. 8. 8.
p Pollard.
Del rec 4. E. 6.
Com. 54. per
Hales iuftice.
1. R. 3. cap. 5.

Vide 29. H. 8.
111.

14. H. 8. 8. per
Brooke iuftice.
Perk. 103. C.

donours et le donee, que eſt conſideration que
le tenaunt en tayle ſerra ſeiſie al ſon vſe demeſne. Et eadem lex del tenaunt a terme
dans, Et tenaunt pur vie, la ſealtie eſt due.
Et ou rent eſt reſerue, la, coment que vſe ſoyt
expreſſe ad vſum le donour, ou leſſour, vncore
ceo eſt conſideratiõ que le donee ou leſſee ceo
auera al ſon vſe demeſne. Et eadem lex ou
home vend ſon terre pur xx. li. per indenture,
et execute eſtate al ſon vſe demeſne, ceſt voyde
lymytatyon del vſe, car le ley per le conſideration del argent ſayt le terre deſtre en le vendee.
Et opinio fuit que vn vſe fuit al comen ley
deuant leſtatute de Quia emptores terrarum,
mes vſes ne fueront common deuaunt meſme
leſtatute, Car ſur cheſcun feoffement deuaunt
ceo eſtatute fuit tenure enter les feoffours et le
feoffee que fuit conſider, que le feſſee ſerra
ſeiſie al ſon vſe demeſne, mes puis ceſt eſtat le
feoffee tiendra de capitali domino, et donquez
neſt conſideration enter le feoffee et le feſſor,
ſans money pay, Ou auter eſpecial matter declare, pur que le feoffee ſerra ſeiſie a ſon vſe
demeſne, Car ou le ſtatute de Marlebr̃ eſt, que
feoffement per le pier que tient en chiualry ſayt
al ſon fits per couen ne tollera le ſeignior de
ſõ gard &c. en ceux caſes le feſſor puis tyel
feoffement, priſt les profits del terre tout ſon
vie. Et eadem lex per *Shelley* de feoffement
ſayt per femme al home de luy maryer, le
femme priſt les profittes puis leſpouſels *Quære
inde.* Car ceo eſt expreſſe conſideration en luy.
meſne. Et per *Norwiche*, ſi home deliuer
money al I. S. pur achater terre pur luy, et
il achate ceo pur luy meſme, et al ſon vſe de-

meſne,

Litt 29.
Perk. 103. D.
30. H. 8. 136.
36. H. 8. 284.

Weſt. 3. ca. 2.
Raſt. Tenure 4.

45. E. 3. 15.
per Finch.

Park. 103. B.

Cap. 6.
Supra 59.

4.
Tenure eſt con-
ſideratiõ en ley.

Termour ſerra
ſealtie.

Rent reſerue
bon conſidera-
tion.

Vſe change per
achate.

Vſe al comon
ley.

Tenure.

A q vſe le feffee
ſerra ſeiſi deuant
leſt. de Tenures,
Et a q vſe puis
diuerſitie.

Feffee per collu-
ſion ſerra ſeiſi al
vſe.
Garde.

Feffee cauſa ma-
trimonij plocuti
ſeiſi al vſe.

Quære.

Difceipt.

mefne, ceo eſt al vſe lachator, et nemy al vſe ceſtuy que lyuer le money, et la neſt auter remedye mes actyon de difceypt, *B. Feoffementes* al vſes. 40. 20. H. 6. 34. per Wangf.

Indictment de mort & poyſoning.

61 ❡ Indictment de mort doyt comprehender le iour de ferur̃, et iour del mort. Et eadem lex del poyſonynge, iſſint que poyt appearer ſil deuie deyns lan ou nemy, iſſint que poit eſtre conus ſil deuie de meſme le plague ou nemy. *B. Indictments.* 41. St. 21. D.

Feffement pur maintenance.

Expoſition deftat.

Remitter.

62 ❡ Nota per *Fitziames* chiefe Juſtyce, *Englefield* Juſtyce, & dyuers auters, Ou diſſeyſour fayt feoffement pur mayntenaunce, et priſt les profittes, le feoffement eſt voyde per leſtatute 1. R. 2. capitulo. 9. quaunt al eſtraunger que auera actyon, car il ceo auera vers le pernour del profittes. Mes il neſt voyde enter le feoffour et le feoffee. Et auxi home que vouche per tyel feoffement vn des feoffees, le demaundant counterpled per meſme leſtatute ratione que le feoffement fuit voyde. Et *B.* ſemble que tiel feoffement ne ſerra remitter en preiudice dun 3 perſon. *B. Feoffements.* 19. 27. H. 8. 23. per Fitzh. 1. R. 2. cap. 9. Raſt. Feoff. 9. 21. H. 6. Counterplede voucher.

Le primer nihil in ſcire facias peremtory.

63 ❡ Home recouer det ou damages, et puis port ent ſcire facias, le primer retourne de nihil vers le det. eſt peremptorie ſil fayt def. *B. Peremptorie.* 63. 8. E. 4. 15. per Danby.

Auerrement de ſon title.

Rec per def. et acc trie diũſity.

Quod ei deforceat.

64 ❡ Nota quod dicitur pro lege, que ceſtuy que plede recouery per defaut doyt auerre ſon title de ſon briefe. Et auxi que le defendant en le recouery fuit tenant del frank-tenement die breuis. Mes ſi le recouery fuit per action trie, il ne beſoigne de prender lun auerment ne lauter. Tamen dictum fuit que en *Quod ei deforceat* il que pled le recouery per default, ne beſoigne 22. E. 4. 32. per Brian.

beſoigne de auerrer le partie tenaunt del franketenement tempore breuis ſui, car il eſt proue
que il fuit tenaunt tēpore &c. per le vſer del
Quod ei deforceat, car ceo eſt leffeɗ de cel
aɗion, pur ceo que le demaund en cel aɗyon
perd per default en le primer aɗyon＊ Uncore il

36. H. 6. 29.

auera le title de ſon briefe＊ Et ceſtuy que
pled recouerie en brief de waſt per default ne

Nontenure neſt
plee en waſt.

**48. E. 3. 19.
per Finch.
Fitzh. 56. A.
40. E. 3. 33.
per Finch.**

beſoigne dauerrer le partie tenaunt. Car Nontenure in ceo aɗyon neſt ple. Auxi ſi vn ſayt
waſt et aſſigne ouſter ſon terme, vncore laɗyon
giſt vers luy de recouer le waſt *B. Pledings.* 6.

30. Aſſ. 14.

65 ⟨ En aſſiſe ſeueral tenancy neſt plee.
Et eadem lex in auters aɗyons ou nul terre eſt
demaunde en certaine. *B. Seueral tenancy.* 18.

Vncertaine de-
maund en aſſiſe.

**Lit 160.
N B. 143.
13. H. 7. 24.
per Towneſ.
Conc Vaviſour
10. H. 7. 8.
2. M. 1. Com
110.
N B. 144. &
48. E. 3. 9.
per Finch.
contra.
Tēpo. H. 8. 348.**

66 ⟨ Tenaunt en tayle ad iſſue et alien
oue garrantie, et leue aſſets, et deuie, liſſue ne
poet recouer per formedon, car le garrantie &
aſſets eſt barre. Et ſi liſſue alien laſſets,
vncore il nauera formedon. Mes ſil ad iſſue
& deuie, la liſſue del iſſue auera formedon, pur
ceo que laſſets neſt deſcend a luy. Tamen
dicitur que ſi liſſue ſur que le garrantie et
aſſetes diſcend port formedon et ſoyt barre per
iudgement & alien laſſets et deuie, ſon iſſue
nauera formed, pur ceo q̃ ſon pier fuit barre
per iudgment. *B. Taile.* 33. Et ſi le tenant
in tayle ad iſſue deux fits per diuers venters et
diſcontinue, et deuie, et auncester collaterall
del eigne fits releaſe oue garrantie et deuie ſans
iſſue et leigne fits deuie ſauns iſſue deuant aſcun
formedon port, le puiſne fits poet recouer per
formedon, car il neſt heire al garrantor, et ſon
frere ne fuit barr̄ p iudgement. Tamen *B.* doubta
inde, car luy ſemble que le diſcent del collateral

Ou laſſets alien
ſerr barre in
formedon, et
ou nemy.

Deux fits per
diuers venters.
Coll' garr
per releaſe.

Quære.

Taile extinct.

teral garrantie extinct le taile, Mes ſi leigne
vſt eſte barre per iudgemēt, donques clerement
le puiſne eſt ale auxi, *B. Tayle.* 33. *Formedon* 18.

Rec de terre en vn com, que giſt en auter.

67 ❡ Aſſiſe in Comitatu **B.** le tenaunt
pled en barre recouer per aſſiſe per luy vers le
plaintiſe de m̄ les tenements in com̄ **O.** et cel
ore plaintiſe dōques tenāt pled en barr̄ per
releaſe de auunceſter le playntiſe oue garrantie,
q̄ fuit voyded p nonage, & ceo troue pur le
playntiſe, per que il recouer vers ceſtuy playntiſe Judgement ſi, ou il accept le terre deſtr̄ in
com̄ **O.** ore ſerr̄ reſceu adire que giſt in Countie

View.

B.   Et dicitur in communi banco, que coment
que ceſt terre fuit dōq̄s miſe en viewe, le

Intendement.

plaintiſe ne ſerra lie per le recouery, car il ne
poet eſte entend vn m̄ terre *B. iudgements.* 62.

Aſſ. in N. & rec pled in H.

68 ❡ Aſſiſe de terre en **N.** le defendant dit
que auterfoits il meſme port aſſiſe de meſm̄ le
terr̄ in **H.** vers meſme le playntiſe, et ceux
terres myſe en viewe, et ceſtuy ore playntiſe
donques priſt le tenauncy et plead in barre,
et dit que **H. & N.** ſont vn meſme ville, et
conus per lun noſme et per lauter, et que **A.**
port formedon de ceux tenements, et plead
certaine &c. et recouer per action trie, &
leſtate le plaintiſe meſne enter le title del diſtr̄
et ſon recouery, iudgement ſi de tyel eſtate
aſſiſe, a que lauter dit, que cheſcū des dits **H.**
et **N.** fueront villes a per luy, et ſic al iſſue, et
troue fuit que fueront ſeuerall villes, et le ſeyſin
et dyſſeiſin, per que fuit agarde que ceſty
tenaunt donques playntiſe recouer.   Et pur
ceo que il ad recouer meſmes ceux terres vers
le playntiſe meſme in **H.** iudgement ſi aſſyſe.
Et

44. E. 3. 45. contra.
23. Aff. 16.

Et *Shelley* Juſtyce tyent fortment que ceſt recouerie de terre in H. neſt plee in aſſiſe de terre
in N. et ideo doyt laſſyſe eſtre agarde, Et
iſſint ſemble a *B. Iudgement.* 66.

Magna
charta C. 15.

69 ¶ Nota lou leſtat de Magna carta cap.
25. dit. Et viſus de franchiplegio tunc fiat
ad illum terminum ſancti Michaelis ſine occaſione. Ceo eſt entend le leete del turne de vic̄.
et non auters leetes. *B. Leete,* 23. in fine.

Leete del turne
de vic'.

Expoſitio.
ſtatuti.

Vide 27. H. 8.
hic 91.
5. E. 4. 2. contr
per Haydon
Vide poſt 81.

70 ¶ Nota q̄ fuit priſe, ſi mon tenant pur
vie vouche eſtranger q̄ ent en le garratie, & ne
poet barrer le demaundant, per que le demaundaunt recouer, et le tenant ouſter en value, q̄
ceſt terr̄ recoū in value ne irra a moy in reuerſion puis le mort le tenant pur vie, ne le reuerſion del terr̄ recouer in value ne ſerra en moy en
le vie le tenaunt pur vie, et iſſint tenetur a ceo
iour. *B. Recouerie in value,* 33.

Rec in value ne
irra al ceſty in
reuerſion.

45. E. 3. 17.
13. H. 7. 22.
per Rede
16. H. 7. 6.
per Keble.
5. E. 6. Com.
72. 9. H. 4. 4.
per Gaſc
Conc P. 36. H.
8. a. Audit que
rela 2. in fine.
48. E. 3. 5.
per Finch.
17. E. 2. B.
Suit 13. econt.

71 ¶ Home ſeiſie de xx. acres, eſt lye en
ſtatute marchaunt, et fayt feoffement de 15. a
ſeueral perſons, et executyon eſt ſue vers lun
del feoffees, il auera *Audita querela* ſur ſon
ſurmyſe, dauer lauters feoffees deſtre contribu-
torie oue luy. Mes ſi execution ſoyt ſue vers
le coniſour meſme il nauera tiel contribution,
car c̄ ē ſur ſon act demeſne. (*B. Audita querela*
39.) Tamē ſi le coniſor deuy, & le conuſee
ſue execution vers lheire, il auera contribution
del feoffee. Iſſint cheſcun de eux auera del
heire. *B. Audita querela* 44: *in fine.*

Feoffee, ou
lheire le conuſor
auera contribu-
tion Contr del
conuſour m.

72 ¶ Det ſur indentures de couenants, ou le
def. aū couenant, de faſſ pluſorz choſez, & le
pl' ſimiliſ de faire pluſours auters choſes, ad
quas quidem conuentiones perimpled vterque
obligatur alteri in 100. li. et lun infreint couenant,

Det ſur indentur
de couenant en
q ſont parols
obligatot.

nant, per que lauter port det, et le defendaunt
plede payment de 10. li. a D. que fuit tout a
que il fuit lye, judgement fi action, & nul ple
per *Curiam*, pur ceo que il ne monftre ent fait,
lou le plaintife declare fur lendenture que eft
fait.   Et vncore ecōtra en pleding de payment
de rent referue fur leas pur ans fait per indentures, car la il poet ceo leuier per diftreffe, et
ideo auerment poet vener en vre.   Mes ecōtra
ou tout infurge per efpecialty ou ceo gift en
payment.   *B. Debt* 173.

73 ⸿ Nota que les Juftices de commen bāke
accord in cafe de corporation, que conus per lun
et lauter, en fuit per nofme conus, neft ple pur
le plaintife, car il doit conufter fon proper
nofme.   Mes fi le defendaunt foit nofme per
le plaintife per nofme conus, coment que le def.
foyt corporate ceo fuffift.   Tamen quere fi ne
foit diuerfitie enter actiō real et perfonal.   *B.*
Corporations, 82.

74 ⸿ Home leffa vn meafō & terre pur ans,
& le leffee couenāt que il & fes affignees repairer le meafon, & puis le leffee graunt oufter
fon t̄m̄, & le affignee ne repaire pas, action de
couenant gift v̄s laffignee, car cē vn couenaunt
que currift oue la terre, (*B. Couenant* 32. *De-*
putie 16.)   Et auxi il gift cleremēt v̄s le leffee
puiz que il ad affygne oufter fon terme.   Et *B.*
femble que fil port feueral br̄z de couenant v̄s
ambideux, que la nē paz remedy tanque il prift
execution v̄s lun.   Et donques femble a luy q̄
fil fuift v̄s lauf, il av̄a Audita querela.   *B.*
Couenant 32.

75 ⸿ Nota fi feoffement foit fait al vfe w. N.
pur terme de fon vie, et puis al vfe J. S. & fes
hr̄s,

Lou payment eft
bon plee en det
fans acquitance,
ou efcript, &
econtra.
Mrans de fait.

Curia.

Conc Cherie
45. E. 3. 5.

Faile de nofme
Corporation ex
parte quer, & ex
parte def. diuerf.

Conc Mark.
1. E. 4. 7.

21. H. 6. 4.
per Newton.

Quære.

Vide 20. H. 6.
29.

Affignee charge
oue couenant
fon grauntor.

Audita querela.

Cefty que vfe en
rem, ou reuer-

hr̄s, la cefty que vſe en remainder, ou reuerſion, poet vend. le rem̄. ou reuerſion in vie W. N. Mes il ne poet faire feoffement tanque puis ſon mort. *B. Feffements al vſes* 44.

10. El. Com. 350.

fion vendera, ſed ne fra feff.

76 ❧ En aſſ. ou treſpas, ſi home entitle eſtraunger & iuſtiſie per ſon commaundement, ceo doit eſtre pled & nemy dōe en euidence ſur nul tort, ou non culpable pled. Iſſint de cōmen, rent ſeruice, rēt charge, licence, & huiuſmodi, ceux doient eſtre pleds et nemy done en euidence ſur general iſſue. Contrary de leaſe del terre pur ans, ſur non culpable plede, le def poit done ceo en euidence (*B. General iſſue* 81.) Auterment de leaſ a volunte, car ceo eſt come licence, que poet eſtre countermaunde, ou determine al pleaſure. Et ſi villeine pled frāke et de frāke eſtate, il poet done manumiſſion en euidence, car ceo eſt manumiſſion en fait. Mes ou il eſt manumitt̄ per aſt en ley, come ſute priſe vers luy per ſon ſeignior, Ou obligation fait a luy per le ſeignior, Ou leaſe pur ans, & huiuſmodi, q̄ux ſont manumiſſions en ley, dount le iury ne poet diſcuſſer, & ideo ceux ſerra plede. *B. General iſſue* 82.

Del licence 4. E. 6. Com 14. per Harris.

12. H. 8. 1. per Brooke.

Litt 45.

Choſes dēe pled & nemy done en euidence. Command.

Comen. Rent. Licence.

Leaſe pur ans, & la volūte diūſity

Manumiſſ. ē fait & en ley diuerſ.

77. ❧ Si ſeignior dun mannour claime le diſmes de tiels t̄res en D. de trouer chaplen en Dal, & le parochians claime ceo auxi pur meſme le purpoſe, dicitur pro lege que le lay court auera iuriſdiſtion enter eux, & nemy le ſpirituall court *B. Iuriſdiſtion,* 95.

Debate de diſm ent lay perſons.

Spiritual court.

78. ❧ Nota ſi le roy ad garde pur cauſe de garde, & le primer gard vīet a pleine age, et ſua lyuerye, lauter garde eſteant deins age, la le garde pur garde ne ſuera liuery, mes ouſter le mayne, car ore le ſñrye de ſon ſeigniour eſt

Vid 13. E. 4. 10.

Ou gard p cauſe de gard ne ſuera liuery, mes ouſt' le maine.

Seigniory reuiue per liuery fuer.

eſt reuyue per le liuerye, iſſint q̃ il ne tient del roy ſicut pryus mes de ſon immediate ſeigniour Sed ſi le gard pur cauſe de gard vſt eſtre de pleine age deuaunt le prymer gard il ſuera liuery, *B. Liuery*, 47.

28. H. 6. 11. Stp. 18.

Quant rem eſt graunt in mortmaine & quaunt reuerſion diuerſitie. Claime.

79 ❡ Seigniour & t̃ le t̃ leſſa pur vie al J. S. le remaind a vn Abbe et ſes ſucceſſoures, le ſeigniour ne beſoigne de faire claime, tãque le tenaunt pur vie ſoit mort, car ſil voyt Wayuer le rem̃ il neſt mortmayne.

Rem waiue. Vſe.

* Mes dun graunt de reuerſyon oue attournement auterment eſt.* Et ſi le teñt fait feoffement en fee, al vſe Al pur vie, et puis al vſe dabb. & ſes ſucceſſours, la il neſt pas mortmaine tanque le tenaunt pur vie en vſe, moruſt, et ceſty en remaind priſt les profits. Nota que appropriation dauowſon ſans licence ē mortmaine *B. Mortmaine* 37.

Appropriation ſans licence eſt mortmaine.

8. H. 4. 15. B. Mortmain 11.

Roy nonſue.

80 ❡ Nota que le roy ne poet eſtre nonſue. Tamen. *B.* ſemble que ceſty q̃ tam pro domino rege, quam pro ſelpſo ſequitur poet eſtre nonſue *B. Nonſuit* 68.

Intracc.

Aſſurance pur lier le taile.

81 ❡ Nota per aſcuns, ou briefe dentre en le poſt eſt port vers baron & feme, lou le feme eſt tenant en taile et ils vouch ouſter, & iſſint le demaund recouer P̃s le baron & feme, et ils ouſter en value ſi le feme tenaunt en taile deuie, & le baron ſuruiue, ceo ne liera liſſue en tayle, car le recompence irra al ſuruiuor, & donq̃ ceo ne liera liſſue en taile. Tñ. *B.* ſemble que ceſt opinion neſt ley, car le recompence irra come le prim̃ terre que fuit recouer irroit. Et voucher per baron & feme ſerra entende pur lintereſt del feme. *B. Recouery en value* 27. in fine.

Vid. 23. H. 8. 37.

Voucher.

Vide deuãt 70.

❡ Plus de hoc An. 23. H. 8. 27.

Plus.

❡ Añ.

¶ *Añ.* 26. *Henrici octaui.*

82 ¶ En action fur le cafe ou le plaintife liuer biens al def. et le def. pur 10. s. affumpfit eux fafement gardr̃, & non fecit, ad dampnum &c. Et per *Fitzherbert & Shelley* Juftices, non habuit ex deliberac̃, eft bone plee. *B. Acc. fur le cafe* 103.

Liuery del biens traũs en detinue.

Negat preignans.

Vide 29. H. 8. 108.

83 Si le tenaunt le Roy alien en fee fauns licence et deuie fõ heire deyns age, le roy nauera le garde, pur ceo que rien eft a luy difcende et que lalienatiõ eft bõ faue le trefpas al roy, que nẽ nifi vn fine per feifir. *B. Alienations* 29. *Garde* 85. Mes autermẽt fi lalíẽnor fuit teñt in taile Et fi lalienation fauns licence foyt troue p office le roy aũa liffues del terre a tempore inquificionis capte, & non ante. (*B. Alienations* 26. *in medio.*) Mes lou le tenaunt deuie & fon heire enter, fur office troue pur le roy del morãt feifie launc̃, la lheire refpond les profitz per luy prife deuant. *B. Intrufion* 18. *in fine.*

Lou lheire deins age ferr en gard et ou nemy.

Alienac per t en feefimple, & per t en taile diũfity.

Relac doffice, diuerfitie.

33. H. 8. 205. 8. E. 4. 4. per Choke. Stp. 84.

8. E. 4. 4. per Choke.

Conc Port. 21. H. 6. 49. 34. H. 6. 8. per Prifot. contra.

84 ¶ Nota per *Fitzh.* et *Shelley* Juftices, que fi home plede plee que va al actĩõ de br̃, il poet eflier de cõcluder al br̃, ou al acc̃, *B. Briefe,* 405. 492.

Collufion al briefe.

85 ¶ Si A. enfeoffe B. fur cõdic̃ &c. de reenter, la fi home impled B. que vouch A. et iffint rec. Ou fi A. reentra fur B. fans caufe, & eft implede & pde, la en lun cafe, & lauter, le condic̃ eft determine, car le terre eft rec̃ v̄s cefty que fift le condition *B. Iudgement* 136.

Condic detmine per iudgement.

37. H. 8. 298.

86 ¶ Home leffa pur 10 ans, & lẽdemaine leffa m̃ le tre a vn auf̃ pur 20. ans, cẽ bõ leafe pur les darraine 10. ans del fecond leafe. *B. Leaffes,* 48.

Leafe durant. leafe.

E 87 ¶ Cefti

Enter per auoid garr.

Seifue dur lecov^{t}ture in dower.

87 ¶ Cefti q̃ plede eñt pur defeat coll' garr̃, doit aũre que il entr̃ en la vie laũñc. Et en dower, fi le ĩ plede diffeifin p le barõ, & le fĕe plede feffemẽt p J. N. al baron. que puis enfeffe l' ĩ, & puis luy diffeife, el dirra q̃ le feffemẽt J. & le feifin le baron fuerõt durant le couerture, et cefty que deraine intreft p leafe del ĩ pur vie, ou en tayle, doyt auerre le vie le ĩ pur vie ou in taile. B. *Pledings* 147.

Auerre le vie le ĩ purvie, ou en taile.

¶ Plus de hoc An. 15. H. 8. 3.

3. H. 7. 2.
4. E. 6. com 46.

19. H. 6. 74.
13. H. 8. 15. per Wilby. Piu.

An. 27. *Henrici octaui.*

Ou pier del realme eft partie, chiualers ferra en le iury.

88 ¶ Nota 'enter Regem & Epifcõp Ronenfem pur treafon, leuefq, nauera chyuallers en fon Jurye, ou chiuallers doyent efte retourne quaunt vn pier del Realme, come Euefque, & huiufmodi e partie, Tamen quere, fi ceo fuit challenge. B. *Enqueft* 100.

Vide 2. M. 1. 465. & St. 153. A. Vide 33. H. 8. 221.

Quaere.

Feffement al 4. & liuery al attorney luu pur touts.

89 ¶ Si home fait feoffement en fee al 4. & luu del 4. fift letter datturney al J. N. pur prender liuerye pur luy & fon companions, que le fift accordant, ryens paffer, mes al cefty q̃ fift le letter datturney tantum B. *Feoffements* 67.

Vide temp. H. 8. 341.

Lou le roy nefeifera fas office.

90 ¶ Nota per ceux del Exchequer, ou home eft attaint per parlyament, & toutes fes terres deftre forfeits, & ne dit q̃ ceux ferra en le roy fans office, la ils ne font en feyf. le roy de graunter ouf̃ fans office, car non conftat de record quales ũ ille funt. B. *Office deuant* 17.

Vide 35. H. 8. 263.

St. 54.

91 ¶ Tenant pur vie, le remaynder oufter, ou tenaunt en taile, le remaindr̃ oufter, eft empled p br̃ dentre en le poft, & il vouch eftraunger, le dd recouer vers le ĩ, et le ĩ oufter en value, ceo liera ceftuy en reñ per *Mountagu* Juftice

Vide 25. H. 8. 70.

Juſtice et allos, car le recompēce irra a ceſty en
rem̄. Mes vncore en le caſe le ſeigniour Zouch
& Stowell en Cancellaria, le ley ſuit determine
auterment per toutes les Juſtices. *B. Semble le*
reaſo, eo q̃ q̄nt il vouch eſtranger, le recompēce
ne irra a ceſty en rem̄. Contrary ſil vouch le
donour ou ſon heire que eſt priuie. Mes puis
cē iour Plur̄ mit ceo in bre de lyer le remainder.
B. Recouery en value 28.

N B. 148.

92 ¶ Si le roy ſoit entitle al terr̄ J. S. p
forfaiture de treaſon, ou felony per act de parliament, ou office, per ceo toutes tenures ſount
determines, ſi bien del roy, cōe de touts auters.
Et la ſi ceſt terre puys ſoit done a auter per
auter Act de parlyament, ſauaunt a toutes auters toutes lour droites, intereſtes titles, rent
ſeruice, & huiuſmodi, cōe nul tiel act vſt eē, la
les ſeignioryes & huiuſmodi ne ſerra reuiues, car
nul ſeigniorie fuit en eſſe tēpore ſecund actus
facti. Et icy ne ſont parols de done, ne reuiuing,
mes parols de ſauing, que ne ſerue mes de ſauer
ceo q̃ eſt en eſſe tempore del ſauinge &c. Mes
tiel prouiſo en le primer act voit ſeruer, car
ceo vient oue lact q̃ entitle le roy. Et ou le roy
eſt entitle al terre p office pur Eſcheat, et puis
eſt enact per parliament que le roy ceo enioiera
ſauaunt a toutz auters lour ſeigniores & huiuſmodi, la tiel ſauing ne doit ſerū (p rōne ſuprad)
car tout fuit extinct deuaunt p loffice & rien
fuit in eſſe tempore del ſauinge (quel fuit enure
enter Regem et Kekwich in cōm Eſſex, ou
Kekwich perdidit ſon ſeygniorye) Mes la doiēt
eſtre parols affirmatiue que les ſeigniours doyent
auer lour ſeigniories. *B. Parliament* 77.

Conc Danby.
35. H. 6. 34.

Marginal notes:
Recouery de lier ceſty en rem.

Roy ne tiendra de aſcun home.

Queux parolz en acts voient reuiuer ſeigniories extincts deuant, & qux nemy.

Office pur le Roy.

Anno

. *Anno* 28. *Henrici octaui.*

St. 198. C.

Enſeint naũa be
nefite de ſõ ven-
ter forſque vn
foits.

93 ¶ Dicitur ou feme eſt arraine et adiudge
deſtre pende, ou arſe ſolonque le crime, et pur
ceo que el eſt enſeint, execution eſt reſpite tanque el ſoit deliuer, & ore el eſt enſeynt arere.
Eo que auterfoytes executyon fuit ſpare pur
meſm̃ le cauſe, ore executiõ ſerr̃ cõmaund deſtr̃
fayt. Et le gaylour naũa paine. *B. Corone.* 97.

23. Aſſ. 2.

12. Aſſ. 11.

Enſeint iudge
deſte arſe.

Office aſſigne
ouſter.

94 ¶ Dicitur q̃ deputation doffice que giſt
en graunt, doit eſtre p fait et non per parol.
B. Deputie 17.

Acc ſur le caſe
pur appeller le
pl' periure.

95 ¶ Nota en action ſur le caſe ent̃ Awſten
pl', et Thom̃ Lewes def. pur appeller luy falſe
& piured, il juſtifie pur ceo q̃ le pl' fuit periure
in Camera ſtellata en tiel matt̃ &c. & bon plee
per curiam. *B. Action ſur le caſe* 3.

30. H. 8. 127.
27. H. 8. 22.

Auowry ſur ſta-
tut, Et per comõ
ley diuerſitie.
Diſclaimer.

96 ¶ Vide per *Fitz.* Juſtice que home poet
auowe ſur le terre per le nouel ſtatut, et donques le tenant ne diſclaimera. Contrary ſil
auow p le comen ley, et relinquiſh leſtatute *B.
Action ſur leſtatut* 6.

21. H. 8. ca.

97 ¶ Dictum fuit pro lege que ſi home leſſa
pur terre pur 10. ans, & meſm̃ le leſſee leſſe ceo
ouſter al auter pur 4. ans, le leſſour fiſt feoffement al eſtraunge per ſufferance del ſecond
leſſee, ceſt bone feoffement ſāz Attournem̃t del
prim̃ leſſee *B. Feffements* 68.

Second leſſee
ſuffer liuery.

Feme hors de
gard' p mariage.
Liũy a 14. ans

98 ¶ Si le roy ad heire en garde que eſt
femme, & luy marie deuaunt lage de 14. ans,
la el ſerra hors de gard al 14. ans, & donq̃
poet ſuer liuery, car les 2. ans de faire 16. ans
ne ſount done, mes de tender a luy mariage,
ideo q̃nt el eſt marie citius el ſerra extra cuſtodiam a 14. ans *B. Garde* 86 *Liuerie* 54.

99 ¶ Ceſty

Tēps H. 8.
352. contra.
28. H. 6. 11.

99 ❡ Cefty que tient terre deyns le counti palantine de Lancaſter de roy en chiualrie, vt de ducato Lancaſtr̄, il ſuera liuery, contra de cefty q̄ tient terre q̄ giſt hors del countye palantine de rege en chiualry, vt del dit vouch. *B. Liuerie* 55.

Ou liuery ſerra de Duchy terre, Et ou nemy.

100 ❡ Nota que general liuery ne poet eſtre, mes ſur office troue. Mez ſpecial liuery poet eſtre ſauns office, & ſans probatiō dage, mes la il ſerra oblige a vn rate & ſome certayne deſtr̄ pay al roy. (*B. Liuerie* 56.) Et p *B. Ibidem* 31. ceo ne poit eſtr̄ claime per le comen ley, come generall lyuery poet, mes eſt al volunt le roy.

General liuery & ſpecial diuerſ. Etate probanda, ne ſerra ſur ſpecial liuery.

101 ❡ Nota que attornement poet eſtre fait per tenaunts al ſñr en ſon court al Seneſchal in abſence le ſñr on purchaſour. Mes attournement al ſeruant le purchaſour extra curiā & in abſence del purchaſer neſt bone, Mes per payement de j. d̄. pur cheſcun tenaunt al ſeruaunt le purchaſer, et en ſon abſence in noſme de ſeyſin de ſour ſeueral rentes, eſt bone attournement, car ſeruaunt poet receiue rent pur ſon maiſter, Quere ſi nul rent donques eſt due, ne le rent iour venus. *B. Attournement* 40.

Lou attornmēt in abſentia perquiſitorie ſerra bō, & lou nemy.

Quære.

Anno 29. *Henrici octaui.*

102 ❡ Per totā Curiam in communi banco Si deux ſont oblige en vn obligatiō coniunctim et diuiſim, Lobligee emplede lun, & ad executiō de ſon corps, & puis emplede lauter & luy condemne, il poet auer execution vers luy auxy, car le priſel del corps eſt bone execution, mes il neſt ſatisfaction, et ideo il poet prender lauter auxi. Mes ſi lun ſatisfie le pl', il naua exec̄ apres,
&

4. H. 7. 8.

Exec ſur obligac coniunctim & diuiſim, & ſatisfaction dīuiſitie.

Vnica execuc'. & ideo ceſt order q̃ le plaintiſe ſur vn obligation nauera niſi vnicam executionē, eſt entende
tiel execution, que eſt vn ſatisfaction. Et lou
ambideux ſont emplede per vn original per
Seueral pcipe. ſeũal Precipe &c. *B. Executions* 132. 45. E. 3. 4.
per Thorpe.

*Pur qi choſe
pardon ſeruera,
& pur que don,
ou reſtitution
eſt neceſſary.*

103 ¶ Nota ſi home ſoit attaint de murder,
ou felony, per vtlagarye vel aliter, & le roy luy
pardon toutes felonies, murders, & executions
eorundem, & vtlagaries, & wayuingz, & ſectam
pacis. Et pardon & releaſe toutes forſaitures
de terres, & tenem̃ts, & de biēs & chattels, ceo
ne ſeruera mes pur le vie, Et pur le t̃re ſi nul
office ſoit ent troue. Mes ne ſeruera pur les
biens ſauns reſtitution ou done. Car le roy eſt
entitle a eux par lutlagarie ſauns office. Mes
le roy nē entitle al t̃re, tanque offyce ſoit troue.
Et ſi office ſoit troue puiz vnc̃ le pd̃o ſerũa, car
ceo aſta relac̃ al iudg. & donques le pardon
meſne ſeruera bien. Contrarie ou office eſt troue
deuaunt le pardon graunt, car dōques le roy eſt
ſeiſie per loffice, et la vn releaſe ou pardon ne
poyt ceo doner. Mes doyt eſtre vn done ou
graunt. *B. Charters de pardon* 52.

Nota q ceux
parols (execuc
eorundc̃) ſõt ne-
ceſſary, 6.E.4.4
per Choke.

*Pardon deuant
office,& puis,di-
uerſ. lou relation
doffice ne defe-
tera meſne act.*

Vide 30. H. 8.
130.

*Pardon daliena-
tion p parliamēt
& letters patēts
diuerſitie.
Amoueas manū.*

104 ¶ Nota ſi alienation ſauns licence ſoit
pardō per act de parliamēt, le partie poet enter
ſans ouſter le maine, vel amoueas manum.

Mes econtra per auter pardon per letters
patentes, *B. Charters de pardon* 53.

*Obligac' deter-
mine contract.*

105 ¶ Si home ſoit endetted a moy per
contract, & puis fait a moy obligation de meſne
le debt, le contract per ceo eſt determyne, car
en debt ſur le contract, il eſt bone plee q̃ il ad
oblygation de meſme le debt. *Iſſint ſi lobligac̃
ſoit fait pur pcel del cōtract que ē entire 3. H.
4. 17.* Mes ſi eſtraunger fait al moy obligac̃
pur

Diuerſitie.

33. H. 8. 206.
10. H.7. 21.24.
Fitzh. 121. M.
9. E. 4. 25.
per Genney, &
Choke fo. 50.
1. H. 6. 8.
per Babing.
22. H. 6. 56.
per Choke.
20. H. 6. 21.
per Newton.

28. H. 6. 4.
21. H. 7. 5.
per Cutler.

Conc B. Det
126 in fine.

13. H. 7. 17.
per Fineux.
3. M. 1. Com
158.

27. H. 8. ca.

Park. 131.
39. H. 6. 25.
per Prifot.
37. H. 6. 33.
per Prifot.
7. E. 4. 28.
per Choke.

2. E. 4. 6.
34. H. 6. 46.
per Prifot.

7. H. 4. 14.
per Tillefley.

32. H. 8. 171.
7. E. 4. 5.
per Litt.

pur m̄ le det, vncore le contract remaine, pur
ceo que eſt per auter perſon, & ambideux ſont
ore dettors *B. Contract* 29.

106 ¶ Dette ſur obligation oue condic̄ ou le
cōdition nē paz enfreint, per que il eſt barre,
il ne vnques ſuera ceo obligation arere, car vne
foites barre eſt pro imperpetuo. *B. Det.* 174.

107 ¶ Fuit agree per omnes que ſi home
voyt, que J. S. auera ſon terre in dāle poſt
mortem ſon feme, & deuie, ore le feme le
deuiſor p ceux parolx auera le terre p ſon
entent apparaunt. ſ. ratione intentionis volun-
tatis. *B. Deuiſe* 48.

108 ¶ Si 2. copercen̄ fōt partic̄ & done
notice al ſ̄ur, il doit faire ſeūal auower̄. Et ſi
home vēde ſon tre per fait endent enrolle deinz
le demy an, iuxta ſtatutum, Lauowrie neſt
change &c. ſans notice, Nient plus que ſur
fine. Tamē *B.* doubta de conuſance de droit
oue ceo &c. Mes ſi home recouer vers le
tenaunt, Ou ſi le tenaunt eſt diſſeiſie, le diſſeiſour deuie ſeiſie, et ſon heire eſt eyns per
diſcent, iſſint que lentre le diſſeiſie eſt tolle,
lauowry ſer̄ change ſans notice. Ead lex ſi
le t̄ fait feoffemt, & deuie le ſeigniour changera
ſon auowry ſanz notice, car rien ē diſcend al
heire le feoffour. Et ou notice eſt neceſſarie,
ceo ſerra fait ſur le terre tenus oue tender de
les arrareges, Car auterment le ſ̄ur perdra ſes
arrerages, ſil auowe ou accept ſeruice dl feoffee
&c. deūat les arreragez pay, Ideo caueatur
inde. *B. Auowrie* III. 146.

109 ¶ Nota que fait de baron et feme ne
ſerra enrolle en communi banco niſi pur le
baron tantum, et non pur le feme, ratione del
couerture.

Semel barre ſur
obligac', eſt pro
imppetuo.

State pur vie per
entent, Et deuiſe
bon p implic'.

Auowrie change
ſans notice.
Et econtra.

Vend' p fait in-
rolle.
Fine.
Rec'.
Diſcent.
Quære.

Comtete q̄l lieu
notice ſerr fait.

Fait enrolle per
feme couert, per
comen ley, & per
cuſtome diuerſ.

couerture. Ne el ne ſerra oblige oue ſon baron
en ſtatut merchant, nec huiuſmodi. Mes ſils
ſot fait enrolle de t̃r en London, et ceo conuſter
deuant le Recorder & vn Alderman, & le feme
examine, ceo liera come fine al cōmō ley pur
lour cuſtome, & non tantum come vn fait, Et
ſuffiſt ſans liuery de ſeiſin.   *B. Faits enrolle*
14 & 15.

London.
Examinac'.
· Fine leuy.

Liuery de ſeiſin.

110   ❡ Home enſeffe le roy per fait & fait
liuery, c̃ ne vault, car le roy ne prēdra, mes p
matt̃ de rec.   Mes ſil enrolle le fait donꝗs ē
bon al roy ſāz liuery, car le roy ne priſt p
liuery.   *B. Faits enrol* 16.   *Feoffements* 69.

Feffement al
roy.

31. H. 8. 155.
12. H. 4. 21.
Vid. 37. H. 6.
10. p Dauers.
4. El. Com 213.
& 242.

111   ❡ Tenetur que ſi feoffees ſeiſies al vſe
dun eſtate taile, Ou auter vſe ſont implede, et
ſuffer le common recouery P̃s eux ſur bargaine
ceo liera les feoffees & lour heires, & ceſtuy
que vſe et ſes heires, lou le achatour, ne re-
couerour nad conuſāce del primer vſe.   Et per
Fitzherbert, ceo liera, coment que ils ount notice del vſe, car les feoffees ount le fee ſimple.
Et per plures, ſi ceſty q̃ vſe en taile ſoit vouch
en vn recouery, & ſic le recouery paſſe, ceo
liera le taile in vſe. s. c̃ey q̃ vſe & ſcz hr̃z.
Et aliter non.   Et hoc *B.* ſemble deſtre p
leſtat̃, que except tenaunt en tayle, que eſt
entende tenaunt en taile en poſſeſ s̃.   Et nemy
c̃ey q̃ vſe en tayle, car ceſty que vſe en taile
nē tenaunt en taile.   *B. Recouery en value* 20.
Feoffements al vſes, 56.

Rec' vers feffees
ſeiſies al vſe en
taile.

Notice del vſe.

Rec' ou ceſty q
vſe en taile. eſt
vouch.

St. expound.

Vide temp.
H. 8. 361.

Vide 30.
H. 8. 147.
Tẽp. E. 6. Cam
443.

1. R. 3. ca. 5.
Raſt. Vſes 4.
Vide 24. H. 8.
60. fo. 12. &
30. H. 8. 146.

112   ❡ Si home leſſa a vn Abbe & ſes ſucceſſours, ou a auter religious perſon pur 100.
ans, et ſic de 100. ans, en 100. ans quouſque
300. ans ſont encurres, ceo eſt vn meſme leaſe,
& tiel leaſe eſt mortmaine per verba ſtatuti de
religioſis.

Leaſe pur 300.
ans, ou 400. ans
eſt mortmaine.
Auterment de
couenant pur
tant dans.

6. El. Com 273.

religiofis. Anno 7. E. 1. s. colore termini,
car le dyt eſtatute ē, q̄ nullus emeret, vel ſub
colore donationis aut termini, aut ratione alterius tituli ab aliquo recipere, aut arte vel ingenio ſibi appropriare preſumat, &c. Et
eadem lex de leaſe pur 400. ans vel huiuſmodi. Contrar̄ ſi home leſſe pur 100. ans vel
ſimilia, & couenant que il, ou ſes heires al fine
del 100. ans, ſerra auſ leaſe pur auſ 100. ās,
& ſic vltra, c̄ neſt mortmaine, car nē q̄ vn
leaſe pur 100. ans, & le reſt nē aliter q̄ couenāt,
mes in primo caſu car ceo eſt pur 300. ans al
primes en effeͨt, et tout per vn meſme fait.
(*B. Mortmaine* 30. *Leaſes* 49.) Et 99. anz
neſt mortmaine. Et auxi leaſe pur 100. ans
neſt mortmaine per *B.* car ceo eſt vſual ſme.
Mortmayne 30.

113 ⁋ Si le roy purchaſe manner de que
J. S. tyent en chiualry, le tenant tiendra come
il tenoyt deuaunt, et il ne rendra liuerie, ne
primer ſeiſin, car il reteigne in capite, mes
tenet, vt de manerio, Et ſi ſon heire ſoit en
garde per reaſon de ceo, il auera ouſter le maiñ
a pleine age. Et dicitur ſi le roy puis graunt
le manner a W. N. in fee, excepī les ſeruices
de J. S. ore J. S. tient del roy come del perſon
le roy, et vncore il ne tiendra in Capite, mes
tiendra come il tenoyt deuaunt, car laͨt le Roy
ne preiudicera le tenaunt.

Mes ſi le roy done terre a moy en fee, tenend mihi et heredibus meis de roy &c. et ex
preſſe nul ſeruice certeyne, ieo teignera in
capite, car eſt del perſō le roy. Et nota q̄
tenure en Capite eſt del perſon le roy. *B.*
Liuery 57. *Tenures.* 61.

F 114 ⁋ Extent

Conc. Nele.
3. E. 4. 13.

3. E. 4. 13.
p Nele cont.

Vide poſt 14.

Vide 33. H. 8.
230.
Vide 3. EL
Com. 241.

33. H. 6. 7.
per Priſot.

8. H. 7. 13.
13. H. 7. 11.
p. Dauers.
Vide 30. H. 8.
141.
Vide 3. EL com.
240. p Carus.

99. ou 100. ans
neſt mortmaine.

Mannour pur-
chaſe per le Roy
ſerra en ſuy cōe
en le grauntor.
Liuery.
Primer Seiſin.
Garde.
Ouſter le maine.

Ou home tien-
dra del roy, cōe
de ſō perſon, &
vncore ne tien-
dra in capite, Et
econtra.

32. H. 8. 187.

31. H. 8. 148.

Extent de liuery
Et de intrufion
diuerfitie.

Attainder de cēy
que vfe p parlia-
ment, Et de at-
tainder de fole t'
per le comen ley
diuerfitie.

114 ❡ Extent de liuery eſt le value del terre per demy an. Mes ſil entrude & entra ſans liuery, il paiera le value per vn an, per experience Scaccarij. Et ou ceſtuy que vſe eſt attaint de treaſõ, & eſt enaɕt p parliament que il forfeitera ſon terre en poſſeſſion, et en vſe, que la le roy neſt que vn purchaſour, et ideo ceux que teigne de ceſty q̃ fuit attaint, ne ſueront liuerie. ‟Quere ſi ſoit enaɕt que il forfeitera c̃ al roy ſes heirs et ſucceſſors. Econtra ſil vſt eſtre ſole ſeiſie, et vſt eſtre attaynt per le comen ley, car la le roy ad la terre come roy, et la ceux que teigne &c. ſueront liuery. Et vncore leſtatute eſt, ſi quiz tenuerit de nobis de aliqua eſchaeta, vt de honore Wallingford Bolen &c. non faciet aliud ſeruicium quam fecit preante. Et ideo ceſt entend del common eſcheate. Et auxi aſcuns honours ſont in capite, come part de Peuerell & aliorum. *B. Liuerie*, 58.

Magna' charta ca. 31. Raſt. Tenures 2

Expoſition dun eſtatut.

Feſſ. a. ij. & a lheire lun.

Mordaunceſt.

Diſcent de re-
uerſion.
Dower.
Forfeiture.
Feoffement.
Droit.

115 ❡ Per optimam opinionem in communi banco, ſi deux purchaſe ioyntment a eux et al heires lun, et ceſty que ad fee deuie, et puis lauter devie, lheire le primer nauera Mord (et *B.* Semble le reaſon eo q̃ le fee ne fuit execũ en poſſeſſyon ratione del ſuruiuor lauter, et neſt en effeɕt ore niſi diſcent dun reuerſion.) Et le feme ceſty que auer fee, nauera dower. Et vncore il poet aſſ forfeit le fee ſimple, Ou done ceo per feoffement. Mes nemy per graunt de reuerſion, 12. E. 4. 2. Et ioine le miſe en briefe d droit, car ceſty en reuerſion, et le tenaunt pur vie poyent ceo faſſ. Quere ſil poet ceo releaſe *B. Mortdauncefter*. 59.

Quære.
Releaſe.

116 ❡ Nota pro lege ſi home ad fee dun ſeigniour, et puis eſt fait Juſtice, ceo fee neſt voide

voide per la ley, Mes apres le fefans de luy
Juftice neft de prender afcun fee, nifi del roy,
Et eadem lex de ceftuy que ad office de fene-
fchall, et puis eft fait Juftice. Et per plures
ou home eft Baylie dun manner per patent, et
puis eft fait Senefcall de mefme le manner per
auter patent, ambideux patents font bõs, Car
les futors font Judg. & nemy le bail. Mez p
plurez fi home foit forefter per patent, & puis
eft fait Juftice de mefm le foreft, le primer
patent eft voide. Come ou perfon eft fait
Euefque le perfonage eft voyd, car il ne poet
eftre ordinary de luy mefme, ne punifh luy
mefme. Et *B.* concord que home ne poet efte
gardẽ del foreft & Juftice del foreft, car locciff.
del dames per le gardein et huiufmodi, eft forfeyture de fon office queux ferra adiudge per
les Juftices del foreft, & il ne poet iudge luy
mefme. Mes home poet efte Senefcal del
foreft per patent, et Juftice de mefme le foreft
per auter patent, et ambideux bone, car
ambydeux fount iudicials. Et Juftices del
foreft poyent faire Senefcall del foreft. *B.*
Officer. 47.

117 ❡ Si le roy graunt terre pur terme de
vie, et puis le patentee deuie, vncore le roy ne
poet ceo graunt ouftre tanque le mort foyt
troue per office, Et hoc ratione ftatuti, que
graunt deuaunt office ferra voyde, *B. Office*
deuant 56.

118 ❡ Si office troue le mort le tenant le
roy, et que fon heire eft de pleine age, et ne
dit quando, la ferra entend, que il eft de pleyne
age tempore captionis inquifitionis, mes que
fuit deyns age tẽpore mortis tenẽtis, et ideo
doit

Side notes:
39. H. 6. 5. per Prifot.

5. M. 1. 498.

10. H. 7. 7. per Vanifor, 15. E. 4. 3. per Brian.

18. H. 6. ca. 6.

Fees graũt a cũt que puis eft fai iuftice.

Senefcal, & aps fait iuftice.

Vn mefme home Baily & Senefc'.

Iuftic' foreft. & gard' de foreft.

Perfon cree en Euefque.

Forfeitur doffic. Senefcall' foreft. & Iuftice. Auchoritie del Iuftice foreft.

Tenant pur vie, le reuerfiõ al roy deuie.

Pleine age ferra expreffe quãdo.

Office doit eſte certeine.

doit eſtre expreſſe certeyne que il ſuit de pleyne age. *B. Office deuaunt* 58.

Remitter ne ſerra ou terr eſt aſſure p parliament in caſu communis perſonæ, ne en caſu Regis.

119 ❡ Nota per *Englefielde* Juſtice en caſe inter Buttō & Sauage, que ou home ad title al terre per vn tayle, et puis meſme le terre eſt done a luy per parliament, que ſon heire ne ſerra remit, car per laƈt de parliament toutes auters titles ſont excludes imperpetuum, Quare ceo eſt vn iudgemēt del parliament. Et ou le terre eſt done expreſſement a aſcun perſon per noſme per aƈt de parliament, il, ne ſes heires naueront auter eſtate que neſt done per laƈt, mes q̃ ceo done tātum eſtoiera. (*B. Parliament* 73. *Remitt* 49. *in fine.*) Et eadem lex, ou le roy auoit title in tayle, et le terre eſt done a luy per parliament in fee, le tayle eſt determine. Iſſint que lheire ne auoydera leaſes ſait per ſon pyer, ne charge, et huiuſmodi, car le darraygne ſtatute lia toutes former titles & ſtates nyent exceptes *B. Parliament,* 73.

Leaſe ou charge p t' en taile.

Vide 34. H. 8. 251.

Rec vers pernor de profits, q eſt en gard le roy.

120 ❡ Office eſt troue puis le mort de ceſty que vſe q̃ il deuie ſeiſe et lheire c̄ en gard le roy, et puis recouerie eſt ewe vers lheire durāt poſſeſſione regis, cōe vers pernour de profits, ante ſtatuƚ de vſes Anno 27. H. 8. les feoffees trauers loffice, Ou ſue ouſter le maine, Ceſt recouery liera lheire. Mes le recoſſer ne poet entre durāte poſſeſſione Regis *B. Pernour.* 32.

Trauers per ſeffees en vſe.

27. H. 8. ca. 10. Raſt. Vſes 9. 4. E. 4. 24. 26. H. 8. 3. 8. Conc. Vauiſor. 13. H. 7. 15.

Trauers morant ſeiſie troue per office.

121 ❡ Troue ſuit que J. S. deuie ſeiſie, Per que vient W. S. ſon fits, & dit que le dit J. S. en ſon vie ſuit ſeiſie en fee, et c̄feffe A. B. in fee al vſe le dit J. S. & ſon heires & deuie, et puiz per leſtatute de vſes An. 27. H. 8. il ſuit ſeiſie en poſſeſſyon, ſauns ceo que J. S. ſon pier deuie ſeiſie, prout &c. Et bon trauers,

Stp. 62.

trauers, Et termor ne poet trauers office per le comen ley, niſi ceo fuit troue en loffice, et donques il puit aſ monſtrãs. de droit, et ouſter le mayne le roy. *B. Trauers doffice* 50.

Termour ne poet trauers. Monſtrance de droit.

122 ¶ Baron et feme purchaſe en fee, et puis ils leaſont pur ans per Indenture, et puis le baron releaſe al leſſee et ſon heires, ceo neſt diſcontinuance, et vncore ceo done franktenement al leſſee durant ſ vie le baron. Per plures ſauns doubt. *B. Releaſes* 81.

Releaſe neſt diſcontinuance.

123 ¶ Dictum fuit pro lege que ſi home ſua execution ſur ſtatute merchant, Ou ſtatute ſtaple, & part del terre eſt extende nomine omnium terrarum, que eſt returñ accord, et le party ceo accepta, il nauera vnques extent, ne reextent del reſt. Et que ſur vn nihil returne ſur vn teſtatum eſt, il poet auer proces in vn auter coñ, car la le iudgement ſerra quod habeat execuc̃ de terris quouſque ſumma leuetur. Tamen aliter *B.* ſemble de tiel retourne de byens *B. Statute merchant.* 40.

26. H. 8. 7. p. Fitzh. 33. H. 8. 226.

Priſt per t' del terre en exec ſur ſtatut.

Proces en auter com ſur nihil returne ſur teſtatũ eſt.

124 ¶ Home fayt feoffement de moytie de ſon terre, le leſſee tyendra del ſeigniour per lentier ſeruices q̃ lentier terre fuit tenus deuaunt, car leſtatute de Quia emptores terrarũ tenẽdo pro particula, ne tient lieu icy, car moitie eſt particula. Eadem lex de 3. parſ et huiuſmodi, que va p mie & p tout. Contrarie de acre, ou deux acres in certein. Et ſi home tient 2. acres per eſperũ, et fait feoffement in fee del vn acre, le feoffee tiendr̃ ceo per vn eſperuer, & le feoffour tiendra lauter acre per auter eſperuer. *B. Tenures.* 64.

Perk. 129. D.

Weſt. 3. ca. 2. Raſt. Tenure 4.

Fitzh. 235. A.

22. E. 4. 36. p Cateſby.

Tenãt fait feoffement de moitie, ceo neſt pro pticula.

125 ¶ Hõe deuiſe ſon ſre a J. S. c̃ ſerra priſe niſi p̃ termino vſſe ſue, Mes ſil dit, payant

22. E. 3. 16. B. Deuiſe 33.

State ou nul ſtate eſt limit.

Lou home auera pur vie, & lou fee fimple p deuife.
Payment per Lheire,
Execut.
ou Affignee.
Quære.

100 li. a W. N. ceo ferra intend fee fimple. *4. E. 6. 406.*
Et fil ne ceo paye en fon vye, vncore fi fon heire, ou executour ceo pay, ceo fuffift. Quere *Vid 24. H. 8. 50.* de fon affignee. *B. Teftament.* 18.

126 ❡ Nota que lou home pur 100.li. vende fon terre fur condition que fi le vendor ou fes heires repaye le fumme citra feftum Pafche, vel huiufmodi, tunc proximo futur̃, quod tunc il poet reenter, ceo neft pas vfurie, car il poet repaier lendemayne, ou afcun temps deuaunt Pafche, et ideo il nad afcun gayne certayne de receyuer afcun profits del terre. Et eadem lex ou defefauns, ou ftatute eft fait pur le repayment citra tale feftum. Econtra, fi le condition foyt que fi le dit vendour repaia tali die, vn an, ou deux ans puis, ceft vfurye, car il eft fure dauer les terres et les rentes ou profits cel an, ou ceux deux ans. Et iffint ou defefauns, ou ftatute eft fayt pur le repayment ad tale feftum, que eft vn an ou deux ans puis, *B. Vfurie.* 1.

Diuerfitie ou le iour eft certaine, & ou incertaine de faire vfury.

Defeifance.

❡ *An.* 30. *Henrici octaui.*

Acciõ fur le cafe pur appell' luy p iure, & iuftific en ceo.

127 ❡ Action fur le cafe pur appeller le *28. H. 8. 85.* pleintife faux periured mā, Et le defendaunt iuftifye quod tali die et anno in Camera Stellata le plaintife fuit periure, et pleade certayne in que &c. per que il luy appel faux periured man, vt fupra, put ei bene licuit, Et bõ plee per Curiam in cõmuni bāco. Per q̃ le pł dit de fon tort demefne fauns ceo que il iura modo et forma. *B. Action fur le cafe.* 104.

De fon tort demefne.

Quel chofe le roy amendera fõ de-

128 ❡ Nota fuit accorde per le learned *33. H. 8. 229.* counfell le roy, que ł roy poet amend fon *Vid 1. E. 5. 7.* declaration

p Vauifour.
& Catefby.
Vide 6. & 7. E.
6. Com 85.

declaration en auter terme in omiſſiō & huiuſmodi, come ou information miſrecite le ſtatute, ceo pǒet eſtre amende, car miſrecital eſt le cauſe de demurrer, car ſi ſoit miſrecite, donquez neſt tiel ſtatute, Mes il ne poet alter le matter et chaunger ceo tout ouſtrement. Tamen meſne le terme il puyt 4. El. Cōm. 243, per *Weſton* B. *Amendment.* 80.

13. E. 4. 8.

clarac' en auter term, & ql nemy. Miſrecital dun eſtatut en information, amend' en aut' terme.

Conc Litt. 39. H. 6. 24. Cap. 16. Raſt. Inrolments 2. Cap. 10. Raſt. Vſes 9.

Litt 230.

129 ¶ Fuit agree que ou terre eſt vende per fayt endent enrolle, iuxta ſtatutum 27. H. 8. la pur ceo que luſe eſt change p le bargayne et ſale per le ſtatute dicto anno 27. ca. 10. et lachator en poſſeſſion, et nad meſne de aret le tenant datturner, la il poet diſtrein et faire auowry ſans attornement. Contra ſur graūt per fine, car la il poet auer vn briefe de p q̄ ſeruic̄. B. *Attornement.* 26. in fine.

Auowry fait ſãs attornement, & econtra.

Fine leuy. Per q ſeruitia.

Conc Filpot 16. E. 4. 1. Vide 29. H. 8. 103.

33. H. 8. 204.

130 ¶ Si intruſion per le heire poſt mortē anteceſſoris ſoit troue p office, et puis le roy ceo pardon per act de parliament, ou p letters patents, vncore le heire ſuer liuery, car ceo neſt reſtore a luy per vn pardon, Mes ſi le pardon fuit graunt deuāt office troue, et al feſauns del pardon lheire eſt de pleine age, il reteignera le tre, et office troue puis le pardō ne luy greuera. B. *Charters de pardō.* 54.

Intruſion, pardō deuant office, Et puis office diſſ. Liuery.

Pleinage.

131 ¶ Si home morgage ſa tre a W. N. ſur condition, que ſi le morgageor, et K. S. repay C. li. per tyel iour, que il reentra, et il deuie deuaūt le iour, Mes. J. S. paya per le iour, le condition eſt perfourme et hoc ratione mortis le morgageor, non obſtant que le payment fuit en le copulatiue. Econtra, ſi ne fuit en le caſe de mort. B. *Conditions.* 109.

Conc. 15. H. 7. 2. & 13.

Condic perform ratione mortis Et econtra.

132 ¶ Nota que en London hōe poet deuiſe per

Deuiſe a comen

perſon en Londō
Et deuiſe ē mort-
maine en Lōdon,
diuerſitie.

per teſtament a commen perſonne, coment que
le teſtament ne ſoyt enrolle. Sed ſil deuiſe in
mortmaine il doyt eſtre Citizen et freeman re-
ſiant, Et le teſtament doyt eſtre inrolle ad prox.
huſtinges *B. Deuiſe.* 28.

5. H. 7. 10.
D S. 21.

Vid 45. E. 3. 26.

Suruiuour ne
tiet lieu en
deuiſe.

133 ❡ Home deuiſe a deux & heredibus
eorum et deuie, et puis lun del deuiſees deuie,
et lauter ſuruiue, il nauera lētier p ſuruiuor,
Mes tātū vn moitie, & lheire del auł iointenāt
lauł moitie, car ceo fuit le entēt del deuiſor
Per Audley Chaūcelor del Anglet. *B. Deuiſe.*
29. Et p *B.* ibm̄ in fiñ, Si vn deuiſe a vn auł
in feod ſimplici, le deuiſee ad fee ſimple.

In feodo ſim-
plici.

Park. 106. G.

Ou touts execu-
tors vendera, Et
ou vn poet.

Quære.

134 ❡ Home voet que ſon terre deuiſable
ſerra vend per ſes executors, et fayt 4. executours et deuie, toutes les executours doyent
vende, car le truſt eſt coniunꝃim miſe en eux,
quere, Car *B.* ſemble que ſi vn, ou deux deu-
yont, que les 3. ou 2. que ſuruiue poient vender, car la eſt le plural number executors, et
mort eſt faꝗ de dieu, (*B. Deuiſe.* 31.) Et per
luy ou tiel will ē fait & aſcū del exeꝏ refuſe &
lauter proue le teſtam̄t, ceux, ou cēy q̃ proue
le teſtam̄t poient vend per leſtatute (*B. Deuiſe.*
29. 31.) ou eſt expreſſe que fuit doubt al commen ley ſi le vend per vn exeꝏ fuit bō ou nemy,
(*B. Deuiſe.* 31.) Et p aliquos ou hōe voet q̃

21. H. 8. ca. 4.
Raſt. Probate
of teſt. 3.

Deuiſe q ſes
exec' vēder poſt
mortem I. S.

le t̄re ſerr̄ vēd poſt mortē J. S. p ſes executorz
& fait 4. executorz et deuie, et puis deux del
executors deuie, et puis J. S. deuie, la les 2.
executors que ſuruiue poyēt vender, car le
temps neſt venus tanque ore *B. Deuiſe.* 31.

Contraꝏ
apporcion.

135 ❡ Dicitur que ſi ieo vend mon chiual,
et le chiual de W. N. al A. pur x. li. & W. N.
repriſt ſon chiual, Et A. rendra a moy lentier
        x. li.

24. H. 8. 52.

x. li. quia chattel nemy poet eſtre ſur contract apportion, B *Apportionment.* 7.

24. H. 8. 60.

156 ❡ Feoffees in vſe ſont leas pur ans, rendant rēt al auter que ad notice del primer vſe, vncore le leaſe ſerra tantum al vſe del leſſee meſme. Et eadem lex per Plures comēt que nul rent ſoit reſerue. Et ſi home fait feoffemēt, et annex ſcedule al fait conteynant le vſe, il ne poet change luſe en apres. Et iſſint ſil expreſſe luſe in le fayt del feoffement. Mes econtra ou il declare le vſe per parols de will. ſ. I will that my feoffees ſhalbee ſeyſed to ſuch a vſe. La il poet changer ceo vſe, quia per will &c. Et que ſi feoffement ſoyt fayt al vſe le feoffor en tayle, et puis les feoffees execute eſtate a luy en fee, luſe del eſtate taile eſt determine &c. B. *Feoffements al vſes.* 47.

Cõc 19. H. 8. 1.

Vid 20. H. 7. 11.

Notice del vſe material. Et econtra.

Quant home poet charger vſe, Et ou nient.

Vſe entaile determine.

137 ❡ Si A. couenant oue B. que quant A. ſerra enfeoffe per B. de 3. acres en D. quod tunc le dit A. et ſes heires, et toutes auters ſeyſies del terre le dit A. in S. ſerra ent ſeiſie al vſe le dit B. et ſez heirz, la ſi A. fayt feoffement de ſon terre in S. et puis B. enfeoffe A. del dits 3. acres in D. la les feoffees A. ſerra ſeiſiez al vſe B. nõ obſtant quilz nauoiēt notice del vſe, car le terr̄ eſt, et ſuit lye oue luſe auauntdit, ad cuiuſcunque manus deuenerit. Et neſt ſemble ou feoffee in vſe vende le terr̄ al vn que nad notice del primer vſe, Car en ceſt primer caſe luſe nad eſtr̄ tanque le feoffement ſoyt fayt del 3. acres, et donques luſe commence. B. *Feoffements al vſes.* 50.

14. H. 8. 9. per Pollard.

De faire vſe de commēce expectant p couenant.

Meſne d' lier terres oue vſe, ad cuiuſcāque manus deuenerint. Notice del vſe.

138 ❡ Nota que fuit couenanted que A. ſerra al B. ſa feme file J. R. iointure per fine, et le briefe fuit port per J. R. vers A. & B. ſa feme,

Conc H. 38. H. 8. int W. Roch. & Radm Lacharne &c.

Couenant pur aſſurance de ioincture per fine.

feme, & ils offer de conuſtre al J. al entent q̄　32. H. 8. 171.
J. renď a eux pur vye B.　Et pur que B. la
feme fuit deins age, ideo el fuit trahe hors, &
releƈt.　Et dōques pur ceo que nul poet prender le primer eſtate per le fine, mes ceux que
ſerra noſme in le briefe de couenant. (Mes
cheſcun eſtraunger poet prēder reṁ) Ideo le
briefe fuit fait inter J. et A. tantū.　Per que A
conuſter les tenements deſtre le droyt J. vt illa
que &c.　Et J. graunt et render ceo al dit A.
pur terme de ſō vie ſauns empeachement de
waſt, le remaynder al dit B. ſa feme pur l̃me
de ſa vie, le remainder al dit A. & ſes heires.
B. Fines leuies. 108.

139　❡ Tenant le roy leſſa pur ans et deuie,　Stp. 13.
lheire ſuera liuery non obſtant q̄ le leaſe endura.
Et eadem lex ou le pier declare ſon will del
l̃re pur ans et deuy.　*B. Liuery.* 59.

140　❡ Si leaſe ſoyt fait a 3. de terre al
comen ley pur terme de vie, Ou pur ans, Ha-
benď ſucceſſiue, vncore ceo eſt vn ioint eſtate,
& ils teignera in iointuř, & ſucceſſiue eſt voiď,
Mes ou le cuſtome de copyholdes eſt, que ceſt
parol (ſucceſſiue) tiendra lieu, ceo eſt bone la
per le cuſtome.　*B. Iointenants.* 53. *Leaſes.* 54.

141　❡ Nota que eſt auncient courſe ē lex-　Vid. 13. H. 7.
11.
chequer, que ſi ſoit troue per office que J. S.
fuit ſeiſie in fee et deuie, ſed de quo vel de
quibus tenementa tenentur .ignorant, que cōmiſſion iſſera ď ceo enquirer certeinment de quo
&c.　Et ſi ſoit troue que de W. N. tunc le
partie auera ouſter le mayne le roy.　Mes ſi　Conc kingſ.
& Fineux.
13. H. 7. 5. & 9.
26. H. 8. 9.
p Bromley.
office ſoyt troue quod tenetur de Rege, ſed per
que ſeruitia ignoratur, ceo eſt bone pur le roy,
et ſerra entend deſtre tenus in capite per ſeruicium

Vide 29. H. 8.
113.
2. E. 6. ca. 8.

cium Militare, car le melius ſerra priſe pur le
Roy. Mes ore in ceux caſes melius inquirend̄
ſerr̄ agard per ſtatutum. *B. Office deuant.* 59.

Melius inquirend'.

142 ❡ Si le roy graunta omnia terras &
tenemēta ſua in D. ceſt bone graūt p ceux
parols generals. *B. Patents.* 95.

Roy graunt per general parolz.

143 ❡ Tenetur, que ou tenant pur vie eſt,
le remaynder ouſter in taile, ou pur vie, et le
tenaunt pur vie eſt implede & vouche ceſty en
remainder, que vouch ouſter vn que ad title de
formedon, et iſſint le recouery paſſe p voucher,
la liſſue ceſty q̄ ad title de formedon poet porter
ſon formedon, & recouer vers le tenaunt pur
vie, car le recompence ſuppoſe ne irra al teūt
pur vie, & ideo il poet recoū, car ſon auunceſter
ne garrāt niſi le remaind, & nō leſtate pur t̄m
de vie, & ideo le teūt pur vie ne poet luy lier
per le recouery, car il ne garrant a luy. Et
ideo en tyel caſe le ſure voye eſt de faire le
tenaunt pur vie de prier ayde de ceſty en remainder, et eux de ioinder & voucher ceſty
que ad title de formedon, & iſſint d paſſer le
recouery, car la le recompence irra a ambideux,
B. Recouery in value. 30.

Diuerſitie ou le rem tantum eſt garr. Et ou leſtate pur vie.

Formedon.

14. H. 8. 56.

Rec' de lier ceſty en rem &c.

Ioinder en aide.

144 ❡ Nota que tenaunt en tayle que leuie
fine oue proclamation ſerra lie, & ſes heires de
ſon corps auxi puis les proclamations faytes, et
non ante, Iſſint que ſi le tenaunt en tayle deuie
deuaunt toutes les proclamations faites, ceo ne
liera liſſue en taile, & lez proclamations ne
poient eſtre faits in plus briefe temps que en 4.
termes. (*B. Fine leuies* 109. *Aſſurances.* 6.)
Mes teūt en tayle q̄ neſt partie al fine, ne ſerra
iſſint lie puis les proclamations, mes que il
auera 5. ans de faire ſon claime, Et ſil faile de

Fine oue procl' de lier tenaunt en taile & ſon iſſue.

Temp. pur faire pclam ſur fine.

5. ans pur liſſue en taile de clai-mer.

eux

Equitie.

Quære.

Priuitie.
Fine confeſſ. &
auoyd.
Intendement.
Auerment.

Fine per con-
cluſion.

Eſtraàger.

Fine oue procla-
mation per t' en
taile, le reuerſi-
on al roy, Et co-
men recouery
diuerſitie.

eux et deuie, ſon iſſue auera auters 5. ans per
lequitie de leſtatute de W. 2. quod non habeat Weſt. 2. cap. 1.
poteſtatem alienandi. Tamen dicitur ſi le pri-
mer iſſue neglect les 5. ans, per que il eſt barrable et deuie, ſon iſſue nauera auters 5. ans.
Car ſi liſſue ſoit vn foites barrable per le fine,
le tayle eſt per ceo lie imperpetuum (Quere)
Et leſtatute dyt que il liera parties et priuies, 4. H. 7. ca. 24.
et ideo ou tenaunt in tayle eſt partie al ſyne Raſt. fines 8.
oue proclamation, et ſon iſſue clayme per formā
doni, liſſue eſt priuie, Car il ne poet luy conueier come heire al tayle niſi vt de corpore
patris ſui, que ē priuitie : Mes fine oue procl
poet eſtre confeſſe et auoided, et donques c̄ ne
lier car leſtatute eſt entende de finibus rite
leuatis. Et ideo il poet dire que les parties al
fine nauera riēs tempore finis &c. Car ſi nul
des partyes nauer ryen tempore finis, tunc ceo
eſt fine per concluſion enter les parties, Mes
toutes eſtraungers poyent auoyder ceo per le
auerment vt ſupra. (*B. Fines leuies.* 109.) Et Poſt. 145.
p leſtatute de 32. H. 8. fine oue proclamation in fine.
per ceſty que vſe in tayle liera luy et ſes heires
puis proclamatiōs faitz. Et vn fine oue proclamation, le reuerſion ou remainder en le roy,
et le conuſor deuie, q̄ les proclamations ſont
pleynment faytes, car neſt barre, ne diſcontinuaunce, ratione que le reuerſion, ou remaind Fitzh. 142. A.
en le roy ne poet eſtre dyſcontinue, ideo la
liſſu in taile poet enter puis t̄ mort del tenāt
in taile. (*B. Barre.* 97. *Aſſurances.* 6) Et *B.* 32. H. 8. ca. 36.
Semble q̄ nec leſtat̄ de 32. H. 8. nec leſtatute Raſt. Fines 9.
de 4. H. 7. ne liera liſſue en taile ne reuerſion al 4. H. 7. ca. 24.
roy p fine oue proclamatiō comēt que les procl
ſoiēt faites. Et vncore leſtatut de 4. H. 7.
voet

voet q̃ puis proclamatiõs faits, il ſerra final
end, et concludera cibien priuies cõe eſtraũgers,
except infants, femes couerts, et hm̃odi &c.
Et liſſue en taile ē priuie.   Tamen *B.* penſa q̃
lentent đ leſtatute ne fuit que liſſu en tayle, le
reuerſion al roy, ſerra lie, Car p̃ luy, puis cel
eſtatute ceo fuit priſe deſtre nul diſcontinuãce.
Et ideo luy ſemble q̃ ne liera liſſue en taile, le
reuerſion en le roy.   (*B. Fines leuies* 121.)   Quære.

32. H. 8. ca. 36.   Tamen quere, Car leſtatute de 32. H. 8. que
voet q̃ lheire in taile ſerra barre p̃ fine oue proclamation puis les proclamatiõs faits, ad vn
exception de ceux dount le reuerſion ou le rem̃
eſt en le roy, iſſint que ne liera tiel iſſue en
taile. *B. Aſſurances.* 6. in fine.   Mes auterment de recouery et exec̃ ewe p̃ br̃e dentre en
le poſt oue voucher p̃ le cõmon ley, Car
32. H. 8. 177.   coment q̃ le reuerſion ou rem̃ ſoit en le roy,   Comen recouery p̃ comen ley, Et puis leſtat' diũſ.
tiel recouery liera, et fuit barre vers le tenant
en taile, et ſon iſſue mayntenaunt, mes nemy
vers le roy.

34. H. 8. ca. 20.
Raſ. Recoue-
ries 4.   Mes a ceſt iour per leſtatute de 34. & 35.
H. 8. recouery vers tenaunt en taile, le remainder ou reuerſion en le roy ne liera liſſue
en taile, mes que il poet enter puis le mort del
tenaunt en taile. *B. Barre* 97. in fine. *Aſſur-*
ances. 6.

146 ❡ Si ceſty q̃ vſe pur terme de vie   Fine leuy per cẽy que vſe pur vie.
leuie une oue proclamation, la nul beſoigñ
denẽ ne faire claim̃ deinz les 5. ans, eo q̃ nē
q̃ vn graunt de ſon eſtate, q̃l eſt loyal, et nul
forfayture, car il nad riens en le terre.   Ne il
ne poet faire forfaiture del vſe.   Vſe forfeit.

10. H. 7. 20.
per Keble.   Eadem lex del une leuie per t̃ pur vie en
poſſeſſion. Tamen *B* doubta inde, et penſe   Quære.
aliter

aliter ſil leuy ē in fee, (*B. Feoffements al vſes.*
48. *Fines leuies.* 107.)   Et per plures ſi ceo
ſoit leuie per ceſtuy que vſe in tayle, ceo liera
luy et ſes heires.   Mes nemy ceſty que vſe en
le reuerſion.   Ne les feoffees puis le mort le
conuſor, car leſtatute de 1. R. 3. eſt, que il
liera luy et ſes heires.   Et feoffees claymants
tant ſolemēt a meſme le vſe quod non eſt ſic
hic, Quere inde, Car *B.* ſemble per meſme le
ſtatute que taile in poſſeſſion eſt remedy per
cel eſtatute, mes nemy taile in vſe, car ceo
videtur luy de remayner al comen ley, come
fee ſimple in vſe cōditional, car neſt vn done
del terre, Tamen quere, Car per luy, per
lequitie de leſtatute de W. 2. de tailes, Deuiſes
in taile ſont priſes, vncore ceo eſt in nature dunc
done, Tamen nota a ceo iour per leſtatut de
32. H. 8. fine oue proclamation per ceſtuy q̃
vſe en taile, liera le taile puis proclamatiō.
B. Fines leuies 107. in fine.

147 ❡ Fuit doubt ſi recouerie ewe vers ceſty
q̃ vſe en tayle, liera lheire en taile.   Mes per
Hales Juſtice, per tiel recouery lentre del feoffees ſeiſies al vſe de ſtate taile ē tol, mes puis
le mort ceſty que vſe que ſuffer le recouery, les
feoffees poient auer briefe de droit, ou briefe de
Entre ad terminum qui preterijt en le Poſt, vel
huiuſmodi.   Et per aſcuns ē nul vſe en tayle
mes ceo ē fee ſimple conditional al comen ley,
vt fuit del taile deuant leſtatut de W. 2.   Et
ceſt eſtatut ne fayt mention mes del donez en
taile que eſt taile in poſſeſſion.   Et ideo quere,
ſi le taile en vſe ne poet eſtre priſe par lequitie
de c̃, vncore fuit doubt ſi liſſues et les feoffees
ſerra lies poſt mortē del ceſty q̃ vſe q̃ ſuffer le
recouery

1. R. 3. ca. 5.

recouery ratione iſtoꝝ verborū in leſtaꞇ de 1. R.
3. q̃ voet, q̃ le recouery ſerra bon vers le vendor
et ſes heires claimant tant ſolement come heire.
Et vers toutz auters claimant taunt ſolement al
vſe del vendor & ſes heires. Et ceſt entend
par aliquos del fee ſimple. Et in caſu ſupra
liſſue en tayle clayme cõe heire en taile en vſe.

32. H. 8. ca. 36.

(B. *Feoffements al vſes.* 56. *in medio.*) Tū vide
ſtatuꞇ de 32. H. 8. q̃ fine oue proclamation leuie,
ou deſtre leuie p̃ tenãt en tayle in poſſeſſion,
reuerſion, remainder, ou in vſe, puis proclama-

Supra 145.

tion ewe, liera ceux tenaunts de ceux tailes et
lour heires imperpetuum. Et vide que meſme
leſtatut eſt tam bene pro temporibus preteritis,
quã futuris. B. *Feoffements al vſes.* 57. in fine.

Expoſition dun
eſtatut.

Fine per tenant
en taile, en vſe
ou poſſeſſ.

Anno 31. *Henrici octaui.*

29. H. 8. 114.

148 ❡ Dicitur pro lege que fine pur alienation eſt le value del terre alien per an. Et eadem
lex de fine pur intruſion ſur le roy. Mes le
fine dauer licence daliener, neſt niſi le 3. part
del ānual value del terre, que ſerra alien. Et pur
licence dalieñ en mortmaine, le fine eſt le value
del t̃r p̃ 3. ans, B. *Alienation,* 29. in fine.

Fine pur aliena-
tion, Intruſion
ou fine dauer li-
cence daliener
en mortmaine,
ou auterment,
diuerſitie.

149 ❡ Det ſur obligation, le defendant pleḋ
condition ſi ſteterit arbitrio J. et N. iſſint que
lagarde ſoyt fait deuaunt tiel iour, et dit que
lagarde ne fuit fayt per le iour, le plaintife
poet dire q̃-ils fler̃ tiel ag. deuant le iour, q̃l le

Pleding de con-
dic' en barre.

8. H. 6. 18.
per Newton.
B. Arbiter-
ment 18.

def. in tiel poynt (et monſtre certaine in quo)
ad infreint, car il monſtra lenfreynder en aſcun
point certaine, ou auterment action ne giſt.
B. *Arbitrement.* 42.

Replication.

150 ❡ Aſſiſe, le tenaunt pleḋ nyent attache

per

Baily examine en affife.

per 15 iours, le Bayly fuit examine, que dit que il luy attache per le chiual dun fermor q̄ fuit vn termor al tenaunt del terre in pleynt, quel matter fuit recorde. Et *B.* femble que neft bon attachement, Car le tenaunt ne puit forfayt les beafts fon fermor. Et Attachement doit eftre fait de tiels chofes que le tenaunt puit forfayt per vtlagary.

Attachment ne ferra de bonis alterius, quam ten.

De queux chofes attachment doit efte.

27. H. 6. 2.

Nota enter Dudley & Leuefon pur le maner de Parton in com̄ Stafford. *B. Affife.* 480.

Ou graunt ferra bone fans attornement.

151 ¶ Nota que fi home ad comen de pafture al certaine number, Ou comen de eftouers al certayne number de carucis, et eux graunt oüfter, c̄ paffa fans attornemēt, pur ceo q̄ neft deftre prife per mains del tenaunt, mes per les bouches des beafts, Et per fcier et carier. Iffint vid q̄t nul attendancie, ne paim̄t eft deftre fait p le t, la le chofe poet paffer fās attornem̄t *B. Attornement.* 59.

Abr. daff. 22.

Vid 2. E. 6. 379

Ad intencionem neft condic.

152 ¶ Per *Plures* Si home fayt feffement en fee ad intentionem pur performe fon wil, ceo neft conditiō, mes vn declaration del purpofe et wil le feoffor, et le heire ne poet enter pur non performaunce. *B. Conditions.* 191.

DS. 123.
Vide 27. H. 8.
15. p Knightly.

Rec' vers cefty q vfe en taile.

152 ¶ Cefty que vfe en tayle fuffer recouery vers luy fur faint tytle deuaunt leftatute de vfes, et deuie, les feoffees ne poyent ceo fauxifyer en affife per voy dentre, mes aueront briefe dentre ad terminum qui preterijt, ou briefe de droit, et fauxifier ceo per ceo action. (*B. Entre congeable* 123. *Fauxifier* 49.) Et fil leuie fine oue proclamation & deuie, fi eftraunge de fon teft demefne enter in nofme les feoffees, ou a lour vfe deyns les 5. ans, ceo auoidera le fin̄, coment que les feoffees ne luy commaund

20. H. 8. 147.

Entre deftrange.

commaund, car per ceo le franktenement eſt en
eux tanque ils diſagree, Ou tanque auter enſ.
B. Entre congeable. 123. in fine.

Conc Litt 67.
21. E. 4. 22.
per Rede.
29. H. 8. 109.

154 ¶ Diciт̃ q̃ feoffemt̃ dũ moity eſt bon.
B. Feſſements al vſes. 19.

Feffement del
moitie.

155 ¶ Nota q̃ fait enrol in London lia
come fine al cõmon ley (ſed non cõe fine oue
procl̃) & ne beſoigne liuery d̃ ſeiſin ſur tiel
fait. Et ceo eſt diſcontinuaunce ſans liuery,
eo que p le cuſtome la, (que eſt reſerue per
diuers parliamentes) ceo liera come fine *B.*
Fines leuies 110.

London.
Fait inrolle.

22. E. 4. 16.
per Genney.

156 ¶ Home done ɬre a deux & heredibus,
& ne dit ſuis, c̃ neſt fee ſimple. Et fuit dit
que ratio eſt pur ceo q̃ deux ſont noſme en le
fait, et ideo eſt incertaine a que de eux (here-
dibᵍ) ſerr̃ referr̃. Mes ſi fuit niſi vn en le fait,
donques ſerra referre al lũ tantum. Mes en
deuiſe fuit dit per aliquos que les parols ſup̃
ſont fee ſimple, contrary en done et feſſemēt,
car lun ſerr̃ priſe entēdment, et lauſ nemy.
B. Eſtates. 4.

Grauntoufeffe-
ment & deuyſe
diuerſitie.

Diuerſitie.

4. E. 6. Com 28.
20. H. 6. 36.
per Porting.

Intendement.

Vide 27. H. 8.
antea 92.

157 ¶ Seigniour et tenaunt, le tenaunt eſt
attaint de treaſon per act de parliament, et de
forſayture toutes ſes terres, et puis il eſt pardon
et reſtore per auter parliament, habend̃ ſibi &
heredibus, ſicut nul tiel attaynder, ne former
act vſt eſt̃. Ou ſi lheire del ceſtuy que fuit
attaynt ſoyt reſtore par parliament en tyel
forme, ore le ſeigniorie que fuit extinct eſt reuiue, et il tiend̃ del common perſon ſicut prius,
et vncore a vn ſoytes le tenure fuit extinct per
le forſayture del terre al roy. *B. Extinguiſh-*
ment. 47. *Reuiuinges.* 8. *Tenures.* 70.

Reſtituc per par-
liament reuiue
ſeigniorie, ou
tenure q fuit
extinct per at-
tainder de trea-
ſon per parlia-
ment.

158 ¶ Si le baron et femme alien terre de
quel

Collateral garr.

quel el eſt dowable, la dauer collateral garrantie,
il eſt bone dauer le garranty del feme vers luy
et ſes heires, et donques ſi el ad iſſue per le
baron, et el et le baron deuie, le garrantie ſerra
collateral al iſſue, pur ceo que le terre vyent
per le pier, et non p le mier, *B. Garranties,*
79.

Office de charge & de profite diuerſitie.

159 ¶ Nota per plures Juſticiarios et alios
legis peritos, que ou home graunt office de
bayly, ſeneſcal, receiuer, parker, & huiuſmodi,
et fee certaine pur ſon labour tantum, la le
graütor poet expulſe tyels officers. Mes ils
auera lour fee, car neſt que office de charge.
Mes ou le ſeneſcal, et parker ount profittes de
courtes, windfalles, deare ſkinnes, & huiuſmodi
caſuels profittes: Dicitur que ils ne poient eſtre
expulſe, et q̃ de tiels offices ils poient aū aſſiſe.
Et dicitur q̃ fuit iſſint priſe tẽpore Jacobi Hu-
berti Attorñ Regis H. 7. Et lofficers poyent
relinquiſher loffices quant ils voient, mes donq̃s
lour fee ceſſera. Et *Whorewood* Attorñ Regis
H. 8. conceſſit caſus ſupradictos. *B. Graunts.*
134.

**Conc M. 5.
E. 6.
34. H. 8. 243.**

Meaſon.

160 ¶ Home leſſa meaſon cum ptiñ, nul
terre paſſa per hec verba cum pertiñ. Contrary
ſi home leſſa meaſon cum omnibus terris eidem
pertiñ, la les terres a c̃ vſes paſſa, Et plures
grants ſont de omnibus terris in D. nuper
monaſterij de G. pertiñ, et maxime ſil auerre
que ceo ad ptaine de tẽpore &c. *B. Leaſes.*
55.

Auerment.

**Conc M. 3.
M. 1.
23. H. 8. 31.
3. M. 1. Com
168.
Vide 6. & 7.
E. 6. Com 85.
3. M. 1. Com
168.
Vide 2. M. 1.
Com. 103.**

Ou ſuerties in London rem puis lacc’ remoue, & econtra.

161 ¶ Si hõe arreſt en franchiſe, ſua briefe
de priuiledge & remoue le corps et le cauſe, et
puys ne vyent pur prouer ſon cauſe de priuiledge, le plaintiſe in le fraunchiſe poet aū procedendo.

cedendo. Et ideo *B.* femble q̃ la, les primer fuerties remaine : Et econtra fil aũ eſtre diſmiſſe p̃ allowance del priuiledge, car donques ſes fuerties ſont diſcharges: Tamẽ luy femble que quaunt ils remoue le corps & le cauſe, il ne remoue nul fuerties, mes tunc la nẽ aſc̃ recorde vers eux, et donques il femble q̃ le priuiledge eſteant allowe, les fuerties ſont diſcharges. Et ecõtra ou le priuiledge nẽ allowe, car donques le priſoner et le cauſe fuit femper remaĩat in le cuſtody d̃ ceux del frãchiſe. *B. Procedendo.* 13. *Suerties.* 28.

31. H. 8. 191. coatra.

162 ☖ Dicitur pro lege q̃ ſi home recouer terre vers J. S. ou diſſeiſie J. S. il poet plede que il ad ſon eſtate, et vncore il eſt eins en le poſt. *B. Que eſtate.* 48.

39. H. 6. 24. per Nedham.

Que eſtate pled per le recoueror, ou diſſeiſor.

163 ☖ Tenãt a terme de vie furrender a ceſty in reuerſion extr̃ terr̃ a que il agree, le franketenement per ceo eſt en luy maintenaunt, et il eſt tenaunt al action vſer p̃ precipe qd̃ redd̃ fauns entre, fed il nauera trñs fans entre. *B. Surrender.* 50.

Conc Brooke 14. H. 8. 21.

Surrender extra terram.

Treſpas.

163 ☖ Concordatur que ſi home ſoit ſue en le Spiritual Court p̃ur diſmes de ſeiſonable boys, le partie greeue poet faire fuggeſtion in Cãcellaria, vel in Banco Regis, que il eſt ſue in curia ſpirituali pur diſmes de groſſe arbres, que paſſe lage de xx. ans, per noſme Sylua Cedua, q̃ eſt feaſonable wood vſe deſtr̃ ſuccide, ou en fait il eſt groſſe arbres et pria prohibition et auer ceo. Et eadem lex ou home eſt ſue en Curia Admirali pur choſe fayt ſur le mier, ou en fait il fuit ſur le terre, la ſur furmiſe que ceo fuit ſur le tˈre il auera prohibition. *B. Prohibition.* 17.

Conc Fitzh. 43. H.

Surmiſe doptaiſi prohibic'.

Admiraltie.

164 ☖ Fuit

Rationabile parte est per le commen ley.

164 ⦿ Fuit dit pur ley, que le bře de Rationabili parte bonorum eſt p le comen ley, et q̃ ceo ad eſtre ſepe miſe in vre, come vn common ley, et nunquam demurre, ideo *B.* ſeble que ceo eſt le common ley. *B. Rationabili parte.* 6. in fine.

Fitzh. 122. L. Magna charta. ca. 18. Raſt. Det to the king. 2.

Vſury & ou nemy.

165 ⦿ Si home morgage ſa tř ſur defeſans de repaimět, de reenter, per quel endenture le vendee leſſa meſme le terre al vendour pur ans rendant rent, la ſi ſoit condition in le leaſe, que ſi le vendour repay le ſome deuaunt tiel iour quod tunc le leaſe ſerra voyd, ceo neſt vſury. Et econtra, ſil ſoyt de repayer tiel iour certaine, vn an, ou plus puis. *B. Uſury.* 2.

Vide 29. H. 8. 126.

⦿ *An. 32. Henrici octaui.*

Acceptaunce per iſſue en taile del ſecond leſſee. Priuitie.

166 ⦿ Si tenaunt en taile leſſa ſo terř pur 20. ans rendant rent et deuie, & le leſſee leſſa c̄ ouſter a vn aut̃ pur 10. ans & liſſue accept le rent del 2. leſſee, ceo neſt pas affirmance del leaſe, car neſt priuitie enter le ſecond leſſee & luy. Cōtra ſil ceo pay come baily le primer leſſee. Et *B.* ſemble ſi le primer leſſee vſt leſſe ouſtř tout ſon terme in parcel del terre leſſe, et cel aſſignee pay le rēt al iſſue in taile q̃ ceo affirme lentier leaſe, Car rent ſur leaſe pur ans neſt apportionable *B. Acceptance.* 13.

Diuerſitie.

Apporcionment.
Variance del licence.
Fine leuy.

167 ⦿ Si home obtaine licence dalien le maner de D. & toutes ſes terres & tenements en D. il ne puit alien per fine, Car fiñ ſerra certaine tants acres de terre, tantes de pree, tants de paſture, et huiuſmodi. Et lalienation ne doit varier del licence. Tamen par *B.* aliter vtitur oue auermēt q̃ tout c̄ vn, *B. Alienatiōs,* 30.

46. E. 3. 45. per Perſay.

Auerment.

168 ⦿ Si tenant le roy de 4. acrez aliē vn
acre

acre al roy, Ou ſil ad 2. files et deuie, & lū
alien al roy, le rent ſerr̄ apporcion ſi ſoit ſeuerable. Et hoc p le comen ley per aliquos.
Quere, car lectura *Fitziames* eſt contrarie per
B. *Apporcionment.* 23.

Apporcionment
per le comen ley
ſur purchaſe.

Quære.

6. H. 7. 3.
p Brian cont.

169 ❡ Si home ſoit oblig. in bond de paier
20. li. lobligor en que diſcharge le condition
va, doyt eſtre priſt al lieu &c. tout le iour, &
lobligee poit veñ aſcun temps del iour. B.
Conditions. 192.

Ceſty que voit
aver auantage de
condicion done-
ra attendance.

20. H. 8. 10.

170 ❡ Per *Fitzherbert* Si Labbe & Couent
vend tout les ſres, & labbey, vncore le corporation remayne. Quere per B. de que il ſerra
Abbe, car la ē nul eſgliſe ne monaſtery. Et
p luy Quere ſi labbe deuie ſils. s. le Couent,
poient eſlier auter, le meaſo eſteant diſſolue.
B. *Corporations* 78.

Abbey extinct.

Quære.

19. H. 8. 19.

29. H. 8.

171 ❡ Nota q̄ eſtatut ſtaple, ne fait inroll
ne ſerra accept de fēe couert p le comon ley,
Contrarie per le cuſtome in London del fait
inroll. Car ceo liera in London cōe fine al
comō ley (B. *Couture,* 59. 76. in fine.) Nec
fine, ſtat, ne fait inroll, ne ſerra ſuffer p inf.
B. *Couerture.* 59. in fine.

Del fine 30. H.
8. 138.

Fait inrol p ſem
couert p le com-
men ley, Et per
cuſtome diūſitie.
London.

Infancie.

11. E. 3.
F. Abbe 9.

172 ❡ Si vn pſon deſgliſe leſſa pur vie, &
deuie, le ſucceſſour accept fealtie, il ſerra lie
per ceo durant ſon vie, Contra ſur leaſe pur
ans fait p luy, ceo ne liera le ſucceſſor p acceptance de rent, car void p mort le leſſour. B.
Deane. 20. *Encūbent.* 18. *Leaſes.* 52.

Leaſe pur vie per
perſon, & leaſe
pur ans diūſity.

24. H. 8. 54.
38. H. 8. 321.

173 ❡ Inquiſition troue que J. S. tient certaine terre del roy vt de honōr ſuo Glouceſter
q̄ nē in capite, ſur q̄ proces iſſiſt vers W. S. q̄
aſī intrude &c. et de ſuer liuery, et pur ceo q̄
cē tenure neſt in capite, & ideo liuery nē due,
le

Demurr ſur
office.

Poſt. 189.

Pur ql tenure li-
uery eſt due al
roy.

le partie demurre en ley ſur le record, car ē nul
cauſe đ liuery.   Et lou hōe declare ſur ſtatute
& recite ceo auterment q̃ il neſt, Ou pleđ ſtaī   33. H. 8. 229.
auterment q̃ il neſt, lauter poet demurr̃ ſur c̃,
car nul tiel ley ſil ſoit miſrecite.   *B. Demurrer
en ley.* 25.

Trouer.

174 ❡ Per *Shelley* et alios, ſi home medle   27. H. 8. 13.
oue biens, cōe p trouer de eux, il ſerra ent   contr per
Fitzh.
charge comēt q̃ il eux liuer ouſter deuaunt
aĉtion port, *B. Detinue de biens.* 1. en fine.

Aĉtes executed
deuant le deuorce

175 ❡ Nota pur ley, que ou le baron et
feme ſont deuorces ou il eſt enheritrix, vncore
meine aĉts executed ne ſerr̃ reuerſe p le deuorce
come waſt, receipt de rēts, priſel de garde, preſentment al benefice, done de byens le feme,

Diuerſitie.

Contra denheritaunce, come ſi le baron vſt diſcontinue, ou charge le terre ſon feñ, Cui ante ·

Cui ante diuor-
cium.

diuorciū giſt.   Et idem de releaſe le baron.
Ou manumiſſiō dez villains & huiuſmodi.   Et
ſi le baron et feme purchaſe iointment, & ſont
diſſeiſie le barō releas, & puis ſont diuorces, le
feme auera le moitie, coment que ne fueront
moities deuāt le deuorce, car le deuorce conuert
ceo ē moities.   *B. Deraignement.* 18.

Det pur Reliefe.

176 ❡ Adminiſtrator dun ſeigniour port
aĉtion de dette del reliefe que chia tempore inteſtati, et le defendaunt plede en barre et trauers le tenure, et ſic al iſſue.   Et ideo *B.* ſemble
que laĉtion giſt cleremēt pur luy, Car le defendant ne demurre.   Iſſint ſi ſoit port per execuī
del ſñr de reliefe due al teſtator.   Rotul 529.   7. H. 6. 13.
per Rolfe.
en communi Banco.   *B. Det* 193. *Reliefe.* 11.
in finibus.

Rec' vers tenant
en taile le reuer-
ſion en le Roy.

177 ❡ Recouery vers tenaunt in taile, le   30. H. 8. 145.
reuerſion, ou remainder en le roy in fee, liera   33. H. 8. 224.
le

Poft. 192. cõt
Conc 2. M. 1.
& 5. E. 6.

le tenant in taile, et liſſue in taile, mes ne liera le roy.

Mes ore per leſtatut il ne liera liſſu in taile, mes q̃ il poet enter, *B. Diſcõtinuance de poſſeſſion.* 32.

178 ℂ Dictũ fuit que ſi perſon demiſe ſ. glebe al lay hõe, la il payer diſmes. Contra del perſon meſme que eux reſerue in ſõ proper mayns. Et que terre prius diſcharge de diſmes ſerra vnquez diſcharge de diſmes. Uncore ſi ceſtuy que ad purchaſe manner et rectorie que eſt diſcharge de diſmes, leſſa part de ſon demeſnes, le leſſor auera diſmes de ceo, pur ceo que il ad le parſonage. *B. Diſmes.* 17.

Lay home paiera
diſmes pur ſpiri-
tual terre, Con-
tra de home ſpi-
ritual.

Conc Moile &
Aſhton 39. H.
6. 45.

179 ℂ Home fiſt deux execut̃s et deuie, lun execut̃ fiſt execut̃ et deuie, et lauter ſuruiue & deuie inteſtate, le executor del execut̃ ne medlera, car le power de ſõ teſtator fuit termine par le mort de luy, et per le ſuruiuor del auter, iſſint que ore lordinarie committera ladminiſtration des byens lexecutour que ſuruiue, et de bonis non adminiſtratis del primer teſtator, *B. Executors.* 149.

Exec' del exec'.

19. H. 8. 8.
per Fitzh.

180 ℂ Home fiſt A. & B. ſes exec̃ & voit que B. ne medlera durant le vie A. & bien, car il ne reſtrayne ſon entire power, car il poet faire vn executor de ſes biens in C. & aut̃ exec̃ de ſes b̃ns in D. Et iſſint deuide le temps vt ſupra. *B. Executors* 155.

ij. Executors dõt
lũ ne medler pur
certein temps.

Tẽp. H. 8. 358.

7. & 8. El.
Com 302.

181 ℂ Si home achate terre et le vendor execute eſtate al vẽdee, habẽd ſibi imperpetuum ſauns parols de heires, ou leatent del bargaine eſt de paſſ. fee ſimple, et le vendor ſur requeſt refuſe de faire aut̃ aſſurance, la giſt briefe de ſub pena. *B. Conference.* 25.

Sub pena pur ex-
ecut eſtate.

182 ℂ G.

Cafus wimbiſh.

182 ❡ G. T. Chiualer ſeyſie en taile a luy & lhrs males de ſõ corps diſcontinue, & repriſt a luy & E. ſa feme, & al heires de lour deux corps, & auoit iſſue T. & W. & deuie, & E. ſa feme ſuruiue, & T. auoit iſſue E. nuptam T. W. & deuie, & puis W. per couin E. ſa mere tenaunt in iointure, port formedon ſur leigne tayle Ꝗs ſon mere, & el appere al primer iour & W. recouer per nyent dedire & T. W. & E. ſa feme heire al G. enter per leſtatute de 11. H. 7. Et lentre adiudge loyal per m̃ le eſtatute, que voet tiels diſcontinuances, alienationz, garr̃ & recoueries ſerr̃ void, (*B. Entre Congeable* 140. *Iudgement*. 153.) Et ne beſoigne adire que le recouery fuit execute, car pur ceo q̃ eſt voide, il ne vnques ſerra execute. Et E. lheire auerre que il eſt meſm̃ le perſon a que le reuerſion appertient, & ne monſtra coment el eſt hr̃e a ceo, & vncore byen per *Molineux* et *Hales* Juſtices, contrar̃ *Browne* et *Mountague* chiefe Juſtyce del common banke. Mes toutes agree que fuit recouery per couin, nient obſtant que fuit ſur voyer title. Et bien, non obſtaunt que il ne monſtra cauſe del couin. *B. Entre côgeable* 140. *Colluſion* 47.

Recouery void.

Auerment.

Rec ſur voyer title fauxifie.

Couin.

183 ❡ Seignior & tenant, le teñt tient per 3. d. 3. acres de terre, le tenaunt enfeoffe le ſeignior in fee dun acre, le ſeigniory eſt extinĉt pur le 3. parte, & remaine pur lauterz 2. partz, Mes ſi le tenaunt vſt leſſe al ſeygnior vn acre pur ans, la le ſeigniory eſt ſuſpende en tout durant le term̃, car ſeygniory poet eſtre extinĉt en parte, mes nemy ſuſpende en parte, ſed pur lentier. *B. Extinguiſhment*. 48.

Extinguiſhment. & ſuſpencion diuerſitie. Seigniorie.

184 ❡ Si couenauntes & agreementes ſont contaigne

Similis caſus inter Villires, & Beamõt fuit adiudge in communi banco. T. 4. M. 1. 4. E. 6. Com 42

11. H. 7. 20. Raſt. Diſcont of Proces 1.

Vide ſupra 168. Litt 48. Conc 11. H. 7. 13. p Dauers. Park. 16. C.

contaigne in Indentures & non vſes, & eſt couenãt per ceo Indẽtures que A. recouer vers B.
ſon Pre en D. al vſe del recoueror & ſes heires,
& al vſes del couenauntes & agreementes en
lendentures, la ſil recouer, le recouery ſerra al
vſe del recoueror & ſes heires, et non al vſes
del couenants, & agreementes in lendenture, ou
nul vſes ſont en lendenture. Mes econtra ſi
vſes ſont conteigne en lendenture, et eſt couenaunted que A. recouer al vſe de A. & ſes
heires, & al vſes en lendenture, la le recouery
irra accordant, & ſerra executed per leſtatute.
B. Feoffements al uſes 58.

27. H. 7. ca. 10.
Raſt. Vſes 9.
31. H. 8. 160.

185 ❡ Si home fait feoffemẽt dũ meaſon,
ac omnia terras, tenementa & hereditam̃ta
eidem meſ. pertineñ, aut cum eodem occupaꝯ
locaꝯ, aut dimiſſ. exiſteñ, p ceo le terr̃ vſe oue
le meaſon paſſer. **B. Feoffementes 53. in fine.**

27. H. 8. ca. 10.

186 ❡ Hõe fait feſſemt deuant leſtatute
dexecution de vſes, al vſe de luy m̃ pur terme
de ſon vie, le rem̃ a W. en taile, le rem̃ al dr̃t
hr̃s le feſſor, le feſſor deuie, & W. deuie ſans
iſſue, le dr̃t hr̃e le feſſor deins age, il ſerr̃ in
gard p le fee diſcẽd, car luſe d̃ fee ſimple ne
fuit vnꝗ hors del feſſor. Et ead lex ou home
don en taile le rem̃ as droit heires le donor, le
fee neſt hors de luy. Contrary lex ou home
fait feoffement in fee ſur condition de luy re-
feſſer, et le feſſee dõe al feſſor pur vie, le remainder ouſter in taile, le rem̃ al droit heires le
feſſor, car la le fee & luſe d̃ ceo fuit horz de le
feſſour, et ideo il ad la vn rem̃ & nemy reuerſion, (*B. Gard* 93.) Et ſi home tyent del roy
deuaunt leſtatute de vſes, & infeoſſe auters a ſõ
vſe pur terme de vie, le remaynder ouſter en
taile,

Recouery al vſe
del couenants &
agreements en
lindenture, & re-
couery al vſe en
indenture diū.

Remainder al
droit heires.

Reuerſion &
rem diuerſ.

Ou home ſuera
liũy, & ou nemy.

taile, le remaind a ſes dr̃t heires, & deuie, &
puis le tenaunt en taile deuie ſans iſſue, lheire
del feffor ſuera liuery, car le fee ſimple ne vnques fuit hors de luy, & ideo ceo diſcend a ſon
heire, & ſil ad ceo per dyſcent, il ſuera liuery.
Et eadem lex, et pro eadem ratione, ſi a ceſt
iour home done in taile, le remaynder a ſes dr̃t
heires. Aliter *B.* ſemble ou home fait feoffement en fee in poſſeſſion & luy diſmiſſe de tout,
et repriſe pur terme de vie, le remainder en
taile, le rem̃ a ſes dr̃t heires, & deuie, & puis
le teñt en taile deuie ſãs iſſue, la lheire que eſt
droit heire, eſt purchaſor. Et ſi le roy ſeiſiſt,
il ſuera ouſter le maine, et ne ſerra arct de ſuer
liuery. Mes ſi le tenaunt in tayle vſt deuie
ſauns iſſue en le vie le tenaunt pur vie, et puis
le tenaunt pur vie deuie, la ſon heire ſuera
liuery, car le fee ſimple fuit veſt en le tenaunt
pur vie per extinguiſhment de meſmė rem̃, &
ideo la le fee ſimple diſcēd. Et nota liuery eſt
que le roy auera le value del terre per demy an.

29. H. 8. 114.
Vide 38. H. 8. 322.

Diũſitie, de ouſtr le maine & liũy.
Et ouſter le maine ē briefe de ouſter le roy del
terre ſauns aſcun profit don al roy. *B. Liuery.*
61.

Liuery de terre ſocage.

188 ℂ Ou home tient certaine r̃re del roy in
ſocage en capite, le roy nauera liuerie de pluis
que de terre ſocage. Idem ou tient d̃l roy in
chiualry & non in capite, le roy nauera plus in
garde, mes tantum ceo que ē tenus de luy im-
mediatement. *B. Gard* 97.

Fitzh. 256. C.
Vide 38. H. 8. 322.
Stp. 10. 13.

Tenure del Roy en Chiualry, & in capite diũſ.

189 ℂ Ceſty que tient del roy en chiualrie
& nemy in capite, ne ſuera liuery, eo que il ne
tient in capĩt, & la quaunt lheire vyent a pleyne
age, il auera ouſt̃ le maine, car nul poit enter
ſur le roy. Mes ſil ſoit de pleine age al temps
del

Vide 33. H. 8.
230.
Stp. 13.

del mort fon aunceftour, dõques il rendra reliefe al roy & alera quite. Sicõe il tenuſt dl vn cõmon perſo. Contra de Tenure in Capite. *B. Liuery* 62.

Supra 173.

Reliefe.

190 ¶ Trefpas fur le cafe quod def. affumpfit deliberaꝛ quer. 4. pannos laneos, et il plede quod affumpfit liberare 4. pannos lineos, fauns ceo quod affumpfit modo & forma, & fic al iffue. Et ē troue que il affuma pur liuer 2. pannos laneos, fed non 4 (fic vide que ceſt iffue, coment que il vient en vn trauers, ne amount niſi al general iffue) Le plaintife recouer damages pur lez 2. & fuit barꝛ et amercie pur le reſt. Mes aliter eſt ſi liffue foit, Si A. & B. enfeffe le tenaunt in Precipe quod reddat, necne, & troue eſt que A. luy enfeffe, mes que A. & B. non enfeoffe luy, ceo eſt troue contra le tenant in toto, Ou contra luy que plede tiel feoffement q̃ eſt iffint troue *B. Iſſues ioynes* 80. *Verdiƈt* 90.

Vide 2. M. 1. 460.

10. E. 4. 2. per Litt.

Accion fur le cafe fur affūpſ.

Special verdiƈt ou liffue eſt fur vn abſque hoc.

Amerciament. Iffue troue in part diuerſitie.

191 ¶ Si home foyt arreſt en London, & troue fuerties al playntife la, et puis eſt difmiffe in banco per briefe de Priuiledge, & puis procedendo vient en mefme le fuit all Court de London, ceo ne reuiuera le primer mainprife, ou fuerteſhip, car vn foites difmiffe & femper difmiffe. Et dicitur que puis que home ad troue maynprife al bill in banco regis, et puis foit al iffue ou demurrer, et puis foit agard de repleder, & d̃ faire nouel declaraꝛ, le mainprife p ceo ē difcharge, Contrary ou ils manuceperunt vſq̃ finē placiti, & ou le originall remaine. *B. Mainprife* 96.

31. H. 8. 161. contra.

Suertie fur arreſt en London.

Priuiledge. Procedendo.

Reuiuinges.

Ou fuertie fur bil in banco Regis eſt difcharge, & ou nemy. Repleder.

192 ¶ Roy done al Comiti de Rutland in taile, & puis intende de doner ceo a luy in fee ſimple,

Extinƈt del taile per furrender del letters patents.

ſimple, et dextinꝗ le taile, & dubitabatur ꝗ le ſurrender del letters patents del tayle & le cancellation del ceo, & del enrolment & bil aſſigned, ne doit extinꝗe le taile, car le taile executed poit eſtꝛ auerre ſauns monſtre le patent. Et formedon giſt puis le taile exe-cuted ſans monſtre le patet. Et fuit priſe que ne fuit bone ſuertie pur le roy pur ſes ſeruices de doñ le reuerſion, tenend le reuerſion per tiels ſeruicez quant ceo veſt, & de except les primers ſeruices duraunt le tayle, car quaunt le re-uerſion eſt ale, le rent et ſeruices reſeruez ſur le taile ſōt alez cibñ in caſu regis, vt in caſu cōmunis pſone. Et ideo le deuiſe fuit ꝗ le roy per nouel patent recitant le prim̄ patent, donera le reſſſion, & le primer rent & ſeruices, habend in fee, tenend p tales ſeruices, & red-dend tiel rēt, & per ceo le roy auera le nouel tenure maintenaunt, & le grauntee ne ſerra charge de double ſeruices & rentes duraunt le tayle. Et fuit agree pur ley, que ſi home perda ſez letterz patentes, il auera Conſtat del letters patentes hors del enrolement, et bil aſ-ſigned, que remain in Cancellaria, Et ideo *B.* ſemble que lenrolment ne ſerra cancell (*B. Patentes* 97.) Et fuit agree p *Wherwood* Attorñ Regis, & optimos legis peritos, que ſi tenant in taile de done le roy ſurrender ſes letters patentes, ceo ne extinꝗera le taile, car lenrolm̄t remaiñ de recorde, extra quod liſſue en tayle poet auer Conſtat, & recouer le ꞇre per que ils fierōt le deuiſe vt ſupra, ſ. que le roy grautera al dit Comiti tenaunt en taile le fee ſimple auxi, & dōques recouery ꝕs luy doit barrer le taile. Et econtra le reuerſion eſteant

Marginal notes:

Formedon ſans mre patent.

Aſſurance.

Conſtat.

Surrender.

4. E. 6. Com 5. contr.

35. H. 8. 273.

Vide 12. H. 7. 12. per Fiſher.

Supra 177. contra.

en

en le roy, (*B. Surrender* 51. in fine) Et dicitur pro lege, ſi le roy done in fee, ou in taile, ou pur vie, le patentee leſſa ceo pur ans, ou graūta, leſſa ou dona part del terre ou del intereſt a auter, & puis ſurrender ſō patent, per q̃ ceo eſt cancell, ceo ne preiudicera le 3. perſon que il perdra ſon intereſt per ceo, car il poet auer Conſtat hors del enrolment, q̃ luy ſeruera, quere inde, Quia vn eſtatut eſt fait de ceo. Et quere ſi le comen ley ne ſerſſa, car patet libro Intraſtionum fo. que home plediſt vn Cōſtat. *B. Patēts* in fine 79. *Surrender* 51.

193 ¶ Diſtum fuit pro lege, que le roy poet graunt choſe in aſtion q̃ eſt perſonal, come dette & damages, vel hm̃oi, Ou choſe mixt, come le garde del corps. Mes nemie choſe real come aſtion de terre et huiuſmodi, come droites, entries, aſtions, & huiuſmodi, que abbeyes poient aſ (Et que le roy auera ceux par ſtatute de diſſolutiō de Abbeys 31. H. 8.) ceux choſes en aſtyon le roy ne poet graunter. Tamen per *B.* vide ſi ne ſoient parols in cell ſtatute de mitter le roy in poſſeſſion, coment que Labbe fuit miſe a ſon Aſtion. *B. Patents* 98.

194 ¶ Si villeine vient a vn cōe executour, ou al vn Eueſque perſon ou huiuſmodi in iure eccleſie, et il purchaſe terre, lexecutor enter, il nauera ceo, iure pprio, ſed come executor, et ſerra aſſets. Et ſi leueſque, ou le perſon enter, il nauera ceo mes en iure eccleſie, pur c̃ que ceux naſſa le villein in iur̃ proprio, ſed in auſ dr̃t, Contrary ſils ount ewe le villaine iure proprio. *B. Villenage* 46.

196 ¶ Fuit tenus pur ley que en briefe dattaint home nauera ſuperſedias pur diſtourber execution,

4. E. 6. ca. 4.

33. H. 8. 211.
2. H. 7. 8.
per Huſſey.

D S. 92.
7. El. Com 292

3. El. Com 235

5. H. 7. 22.
4. E. 6. Com. 49

Patentee leſſe ou done, & puis ſurr ſon patent.

Conſtat.
Quære.

Choſe in accion perſonal mixt, & real diuerſitie.

Aſſets inter maines.

Diuerſitie.

Attaint.

execution, car le verdict ferra entend voler
quoufque eft reuerfe &c. Et que le Regifter que
done fuperfedias la neft ley. Contrarye fur briefe
derrour, Car poet eftre intend que errour eft
pur le fuit le def. &c. *B. Superfedias.* 24.

Errour.

4. E. 6. Com 49

167 ⟨ Si home port dette de 10. li. le defendaunt gage fo ley. Et puis le plaintife
port actyon fur cafe vers mefme le def. quod
affumpfit foluere les 10. li. &c. Le def. puit
plede que de mefme le fumme le plaintife port
auterfoits action de det, en que le def. gage
fon ley, iudgement fi action. Et bon plee, car
il fuit vn foits barre de mefme le fumme. Et
en action fur le cafe quod def. affumpfit de
payer 10. li. al plaintife, quel il deĝ a luy pur
vn chiual, et vn vache, le def. poet dire que il
affumpfit foluere 10. li. al plaintife que il deuer
a luy pur vn chiual q̃ il achate d luy, quel
fumme il ad paye al plaintife, fans ceo que il
affumpfit foluere 10. li. quas debuit. querent pro
vno equo & vna vacca prout &c. Vel abfque
hoc quod debuit al pł 10 li. pro equo & vacca,
prout &c. *B. Action fur le cafe* 105.

*Barre en accion
fur le cafe, per
ley gager ē det.*

*Conc 2. R. 3. 14
P. Brian.*

*Plee pur auoyder
double charge.*

Trauers.

198 ⟨ Action fur le cafe eo que le def.
troue les biens le plaintife et eux liuer as perfons difconus, la non liberauit modo et forma
neft plee, fans dire non culpable, ou le chofe
reft en fefans. Et fi laction fuit quod cum quer
poff. fuit &c. vt de bonis propriis, & le defendant eux trouer, & ceux conuert en fon proper
vfe, il nē plee quod quer non fuit poffeffionatus
vt de propriis, mes dirra non culpable al mifde-
meanour, et donera in euidence quod non fueront
bona querentis, & tamen verum quod non culpable erga ipfum. *B. Actió fur le cafe* 109.

*Acció fur le cafe
fur trouer biens.*

Conc 3. M. 1.

*2. E. 6. 382.
Vide 4. E. 6.
405.*

Euidence.

199 ⟨ Nota

21. E. 4. 21. per
Choke & Nele.
Park. 94. E.
190. E.
D S. 79.
37. H. 6. 30.
per Prifot.
1. H. 6. 16.
per Curiam.

21. E. 4. 52.

3. M. 1. Com
150.

199 ¶ Nota ſi executours plede pleinement adminiſter in acc̄ de det, & done en euidence paymēt de legacies, le pl' en aſtion de dette poet demurre en ley ſur ceo, Car tiel adminiſtration neſt allowable in le ley deuant les dettes pay. *B. Aſſets enter maines* 10.

200 ¶ Nota lou home pled recoũy p eſtrauḡe noſm̄ del choſe dđ. (*B. Auments* 42.) Cōe ſi Preč qđ redđ ſoit port đl mañ de B. vel hm̄dí, le ĩ plede fin̄, recoũry, vel hm̄dí del mañ de O. il doit auerre que lun manour et lauter ſount vn meſme manour & nemy diuerſ. Contrarye ſil plede fine ou recouery de prediſto manerio de *B.* Car hoc verbum (prediſt) eſt en effeſt vn auerment que tout eſt vn (*B. Pledinges* 143.) Et lou home plede recouerye per eſtraunge noſm̄ del parties, il doit auerrer q̄ le primer perſon, et ceſty perſon, ſont vn meſme perſon, et nemy dyuers, Aliter *B.* ſemble ou il ceo plede per hoc verbū prediſt. *B. Auerments* 24.

201 ¶ Eueſque charge, Ou grāt office oue laſſent le dean & chapter et deuie, ceo ne vault per aliquos, Car doit eſtre confirme p le Deane & chapter. Et hoc accidit in le graūt del office del Seneſchal del eueſq̄ de Londō, enter Aldred Fitziames, & John Edmundes del Middle Temple, Lou leueſque graunt le ſeneſcall' de ſes ťres al Aldred Fitziames, per aſſent le Deane et chapter & deuie, per que le grantee parde loffice vt dicitur, pur ceo q̄ le Deane & chapter nauer ceo confirme. Tamen plus fuit en le graunt de leueſque, come miſnoſmer & huiuſmodi, car le dit Aldred Fitziamez fuit noſme Etheldredus, ou ſerroyt Aldredus,

Demurre ſur euidence.
Legacies ne ſerra pay deuant deta,

Ou home doit aſ que lun & lauter ſont vn, et nemy diuera, Et ou ecōtra.

Prædiſt ſerue pur auerment.

Leueſque charge oue laſſent Decani & Capit.

Miſnoſmer.

dredus, et iſſint fuit miſnoſme. Auxy fuit default in le ſeale (*B. Charge* 58. *Confirmations* 30) Et auxi le fait fuit quod ſigillum noſtrum appoſuimuz que puit eſtre referre al Eueſque tantum, & non al Eueſq̖ Deane et chapiter. Et ideo p plures ad hunc diem le graunt fuit auoide pur ceux cauſes, & non pur lauter cauſe. Et iſſint graunt oue aſſent del Deane et chapiter oue toutes perfeȼions ē bone. *B. Confirmations.* 30 in fine.

Sigillum. Relation.

202 ⓒ Si Eueſque ſoit patron, & le perſon fait leaſe ou graunt p fait la leueſque, patron, & lordinary, & le Deane et chapter doient confirme, ſi le gr̃t ou leaſe ſerr̃ ſure, Et econt̃ ou lay home eſt patron in fee, et il et lordinary confirme, ceo ſuffiſt ſauns le Deane & Chapter, car en le priṁ caſe, leueſque Patron ad intereſt in inheritaunce al Eueſcherie. Mes in lauter caſe il nad que vn iudiciall power, ideo ſuffiſt que ceſty que ad le power all temps &c. confirme car ceo eſt iudicial aȼ. Mes in lauter caſe, il lie linheritance, que il ad in iure ecclſie, quel ne poet faire vers ſon ſucceſſour, ſans confirmation p le Deane & Chapter. (*B. Confirmation* 21. *Charge* 40, *Leaſes* 64.) Patet hic que le patr̄o doit auer fee ſimple, & hoc iure proprio per cauſe del Deane & Chapter deſtre ioyne oue leueſque ou il ē patron. *B. Charge* 40.

Ou confirmation ſerr per leueſque deane, & chapiter, Et econtra.

Intereſt & iudicial power diūſ.

Patron ad fee.

203 ⓒ Nota q̄ ſi le roy pur luy et ſes heires graunt catalla felonum & fugitiuorum, vel huiuſmodi, queux giſont en grant, & il deuie, le graūtee ne beſoigne confirmation del nouell roy. Mes ſi ſoit faire ou market vel hṁodi, & ſoit abuſe ou miſuſe come poet eſtre. Ou ſi ſoit iudiciall ou miniſteriall office ou power, c̄oe deſt?

Ou le confirmac del nouel roy eſt neceſſary, Et ou nemy.

Fraunchiſe.

Caſus Hill pur le Parſonage. & glebe de Stoke ſuper Derne, in com Salop, lou le pſon, patron, deane, & chapitr ſier laſſurance. B. Charge 40. in fine.

1. R. 3. 4.

deſt̃ Juſtice de peace, Eſchetor, vel hm̃di, la il doit
auer confirmation del nouel roy (*B. Confirmation*
19. & 29.) Tamē *B.* ſemble q̃ le graūt de choſe q̃
giſt en graunt ē bone clerement, ſans ceux parolz,
pur luy & ſes hr̃s, Mes de garrantie, couenant,
annuitie, vel hm̃di, la il doit faire ceo pur luy
& ſes heires. *B. Confirmation.* 19.

Ceux parolx pur luy & ſes heires, in graunt le Roy, Et econtra.

Conc M. 4.
M. 1. in caſu.
Mainwaring.

204 ❧ Nota ou ē troue p office q̃ J. N. t̃ le
roy fuit ſeiſie & deuie ſeiſie, & q̃ W. ſon heire
intrude, & puis per act de parliament le roy
pardon touts intruſions, in ceo caſe lentre &
loffence ē pardō, mez nemy liſſues & profits,
car d̃ c̃ leſchetor ſerr̃ charge per viam compoti,
ſil ad eux receiue ou nemy, car q̃nt loffice eſt
de record il doit eux receuer, Niſi ou eſt troue
in loffice q̃ tiel home prët ent les pfits. Mes
ou le roy pardon, ou nul office eſt troue, lhr̃e
eſt diſcharge ci-bien des iſſues & profites, Et
auxy de liuery. Cōe de intruſion per reaſon
del pardon, car p ceo tout ē pdō, Et la coment
que loffice vient puis que troue lentruſion del
hr̃e, vncore tout ē ale p le pardon & ceo
ſeruera, pur ceo q̃ tout fuit pdon deuant, a q̃
le roy fuit intitle de recorde. *B. Charters de*
pardon 71. *Intruſions* 21. *Iſſues retornes* 22.

Ou pardon dentruſion excuſe liſſues liuery, &c. Et ou nemy.

30. H. 8. 130.

26. H. 8. hic 83.

205 ❧ Office auera relatiō al mort launc.
q̃nt al terre diſcend al hr̃e le t̃ le roy & q̃nt
al intruſion (*B. Relation.* 18 in fine.) Sed
ecōtra q̃nt al alienation fait p t̃ le roy ſans
licēce, ceo nauera relation deuāt le trou̅ de
ceo (*B. Relation* 18. *Intruſion* 19.) Et tiel
entrie p purchaſe nē appelle intruſion, mes vn
treſpas, & iſſint ſont les parols del pardō inde,
qd̃ Pardonamus trangreſſiō p̃dictam &c. *B.*
Intruſion 19.

Diuerſitie.

206 ❧ Si

Prefcription ale per graunt.

206 ❡ Si home ad liberties, rent commen vel hm̃di per prefcriptyon, et puis prift ent graunt del roy per patent, ou dun auter per fait, ceo determinera fon prefcription per conclufion. *B. Prefcription.* 102. *Eftoppel* 210). Car efcript determinera contraɛt & matters in faitz. *B.* (*Prefcription* 102.)

29. H. 8. 105.

Reenter per ii. ou vers ii. ou lū deuye.

207 ❡ Si home enfeffe 2. fur cōdition que ils enfeoffe W. N. deuãt Michael, et lun deuie lauť fole fayt le feoffement ceo eft bone. Eadem lex fi 2. leffe terre rendaunt rent, et que fi foit arere p· 2. mois, & loyalmēt demaund per les dits leffours, que ils poient reenter, lun deuie, et lauter que furuiue ceo demaund et neft pay, il poet reenter. Et eadem lex fi le leafe fuit fait a 2. oue parrols que fi foit arrere & demaund de eux 2. &c. et lun deuie, et le leffour demaund ceo de lauter que furuiue, et il ne pay, ceo eft bone demaunde & le leffour poet reenter. *B. Ioyntenants* 62.

41. E. 3. 18. per Finch.

Ou home auera petition, & ou trauers.

208 ❡ Tenetur pro lege, fi le roy foit intitle per double matter de recorde, come eft enaɛt per parliament que J. S. ferra attaint d̃ treafon, ou felonie, et forfetra toutes fes terres, Et auxi office eft ent troue, la le partie que droit ad, ne poet traɛtfe mes eft mife al petition. Et eadem lex fi le roy ceo graunt oufter puis le double matter de record troue. (*B. Petition.* 35. *Trauers doffice,* 51.) Mez ou le roy nad auter title nifi per faux office, la le partie que poet faire title, poet trauers tam verfus regem, quam verfus partem, fi le roy ad ceo graunt oufter, Mes ore ceft aide per ftatute, *B. Trauers doffice* 51. in fine.

3. H. 7. 3. per Keble.
3. E. 4. 25. & 4. E. 4. 25.

10. H. 6. 15.
4. E. 4. 25.
Conc. Laicon 35. H. 6. 61.

2. E. 6. ca. 8.

209 ❡ Si leffee pur ans deuife fon terme, Ou

Vide temp.
H. 8. 334.

Remainder de chattel deuife.

Ou auter ſon chattel ou biens per teſtament a vn pur terme de ſa vie, le remainder ouſter a auter et deuie, et le deuiſee enter, et ne alien le terme, ne done ou vend le chattel, et deuie, la ceſty ē remaynder ceo auera. Mes ſi le primer deuiſee vſt ceo alien, done, ou vend, la ceſty in remainder vſt eſtre ſaūs remedy d ceo.

Diuerſitie.

(*B. Chattels* 23. *Done.* 57. infra. Et iſſint *B.* ſemble ſi ſoient forſaits in ſon vie, ceſtuy in remainder nad remedy. *B. Done* 57. in fine.

Forſeiture.

35. H. 8. 274.

210. ☾ Home ne poet faire manner a ceſt iour, non obſtant que il done terre a pluſours ſeperaliter in tayle, a tener de luy per ſeruices, et ſuit de ſon court, car il poet faire tenure, mes nemy court, car court ne poet eſtre niſi per continuance, cuius contrarium memoř hominum non exiſtit. Et dicitur pro lege, que ſi māner ſoyt, et toutes les franktenures eſcheate al ſeigniour preter vn, ou ſil purchaſe toutes preter vn, la puis ceo. s. manner eſt extinct, Car ne poet eſtre manner niſi ſoit court bař a ceo. Et court baron ne poet eſtre tenus niſi deuaunt ſutours, et non deuāt vn ſutor, ideo vn frank-tenant tantū ne poet faire manner. *B. Compriſe.* 31. *Manour.* 5.

Feiſans de manour.

23. H. 8. 23.

Court baron.

Suitors.

19. H. 6. hic 7.
Tēp. H. 8. 332.

32. H. 8. 198.

4. M. 1. Com 173.

211. ☾ Nota ou leſtatute de 31. H. 8. done al roy, les poſſeſſions de abbeys, et touts droits ētries, actions, conditions & huiuſmodi q̄ labbies poiēt auer ewe, & que il ſerra in poſſeſſion ſauns office, & que il ſerra adiudge in actual et real poſſeſſion de ceux in tiel plite & ſort q̄ ils fueront tempore cōfectionis ſtatuti illius: Uncore. ſi abbe fuit diſſeiſie de 4. acres de terre, le roy ne poet ceo graunt ouſter deuant entrie fait per luy in ceo, pur ceo que ē choſe in

Choſe in accion veſt in le roy per leſtatut de 31. H. 8. cap.

in aftion reall. Et nyent ſemble al choſe in
aftion perſonall, ou mixt, come det, gard, et
huiuſmodi, p Aliquos. Et aliqui econtra per
reaſon de ceux parols que le roy ſerra in
poſſeſſion, Tamen p *B.* hoc videtur, que il
ſerra in tiel poſſeſſion come labbe fuit. s. de
choſe doūt labbe auoit poſſeſſion, le roy ad de
ceo aftual poſſeſſion, Et de tielz dont labbe
nauoit que cauſe dētre, ou droit in aftion, de
ceux le roy ſerra veſt dū title dētre & title
dacē. Mes í choſe a q̄l il ad tiel cauſe dētrie
ou dacē nē pur ē in luy in poſſ. Et ideo ne poet
paſſer del roy p general parols, mes *B.* ſemble
ſi le roy recite le diſſeiſin, et coment le droit
& aftion eſt dōe ent a luy p leſtatute, et graūt
ceo eſpecialment q̄ ceo eſt bō, *B.* *Choſe in*
Aftion. 14.

Condition ne
ſerra apporcion.

212 ⸿ Home done terre in tayle ou leſſa t̄
pur vie, ou pur ans rendāt rēt oue. vn condition que pur defaut de paymēt de reenter, la
ſil leſſa parte del t̄re al donour ou leſſour :
Ou ſi le donour ou leſſour enter en parte del
terre, il ne poet reenter pur rent arere apres,
Mes le condition eſt ſuſpende en tout: Car
condition ne poet eſtre apportion, ne deuyde *B.*
Extinguiſhment. 49. *Conditions.* 193.

Park. 163. C.

Condicions per-
forme.

213 ⸿ Det ſur obligation de perfourme
touts couenants cōtayne in certeine Indentures,
il neſt plee q̄ il ad perfourme toutes les couenants generalm̄t, s. quod pformauit omnes &
ſingulas conuentiones in Indētura predict̄ ſpeci-
ficat̄ ex parte ſua perimplēd, ſils ſoūt in laffirmatiue. Mez mōſtra certein in cheſcun point, coment il ad eux perfourme, (*B. Conditions* 198.

20. H. 8. 9.
26. H. 8. 5.
per Engleſ.
6. E. 4. 5.
per Rogers
27. H. 8. 1. 27.

Pled' de coue-
nants performe.

Couenaunt 35. Et ou in couenant le defendant
dit

dit que les couenaunts font que il payera 10. li.
per tiel iour, et luy enfeoffe per mefme le iour,
quas quidem conueñ idem defend bene perim-
pleuit, ceo neft bon plee, car il mõftra coment il ad
ceo performe certeine. *B, Couenaūts* 35. in fine.

214 ❡ Nota pro lege que cefty que diftraine   Pound ouert.
auers poet eux metter in clofe meafõ fil voet
Vide 4. E. 6.
Com 68. per
Mountegue.
eux dofi vlãd, car le diftreffe in pounde ouert,
neft mes al intent que le owner poet dofi a eux
viand. *B. Diftreffe.* 66.

215 ❡ Concordatur pro lege, que fi terre   Entre ou dif-
efcheate al Roy que eft in leafe pur ans, Ou   treffe fur le
charge oue rent charge, et office eft troue pur   patentee le Roy,
le roy del efcheate (le leafe ou graunt nyent   Contrary fur le
troue in loffice) le leffee ne poet enf, ne le   roy.
grãtee ne poet diftrein, mez fi le roy graunt le
fre oufter, le leffee poet enf, et le graütee poet
diftreine. Tamen home q̃ claime franktenemēt   Qui trauers
in le terre ne poet enf faũs trauers loffice p   office.
34. H. 6. 19.
per Danby.
B. Entre congeable. 124. Conceditur pro lege   Auter de mefme
ou deux fount dune mefme nofme (come fi font   le nofme leuie
2. R. B.) et lun leuy fine del auf fre, la lauter   le fine.
auoydera ceo per plee. s. A dire que font 2.
del nofme, et que lauter R. B. leuie le fiñ, &
nemy cefty R. *B. Fines leuies.* 115. in fine.

216 ❡ Si le tenaunt in Precipe quod reddat   Effoine fur le
pria le viewe p Attorney, fon attorney ferra   view ou vou-
effoine fur le viewe, mes fil mefme prie le   cher.
viewe in proper perfon, donques per plurez
nul ferra effoine fur le viewe, mes le tenant
mefme, Car puis proces fur vn voucher il
mefme ferra effoine et per confequens fimiliter
Iffint de ayde
prier. 5. H. 7.
8. & 9.
ferra fur le viewe. Et nota que graunting
deffoine ou effoine ne gift nē error. Cõtrary   Errour.
del denying deffoine ou il gift. *B. Effoine.* 116.   Diuerfitie.

217 ❡ Si

**Que auer prop-
tie en vn eftray.**

217 ¶ Si home, prift auers come eftray, &
eux garde per 3. quarters del an, & puis ils
eftray de luy, & aut eux happa, le primer
feigniour q̃ eux gard p 3. quarts, ne poet eux
reprender, pur ceo q̃ il nad propertie in eux
tanq̃ il ad eux gard p lan & iour, et procl
paffe in 2, prochein market villez & 2. market
iours, lun in lun ville, et laut in lauter ville.
Car le poffeffion le 2. feifor eft bone, vers cefty
q̃ nad propertie. *B. Eftray.* 11.

Conc Eliot.
12. H. 8. 10.

**Homage.
Corporation.**

218 ¶ Nota in Scaccario que deane &
chapiter, & auters corps politike ne fra homage,
car ceo ferr fait in pfon, et corporation ne
poet apere in pfo, mes p Attorney, Et homage
ne poet eftre fait per attorney, mes folemt in
pfon *B. Fealty.* 15.

**Coutur ne voyd'
coll' garranty
fur difcont.**

219 ¶ Nota fi le baron difcontinue le droit
fon femme, & Auncefter collateral del feme
releas oue garrant & deuie, a que le feme eft
heire, & puis le baro deuie, le fee ferra barr in
Cui in vita per ce garrantie, non obftant le
couerture, pur ceo q̃ el eft mife a s. actio p la
difcont, car cofture ne poet auoyder garranty,
mes ou lentre le feme e loyal, q̃ il neft fur vn
difcontinuance. *B. Garranties.* 84.

Preignancie.

220 ¶ Informac en fcaccario. Vz A. B. pur
achat laines inl fhearing time & Laffumpfio
tali an de C. D. contra formam ftatuti, ou il
neft pas drape, ne il ne fift et drape ne yearne,
Il dit q̃ il ne achata pas de C. D. cotra forma
ftatut prout &c. Et nul iffue car ne pas material, ne trauffable fil achata de C. D. ou de
E. F. ou de aut, mes fil eux achata contra
forma ftat, necne. Et ideo liffue ferra, ne
achate pas modo & forma &c. *B. Iffues ioines.*

24. H. 8. c1.

81. *Negatiua preignans* 54. *Trauers* per 367.

10. E. 4. 6.
per Litt.
St. 152. A.
10. E. 4. 6.
per Litt.

221 ❡ Pier del realme ſerr̃ trie p ſō pierz ſil ſoit arraine ſur indictm̃t, Cōtrary ſil ſoit arraine ſur appeale, car al ſute del parties il ne ſerra trie par ſes piers. Et ſic fuit fines ſeigniour Dacres del South. hoc an, et pēd pur felony pur mort dũ hōe que fuit troue in ſo cōpani a vn hunting in Suſſ. *B. Iurors.* ĩ fiñ *Trials* 142.

Vid St. 38. C.

222 ❡ Fuit aiudge in Curia hoſpicii dñi Regis apud Greenewich Ɵſꝰ Edmũdũ Kniuet militē, que il ſerra diſherit, impriſon imppetuũ, et ſo maine coupe, quia pcuſſit quendā hominē ibidem le roy eſteant la in ſo court *B. Paine.* 16. in fine.

223 ❡ Hōe grãt proxim̃ p̃ſentatiōe, & ad feme & deuie, le grãtee aſia le priñ p̃ſentation, lheire le ſecond, & le fēe pur dower ĩ 3. *B. Prēſetatiō.* 55.

Vid 20. H. 8. 13

224 ❡ Fuit agree q̃ ſi t̃ in taile le reũſion al roy. ſuffer recoſſy, ceo liera luy, & ſon iſſue, ſed nemy le roy p le comē ley. Uide nũc ſtatutũ ind̃ q̃ ne liera liſſue. *B. Recouery en value.* 31. *Taile* 41. in fine.

32. H. 8. 177.

225 ❡ Si home leſſe ſon maner except les boys & ſubboys, per ceo le ſoile del boys eſt except per *Baldwine* chiefe Juſt. del cōen bank. *Fitzh.* iuſt. & *Knightle*, & *Mart.* ſeriants. Contrar̃ *Spilman*, & W. *Conigſ.* Juſtic̃. *B. Reſeruation.* 39.

Conc Tank.
46. E. 3. 22.
Vide 14. H. 8.
per Brudnel.

226 ❡ Nota ſi ſtatute ſtaple ſoit extend et iſſint remaine per 7. ans ſauns Deliberate fait, vncore il poet ati vn Deliberat̃ al fine de 7. ans. Mes ceſty que ad le terre a luy liſt per liberate ſur ſtatute, ne poet faire ſurrender conditional

Trial de pier del Realme arraigne ſur indictment, & appeale diũſity.

Paine pur percuter vn home en preſence le roy.

Graunt de prox. preſentac.

Soile except per excepc del boys.

Deliberate.

Surrender.

conditional al conuſor et enter pur le condition
enfreint puys temps del extent incurres, Cōe
ƀre de x. li. per an eſt liuer en execution pur
xl. li. ceo poet incurrer in 4. ans, la le Conuſee
per tyel condition ne poet enter puis les 4. ans
incurres, car il doit prender les pſits ſur ſon
extent mainteñt. Et il ne teigña ouſter ſon
temps niſi in ſpeciali caſu, come ou le ƀre eſt
ſurround oue ewe ſoden tempeſt vel huiuſmodi.
Et le iudgement ſerra quod teneat terram vt
libm̃ tenementum ſuum quouſque denarii leuentur. *B. Statute merchant.* 41.

Quāt poit home tener le terre vltra terme ſur ſtatute. Iudgement.

Conc Brian.
15. E. 4. 5.
Conc 7. H. 7.
12. p. Reporter.

29. H. 8. 123.
4. E. 6. Com 61

227 ❡ Dicitur pro lege que ſi le conuſor ſur
ſtatute ſtaple ad vn reuerſion, & graunt c̄ ouſter,
& puis le tenant pur vie deuie, ceſt terr̃ ne
ſerra miſe in execution, car le reuerſion ne
vnques fuit extendable in les maines le conuſor.
B. Statute merchant 44. in fine.

Reuerſionnient extend.

228 ❡ Si diuers Seſſions ſont in vn meſme
parliament, & le roy ne ſigne bille tanque al
darrein, la tout neſt que vn meſme iour, &
tout aueř relatiō al primer ioure del primer
Seſſions, & le primer iour & le darrein, tout
ně q̃ vn meſme parliament & vn meſme iour in
ley, Niſi ſpecial mention ſoit ſayt in laꝗ quant
ceo prendera force. Mes cheſcun Seſſion in
que le roy ſigne le billes eſt vn iour aperluy et
vn parliamēt aperluy & nauera auter relation mez a meſmes les Seſſiōs. *B. Parliament.*
86. *Relation.* 35.

Del relation de act de parliamt, diuerſitie.

H. 6. & 7. E. 6.
Com 79. per
Juſticiarios.

H. 6. &. 7. E.
6. Com 79.
p. Hales Juſt.

❡ Nota que in Court baron le tryal eſt par
ley gager, Mes ils poient eſtre per iurie ex
aſſenſu partium. Et que les maximes & les
general cuſtomes del realme, que eſt le comen
ley, ſerra trie p les Juſt. Et eadem lex de
expoſitions

Trial in court baron per ley gager.

Conc Fineux.
12. H. 7. 18.
D S. 14.
D S. 15.

expofitions de ftatuts, Et per le ley ciuel, les Judges ount le conftruction del ftatutes fimiliter. Mes particuler cuftomes ne ferra trie nifi per patriam. *B. Trials.* 143.

229 ❧ Nota fi home en action, ou recite pleadinge alledge ftatute et ceo mif-recite in matter, ou in an, iour, ou lyeu, lauf poet demurr generalmēt, car la eft nul tiel ftatute, et donques eft

nul tiel ley, car chefcun q̄ medle oue ceo doit monftre la ley veracr. Mes in cafu regis il poet eftr amēd, & hoc in alio termino. Contrary pur commen perfon. *B. Parliament.* 87.

230 ❧ Vid in Scacc. 3. E. 3. Ro. 2. fuit troue q̄ home tient del roy in Chiualrie in capite, vt de honore fuo de **Rayleghe**, Et fuit prife nul tenure in Capite, mes tenure del honour, & ideo fon heire auera ouftre le maine de fes auter terrez, q̄ ne ferra fi vft eftre in

Capite, car dōq̄, le roy aßa tout in gard p fon prerogatiue Tamen aliter eft fi le honour foyt annex al Coroñ, Car donquez le honor eft in Capite. Et An. 11. H. 7. le honor de **Rayleghe** fuit annex al Corone. Ideo ore ceo ē in capite. Et ou le roy dōe fre, teñendū de luy per fealty & 2. d̄. p oībus feruiciis, ceo ē Socage in Capite, car ē del parfon le roy, Et econtr fi fuit, tenendū vt de manerio de R. *B. Tenures.* 94.

Añ. 34. *Henrici octaui.*

231 ❧ In action fur cafe q̄d bona quer deueñūt ad man⁹ defend, et il eux degafta, le defend̄t dit q̄ nō deueñer ad man⁹ &c. Et bō

L   plee,

plee, et done in euidēce q̃ ils ne fuer̃ le ꝓper bñs le pł. *B. Acc. ſur le caſe.* 103. in fine.

Vide 33. H. 8. 198.

Lieu en accion ſur le caſe.

232 ❡ Accion ſur le caſe fuit port in London p A. B. quod cum ipſe poſſeſſioñ fuit de certein vine et aut̃ ſtuffe (& mr̃ certē) in tiel nief ad valētiā &c. Et ne mõſtra lieu certen ou il fuit ent poſſeſſe, & vncore bone, Et alledge q̃ le defendt tali die, Anno, et loco, in Loūdres aſſūpſit pur 10. li. q̃ ſi le dit nief & bñz ne vyent ſaffe al Lond & miſe ſur la terre, qd tunc il ſatisfia al pł. 100. li. & q̃ puis le niefe fuit robbe ſur le trade in le mier p q̃ il port laᵭiō pur nō ſatisfier. Et le verity fuit q̃ le bargaine fuit fait vltra mare & nō in Lod̃.

Aſſumpc neſt local. Lieu en det nient trauerſable.

Mes in aᵭiō ſur caſe ſur Aſſūpſit & hm̃odi, q̃ neſt pas local, le lieu neſt pas materiall, (Nīet plus q̃ in det) car il alledge q̃ les dits biens in parochia ſanᵭi Dūſtani in Orient̃ Londō, antequā ad terrā poſiī fueront, vel diſcarcai, aſportai fueront per ignotos &c. Et laᵭion giſt bien in London coment q̃ils fueront periſh ſur le haut mier. *B. Acc. ſur le caſe* 107

2. M. 1. 451. Tēp. H. 8. 366.

Adminiſtrac comit pēd' le bre.

233 ❡ Det ē port vers Lordinarie que pend le briefe commit ladminiſtration a J. S. le primer briefe abatera, car lordinarie eſt compellable de cōmitter ladminiſtratiō p ſtatute *B Adminiſtrators.* 39.

31. E. 3. ca. 11. Raſt. Adminiſters 1. & 21. H. 8. ca. 5. Raſt. Probate of teſt. 3.

Que eſtate en auter perſon.

234 ❡ In repleuin, ſi le defendt auowe pur ceo que A. fuit ſeigniour et fuit ſeiſi p le mainez B. donques tenant &c. de tiels ſeruices, poet conueier leſtat̃ le dit B. in le tenancy al pleintiſe in repleuin, per q̃ eſtate, ſās monſtre coment, Mes il ne poet cōuey a luy meſme leſtate le dit A. in le ſñorie per q̃eſtate ſās mr̃e comēt,

Diuerſitie.

comēt, car le ſeigniorie eſt la in dđ et nemy le tenancy. *B. Auowrie* 7. *Que eſtate.* 2. in finibus.

235 ❡ Nota que ceſty que auowe ſur le terr̄, cōe deins ſon fee ou ſeigniorie per leſtatut allegera ſeiſine, cōe en auter auowrie, et donques cōcludera ſon auowrie ſur le terre come deins ſon fee et ſeigniory, Et en tyel auowrie cheſcun pleyntiſe in repƚ (ſoit il termor ou auƚ) poet aƈ cheſcun reſpons al auowrye, come de trauerſer le ſeiſin, le tenure, & huiuſmodi q̃ ſont bon reſpons in Auowrie, Ou pleade releaſe, vel huiuſmodi come tenāt del franktenement ſerra, comt̄ q̃ il ſoit eſträge al auowrie, car tiel auowrie neſt fayt ſur aſcun perſon certeine, ideo cheſcun eſt eſträge a cel auowry, & iſſint le pleītiſe poet auer cheſcun reſpons q̃ eſt ſufficient, *B. Auowrie.* 113.

236 ❡ Home emblee biens in vn countie, & ſua oue eux in auƚ coūtie, il poet eſtre indiƈe, ou appelle in aſcun des counties, car il eſt felonie in cheſcun des Counties, car felonie ne altera propertie *B. Corone.* 170.

237 Nota que ſi 12. vient pur faire robberie, affray, riot, vel huiuſmodi qui ſont illoyals aƈtes, vn de eux enter in le meaſon, et tua home, ou fait auƚ illoyal aƈt, touts lauters que veigne oue luy pur faire illoyal aƈt ſont principals. Et eadem lex in le caſe de Fines Sñr Dacres, que vn de ſon companie tua home in hūting in vn foreſt, & le Seigniour Dacres, et lauters hunters, come Mätel, & alii fuer̄ principals, & fuer̄ touts pends, *B. Corone.* 171.

238 ❡ Nota en treſpas local que ſur enqueſt

Auowrie ſur le terre per ſtatut 21. H. 8. ca. 19. & reſpons in ceo.

Endiƈtment.

Appelle.

Que ſerra dit principall.

4. H. 7. 5. per Frowƈre. B. Coron 139. St. 182. C.

1. M. 1. Com 91.

33. H. 8. 221.

Damages abridg
& ēcreafe fur en-
queſt doffice.
Contra fur iſſue
trie ent pties.
Coſtes.
Ou attaint giſt
& ou nemy.
Defefans al eſ-
traunge, Et ou
al vn def. diāſ.

queſt doffice denquire de damages, le court les
poet abridger, ou increaſer. Mes econtra fur
le principal. s. fur iſſue trie enter partie &
partie, (Mes la poet increaſer coſtagez) car la
le pty eſt a ſo attaint, Mes fur enqueſt doffice
il ne poet auer attaint. *B. Damages.* 144.

19. H. 6. 10.
27. H. 8. 2.
contr.
3. M. 1. 466.
34. H. 6. 12.
per Moile.

239 ¶ A. eſt oblige a B. in 100. li. & B.
fiſt defefans a W. S. q̄ ſi W. S. pay 40. li. que
le obligation ferra voide, ceo ne valt per opinionē, pur ceo que A. que pledera ceo, eſt eſtraunge al fait, Mes lou 2. ſont oblige a moy
& ieo face defefans al vn, ceo feruera lauter de
pleder ſil poet ceo monſtre. Cōe in trñs P̃s 2.
releaſe al vn feruera lauſ, ſil poet ceo monſtre.
B. Eſtranger al fait. 21.

Monſtrans.

Litt 82.
14. H. 8. 10.
per Brudnel.
Conc Huſſey.
22. E. 4. 7.

240 ¶ Fuit agree p omnes Juſticiarios fur
graund deliberation in le caſe del Mantel ar-
miger dl Coūtie d North q̄ fuit attaīt oue le
feignior Dacres del South pur le mort dū hōe
(quod vide deuant 237.) q̄ lou il a ſon mariage
31. H. 8. puis leſtatut de vſes fait 27. H. 8.
couenant q̄ pur 100. li. et in cōſideraē del mariage, q̄ il et ſes heirs et touts pſos ſeiſiez de
ſes ēres & teñts in H. ferra ent ſeiſi al vſe de
ſon feme pur l̃ĩ de ſon vie, & puis al heirs de
ſon corps p luy engend̃, q̄ ceo changera vſe
aſſets bien et treſbone. Et p ceo le terre fuit
ſaue, et nō fuit forfait. *B. Feffements al vſes*
16 in fine.

Couenant
chaūge vſe.

241 ¶ Home purchaſe ēre, & cauſe ſtate
deſtre fait a luy & ſon feme & al 3. auters in
fee, ceſt ferra priſe al vſe le baron tantū, &
nemy al vſe le fēe ſauns eſpeciall matter de ceo
inducer. Et ſic vide femme poet eſtre ſeiſie al
vſe ſon baron, Et p luy tiel feoffement fuit añ.

Feme ſeiſi al vſe
ſon baron.

Vide 4. E. 6.
Com 44.

3. H.

3. H. 7. et entende vt ſupra. B. *Feoffements al* vſes. 51.

242 ¶ Richardus Fermor de L. fuit attaint in Premunire, et ſez terres fuerōt forfait in ſee imppetuum, et nō tantū pur terme de vie. Et ſic vide que neſt tantum vn forſeyture pur terme de vie, Ut in attaint. Car lun eſt per ſtatute, et lauter per le commen ley. B. *Præ-munire.* 19. in fine, Forfayture 101.

Forfeiture en at-taint, & premu-nire diuerſitie.

Attaint.

31. H. 8. 159.

243 ¶ Fuit dit pur ley que ſeo poye ouſter mon bayle, receyuor, et huiuſmodi donant a eux lour fee, car le reſt ē charge & nul p̄ſt B. Doubta de Seneſcal car aſſiſe giſt de tiels ouſters. B. *Graunts.* 93. in fine.

Ouſtr le officer.

Quære.

244 ¶ Det ſur eſcape in Scaccario v̄s vic̄ de Lōdrez de leſſ. hōe p eux arreſt per capias ad ſatisfaciendum et in execution, deſcape, Les def. ne poiēt dire q̄ ne eſcape pas, et done in euidence, que il ne fuit arreſt car larreſt eſt cōfeſſe, ſil dit q̄ il ne eſcape pas B. *General iſſue.* 89.

Ne eſcapa pas pled', Et nient arreſt done en euidence.

245 ¶ Detinue de fayt indent, ou obliga-tion de leaſe pur terme dans, le defendaunt ne gage ſon ley, car ceo cōcerñ t̄re, et chattel real. Et ſic nup fuit adiudge in bāco Regis. B. *Ley gager.* 97.

Ley en detinue de indenture de leaſe.

Conc 22. E. 411.

246 ¶ Hōe gage biēs en pledge pur xl. li. apprompt, et puis le debtor eſt conuict̄ in 100. li. in det a vn aut̄, ceux biens ne ſerra myſe in execution, tanq̄ le xl. li. ſont payes, car le creditour ad intereſt in ceo. Et auxi biens priſe pur diſtreſſe ne poient eſtre miſe in exe-cution, B. *Pledges.* 28.

Gage liuer pur dette.

Diſtreſſe eſt come gage.

38. H. 8. 327.

247 ¶ Nota per *Whorewood* Attorñ Regis & alios, ou information eſt miſe in leſchequer ſur

Ou le Roy poet waiuer fon iffue & ou nemy.

fur penal ftat, Et le defendãt fait barre & trauerfe le plee, que la le roy eft tenus deftoier al primer trafis, q̃ tenð vn iffue et ne poet waiuer tiel iffue tenð, et trauers le forñi matter del plee, Cõe il poet fur trauers doffice & hm̃di ou le roy ē fole pty, & intitle p matł de recorð, car s' lēformac̃ neft office troue deũãt. Et auxi fubieƈt eft party oue le Roy pur recoɓ le moitie vel hm̃odi. *B. Prerogatiue.* 116.

Vide 6. & 7. E. 6. Com. 85. & 3. El. Com 263.

13. E. 4. 3. Stp. 65. 38. H. 8. 237.

Burrough & vpland.

248 ¶ Fuit concorð in Scacc̃ q̃ Cities & Borowz paierõt al difm̃z. Et vplands al quinzifmes. *B. Quinzifme* &c. 8.

Infra 249.

Difme & quinzifme, quia ea foluat, & vnde leuentur.

249 ¶ Nota per expofitionem de ceux del exchequer q̃ taxe et tallage neft auter mes difme, quinzifme ou auter fubfidie grant per parliamẽt. Et le quinzifme eft de layes. Et le difme eft del clerge, et eft deftre leuie de lour terre. Et le difme, et le quinzifme des lay gents eft del biens. s. decimam partem bonorum in Ciuitatibus & Burg. Et quinfefimam partē bonorum del lais en patria q̃ fuit leuie in auncien tẽps fur lour biens. s. del auers fur lour łrez que fuit valde troublous. Mes ore ceo eft leuie fecundum ratũ terrarũ fuarum per verges de terre, et auters quantities, iffint que ore touts fcient lour certeintie in chefcun vill et paies per tout le realme. Mes il eft vncore leuie in afcuns lyeus fur lour biens. Mes in le plufors lieus fur lour terres, qð fuit conceffum p Barones. *B. Quinzifme* 9.

Releafe de touts demandes barr enter & feifer.

250 ¶ G. Chauncery fuit poffeff. dun endenture et perdera ceo, et J. S. troue mefme lendenture, al que le dit G. C. releafe toutes aƈtions & demaunds, et puis le dit J. S. dona mefme lendenture al John Tifõ, & puis le dit G.

G. Chauncerye port acc̃ de detinue vers le dit
J. T. q̃ plede q̃ le dit J. S. troua le endenture,
et q̃ le dit G. C. releaſe al dit J. S. touts actions et demaundes, & puis le dit J. S. done le
dit endenture al dit J. T. Judgement ſi aɛtyon.
Et fuit agree in communi banco, le caſe eſteant
de terre d̃d ibidem q̃ co̅ bone barre, et que le
releaſe del toutes demaunds excludera le party
de ſeiſer le choſe, et del ſon entre en le terre,
et del propertie del chatel que il auoit deuant.
Et fuit moue in banco Regis, et ils fueront
de meſme le opinion, et dixerunt quod ratio
eſt, eo que entre en terre, et ſeiſer del biens
ſont demaunds en ley. *B. Releaſes* 90.

6. H. 7. 15.

Vide 29. H. 8. 119. 2. M. 1. Com. 114.

251 ❡ Nota per *Curiam* ſi tenant en taile
fait feoffement a ſon vſe en fee deuant le ſtatute
de vſes fait 27. H. 8. et deuie deuaunt le dit ſtatute, ſon heire deins age, & puis leſtatute eſt
fait deuaunt le pleine age lheire, p q̃ lheire eſt
en poſſeſſion p leſtatut, il ne ſerra remitte per
ceo. Contrarie de diſcent puis leſtatute, car c̃
ſerra remitter. *B. Remitter* 49.

Leſtatut de vſes 27. H. 8. ne fait remitter.

Diuerſitie.

252 ❡ Si home ad title dentre et nemy
droit dentre come per eſchete mortmaine, aſſent
per feme al rauiſhor et huiuſmodi, et priſt ſtate
del terre tenant, il ne ſerra remitte, car il nad
niſi vn title. (Et home ne poet eſtre remitte,
mes in reſpeɛt dũ droit deuaunt. Come ou
home eſt diſſeyſie et priſt eſtate del diſſeiſour,
il eſt remitte, car il auoit droit dentre deuaunt)
Et eadem lex ou home decay ſon tenements, ou
conuert terre de tillage in paſture enconter leſtatute, et fait ſtate par vie a ſon ſeigniour, il
nauera auter ſtate, car il nauera niſi title dentre,
et nemy droit dent̃r Quere, car non adiudicatur
p. *B. Remitter* 50.

Title dentre ne fait remitter cõtrary de droyt dentre.

4 H. 7. ca. 19.

Quære.

253 ❡ Si

Seif. per maines de intrudor.
Liuery.
Diftreffe fufpend nemy feigniory.

Scifin regis ne perdr larr.

253 ❡ Si home tient del roy et tient auter terre dauter feigniour et deuie, fon heire deins age, q̄ entrude a fon pleine age, et pay le rēt al auter feigniour, ceo c̄ bone feifin, & luy liera puis que il ad fue liuerie, car le feigniorie ne fuit fufpend per le poffeffion de roy, mes tantū le diftreffe, car puis liuerie lauf feigniour poet diftrefn̄ pur larrerages due deuaunt Per optimam opinionem tunc. Vide nunc Statutum inde que lofficers le roy rend annuatim le rent al feigniour, et lheire ne ferra charge oue ceo per diftreffe puis fur liuery fue, come il fuit al comon ley. *B. Seifin* 48.

13. H. 7. 15.

33. H. 6. 35. per Dauers. St. 9.
26. H. 8. 8. per Norw.
2. & 3. E. 6. cap. 8.

Accio fur le cafe pur feifauns faux drapes.

254 ❡ Aĉlion pur fefauns faux drapes in Barthelmewe faire contra ftatuĺ. Lauter dit que il eux fift bene & voyerment a D. in com̄ F. fans ceo que il eux fift in Barthelmewe faire in L. prout &c. Et bone plee. *B. Trauers* per 368.

Cuftome per totam Angliam, Et cuftome en vn Citie, ou countie diūf.

255 ❡ Information in *Scaccario* vers marchaunt pur lader vyne in eftrange niefe, le defendaunt pled licēce le roy fait a J. S. de ceo faīr, quel J. S. auer graunt fon aucthoritie inde al def. et quod habetur cōfuetudo inter mercatores per totam Angliam, que vn poet affigne tyel lycence oufter a vn auter, et que laffignee enioyer c̄ &c. q̄ fuit demurre en ley, Et fuit agree pur ley, q̄ hōe ne poet prefcriber cuftome p totam Angliā, car fi foit per totam Angliā, ceo ē vn commē ley, et nemy vn cuftome. Contrary fi le cuftome vft eftre pled deftr̄ ē tiel citie, ou coūtie, cōe Gauelkind, Borowēglifh, Gloceft. fee, & hm̄di. *B. Cuftomes* 59.

Plus.

❡ Plus de hoc An. 24. H. 8. 55.

❡ *An.*

❡ *An.* 35. *Henrici octaui.*

256 ❡ Nota pro lege que prouiſo ſemper miſe ſur le parte le leſſee, ſur les parols de ha-bend fait vn conditiō, Tñ ecōtra dun prouiſo de part le leſſor, Come eſt couenaunted en lindenture que le leſſee faiſ̃ les reparations. Prouiſo ſemper que le leſſor trouera le graund meriſme, ceo neſt condition. Nec per aliquos il neſt condition quant ceo vient enter enter alias cōuentiones ſur le pt le leſſee, Cōe ē couenāted puis le (heñd) et puis le (reddēd) que le leſſee eſcouſ̃ ſes ſoſſes vel hm̃odi, Prouiſo ſemper que le leſſee cariera le foyne de ceo a tiel campe, ceo neſt condition de forfaiture le leaſe pur non feſans de ceo. Contrary ſi tiel prouiſo ſoit miſe immediatment puis le (habē-dum) que fait le ſtate, ou puys le reddeñd, Quere per. *B. Conditions.* 195. Ou prouiſo ſerra condic, & ou nemy.

Quere.

257 ❡ Si hōe morgage ſa tr̃ ſur defeiſans de repaiment, d̃ reenter, et le bargain deſtre void. Et le vendee leſſa la l̃re al vendor pur 10. ans per endenture de defeſans, et ouſ̃t graūt a luy q̃ ſil pay 100. li infra terminū dict 10. annorū, qd̃ tunc le vēd̃ ſerr̃ voyde &c. Et le leſſee ſurrender le terme, vncore le tender del 100. li. eſt bone deins les 10. ans, pur ceo que les 10. ans eſt certayne, coment q̃ le leaſe eſt ſurrender, ou forfayt, Et econtra, ſi fuit de re-pay infr̃ terminum predictum, ſans ceux parols 10. ans, Car ē lū caſe le terme. s. le leaſe eſt limitation del paymēt, & en lauter caſe les 10. ans, per *Whorewood* en lectura ſua in quadra-geſima. (*B. Conditions* 203. *Defeſauns* 18.) Infra terminum 10. an. & infra terminum pd' diuerſitie.

Surrender.

Forfeiture.

Lectura.

M Eadem

Eadem lex ſi B. tient certayne terre pur terme
de 10. ans de A. et il eſt couenaunt enter A.
et B. que ſi B. pay 100 li al A. infra dicī 10.
ans, que adonques il ſerra ſeiſie al vſe B. in fee,
et B. ſurrender ſon terme al A. et puis luy pay
100. li. infra les 10. ans, la B. auera fee, Car les
ans ſont certaine. Et econtra ou eſt couenant
q̄ ſil pay 100. li infra terminum prediƈtum, & il
ſurrender, et puis pay les 100. li ceo ne vault,
car la le terme eſt determine, mes in lauter caſe
les 10. ans remaine, non obſtant le ſurrender.
B. *Expoſition* 44.

258 ⸿ Nota ou aƈtion penal eſt done p
ſtatut đ recouer graūd ſume per aƈtion de det
pur engroſ. vel huiuſmodi, la le p̃t ne recouera
coſtes ne damages in cel acē de det B. *Dam-*
mages 200. *Coſtes* 32.

Conc T. 4. M. 1

260 ⸿ Home done terre al barō & fēe pur
terme de lour vies, et diutius eorum viuentis,
le remainder al heires de lour corps, ceſt vn
taile executed ratione del immediat remainder,
nō obſtantibus verbis ſtatuti, quod voluntas
donatoris in omnibus obſeruetur, p omnes Juſticiarios. B. *Eſtates* 75.

Weſt. 2. ca. 1.
Raſt. Taile 1.

261 ⸿ Home fait vn fait de feffemēt a aul̄,
& liuer le fait a luy en le terre, ou ſur le terre,
cē bone feffemēt Per omnes *Iuſticiarios* in communi banco. B. *Feoffementes* 74.

262 ⸿ Nota que ſi le br̄e de Dedimus poteſtatem de leue fine ne port teſte puis le briefe
de couenant, ceo eſt error, car le dedimus poteſtatem dit, cum breue noſtrum de conuentione
pendet enꝑ A. B. & C. D. &c. B. *Fines leuies* 116.

Temp. H. 8.
339.

263 ⸿ Nota ſi hōe ſoit attaint de treaſon
per parliament, per ceo ſes terres & biens ſont
forſaites

4. H. 7. 11.
per Towneſ.

forfaites ſauns parols de forfaiture de terre ou biens in laꝛ. *B. Forfaiture* 99.

5. H. 7. 37.
36. H. 8. 287.
Tℰp. H. 8. 335.
5. H. 7. 37.
per omnes.

264 ❧ Nota per omnes *Iuſticiarios* Anglie q̃ ſr̄ en Chiualrye per nonage lheire ne ouſter le grauntee de wrecke, ou de proxima preſentatione, Nec le termors que ſont eins per le pier lheire. *B. Graunts* 85. *Gard.* 66 *Leaſe* 31. in finibꝰ. Iſſint de leaſe pur terme de vye. *B. Garde* 61. in fine.

Seigniour en chiualrie ne ouſtr le termor &c.

265 ❧ Home deuie ſeiſie de r̃es tenus in Chiualrie, ſon frere et heire deins age, le ſeignior ſeiſiſt le garde, le feme del tenaunt priuemēt inſeint oue fits, et puis le femme eſt deliuer, le frere eſt hors de garde.

Ou vn pſon ſerra bis en gard, & ou nemy.

Mes ſi lenfaunt deuie le frere vncore deins age, la le frere ſerr̃ ē gard arere. Et eadem lex ou file eſt heire & puis fites ē nee, le file eſt horſe de garde, & ſi le fites deuie ſauns iſſue le file deins age, el ſerra en gard arere, Sic vide que vn meſme perſō poet eſtre bis in garde per 2 ſeueral aunceſters. Mes ou le ſeignyor ſeiſiſt le fits pur garde pur terre a luy diſcend de ſon pier, et graunt le mariage de luy a vn auter, et puiz auter terre tenus in chiualrie tenus de meſme le ſr̄ deſcende a meſme le fits de mon mere, la B. ſemble que le ſr̄ nauera le gard arere, eo quil luy auer, et graunt ſon mariage deuaant, Et le corps eſt choſe entier, *B. Garde* 119.

Graunt dun garde.

266 ❧ Si hōe dit en ſon garrātie, Et ego tenementa predicꝛa cum pertinentijs preſato A. B. le donee warrantizabo, et ne dit, ego & heredes mei, il meſme garrantera, mes ſon heire neſt tenus de garranter, pur ceo q̃ (heires) ne ſont expreſſe ē le garrantie. *B. Garranties* 50.

Garrantie ſins hered'.

267 ❧ Nota

3. M. 1. Com 155. 159. 161. & 162. contr.

267 ❡ Nota que ſi home leſſa ſon manour, ou meaſon pur terme de vie, et puis done, ou graunt totū maneriū vel meſuagium ſuum, ceo ne le vault, car il eſt reuerſion del leſſor, et le meaſon ou manor del leſſee durant ſon terme. Et Attornement ne ayda ceo ou le graunt eſt voyd. Mes ſil vſt graūt ſon intereſt en le manor ou meſe, ceo vſt eē bone vt dicitur per *Whore-woode*, B. *Grāts* 150.

Reuerſ. p noſme terre.

Attornement ne aid void graunt, Reuerſ. paſſe per verbā intereſſe.

Ley gager ne giſt en Quo minus.

268 ❡ Dictum fuit pro lege q̃ home ne gagera ſon ley in quo minus. B. *Ley*. 102. *Quo minus* 5. in finibus.

8. H. 5. Fitzh. Ley 66.

Done de biens per le roy.

269 ❡ *Shelley* Juſtice fuit preciſe q̃ done le roy ē bone de chattels mouables ſauns eſcript, cōe de chyual et huiuſmodi. B. *Prærog.* 60, & 71. in finibus.

2. E. 6. 393.

Preſentment lun iointen mit lautr hors de poſſ.

270 ❡ Per *Whorewood* Attournā Regis clerement ſi deux ioyntenauntes ſont, lun preſent ſole et ſon clerke induct, lauter eſt horſe de poſſeſſion, B. *Quare impedit* 52. in fine.

Contr p. 36. H. 8. B. Quar imp 2. in fine p Bromley, & Hales ſeriātz.

Relac de forf. p act de parliamēt.

271 ❡ Nota que lattainder de treaſon per act de parliament naſſa cigne relation que al primer iour del parliament, niſi ſoit per ſpecial parols que il forfetera ſon terre que il auoit tali die et puis. B. *Relation* 43.

Iury diſcharge per ieofaile.

272 ❡ Fuit en vſe en banco regis coment que le iury ſoit priſt de paſſer, la ſi ſoit ieofaile apparant en le record, lenqueſt ſerra diſcharge. B. *Repleder* 54.

P. 7. E. 4. 1. accord.

Surrender.

273 ❡ Si le roy done en taile per ſes letters patentes, et puis le donee ſurrender ſon letters patentes al roy, le taile per ceo neſt extinct. B. *Taile* 38.

32. H. 8. 192.

Tener per ſuit de court.

274 ❡ Tenetur que ſi home fiſt feoffement de terre ante ſtatutū de Quia emptores terrarū a tener de luy. Et de faire ſute a ſon court, ceſt

Weſt. 2. ca. 2. Raſt. Tenure 4.

ceſt bone ſil ad Court. Mes home ne poet commencer vn court per tenure fait, ou il nad *Court.*
mannor deuant. Car la les feruices ferront *Mannour.*
33. H. 8. 210. tenus d ſon perſon. (*B. Tenures* 34.) Et hōe
ne poet faire manour a ceo iour, coment que il
done terre en taile a tener de luy, et per ſuit de
ſon court, Car il ne poet faire court, car court
ne poet eſtre mes per continuaunce : Et ſic home
poet faire tenure, mes nul manor ne court, Car
mannor et court ne poet eſtre mes p vſage ewe
de tempore cuius contrar. memoria hominum
non exiſtit. *B. Tenures* 34. et 102.

275 ¶ Si home tient 3. feuerall mannours *VVill de 3.*
de 3. feueral ſeigniors in Chiualry, et cheſcun *mannors per*
de egal value, il ne poet faire ſon wil de 2. del *ſtatute 32. H. 8.*
manours, relinquant le 3. mannour al heire.
Mes de 2. partes de cheſcun mannour, Car aliter
il preiudicera lauters 2. ſeigniours. *B. Teſta-*
ment. 19.

An 36. *Henrici octaui.*

276 ¶ Nota per omnes legis peritos, et per *Quecommittera*
ceux del arches, quod tempore vacationis dun *adminiſtration*
archeueſq̃, ou dun Eueſq̃, le Deane et le Cha- *vacante Epiſ-*
piter committera ladminiſtration. *B. Admin-* *copatu.*
iſtrators 46.

277 ¶ Accord fuit q̃ ſi Eueſque Deane et *Contra formam*
Chapiter done lour terre in fee ſauns licence le *collationis.*
roy, que eſt founder et eſt troue iſſint per office,
le roy auera le terre. Et auſ founder poet auer
contra formā collationis. Et ſil alyen ſine aſſenſu
Litt 145. decani et Capituli, donques giſt briefe de en-
greſſu ſine aſſenſu capituli. *B. Licences* 21.

278 ¶ Fuit agree in chauncery, que eſt nul *Mittimus.*
Cerciorari in le Regiſter pur remouer recorde
horſe

horſe dun court in commen banke immediate
ment, mes ſerra certifie in le Chācery per ſurmiſe, et donques deſtre˙miſe en commen bāke
per mittim[9]. Et indiƈtmentes poient eē remoue
horſe del païſs per Cerciorari all Chauncerye, et
puis eſtre myſe al Juſtices del banke le roy p
Mittimus, et dōques ils procedeꝛ ſur ceo *B.*
Certiorari 20 in fine.

279 ℂ Dicitur pro lege, que ſur leaſe pur
ans rend rent oue reentre, le leſſee doit eſtre
priſt tout le iour & faire attendaunce de ceo
offer, & ſuffiſt par le leſſor đ vener aliquo tempore diei.   Tamen lentre eſt que lun & lauꝑ
attend lentier iour, quere inđ *B. Conditions*
192. in fine. *Entre congeable* 2. in fine.

280 ℂ Nota p lege, que ou alien nee vient
en Engleterre et ameſne ſon fits oue luy, que
fuit nee vltra mare, et eſt alien come ſon pere
eſt, la le roy per ſes letters patentes ne poet
faire le fits heire a ſon pier, ne a aſcun auter.
Car il ne poit alter ſō ley per ſes letters patents,
nec aliꝰ niſi per parliament, car il ne poet diſin-
heriter le droit heire, Ne diſapoint le ſeigniour
de ſon eſchete. Et le fits de alien, ꝙl fits eſt nee
c̄ Angliterre il eſt anglois et non alien, *B.*
Denizen 9.

281 ℂ Fuit accorde ꝙ eſtraunge al fine, ou
recouere ne ceo pledra pur eſtoppel, Contra ſil
claime meſme le terre de ſouth le fine, ou recorde
p ceux que fueront pties, Ou claime meſme
leſtate, ou part de ceo. Et ꝙ ceſt eſtate continue,
Car donques il eſt priue in le per. *B. Eſtoppel*
216. in fine.

282 ℂ Home fait feoffement en fee al ſon
vſe pur terme de vye, et que puis ſon diſceſſe
                                          J. N.

J. N. prendra les profittes, ceo fayt vn vſe en
J. N. Contrary ſil dit que puys ſon mort ſes
feoffees prendra les profittes et liueront eux al
J. N. ceo ne fait vſe en J. N. car il nad eux
niſi per les maines les feoffees *B. Feſſements
al vſes* 52.

Conc Rede
12. H. 7. 26.

3. M. 1. Com
150.

*fait vſe. Et ou
econtra.*

283 ❡ Deane et Chapter et tiels corporations ne poyent departer de riens mes p fait.
Et vncore quaunt ils graunt terre pur ans, lour
leſſee poet ceo graunter ouſter ſans fait. *B.
Graunts* 152.

*Ou fait eſt necef-
ſary, & ou nemy.*

Corporation.

283 ❡ Un ſtatute fuit conus per vn nome
en le noſme de J. S. de D. in cõ E. boucher,
& fuit priſe ſur proces, & dit en auoydaunce
del ſtatute, que il ſuit demurre ſemper a S.
et nemy a D. & fuit huſb. & nemy boucher et
q̃ J. S. d̃ D. conuſt leſtat, ſans c̄ q̃ il eſt in le
perſon que conuſt c̄, Quel plee fuit refuſe pur
graund inconuenience q̃ poet vener de c̄. *B.
Miſnoſmer* 34. in fine.

*Statute ſtaple ou
merchant
auoyd' p miſno-
mer.*

Trauerſ.

24. H. 8. 60.
Plures tient
tempore M.
1. q vſe poet eſ-
tre vſe change
pur confid paſſ.
Vid T. 8. El.
309. contra.

284 ❡ Home ne poet vender terre al J. S.
al vſe le vendor, Ne leſſer terre a luy rendaunt
rent, habend al vſe del leſſor, car ceo eſt cõ-
trarie al ley et reaſon, Car il ad recompence
pur ceo. Et per *Hales* hõe ne poet changer vſe
per vn couenãt que eſt executed deuant, come
de couenant deſtre ſeiſie al vſe de W. S. pur
ceo que W. S. eſt ſon coſin. Ou pur ceo que
W. S. preantea done a luy 20. li. niſi les 20. li.
fueꝛ done pur auer meſme le terre. Mes ecõtra dun conſideration preſent, Ou futur pur
meſme le purpoſe, come pur 100. li. paye pur
le terre tempore conuencionis, Ou deſtre paie
ad diem futurum, Ou pur marier ſon file, vel
huiuſmodi. *B. Feoffements al vſes* 54.
285 ❡ Nota

*Vſe ne poet eſtre
contrary al cõ-
fidernc.*

*Quel eſt ſufficiẽt
couenant de chã-
ger vn vſe.*

7. & 8. El. Com
302.

285 ¶ Nota que fuit deuife daſt leafe pur ans de lier tenaunt ē taile que le tenaunt en tayle et le leſſee conuſter les tenementes deſtre le droit dun A. eſtraunger, et que A. grante et render per meſme le fine al leſſee pur 60. ans, le remainder al leſſour et ſes heires, et fuit oue proclamation, que liera le taile puis proclamations faits.

(Et ſic vide q̄ le deuiſe poſtea 342. ne voet ſeruer pur taile, mes pur fee ſimple, car ceſty que prent per fine ne ſerra conclude ſil ſoit

enfant, ou feme couert, ou liſſue en taile del conuſor.) Et in ceſt caſe nul rent poet eſtre reſerue, car A. fuit eſtraunger al terre, Per que

Vide temp. H. 8. 343.

le leſſee graunta 10. li. de rent et extra terram illam oue clauſe de diſtreſſe duraunt lans, ou terme auantdit, al leſſour. *B. Fines leuies.* 118.

286 ¶ Dicebatur, ou home pled plee in Banco vltra mare, il ſerra condemne a ceſt iour, pur ceo que ne poet eſtre trie in Angleterre. *B. Iuriſdiƈtion* 29.

Conc Thorpe 41. E. 3. 4.

287 ¶ Home eſt purchaſor oue ſa femme a eux et al heires le baron, et puis le baron leſſa pur ans & deuie, le femme entra, ceo auoidera le leaſe pur ſa vie. Mes ſi el deuie duraunt le terme, la le reſt del terme eſt bone a leſſee vers le heire le baron. Et eadem lex de rent charge graunt extra ceo, Car le baron auera le fee ſimple tempore &c. Et poet charger ceo bien.

Vid 37. H. 8. 308.

Et nota per omnes *Iuſticiarios* que le garden del heire in Chiualry ne ouſtra le termor Launceſter le heire. Et eadem lex del ſeigniour per eſcheate. *B. Leaſes* 58.

35. H. 8. 264. Contr Fitzh. 142. C.

Conc Fitzh. 198. F.

288 ¶ Si A. ſoit oblige a B. en 40. ſ. ad vſū I. S. la I. S. poit releaſer lobligatiō pur ceo q̄ (ad vſū) eſt expreſſe in lobligation. Et econ-

Vide Billing. 2. E. 4. 2.

tra

tra ſi ceo ne appiert in lobligation. *B. Obliga-* *tion* 72.

(ad vſum neſt Expreſſe.

289 ❧ Si le roy graunt Bailliwike ou Shirife-wike a J. S. abſq̄ compoto reddend, le parol abſque compoᵗ ne vault, car ceſt contrarie al nature del choſe graunt. *B. Pattents* 99.

Bailliwike ou ſhirifewike graunt abſque cōpoto.

290 ❧ Nota pro lege que il eſt bone pleding adſr̄ q̄ J. N. & W. N. fueront ſeiſie in dominico ſuo vt de feodo, ad vſum T. P. et ſes heires ſauns monſtrans le commencement del vſe, come adire que A. fuit ſeiſie in fee, et enfeoffe I. N. & W. N. ad vſum T. P. &c. Mes home ne poet pleder que A. B. fuit ſeiſie en taile ſans monſtre le done, car lun eſt pticuler eſtate & nemy lauter, *B. Pleadinges.* 160.

Infra 291.

Ou home monſtr le cō-mencement dun vſe, Et ou nemye.

Fee ſimple.
Fee taile.

291 ❧ Et nota que home fra bone. title in aſſiſe adire que I. N. fuit ſeiſie en fee al vſe de T. P. quel T. P. infeoffe le plaintife, que fuit ſeyſie et diſſeyſie &c. ſans monſtre quel perſon fiſt le feoffemēt al vſe T. P. Ou coment luſe commence. *B. Titles* 61.

Supra 290.

292 ❧ Nota quant record eſt remoue extra Curiam de recordo, come London &c. in banco regis, vel in cōmuni bāco, la ila ne procedera ſur le original que fuit in London, mes in banco regis le partie poet adire luy meſme per bille de Midd port la vers le party ſur ſon ap-paraunce, Et in communi bāco de porᵗ original returnable m̄ le iour. *B. Priuiledge* 48.

Priuiledge di-miſſera le plaint.

Bill de Midd'.

293 ❧ Nota per *Bromley, Hales,* & *Portman* Juſtices, & *Rich.* q̄ fuit primus Canc̄ Anglie, Et Apprentici⁹ Cuᵗ, que ſi le conuſee purchaſe parcel del terre puis leſtatut conus, ou recogniſe, ceo neſt diſcharge del ſtatute vers le conuſor meſme. Mes les feoffees del conuſor, de autera

45. E. 3. 22. per Finch.
13. H. 7. 22. per Keble.

Diuerſitie inter purchaſe puis leſtatut, & de-uant exec. Et ou eſt purchaſe puis exec ewe.

N   pcela

pcels ſerra ent diſcharge. Mes ſi le Conuſee ad le terre a luy liuer en execution, & purchaſe parcel del terre le conuſor, que ceſt diſcharge del entier ſtatute, *B. Statute merchant.* 42.

Vide temp. E. 6. 441. 11. H. 7. 4. 5. E. 6. Com 72.

Execution p execu-tors in noſme le conuſee q eſt mort.

294 ❡ Dictum fuit pro lege que ſi le conuſee ſur ſtatute ſtaple deuie, & ſes executors ſuont execution en le noſme le teſtator, ſicome il fuit en vie, & le vic priſt le corps in noſme le teſtatour &c. vncore ceo neſt pas executiō pur lexecutors, mes ilz poyent puis aſt execut̄ en lour noſm̄ demeſne, car le prim̄ executiō en le noſme ceſty que fuit mort deuaunt le teſt del briefe fuit void, & le corps ne poet remaine pur ſatisfier ceſty que fuit mort deuant. Ne le vic ne poet liuer le terre ne biens a ceſtuy que eſt mort iuxta formam breuis. Et p *B.* libro In-tractiō Placitorū, lexec. del conuſee aueront executiō ſur ſtatute merchant, ſans ſcire facias. Et hoc ſur ſurmiſe vt luy ſemble. Et ſi le co-nuſor ſoit retourne mort, vncore execution pro-cedera de ſon terres et tenementes ſauns Scire facias ❡s ſon heire. Et lextent & liberate ſerra ſerue immediatment. Tamen per *B.* nul remedy appiert la pur les biens le conuſor quāt le conu-ſor eſt mort, dauer aſcun execution deux, *B. Statute merchant.* 43.

Execuc pur lexe-cutor le conuſee.

Liber intracc fol.

Conuſor retorne mort.

Fait chiualer puis le com-miſſion.

295 ❡ Nota pro lege que ou commiſſiō del peace iſſuit al J. N. et auters, & puis J. N. eſt fait chiualer, vncore le commiſſion remaine pur luy (Tamen Anno primo E. 6. cap. 7. eſt vn ſtatute fayt, que feſance del plaintife chiualer ne abatera lāction: Ne le commiſſion, in que tiel p ſon eſt noſme) Et ou home erudite en le ley, eſt miſe en commiſſiō, & puis eſt fait ſeriant del ley, vncore il remayne in aucthoritie per m̄
le

Conc 35. H. 8.

le commiſſion. Et qn̄t Juſtice del bank eſt fait
chiualer, vn℮ il remaine Juſtice, & c℮ commiſſion luy ſeruera. B. *Commiſſions.* 22.

295 ¶ Fuit agree per *Iuſtitiarios* que ſi
french home inhabitat en Anglia, et puis guerre
eſt proclaime, en℘ Angliā & Franciam, nul poet
prend ſes biens pur ceo que il fuit icy deuaunt,
mes ſi Frenchman vient icy, puis le guerre
proclaime, ſoit ceo per ſon bone volunt, vel per
tempeſt, ou ſil luy meſme yelde & rend, ou
eſtoyt a ſon defēce, cheſcun poet luy arreſt &
prender ſes byens, et per ceo il ad propertie en
eux, & le roy naſſa eux, Et iſſint fuit miſe in
vre eodem Anno enter Anglicos & Scotos, & le
roy m̄ achate diuers priſoners & biens eodem
Anno, quāt Bullen fuit cōquere de ſes proper
ſubieēles, B. *Propertie & Proprietate probanda,*
38. in fine.

Plus de hoc An. 25. H. 8. 71. 35. H. 8.
270.

¶ *An.* 37. *Henrici oĉtaui.*

296 ¶ Nota que ſi deux Jointenaunts ſont
que tient del roy in capite, & vn releaſe al
auter tout ſon droit, ceo neſt alienation, ne il ne
beſoigne licence ne pardon de ceo, car ceſty a
que le releaſe eſt fait eſt eins per le primer
feffor, & nemy per ceſty que releaſe, Ne il ne

ferra fine pur tiel releaſe, Et ſic eſt vſus in
Scaccario que ceo neſt alienation, Mes ſi trez

Jointenātz ſont, & lun releaſe al vn des auters,
la il eſt eins de ceo per luy que releaſe, Cōtra
ſil vſt releaſe a toutes ſes companions. Et ou
home releaſe per fine al tenaunt le roy, ceo neſt
alienation.

Fine fur releafe, & fur condit dedir cõe ceo &c. diuerfitie Eftoppel.

Non culp en appele.
Se defend'.

Euidence.

Iuftifie.

Indiⅽtmēt coram Coronator, & deuant auters Iuſt. Diuerfitie.

Attornement neceſſarie. Et ou nemye.

Arbitrators.

alienation.   Contrariũ de fine fur conuſance de droit, come ceo que il ad de ſon done, car ceo eſt eſtaⅽ fait p cõcluſiõ.   *B. Alienations.* 31.

297 ❡ Nota per *Iuſticiarios* ambarum bancarum, home nauera pas plee in appeale q̃ le mort luy aſſault, & il luy tua en ſon defence, mes pledera nõ culp̄ modo·& forma, & donera ceſt matter en euidence, & le iurie eſt tenus de ceo conuſter, & ſi ils ceo troua, il irra acquiⅽ in forma prediⅽ, Ne il nauera ceo pur plee oue traⅰs del murder, car le matter del plee eſt murder, Ne murder ne poet eſⅽ iuſtifie, & quant le matter del plea ne vault, la vn trauerſe ne vault.   *B. Appeale.* 122. *Corone.* 1.) in fine.   Et ou le Jurie acquite le defendãt fur indiⅽtment deuaunt lez Coroners, ils doient trouer que occiſt le home.   Et la ils poiⅽt dire q̃ meſme le def. luy occiſt ſe defendendo.   Mes ſur indiⅽtment deuaunt auⅰs Juſtiⅽ ſuffiſt adire non culp̄ tanⅽ, ſans pluis.   *B. Appeale* 122.

298 ❡ Vide per *Whorewood* Attornaⅽ regis, ou home leſſa pur 40. ans, & puis leſſa meſme le ⅬΡre a auter, habenⅾ a fine primi termini pro xx. ans, ceo ne beſoigne attournement, Et econtra ou il graũt le reuerſ. habenⅾ m̃ le reuerſion a fine primi termini pro xx. ans tunc proximo ſequen, la doit eſt̃r atturnement (Quere & viⅾ meliꝰ hic, 467.)   Et ſi hõe leſſa pur x. ans, & puis leſſa ceo a auⅰ pur xx. ans, ceſt bon pur x. ans ſans attornemⅽt.   Cõtra ſi fuit parol de reuerſion.   *B. Attornement.* 41.

299 ❡ Fuit tenus clere in banco regis, que ou M. & auters deux ſont oblige deſtoier al agard I. N. iſſint que ceo ſoit fait & liuer per larbitrators in eſcript al parties deuaunt Michelmas,

1. M. 1. Com. 101.

4. E. 6. Com. 12. 14. H. 7. 2. per Fineux. 13. E. 4. 3. St. 181. B.

Vide 2. E. 6. Com. 379.

26. H. 8. 86. Cõc M. 1. E. 6 Vide temp. H. 8. 349. & poſt. 308.

mas, et ils font lagard, & lyuer ceo al vn per
Michelmas, et ne poient trouer lauter per le
iour, que ceo ne liera lauters, a que ceo ne fuit
lyuer. Et ratio *B. femble* eo que en cel cafe
ils poient auer fait 3. partes, & liuer a chefcun
party vn. *B. Conditions.* 46. in fine.

300 ❡ Nota per les Doctors del ciuel ley, &
feriants del common ley, fi home fait fon teftament, et nofme nuls executors, ceo neft teftament, mes vncore eft bone will de terre in ceo,
car ceux ne font teftamentarie, Mes in primer
ou executors fault, vncore les legacies ferrount
payes. Mes fi appiert que il fayt part del teftament & nemy lentyer, la les legacies ne ferront pales. Et ou home fait teftament &
executors, & ils refufe, vncore les legacies ferr̃
payes car nul default en le teftator, Et le teftament ferr̃ annex al letters dadminiftrac̄. *B.
Teftament.* 20.

*Teftament ne
poet eftre fans
execut'.*

*Ou legacie, ou
deuifes ferr bon
coment q le de-
uifor ne nofme
in fait execu-
tors.*

301 ❡ Dicit̃ pro lege, que fi home done
omnia terras & tenementa fua in D. per ceo
leafes pur ās ne paffa, car hec verba terre &
tenemēta ferra entend franktenement al meines,
B. Done. 41.

*Que paffa p pa-
role, Omnia tra
& tenementa.*

302 ❡ Si terre foit done pur l̃m de vie, le
rem̃ al dr̃t heires W. N. q̃l W. N. eft attaint
de felonie & deuie, & puis le t̃ pur vie deuie,
le rem̃ ne prendra effect, ne nul auera ceo terre,
car il nad heire ratione attincture. Et tout que
ceo foyt vn nofme de purchafe, vncore nul poet
ceo prend, mez cefty q̃ eft heire. (*B. Difcent.*

*Rem al droit
heires.*

*Nul poet efte hre
al home attint.*

59. *Done.* 42.) Et ou terr̃ in Gauelkind eft
done al vn pur vie, ou en taile, le remainder al
droit heires de W. N. q̃ ad iffue qual̃ fitz &
deuie, et puis le tenant pur vie ou t̃ donee
deuie,

Gauelkind.

deuie, leigñ fits aſſa le ꝉre, car il eſt dꝛt heire al
cōmon ley & cē vn noſm̃ de purchaſe q̃ ſerꝛ
order p le cōmen ley.   Mes econꝭ de diſcẽts al

Diuerſitie.

hꝛes en Gauelk. car donques ceo alera a toutes
les Fitz.   *B. Diſcent & Done.* 42. *Noſme.* 6.

Vid 26. H. 8. 4.

Caſus Sir Iohn Huſſey.

303 ⚏ Nota q̃ Sir John Huſſey Chiualer
infeffe certaine perſons in fee al vſe de Anne ſa
feme, pur terme de ſon vie, et puis al vſe del
heires males de ſon corps, et pur default de tiel
iſſue, al vſe del heirz males del corps de Sir
William Huſſey ſon pier, & pur default de tiel
iſſue, al vſe de ſon droit heires, & puis auer
iſſue William Huſſey eigne, et puis Sir John
fuit attaynt de treaſō An. 29. H. 8. & miſe al
execution, & puis Anne deuie, & le dit W. H.

B. Done 61.

Ouſter le maine.
Heires males noſme de purchaſe.

le fits prie ouſter le maine le roy.   Et per
Whorewood Attorñ Regis il ceo auera, car ceo
noſm̃ hꝛes males del corps, neſt q̃ noſme de
purchaſe, Et Sir W. H. nauera ceo cōe heire
a Sir John, mes come purchaſer (*B. Noſme.* 1.
Liuery 1. *Diſcent.* 1.)   Sicome terre eſt done a
vn home et a ſes heires males de ſon corps & il
ad iſſue 2. fits, leigñ ad iſſue file, & le pier &
leigne fits deuie, le puiſne frere auera le terre &
vncore il neſt heire a ſon pier.   Et eadem lex
ou ꝉre eſt done a home, & a ſes heires females
de ſon corps, & il ad fits & file & deuie, le file
auera le terre & nemy le fits. (*B. Noſme.* 1. 40.)

Litt. 5.

Treaſon.

Et ſic ou ꝉ en tayle eſt attaynt de treaſon ante
ſtatutum de 26. H. 8. ſon fits auera le terre car
il ne claime tantum come heire, mes p leſtaꝉ &

Litt 169.
3. El. Com.
237. Cap. 13.

Diuerſitie ou launc' ad aſcun eſtate, Et ou ne-mye.

p formā doni. (*B. Noſme.* 1.)   Tamen Aliqui
fueꝛ, in contraria opinione, et priſteront diuerſitie
ou le done.eſt al pier meſme, et ou eſt al heires
de ſon corps p remaind. (*B. Noſme* 1. & 40.)

Raſt. Treaſon
12.
Weſt. 2. ca. 1.

Et

9. H. 6. 24.
p Ellerker.

Et pur ceo en 9 H. 6. ſi terres ſont dones a
terme de vie, le reɱ al heirs females del corps
I. S. que eſt mort, et ad iſſue fits & file, et puis
le tenaunt pur vie deuie, le file nauera terre,
car el neſt heire : Car p *Hare* maſter del Rolles
aunclent apprentice, il y eſt difference inter
done en poſſeſſion a vn home et a ſes heires
females &c. Et done al eſtranger le reɱ al
hɼes females dun auter, car la il doit eſte heires
en fait quant le reɱ chia, ou aliter le reɱ eſt
void imperpetuum. (*B. Done* 61.) Car comēt
que le caſe tyent lieu en les 2. caſes miſes per
Whorewood, ceo eſt pur ceo que done fuit vn
foytes veſt que fuit en le pyer, et ideo bona lex
ibi. Contraɼ in principal caſu ou le reɱ neſt
veſt. Tamen per aliquos loppinion *Whorewood*
eſt le meliour, car ou terre eſt done al home et
ſa feme a terme de vie, le remainder al heires **Remainder.**
males de corps del home, ceſt remaynder ne
poet eſtre veſt en le vie le feme. Car neſt taile
in le hoɱ ratione del ſtate del feme, Uncore ſil
ad iſſue 2. fits et leygne ad iſſue file & deuie, le
pier et mier deuie, le puiſne fits auera le terre,
come heire male, & vnꝰ il neſt heire in fait,
Eadem lex ſi tiel done fuit, le reɱ al heires **Remaind'.**
females del corps del home que ad fits & file
& deuie, le file aſſa le terre, comēt q̄ il neſt
heire, Eadem lex ou terre eſt done a W. N. pur **Remaind'.**
vie, le reɱ al J. S. pur vie, le reɱ al heirez
males del corps le dit W. N. que ad 2. fits,
leigne ad iſſu file & deuie, W. N. & J. S.
deulont, le puiſne fits auera le ꝑre come heire
male, vncore il neſt heire en fait, mes ſon mere
eſt heire a ſon pier, car nē matter del primer **Rem en abey-**
veſt, ne del reɱ, Car ou le priɱ ſtate a ꝼme de **ance.**
vie

vie eſt executed, le reṁ ouſtr̃ vt ſupra, reṁ poet
depenḋ in abeiance quouſque &c. vt ſupra, Mes
econtra de remaindr̃ al droit heires, car nul poet
auer ceo, mes ceſty que ſerra heire in fait, (B.
Noſme. 40) Et iḋ fuit agre q̃ l' 2. reṁ al droit
hr̃es Sir John *Huſſey* fuit forſayt p lattainḋ. B.
Noſme. 1.

Vide ſupra 302.

B. Noſme 1.

Rem heredibus maſculis de cor, & rectis hered' Diuerſitie. Forfeiture.

304 ❡ Fuit agree q̃ acc̃ ſur le caſe ne giſt
vers executors ſur laſſumpſion del teſtator, comēt
q̃ ilz ont aſſets B. *Action ſur le caſe.* 4. in fine.

Accio̅ ſur le caſe vers executors.

5. M. 1. Com. 182. conc.

305 ❡ Fuit agree ſi hõe ſoit purſue come
felon, & il ſua & waiua ſes biens demeſne, ceux
ſont forfait, cõe ſils vſſēt eſt bn̄z emblees. B.
Eſtray. 9.

VVaiue ſes pper biens pur felony.

St. 186. A.

306 ❡ Si 2. iointenantes ſont que tiēt del
roy in chiefe, et lun releaſe al aut̃ in fee, et puis
ambideux reſpite homage en le Eſchequer, per
ceo ceſty que releſſe ad gaine le moytie per cõclu-
ſion, Come ſerra ou 2. ioine in ſuit de liuery
hors de maynes le roy, ou lun naḋ riens per
opinionem aliquorum. Et idem de partition p
2. lou lū naḋ riēs. B. *Eſtoppel* 218.

Reſpite de homage per ij.

Liuery.

Partition.

33. H. 6. 7. per Laken. D S. 33.

307 ❡ Si home ſoit ſeiſie dun acr̃ de terre
en fee, et auter ſeiſie al ſon vſe in fee dl aut̃ acr̃,
et il fait feffemēt dambideux acres, & liſty del
acre que il ad in poſſeſſio̅, per ceo lacre in vſe
ne paſſer, coment que il fiſt le liuerie in lun, in
noſm̃ del ambideux, car ceo neſt ſon acre, mes
lacre del feffees, et leſtatute dit que ſon feoffement ſerra bone, mes ſi neſt feoffement niſi il
fait liuery in meſme le terr̃. Et ecõtra ſi liuery
fuit fait en le tr̃ en vſe, ratione ſtatuti &c. B.
Feoffements. 77. *Feoffements al vſes.* 55.

Acre in poſſeſſio̅ & auter in vſe.

Conc Frow. 9. H. 7. 25. & 7. E. 4. 20. 3. M. 1. Com. 154.

1. R. 3. ca. 4.

308 ❡ Si home leſſa pur vie a J. S. & lende-
maine leſſa a W. D. pur xx. ans, le ſecond leaſe
eſt

Leaſe pur vie, & leaſe pur as puis.

Conc H. 1. E. & Vid ſupra 298.

eſt voide ſi ne ſoit graunt de reuerſion oue attornement, car en le ley le franktenement eſt plus
digne et perdurable q̃ leaſe pur ans.   Tamen

Vide 36. H. 8. 287.

ſi le leſſee pur vie deuie deins le terme, le leaſe
pur anz c̄ bon pur le reſt del ans a vener, *B.
Leaſes.* 48. in fine.

Admit P. 1. E. 6. in Cancell'.

309 ❡ Fuit concord p *Plures*, que ou J. N.
conuenit & conceſſit a W. S. q̃ il aſſa xx. acres
in D. pur xx. ans, que ceo fuit bone leaſe, car
hoc verbum (conceſſit) eſt cy fort cõe dimiſit vel
locauit.   *B. Leaſes* 60.

*Conuenit.
Conceſſit.
Dimiſit.
Locauit.*

310 ❡ Si conuſaunce de plee ſoit graunt per
le roy, il doit monſtre vbi, vt in Guyldhald,
vel huiuſmodi, & coram quo, vt coram ſeneſ-
callo ſuo &c.   Et le roy poet graunt toll', faire

*Cognitio pla-
citorum.*

2. H. 7. 13. per Keble.

market, & huiuſmod, Mez nemy dauer aſſiſe de
freſhforce, Ne tolle trauers, ne throughtolle, Ne

*Tolle.
Faire.
Market.
Aſſiſe de freſh
force.*

37. H. 6. 27. per Litt.

que le Fre ſerra deuiſable, borough engliſhe,
Gauelkinde, nec huiuſmodi, car ceux ſont per
cuſtome, que ne poet commencer a ceo iour per
graunt, car le roy ne poet faſr vn ley, per ſõ

*Borough
Engliſh &c.*

Abr. daſſ. 56.
9. H. 6. 27.
per Marten.
44. E. 3. 18. per
Thorpe.
Conc Fitzh.
26. H. 8. 1. &
21. E. 4. 48.
p Huſſey.
3. H. 7. 6.
11. E. 4. 1.
per Litt.

graũt, Et que per graunt d̃ cogniſãce placito-
rum, il ne tenera plee daſſ. ne de certificat
daſſiſe.   Et dicitur pro lege que faux conſideration in letters patents ne auoyde eux, cõme ou
le roy pro 10. li. ſibi ſolut̃, dedit talem terram,
et le 10. li. neſt paye, le patent neſt voide, ne
ſerra repeale, Contrarie de patēt graunt ſur
faux ſurmiſe, come de fauxifier que le terre vient
al roy p attaind J. S. que nē voyer vel hm̃odi,
quere diuerſitie, *B. Patents.* 100.

*Diuerſitie inter
faux ſuggeſtion,
ou ſurmiſe, &
faux conſide-
ration.*

Quere.

Vide St. 3. B.

311 ❡ Un chapleine auera affixe vn auncien
ſeale a vn patent de non reſidēce, fait per luy
meſme, de part le roy, & fuit impriſon en le
Fleete pur ceo.   Et fuit tenus miſpriſion, et

*Miſpriſion de
treaſon.*

o   nul

nul treaſon per Juſticiarios, et il eſcape & ne
fuit miſe a mort.   Car il fuit dit que pur ceo
que il ne counterſayt le ſeale le roy, mes priſt
auncient ſeale, ceo neſt treaſon B. *Treaſon*. 3. in
fine. 5.

Capias ad ſatiſ-
fac', niēt retorn.

312. ❡ Scire facias ſur reꝯ de det & dam̄.
Le def. dit que auterſoites le plaintife ſua cap̄
ad ſatisfaꝯ per que le vicount ad priſe ſon corps,
iudgemēt &c.   Et la dicitur que capias ad
ſatisfac. neſt de recorde deuaunt retorne de ceo,
Ideo nul plee.   Tamen B. ſemble le plee bone

Acquit', ſaue
harmeles, &
diſcharge.

per le priſel del corps, coment que nul briefe
ſoit returne (*B. Executions.* 6.) Dicitur per Curiam in banco regis, En det ſur obligation de
gard ſans dammage. s. harmeles, ou le defendant
plede q̄ il ad luy ſaue harmeles, il neſt plee
ſans monſtre coment, Car ceſty que plede diſcharge ou ſauing harmeles, doit plede ceo certaine, quaunt il plede en laffirmatiue.   Et

Diuerſitie,
Non damnifi-
catus eſt.

econtra ou il plede in le negatiue, car ſi le plaintife ne ſoyt dampnifie, il poet plede quod nō
dampnificatus eſt generalment, *B. Conditions* 16.
198. in finibus.

Plus,

Plus de hoc An. 38. H. 8. 313.

38. H. 8. 315.
4. H. 7. 12.
per Keble.
22. E. 4. 43.
per Cateſby.
35. H. 6. 11.
per Cur.
40. E. 3. 20.
Conc M. 35.
H. 8. B. Cond
18. in fine.
38. H. 8. 31.
6. H. 7. 6.
per Huſſey.
Admitt 18.
E. 4. 27.

An. 38. *Henrici octaui.*

Le roy tenant en
taile ne poet diſ-
continue p graūt
per patent.

313 ❡ Nota que fuit agree in caſu entr̄
Regem & Antonium Lee militem, ſi le roy
tenaunt en taile de done dun auter fait leaſe
pur ans, ou pur vie, & ad iſſue & deuie, liſſue
poet faire auter graunt ſans reciter eux. Car
ils ſont void per le mort le roy teūt in taile, que
graunt, et lheire le roy ceo auoydera, iſſint que
ceo ne liera mes durant le vie le grauntor. Car

Similiter fuit
agree 37. H. 8.
B. Patēts 101.

Vid tēp H. 8.
350.

graunt

graunt ſauns garrantie ou lyuery neſt diſcontinuance, Et le roy ſur ſon graunt ne fait liſry,
Et auxi cheſcun diſcontinuance eſt tort que le
roy ne poit faire, Et ead lex ſil vſt graunt ceo
en fee, ceo neſt diſcōtinuance. (*B. Patents.*

101. *Diſcontinuaunce de poſſeſſ.* 35. *Taile.* 39.
Leaſes. 61.) Et ſic vide que le roy poet eſt
tenaunt in taile, car q̄t home done al roy in
tail, le roy ne poet aū greinder eſtate que le
donor voet depart̃ a luy. *B. Taile.* 39.

Iſſint fuit deter-
mine in le caſe le
ſeignior Bark-
ley.

314 ¶ Nota que pur aſſurance de terre que
le heire ne vēda, fuit deuiſe que home ſerra
feoffement en fee a deux al vſe de luy meſme
pur terme de vie ſans empechement de waſt, &
puis al vſe de ſon fites & ſes heires quouſque le
fits aſſenta et concluđ de aliener ceo, ou aſcun
part de ceo, ou de ceo charger ou encūbrer, et
puis immediatment ſur tiel conſent et concluſion
al vſe de A. & ſes heires quouſque vt ſupra, &
tunc &c. ad vſū B et ſes heires quouſque &c.
et ſic de pluribus &c. et per tiel aſſent et concluſion p le ſtatute de vſes Anñ 27. H. 8. ca. 10.
lauter ſerr̃ in poſſeſſ. &c. *B. Aſſurances.* 1.

Aſſurance que le
heire ne venda.

315 ¶ Si home ſoit oblige in obl' de paier
10. li. al obligee a Paris vltra mare, a cert̃ iour,
ſi loblig. pay a aut̃ lieu, & meſme le ioure en
Englet̃, & laut̃ ceo accept, ceo ē bō clerement.
(*B. Conditions.* 206) Et dicitur en dette ſur
obligation de acquite et ſaue ſans damage, quod
nō damnificatus eſt, eſt bone plee, car ceo eſt en
le negatiue, et ideo bon ſās monſtre coment,

Payment a
auter lieu.

Pled' de condic'
en negatiue, &
en affirmatiue.
diuerſ.

Mes ou il pleade que il ad luy garde ſauns
damage in laffirmatiue, il mōſtra comēt, *B.
Conditions.* 93. in fine.

316 ¶ Fuit dit que *Baldwin, Shelley, &
Moun-*

Mountague Juftices determine pur ley, que ou home ad feffees a fon vfe deuaunt leftatutes de vfes faitz Anno. 27. H. 8. & puiz mefm leftatut & auxi puis leftatut de 32. H. 8. de wils, il voet q̃ fez feffees faire eftate al W. N. & fes hr̃ez de fon corps et deuie, que ceft bone wil & deuife ratione intencioñ &c. *B. Deuife.* 48. in fine.

Deuife q feffees faire eftate ou il nad feffees.

317 ❡ Nota per totam *Curiam* in banco regis que Alien ne poet por̃ action perfonal, & ferra refpond fauns eftre difable pur ceo que il eft Alien nee. Et econtra in action real (Et idem *B.* femble in Actyon myxt) Et il poet auer propertie et achate & vend̃. *B. Denizen* 10. *Nonabilitie.* 40.

Nonabilitie & abilitie dalien diuerfitie.

Propertie.

1. E. 6. 375.

318 ❡ Quere per *B.* fi Attaint ne gift fur verdict en Appel de mafhem a ceft iour per leftatute de 23. H. 8. Cap. 4. Car hoc An. dubitabatur. *B. Attaint.* 10. in fine.

Attaint fur appelle de maihẽ.

319 ❡ Nota que home que leffa p fait polle pur ans, ou p parol, poet void c̃ leafe adire q̃ il nauoit rien in le r̃re tẽpore dimiffionis. Contrarie fur leafe p Indenture car ceft eftoppel. *B. Eftoppel* 8.

Leafe confeff. & auoyd.

Litt 12.
Conc Danby 34. H. 6. 48.
Vid. 5. H. 7. 19.

320 ❡ Dicit̃ q̃ hõe cõe cõftable ne poet arreft vn aut̃ pur affray puis q̃ laffray c̃ paffe f̃as warrant, cõt̃r deuãt l'affray, & in tẽpz d̃l affray &c. Et eadẽ lex de Juftice de peace. *B. Faux imprifonment* 6. in fine.

Authoritie de Conftable, ou Iuftice de peace.

321 ❡ Si vn perfõ leffer r̃re pur terme dãs rend̃t rent & deuie, le fucceffor rec̃ le rent, le leas neft bene f̃z luy, car il nad fee fimple. Ne il ne poet auer briefe de droit, mes Juris vtrū, ideo le refceit del rent per fon fucceffor ne affirme le leafe, car ceo fuit voide p mort le perfon que leffa. *B. Leafes* 18. in fine.

Acceptance de rent per fucceffor de perfon.

Perfon nauera bre de droit.

32. H. 8. 172.
2. E. 6. 381.

44. E. 3. 11.
per Cur.
Fitz. 5. cont.
Litt 144.

322 Nota

Stp. 13.
2. M. 1. Com
109.
2. El. Com 204
Vide 32. H. 8.
188.
Stp. 13.
44. E. 3. 12.
Fitzb. 257. L.
Vide lextēt de c
32. H. 8. 187.

322 ¶ Nota que lheire cefty que tient del roy in capite in focage ne rēdra primer feifin al roy pur touts fes ľres, mes tantū pur ceux terres tenus in focage in capite, Cōtraľ de cefty q̃ tient in Chiualrie in capite, p experientiā Scaccarij. Et lhľe q̃ fua liuery, auera in chefē cōm vn feneral liuery. Et nota q̃ liuery eft ou lheire ad eftre in garde, et vyent a pleyne age, il auera liuery extra manus regis. Et primer feyfin eft ou lheire c̄ de pleyne age tempore mortis anteceff>oris, Vel ou fon tenāt tient in Socage in capite et deuie, la le roy auera primer feifin del terre, q̃ amount al autiel charg al hľe, cōe de liuery eft. *B. Liuery* 60.

14. H. 8. 24.
per Cur.
Cōc. 28. H. 6. 8.
& 4. E. 4. 24.

323 ¶ Nota quant les partiez in aĉtion font demurre in iudgement & ont iour oufter, la a ceft ioure le pľ poet eftre demaunde, et poet eftre nō fue, Cibien come al ioure done puis iffue ioyne. *B. Nonfute* 67.

324 ¶ Dicitur que fi commiffion de oier et terminer expire ou difcontinue, dōques les inditemͤts & record ferra mife in bāco regis, & la ils ferra finifhe (Uide coment P. 369.) *B. Oyer et terminer* 1. in fine.

325 ¶ Memorandum, que al parliament tenus p adiornemͤt H. hoc Anñ fuit admit p briefe le roy & iffint accept, que fi vn Burgefe foit fait Maior dun ville q̃ ad Judicial Jurifdiĉtion, & auľ e malaď, q̃ eux font fufficiͤt caufes deleĉter nouels, p que ils iffint fieront per brief le roy extra Cancellaľ compreignant ceft matter, que fuit admitte & accept in cōmuni domo parliamentͨ. *B. Parliament.* 7.

4. E. 6. 407.

326 ¶ Si in Affife tenaunt plede quͤ fon pier fuit feifie in fee & deuie p proteftation feifie.
Dicitur

Socage in capite
& chiualrie in
capite diūfitie.

Diuerfitie inter
liuery & primer
feifin.

Nonfute fur demurre.

Commiffion de
oier & terminer.

Eleĉt nouels
Burgeffes.

Seifin in fee trauers in affife.

Dicitur q̃ le pl' poet faire title per eſtraunger, ſans ceo q̃ pier le tenãt fuit ſeiſi in fee &c. *B. Trauers* per 26. in fine.

Roy wayuer ſon iſſue, Contr dun Informer.

327 ❡ Information in Scaccario Le defendaunt plede plee et trauers vn material point in le information ſur q̃ ſot a iſſu, la l̃ roy ne poit waiſ cẽ iſſu, Cõe il poet in auſ caſes ou l̃ roy ſole eſt party ſauns vn informer vt ſupra, Per Attornatũ Regis, et alios legis Peritos. *B. Trauers* p 369.

34. H. 8. 247.
Vide 7. E. 6.
439. contra.

34. H. 8. 247.

328 ❡ Nota q̃ in Januarie hoc An. H. Howarde Coũte de Surrey fitz et heire apparãt de Thomas Duke de Norfolke, fuit attaint de haut treaſon, pur ioyner larmes de Engleſre deuãt le conqueſt, et auſ armes pu⁹ a ſõ armes demeſne. Et auſ pretences vers le prince. Et il ſuit trye per chiualers & gentle homes, et nemy per dominoz, nec per pares regni, pur ceo que il ne fuit Earle per creatiõ, mes per natiuitie cõe heire apparãt dũ Duke q̃ nẽ dignitie in le ley, Car ſil vſt eſtre de dignitie p creation, et ſeigniour de parliament, il ſerra trye p ſon pieres. *B. Treaſon* 2.

Vide 33. H. 8. 221.

Ou triall ſerra per pares.

Plus.

❡ Plus d̃ hoc An. 30. H. 8. 138. 37. H. 8. 302.

❡ *Tempore Henrici octaui.*

Licence pur leſſee pur vie le Roy.

329 ❡ Tenaunt le roy in Capite ne poet alien a terme de vie ſans licence, car il alter le franktenemnt. *B. Alienations* 22. in fine.

45. E. 3. 6.

Relation.

330 ❡ Nota lou le ordinary commit ladminiſtrac̃ il poet ceo reuoker & cõmit c̃ a vn auſ (mes meſne acts fait p le primer adminiſtrator eſtoyera.) Et ſic fuyt miſe in vre inter Browne & Shelton pur les biens Rawlins, le adminiſtration

27. H. 8. 26.
per Fitzh.

Power & intereſt certaine diũſity.

4. H. 7. 14.
p Tremaile.

5. E. 6. 415. adminiſtration fuit cōmit a Browne & reuoke &
cōmit a Sheltō, car neſt vn intereſt, mes vn
power ou aucthoritie, Et powers & aucthorities
polēt eſtre reuokes, cōtra de intereſt certeine.
B. Adminiſtrators 33. in fine.

43. Aſſ. 41. 331 ¶ Aſſiſe eſt port Ꝑs tenāt p eſtaꝫ merchāt, & Ꝑs le conuſor q̄ eſt ꝭ del franktenemͭt, &
laſſiſe acquit le ꝭ p eſtatute merchāt & attaint
lauꝉ de diſſeiſin, le ꝭ p eſtaꝫ merchāt nauera
attaint, nec le ſeignior ou ꝫ eſt recoꝯ Ꝑs luy &
lheire ou il ad lheire en gard, nec le Ꝑmor ou Ꝑre
eſt recoꝯ Ꝑs luy & ſon leſſor, pur ceo q̄ ils ne
perꝺ aſcū frāctenemͭt, et ratione que ſont acquit
p W. *Whorewood* attorñ Regis, Tamen p *B.*
ceo nē reaſonable ou ils ſot noſmes & pde
lour intereſt, vncore luy ſēble q̄ ceſty q̄ ē acquit
naūa attait, mes ſils ſot trouez diſſeiſors, ils
aꝰront lattaint p luy, *B. Attaint* 82. in fine.

Attaint pur ter-
mor.
Garden & tenant
p ſtatut merchāt

Conc tēp. E. 6. 332 ¶ Fuit tenuz q̄ ſi Eueſq̄ certifie q̄ tiel
26. H. 8. ca. pſon ne paie ſes tenthes iuxta formā ſtatuti q̄
voit quod ipſo facto le benefice ſerra voide, q̄
in ceo caſe home nauera auermͭ cōtrarye a cel
certificate. *B. Certificate deueſque.* 31. in fine.

Auermͭ contr
certificat de-
ueſque.

Vide 33. H. 8. ☞ Dictum fuit pro lege in cameria ſtellata
210. into *Browne* Juſtic. et Lion grocer de Londres,
que court baron poet eſtre tenuz deuant 2. ſutors, car le plural number ſufficit. *B. Suit* 17.

ij. Sectatores
tantum en cur
baronis.

39. H. 6. 25. 333 ¶ Fuit dit que ſi ſeignorie reſt in ho-
per Moile, & mage fealtie & rent, et hōe recouer le rent, per
44. E. 3. 19. ceo eſt le homage recouer, Car Precipe ne giſt
per Cur, & de ceo *B. Incidents* 24. in fine.
Park. 24. cont.

Rec de rent ſer-
uice bone title al
homage & feal-
tie.

2. E. 6. 388. 334 ¶ Concordatur pur bone ley q̄ le occu-
patiō dun chattel poet eſtre deuiſe p voie de
Vide 33. H. 8. rem̄, Mez ſi le choſe m̄ fuit deuiſe al vſe, le
209. remainder eſt voyd, Car done ou deuiſe dun
chattel

Lou le propertie
eſt deuiſe, & lou
loccuaꝑac diūſ.

chattel pur vn houre c̄ ꝑ imperpetuo, & le
donee ou deuiſee poet ceo doner, vender &
diſpoſer, & le rem̄ eſt voide depend ſur ceo.
B. Deuiſe 13. in medio.

Hōe tue al ſword
& buckler, ou al
iuſting.

335 ℂ Nota per *Juſtices*, que il eſt felony
de tuer home`in iuſting, ou lou homes lude al
ſworde et buckler, et lun occiſt lauter, & huiuſmodi, non obſtāt le cōmaundem̄t le roy, car le
cōmaundement fuit cōtra legem. *B. Corone*
228.

11. H. 7. 20. cōc
p Fineux.

Roy ne ouſtera
termour.

335 ℂ Conceditur p oēs *Iuſtices* q̃ le roy ne
ouſtera le termour ſon t̄ ratione q̃ il ad lheir̄
ſō tenāt in gard p office troue p luy. Ne executiō ſur ſtatute merchaunt fait vers ſon tenant,
Ne rent charge graūt per ſon tenant, ne graunt
de proper preſētac̄ dun auowſon. *B. Garde*
44.

35. H. 8. 264.
Poſt. 242.

11. H. 6. 7.
per Babing.

Murder.
Homicide,
Verdict.

335 ℂ Home eſt arraygne de murder et
troue nō culꝑ, mez que il eſt culꝑ de homicide
ou manſlaughter de m̄ le perſon, il ſerra pēdux,
car ceſt bon Ɐdict, Car in murder eſt cōpriſe
manſlaughter, & iſſint fuit adiudge in banco
regis. Et in vn caſe en marches wallie, q̃ fuit
agree per touts les *Iuſtices*. *B. Corone* 221.

1. M. 1. Com
101.

Defaut puis
reſceit.

336 ℂ Si femme ſoit reſceiue in default ſon
barō & pu⁹ el fiſt default, iudgement ſerra done
ſur le default le baron. Et nul mencion ſerra
fayt del reſceit. *B. Default* 85.

22. H. 6. 14.
per Cur.

Que auer attaint
ou errour.

337 ℂ Fuit tenus que attaynt ale oue le
terre, Come briefe de Error alera. *B. Fauxiſier* 50. in fine.

Fitzh. 21. L.

Rec vers ceſty q
vſe in taile p ſuf-
ferance.

338 ℂ Nota recouery fuit ſuffer per Graſeley del countie de Staff. per aduiſe de *Fitz.*
ſeriant & auters, & Graſeley fuit tantū ceſtie
q̃ vſe in taile, & puis Graſeley deule ſans iſſue,
&

Vide 30. H. 8.
147.

& ſon frere recouer le terre en le Chaūcery,
car a cel temps fuit priſe que recouery vers ceſtie
que vſe in taile ne ſeruera mes pur terme de
ſon vie, per q̃ neſt niſi grant del ſon eſtate. *B.*
Feſſemts al vſes 48. in fine.

339 ❡ Si feſſement ſoit fait deinz le viewe,
quant ceo eſt plede, Dicitur q̃ expreſſe mencion
ſerra fait in l̄ pledinge que le terre fuit deyns
le viewe. *B. Feoffements* 57. in fine.

Pled' feffement infra Viſum.

340 ❡ Feoffement eſt bone del terre per fait
per liuery del fait deinz le viewe, iſſint que le
feſſee entra accordāt. Mes ſi le feſſor deuie
deuant q̃ le feſſee enter, donques le t̃r̃ ē diſcend
al heire le feſſor, & le feſſemēt ne prendra
effeɔ. *B. Feffements* 72.

Feffement infra Viſum terre.

10. E. 4. 1.
per Choke.
Vide 27. H. 8.
hic 89.
40. E. 3. 41.
per Finch.
18. E. 4. 12.
per Collow.
& Towneſend.
Vide 36. H. 8.
285.

341 ❡ Home fayt feoffement p fait al 20.
et liuer le fait & ſeiſin al vn in noſme del touts,
cē bōe al touts, Mes ſil enfeffe 20. ſans fait,
& liuer le ſeiſin al vn in noſme del toutes, ceſt
nul feſſemt a nulluy, mes al ceſtie que priſt le
liuerie. *B. Feffemēts* 72.

Feffement a plures, & lliūy a lun pſon pur toutes. Diuerſitie.

342 ❡ Leaſe poet eſte fait per fiñ pur terme
de ans rendant rēt, & primes le leſſee conuſter
les tenements deſtre le droit le leſſor come ceo
&c. et donques lauter grant & render a luy pur
terme de 60. ans, reddend̄ inde annuatim 10.l̄.
p an &c. & oue clauſe de diſtreſſe. *B. Fines*
leuies 106.

Leaſe pur ans fait per fine.

342 ❡ Fuit agree ſepe per oēs que leſſor ne
poet ouſter le t̃mor, nec huiuſmodi. Nient
plus que il poet auoider rent charge graunt per
luy, *B. Garde* 106.

343 ❡ Nota que ou deuiſe fuit offer al
Bromley Juſtice que le leſſours et le leſſee conuſtre
les tenementes a W. N. come ceo que &c. et

Optimus ordo, pur fine pur leſſee pur ans, per tenannt in taile.

P   il

il render al leſſee pur 60 ans, rendant 10.li. de rent a luy, oue clauſe de diſtreſſe, & per meſme le fine il graunt le reuerſion al leſſour & ſes heires, et il ceo refuſe, eo que ne fuit vſual dauer graunt del reuſſion in tiel fine, Tamen dicitur que *Baldwin* chiefe Juſtice, vſe de prender tiels fines, & ſimiliter a ceſt iour B. *Fines leuies* 118. in fine.

Refervation. Vide 36. H. 8. 285.

344 ❡ Nota per *Fitz.* Juſtice que fine leuie per A. & B. ſa feme, ou le noſme la fēe eſt M. luy liera p eſtoppel, & le tenāt poet pleder q̃ il per noſme B. leuie le fine, & ſic fuyt en vre per ipſum, & fuit pled accordant. B. *Fines leuies* 117.

Eſtoppel per fine leuy. Fitzh. 97. A.

Per nomen.

345 ❡ Nota per *Bromeley* chiefe Juſt. & alios, q̃ bře derř fuit port in banco regis, eo q̃ fine fuit conus per Dedimus poteſtatem deuaunt vn q̃ ne fuit Judge, Abbe, Chiualer, ne Seriant. Et pur cel cauſe eſt refuſe dadmitter aſcun que ſoyt priſe per tiels, car leſtatute de finibus & Attorñ ne dõe power a nul niſi al iuſtices, Abbe & Chiualer. Quere per B. ſi ſeriant del ley ne ſoyt priſe come Juſtice per lequitie de leſtatute. B. *Fines leuies* 120.

Que poit prender fine per leſtatute de Finibus & attornatis.

Quære.

346 ❡ Nota quod dictum fuit pro lege q̃ terre ne poet eſtre done in frankemariage oue home que eſt coſin al doner. Mes doit eſtre oue fēe q̃ eſt coſin al donor. B. *Frankemariage* 10.

Frankmariage, oue home. 7. E. 4. 12. ecõt p Moile & Fitzh. 172. H. Conc Litt 4. Park. 48. E.

347 ❡ Nota Dicitur p lege q̃ dõe in frankemariage le remainder al J. N. in fee neſt frankemariage, Car garrantie & acquiſ ē incidēt al frāck mariage ratione del reuerſion in le donor que ne poet eſtre ou le donor miſt le remainder & fee al eſtraunge ſur meſme le done. B. *Frankmariage.* 11.   348 ❡ Dicitur

Frankmariage, le rem en fee. Vide 4. E. 6. Com 14. per Harris.

Fitz. 136. B. del acquit.

DS. 76.
8. H. 7. 10.
7. E. 6. Com
96.

348 ❡ Dicitur que pur hariot cuſtome hōe ſemper ſeiſera, & ſil ſoit eſſoine, il poet auer detinue. Et pur hariot ſeruice eſſoin, il poet diſtraigñ mes nemye pur hariot cuſtome. *B. Hariots* 6. in fine.

Hariot cuſtome & ſeruice diuerſ. Detinue.

14. H. 8. 66.

348 ❡ Dicitᵣ q̃ ſi liſſue en taile ſoit barre p iudgem̄t per reaſon de garr̃ et aſſets diſcend, et puis il alien laſſets, et ad iſſue et deuie, liſſue del iſſue naſſa formedon del primer terre taile. Mes ſi tiel choſe happa deuāt q̃ il ſoit barre per iudgement, liſſue de liſſue auera formedō. *B. Formedon* 18.

Diuerſitie.

Vide 37. H. 8.
298.
Conc Litt.
2. E. 4. 11.

349 ❡ Fuit tenus per *Bromley* Juſtice & alios, que ſi hom̃ leſſa pur 20. ans, & lende-maine leſſa pur 40. ans, le ſecond leaſe prēdra effeᏜ pur 40. ans. s. puis le 20. ans paſſe. *B. Leaſes* 35. in fine.

Home leſſa pur 20. ans, & puis leſſa pur 40. ans.

Conc tēp. E. 6.

350 ❡ Nota q̃ fuit agree q̃ ou le roy graunt terre que eſt in leaſe pur terme dans dun que fuit attaint, ou dun abbey, et huiuſmodi, q̃ le graūt ē bone ſans recital del leaſe cēy que fuit attaint, ou del Abbey. Car il ne recitera aſcun leaſe, niſi leaſes de record. *B. Patents* 93.

De quel leaſe re-cital ſerr en pa-tent le roy. Et de quel nemy.

Vide 38. H. 8.
313.

351 ❡ Home eſt lie al peace, & procure auter denfreinder le peace, ceo ē forfaiture de ſon bonde, vt dicī fuit, *B. Peace* 20.

Breache del peace.

28. H. 8. 99.
contr.

352 ❡ Nota q̃ home ne poet ſuer liuery in Cancellaria pur terre in Gales, Ne en County Palantine, p experientiam. *B. Liuery* 63.

Liuery en Gales, & Countie palā-tine.

353 ❡ Nota per aliquos le roy nauera pre-cipe qd̃ reddĩ (come briefe deſcheit) mes ſon title ſerra troue p office. *B. Prærog.* 119.

Prec' qd' reddat pur le Roy. Eſcheate.

354 ❡ Fuit dit que ou lentereſt le Roy ē certaine & determine, le ptye poet enꝑ, q̃re ꝑ. *B. Reſeiſer* 36. in fine.

Ent' puis l' int' eſt le Roy det'-mine. Quære.

355 ❡ Fuit

Det & detinue in vn mefme bre.

355 ❡ Fuit agree que home poet auer det & detinue p vn mefme bře per feueral precipe, car lun ſerra debet, & lautř detinet. *B. Seueral Precipe* 5. in fine.

11. H. 6.

Tenant per fuf-ferance & a volūt.

356 ❡ Nota pro lege que eſt nul ť p fuf-feraunce mes ceſty q̃ primes enter per authoritie et loialment cōe lou home leſſa pur ans ou pur ľme dautř vie, & tient ouſter ſon terme, puis le terme expire, ou puis le mort ceſty que vie. Et tenant a volunt eſt ou hōe leſſa ſon ľre a auľ a volunt, Quia cēy q̃ enī de ſon teſt demeſne eſt deſſeiſor. *B. Tenant p copy* 15. in fiñ.

Vide 22. E. 4. 38. p. Huſſey.

Diſſeiſor.

357 ❡ Dicitur q̃ ceſty q̃ pled recouery en bře de droit in court barō in barre daſſ. deuant les Juſt. daſſ. il doit monſtř ceo exēplifie fub figillo Cancell. et aliľ il neſt plee. Mes dun record in communi banco, il poet aľ vouche ceo la, et aľa iour dameſner ceo eyns. Eadē lex p *B.* daſcun auter court de recorde. Tamen ecōtra in court barō, car la c̃ e̓ vn recoſſy, mez nul record, car ceo ne̓ court de record. *B. Record* 66. in fine.

Court baron, & court de record, diuerſ.

358 ❡ *Audely Chauncellor* dēgleterre tient clerement que ſi hōe vēde ſon ľre deuant leſta-tute de vſes, ceo changera luſe del fee ſimple. Et eadem lex del vend per Indenture per ſta-tute 27. H. 8. ſans parolz heirs. *B. Conſcience* 25. in fine.

Vendee aľa fee ſans parols hres.

32. H. 8. 181. 4. E. 6. 406. 6. E. 6. 422. 27. H. 8. ca. 16. Raſt. Inrolmts

359 ❡ Fuit agree que Keines de age đ 20. ans, ne ſub 20. ans ne poient eſtre ſuccide per tenant pur ľme dans, ou terme de vie, car eux ſont del nature de timber, et poient eſtre timber, et per ceſt voye eux ne vnq̃s creſſ. deſtre timber *B. Waſt* 134.

Succid' de keines de 22. ou ſub 22. ans dage, ſerra waſt.

Vid 4. E. 6. 411.

360 ❡ Dictum fuit pro lege que neſt plee in treſpas

24. H. 8. 47.
27. H. 8. 26.
2. E. 4. 6.

trefpas fur leftatute de 5. R. 2. pur le def. adire
q̄ le lieu ou eſt 20. acres que eſt parcel del maner
de B. que eſt ſon franktenemēt. Car le def.
doit luy ētitler a vn loyall entrie, Car diſſeiſor
ad frākteñt, et vncore ingreſſus ē vbi ingreſſus
non datur per legem. *B. Acc. fur leſtatute* 27.

Son frankte-
nemt en accion
fur leſtatut de 5.
R. 2.

Diſſeiſor.

Vide 29. H. 8.
111. & 5. E. 6.
413.

361 ❡ Per *Fitz.* Juſt. ſi les feffees al vſe dun
eſtate taile, vende le t̄r al ceſty q̄ ad notice del
primer vſe vncore lachator ne ſerra ſeiſi al primer
vſe, mes al ſō vſe demeſne ratione del bargaine
et ſale, car les feoffez oūt le fee ſimpl̄, & ideo
lour vēdition eſt bone. *B. Feoffements al vſes*
57. in medio.

Vendee aūa fee
coment q il ad
notice del vſe.

Fitzh. 141. D.

362 ❡ Fuit dit, ſi home port br̄e dentruſion,
maritagio non ſatisfaƈto, pur le ſingle value, et
fiſt menciō in le briefe del tender del mariage
al heire, et que il refuſe &c. Que le tender
neſt trauerſable. *B. Forfeiture de mariage* 7.
Intruſion 23. in finibus.

Tender trauer-
ſable.

363 ❡ Founderſhip ne poet eſcheter p mort
ſans heire ne eſt̄r forfeit p attaindr̄ de felony
ou treaſon, car eſt choſe annex al ſanke, q̄ ne
poet eſtre deuide, vt dicitur puis laugmentation
court priſt cōmencement Car home q̄ eſt heire
a auter ne poet faire auter deſtre heire. *B. Corodies* 5. in fine.

Founderſhip eſ-
chete, ou forfeit.

Heire.

32. H. 6. 37.
per Danby.

364 ❡ Conceſſum fuit in caſu Th. Inglefield
militis, Ou le roy recite qd cum A. B. tenet
maneriū de D. pro termiñ vite ſue de conceſſione noſtra &c. Sciatis nos conceſſiſſe C. S.
reuerſ. manerii prediƈti &c. Habendum &c.
que ceſt bon grāt. Ideo *B.* ſemble q̄ ſi le roy
miſrecite date del primer letters patentes, vel
huiuſmodi, vncore ſil bien recite leſtate et le
choſe, et le noſme del leſſee, que donques le
graunt

Recitall en pa-
tent.

Roy prendra
notice.

graunt del reuerſion eſt bon. Car oꝗ le roy
prēt notice de ſon tenaunt pur terme de vie, et
de ſon eſtate, & graunt le reuerſion, il nē deceiue in ſon grant, car il prent ſur luy noticꝰ del
formꝰ intereſt pur vye, et donquez le date del
primer patent neſt pas material *B. Patents* 96.

Relaſ de forſ. de
felony p verdiꝗ
& per vtl' diaſ.

365 ¶ Tenetur pur bone ley, que per attainder de felony per verdiꝗ, home forſeitra
touts ces terres ꝗ il auoit iour del felony fait,
Ou vnꝗ, puis, car ceo auera relation al aꝗ cōtra ſur attainder per vtlary, Car *B.* ſemble la
que il ne forſ. niſi ceux que il auer tēpore
vtlagarie pronunciaꝰ ou puis. Car vtlagarie
nad relation, come verdite ad. *B. Relation* 42.
in fine.

30. H. 6. 5.
Park 6. C.
St. 192. A.

30. H. 6. 5. &
St. 192. A.
Contr Park.
6. B.

Fait port date
vltra mare.

Lieu trauerſ-
able.

366 ¶ Nota ſi aꝗion ſoit ſue ſur vn fait
portāt date a Cane in Normaindie. ſ. daꝰ
apud Cane &c. que le pleyntife counterꝰ, ꝗ le
fait fuit fait a Cane en cōm Kanꝰ et bien, Car
le lieu neſt trauerſable. (*B. Faits* 95. in fine).
Et auxi ou in verity il fuit eſcrie in Cane, eſt
ſuable in Angꝉ ou ceo port date ąlarge, & a
nul lieu certeyne. Mes ſi ſoit (daꝰ apud Cane
in Normandy &c.) quere ſi laꝗion giſt &c.

Conc 48. E. 3. 3.

34. H. 8. 332.

21. E. 4. 74.
per Curiam.

Retorne de ex-
tendi facias li-
berate.

367 ¶ Dicitur ſi br̄ dexecutiō oue extēdi faꝰ
iſſuiſt ſur vn ſtatut merchāt, ꝗ le br̄e doit eſtre
returne, et le tr̄ ſur ceo liuer al conuſee p liberate inde. *B. Statut merchant* 32. in fine.

Home fait fin
ſur endiꝗment
dextorcion, ou
treſpas, & puis
pled non culp.
Lentre en feſanſ
fine.

367 ¶ Si hōe endite dextorcō ou trn̄s luy
miſt in grace le roy, et fiſt fine, et puis le party
ſua vers luy de ceo per bill, ou briefe, et il plede
non culp̄, il auera le plee, et le feſans del fine
al roy ne luy eſtoppera. Car la lentre eſt quod
petit ſe admitti p finem, & ne ceo confeſſe pre-
ciſement, et ideo neſt eſtoppel. Tamen *B.*

ſemble

9. H. 6. 60.
per Curiam.

9. H. 6. 60.
p Babington.

ſemble de faire le fyne per proteſtatyon que il
neſt culpable, et donques ceo eſt tout clere. *B.*
Eſtoppel 132.

368 ¶ Terre fuit done per le roy p̄ erectione
collegii cardinalis Eborum, & le college ne
fuit erect, et ſur office ent troue le roy ſeiſiſt.
B. Office 4. in fine.

¶ Vide *B.* *titulo Voucher* 84.

¶ Plus 4. E. 6. 359. & 5. E. 6. 413.

Marginal notes:
Proteſtation.

Foundation niēt
obſerue.

Plus.

Anno primo Edwar. 6.

NOta p̄ omnes *Iuſticiarios,* q̄ ſi hōe ſoit
indite de felony, tēpore H. 8. le roy
deuie, il ſerr̄ arrayne de ceo tempore. E. 6.
Mes per aliquos cē indictment ſerra remoue p̄
Cerciorare del aūcient cuſtos rotulorum, et miſe
al nouels cōmiſſions. *B. Corone* 177.

369 ¶ Nota que endictmentes et recordes
que ſont priſe deuant Juſtices de oyer et terminer, & nient determine deuant que lour commiſſion ſoit fine, ceux ſerront miſe in banco
regis darraigner les pties la. s. per Cerciorari
hors del Chaūcery, quel ſerra al commiſſioners
del oyer & t̄miner, et puys ſerra myſe in banco
Regis p̄ mittimus. (*B. Corone* 178. *Oyer et*
terminer 2. in fine.) Mes indictemts priſe
deuāt Juſt. de gaole deliſty & niēt determine
ſerr̄ liūeries al clerke del peace. Ou remaynera
oue le *Cuſtos Rotulorum* del County ou &c̃. et
quant auters Juſtices de gaole deliuerie veigne
la, ils poyent proceeder ſur eux ſur iudgement
de mort, et hoc auxi per ſtatutum inde. Et *B,*
ſemble que ils procedera per lequitie de ceux
parols,

Left marginal notes:
1. E. 3. 4. per
Borous.

38. H. 8. 324.

Cōc 44. E. 3. 43.

2. E. 6. ca. 7.

Right marginal notes:
Indictment tem-
pore vnius regis
ſeruera in tem-
pore alterius.

Cerciorarj.

Endictment
niēt diſcuſſe
pendant le com-
miſſion doier &
termin.

Cerciorarj.
Mittimus.
Indictmēt de-
uāt Iuſtic doier
&c. Et deuant
Iuſtic' de gaole
deliuer Diuerſi-
tie.

Clergie.
Sanctuarie.

parois, al allower de Clergie ou Sanctuary, et hmodi *B. Corone.* 178.

Acceptance per cesty en remainder.

370 ¶ Tenant in taile le remainder ouster, lessa pur ans rendaunt rent, & deuie sauns issue, et cestuy en rem accept le rent, ceo ne luy liera, ratio est, eo que quant le taile est determine, tout q̄ ē cōprise deins ceo, ē determiñ, Et issint le lease voide. Et cesty in remainder ne clayme per le lessor. *B. Acceptance.* 19.

Vend' de terre p exec puis disseisin recouery, fine leuy ou discent.

371 ¶ Si home deuise son Ꝑre deste vend per ses executors, et deuie, le heire enter et puis est disseisi, vncore les executors poyent vend, & le vendee poet enter. (*B. Deuise* 36. *Entre congeable.* 134.) Eadem lex si le heire suffer recouery, ou leuie fine. Et eadem lex

Vide 9. H. 6.
24. p. Paston.

Title dentre, & droit dentre, diuersitie.

per aliquos ou home disseisie le heire, et deuie seysie, et son heire enter, les executours vend, et le vendee poet enter, car il nad droit, ne nul action est done a luy, Car il nad mes vn title de entre per le vendition, et ideo il poet enter, car auterment il nad ascun remedy per *Hales*

Mortmaine.

Justice. (*B. Deuise* 36.) Et per *B.* si alienation en mortmaine soit, et le alienee est disseisi, et le disseisor deuie seisie, so heire est eins per discent, vncore le seigñ poet enter deins lan, car il nad nisi tantū vn title dentre, et ne poet auer actiō. Mes econtra de cēy q̄ ad droit dentre et poet auer action. *B. Mortmaine.* 6. in fine.

47. E. 3. 11.

Dower de rent referue sur leas pur ans, & pur vie.

372 ¶ Feme ne serra endowe de rent referue sur lease son baron pur terme de vie, car le rent nest inheritaunce, et est determinable per le mort le lessee, Et vncore lheire auera

7. H. 6. 3.
per June.
Park. 68.

Iudgement & cesset execuc.

ceo, car est incident al reuersion. Et ou home seisie en fee, lessa pur ans rendaunt rent, et puis prist

Park 67.

prift femme et deuie, le femme auera dower
de le terre, mes nauera execution duraunt le
terme dans, car eigne title &c.   Et el ne poet
eftre endowe del rent pro caufa antedicta.   *B.*
Dower. 89.

Park 69.

373 ❡ Nota que de terre de Duchie de
Lancafter et auters terres q̃ le roy ad come
Duke, vel hm̃odi fon age eft materiall, et poet
auer fo age come auter comon perfon poet,
car il ad ceux come Duke & non cõe Roy.
(*B. Age.* 52. et 78.)   Come fi le roy alien
terre parcel de fon Duchy de Lancafter deyns
age, la il poet voider ceo par nonage, car il ad
le Duchy come Duke et nemy come roy, Contrary del terr̃ que il ad com̃ roy, car roy ne
poet eftre difable per nonage, come common
perfon ferra (*B. Prerogatiue.* 132.)   Tamen
p leftatute de 1. E. 4. (que eft priuate act
nient printed mes inroll en le Duchie chamber,
per que roy H. 6. fuit attaint de treafon, et
que toutes les terres del dit duchy ferra forfayt
et ferra vn Duchy feperet et incorporat &c.) il ẽ
annexe al Corone, Mes per vn auter priuate
act 1. H. 7. il eft difannexe et fait vt in tempore H. 4. *B. Age.* 52.

4. El. Com 213.
221. contr.

4. El. Com. 213

Vide leftat
Com 218.

Com̃t feperat
Vide Com 219.
Vide de c Com
219 & 220.
Vide ceo act
Com 214.

Ou le roy alla fon
age & ou nemy.

Ou le roy auera
prerogatiue &
ou nemy.

374 ❡ Et ou tenure eft troue del roy, vt
de ducat̃ fuo Lancaftrie, que en veritie eft faux,
vncore ceo ne befoigne deftre trauers, car le
roy ad ceo Duchy come Duke et nemy come
roy, Et home ne ferra mife a trauers nifi ou le
office eft troue pur le roy, vt pro rege Anglie,
car donques il ad prerogat̃, et vt Duke nul pre-
rog. *B. Trauers doff.* 53.

38. H. 8. 317.

Alien.

375 ❡ Fuit dit in banco regis, que adire,
que le plaintife eft alyen nee iudgement fi ferra

Q   refpond,

respond, nest plee in action personal, Contrary in action real. Tamen ceo ad estr ē question puis cel temps en mesme le court, Et fuit dit que alien nee nest plee en trespas si il ne dit ouster que le playntife est de allegeaunce dun tiel, enemy le roy, Car nest plee en action personal vers alien que est de allegeaunce de tiel prince que est de amitie le roy. *B. Nnnabilitie.* 62.

376 ❧ Per *Mervin* Justice vn Constat est pledable, Contrary dun Inspeximus, car en lun cas le patent remaine, & en lauter il est pdon. Et p *B.* in libro intrationum, vn cōstat fuit plede, & aide graunt del roy sur ceo. *B. Patents.* 97. in fine.

377 ❧ Fuit agree q̄ vn q̄ estate ne serra allowe in vn q̄ est meane en le conuesance, Cōe adire que A. fuit seisie in fee & infeoffe B. que estate C. ad, que infeoffe le def. car le que estate serra allowe solomēt en le def. ou tenant mesme, 1. q̄ estate le t̃ ad. *B. Que estate.* 49.

378 ❧ Nota per omnes, ou tenaunt en taile, ou pur terme de vie ē implede, cesty in rem, ou reuers. poet maintaine et done de son proper deniers pur maintaine, pur sauegarde de son interest, car fuit agree que cēy q̄ ad interest en le t̃re poet maintener pur sauer ceo. *B. Maintenance* 53.

❧ Plus 37. H. 8. 398.

An. secūdo Edwardi. 6.

379 ❧ Home seisie in fee lesse pur 10. ans & prist feme, & ent conuey estate a luy & son
fee,

fée, et al heires le baron, & puis le baron et le feme leſſa al auter pur xx. ans rend rent, le baron deuie, le feme accept le rent durant les x. ans, p c̃ le ſecond leaſe pur xx. ans nẽ affirme, mes puis le 10. ans fine, el poet enter, car acceptance deuant q̃ le leaſe commence ne poet ceo faire pfect. *B. Acceptãce.* 18. commencement del leaſe.

Vide 37. H. 8. 298. & 3. M. 1. 467. 379 ❡ Home leſſe ẽre pur ẽme de xx. ans, et le leſſee leſſa ceo ouſter pur 10. ans rendaunt rent, et puis graunt le reuerſion del terme et rent al eſtraunge, ceo ne paſſera ſans attornement, ratione del attendauncie del rent, Contra ſi nul rent fuit reſerue ſur le ſecõd leaſe pur 10. ans, car donques eſt nul attendauncie deſtre fayt, ne Action de waſt, ne huiuſmodi deſtre port. Car vt *B.* ſẽble, attornement neſt neceſſarie, mes dauer auowry ou acc̃ de waſt. *B. Attornement.* 45. Attornement ſur graunt de reuerſion de terme. Diuerſitie. Vide 31. H. 8. 151.

Vid 15. E. 4. 10. 6. El. Com 268. contr. 376 ❡ Si le fits & heire del tenaunt le roy, ou dauter Seignior ſoit fait chiualer en le vie ſon pier, et puis le pere deuie, lheire ſerra en garde, Car aliter launc̃ poet procure ſon fits deyns age, deſtre fait chiualer per colluſion, al entent pur defrauder le Seigniour del garde, que ne ſerra ſuffer. Et ſic accidit de Seigniour Anth. Browne d Surrey que fuit fait Chiualer tempore patris ſui, q̃ deuie le fits deyns age, & fuit tenus il ſerra en garde, non obſtaunt que il fuit chiualler, per que il agree oue le roy que ore ẽ pur ſon mariage. Auterment *B.* ſemble ou il eſt en garde et eſt fait chiualer en garde, ceo luy mittera extra cuſtodiam. Et per luy leſtatute que eſt, Poſtquam heres fuerit in cuſtodiã cũ ad etat̃ peruenerit. s. 21. annorũ, ĥeat hereditatem ſuã ſine releuio, et ſine fine, Ita tamen Chiualer in gard. Viſcont Mountegue. Diuerſitie ou hõe eſt fait chiualer deins age en vie launc. Et ou il eſt fait chiual' deins age puis le mort launc. 6. El. com 268. Magna cart. Cap. 3. Raſt. ca. 1.

tamen quod ſi ipſe, dum infra etatem fuerit
fiat miles, nihilominus terra ſua remaneat en
cuſtodia dominorum vſque ad terminum ſupra-
diſtum, Eſt entend ou il eſt fait chiualer deins
age eſteant en garde puis le mort launc̃. Et

Expoſic leſtatut. nemy ou il eſt fayt chiualer en vie launc̃. *B.*
Gard. 42. & 72.

Acceptance per 380 ❡ Eueſ{que} leſſa p̃re deueſcherie pur ans
ſucceſſ. deueſ- rendaunt rent et deuie, le ſucceſſor accept le
que. rent, ceo luy llera, car eueſ{que} ad ſee ſimple et
puit auer briefe dentre ſine aſſenſu capituli,
Perſon. Cōtra in caſe dū Perſon, ou Prebende, que ne
Prebend. poient auer niſi iuris vtrum. *B. Acceptance.*
20.

Leaſe deueſque. 381 ❡ Auxi fuit agree pur ley en Cancel- **Iſſint dū Abbe.**
laria per *Iuſtitiarios* que ſi leaſe pur ans ſoit **14. H. 8. 12.**
per Carel. &
fayt per Eueſ{que} que ceo neſt voyde mes voy- **21. H. 7. 38.**
dable, car il auer ſee ſimple, Contra de tiel **per Lee.**
leaſe per perſon, ceo eſt voide per ſon mort,
car il nad le ſee ſimple, mes ceo eſt en abey-
ſance. Et leueſ{que} poet auer briefe de droit, ou
briefe dentre ſine aſſenſu capituli, Ou perſon
nauera niſi vn Juris vtrum. Et ideo ſi ſucceſ-
Deane. ſor de Eueſque, Deane, Prebend, et huiuſmodi
Perſon. que ont ſee, et leſſe et deuie, accept le rent,
Prebend'. ceo affirme le leaſe eſtre bone, Et econtra de **38. H. 8. 321.**
tiel acceptaunce per ſucceſſ. de perſon que fiſt
tiel leaſe, car ceſt leaſe eſt voyde maintenant.
Mes ſi Chaūtery prieſt fait leaſe, ſō ſucceſſ.
auoydera ceo non obſtāt que le predeceſſor
auera ſee, pur ceo que il eſt donatiue, ou pre-
ſentatiue, et donques tiel leaſe neſt perdurable,
Confirmation. Niſi ſoit confirme per le patron en lun caſe, &
per le patron et lordinarie en lauſ caſe, *B.*
Leaſes. 33. in fine.

382 ❡ Aſtion

33. H. 8. 198.

382 ¶ Action fur le cafe pur chofe que gift in fefauns, come pur arfer des biens, ou faites, et huiufmodi, non culp eft bon plee, Contra pur non fefans de chofe que il doit faire, come faire ou repaire pont, meafon, parke, pale, efcourer foffe, et huiufmodi, et ne fayt la non culp neft plee, *B. Action fur le cafe.* 111.

Non culp bone ple in acc' fur le cafe & ou nemy.

383 ¶ Le heire de home occife, auera appele fibien de homicide fon auncefter, coe de murder. *B. Appeale.* 124.

Appelle pur homicide.

384 ¶ Repleuin, le defendaunt dit que B. fuit felfie en fee et leffa al E. pur 40. ans, quel E. graunt fon interest al defend Anno 28. H. 8. per que il fuit poffeff. et diftreigne pur dammage fefaunt, Le plaintyfe dit que mefme cefty E. Anno. 32. H. 8. graut fon interest a luy, il ne trauerfera le graunt in Anno 38. Car il ad ceo confeffe & auoyde per leigne graunt obtaine, *B. Confeffe et auoyde.* 65.

Ou home cō- feffe & auoyd, la ne trauerfer.

385 ¶ Nota que fuit tenus q̃ ou ftable eft prope vn meafon enheritable, come parcel del meafon, et hōe debrufe ceo p noctem, al entent de robber in ceo, ceft felonie, coment que il prift rien, car eft burglarie. *B. Corone.* 179.

Burglarie.

Vide 2. H. 7. 13 per Keble.

386 ¶ Le roy fait Duke ou Coūte & done a luy xx. li. de tre vel huiufmodi per mefme le nofme, iffint que le creation & le graunt eft tout per vn mefme patent, vncore ceo eft bon. Et eadem lex de fefauns de corporation et done a eux terre per mefme le patent et nofme. *B. Corporations.* 89.

Creation & done in vn mefme pa- tent.

Patent a ij. in- tents.

387 ¶ Si South fenefcal tyent court baron, & graunt copiholdes al tenants per copie de court roll faunz aucthoritie del feigniour ou haut fenefchal, ceo eft bone graunt, car en plena

Ou fenefcall, vel fubfenefcall poet leffe per copy, & econtra.

plena curia, Contrarie fil ceo fayt extra Curiam
fans tiel aucthoritie. Tamen le haut fenefcal
poet dimitter cuftomarie terre per copy extra
Curiã per aliquos. Quere inde per *B.* fil nad
efpecial aucthoritie de fũr pur demifer. *B.*
Court baron 22. *Tenãt per copie.* 26.

388 ¶ Ou home deuife que W. O. aũa le
occupatiõ de fon plat pur terme de fa vie, Et
fil deuie deyns le term̃ q̃ ceo remainera al J. S.
ceft bone rem̃, car le prim̃ nad forfqz loccupa-
tiõ, & laul̃ puis luy aũa propertie, *B. Deuife*
13. in fine.

Deuife loccupac'

T̃ĕp H. 8. 334.

389 ¶ Nota fi feffees font enfeffe al vfe le
feffor pur terme de vie, et puis al vfe A. in
taile, deuant leftat de 27. H. 8. de vfes, et
puis leftates en vfes font veft in poffeffion per
m̃ leftatute, et puis le tenaunt pur vie deuie,
& le tenaunt en tayle enter et difcontinue et
deuie, et liffue port formedon fur ceo matter, il
fuppofer le feffor deftre donor, et non les feffees. Et le briefe ferra general quod dedit &c.
Mes le declaration ferra fpecial & declare lentier matter que le feoffor fuit feifie in fee et
infeoffe les feffees al vfes vt fupra, et m̃re le
execut̃ del ftates per leftatute de vfes fait 4. die
Februarij. Anno 27. H. 8. briefement & non
alarge, Et le feifin &c. Et le mort del tenant
pur vie & ĩ en taile, et quod poft. mortem &c.
Difcend ius &c. *B. Formedon.* 49.

Formed' fur
taile q com-
mence en vfe,
& eft execut fur
leftatute, 27.
H. 8.

Ceft matt fuit
in vre P. Rot.
505. in cõmuni
banco, int Bar-
neis pet, et
Browne tent,

General bre, &
fpecial declara-
tion.

7. E. 6. 436.

Vide 1. M. 1.
444.

390 ¶ Si home foit conuict de felonie, et
remaine in prifon, et puis le roy luy pardon, la
les Juftyces de gaile deliuerie poyent luy bayler
tanque le prochein feffions de gaile deliuery,
iffint que il poet donq̃ veft oue fon pardon, et
pleder c̃, *B. Mainprife.* 94.

Power del Iuftic'
del gaile deliũy.

391 ¶ Nota

391 ❡ Nota in cafu *Culpeper* fuit dit que le roy mefme ne poet recorder ou receiuer furrender de terr ou letters patents faites a luy in extra Curiam, Mes ceo doit eftre deuant fon Chauncellor, ou auter Juftice a ceo aucthorifed, ceo fra. *B. Recognifans* 16. *Surrender* 53. in finibus. *Prerogatiue.* 135.

Roy ne record furrender.

392 ❡ Si home leffa pur ans le rem oufter pur ans, et puis le primer termor graunt fon intereft al leffor, ceo ne furrender ratione del mefme intereft del terme in remainder. Et termor fait fon leffour fon executour et deuie, ceo neft Surrender, Car il ad ceo a auter vfe, Contra *Whorewood* inde, *B. Surrender.* 52.

Mefne rem furr.

Termor fait lef-for fon executor.

393 ❡ Quare impedit fur graut de proxim prefentatione graunt a J. N. gent, et en le briefe port per J. N. ceft parol (gent) eft omitte, et le def. demaund oyer del fayt, et habuit et le variaunce nul matter, car le Action de Quare impedit eft found fur le difturbaunce, et non fur le fait. Come action de dette eft found fur obligation. *B. Variaunce.* 109.

Quare impedit, & le bre, & le fait vary.

❡ Fuit conceffum per *Sholley* Juftice, et alios, que fi le roy done chattel fans fait, et le donee ceo prift per fon commaundement, ceo e bone, *B. Donc.* 16. in medio.

Done de chatell per le roy.

394 ❡ Nota pro lege per *Cancellar.* Anglie & *Juftisiarios*, que fi le tenant que tient del roy en Capite en Chiualry, done tout fon terre al eftranger per act execute in fon vie, et deuie, vncore le roy auera le 3. part en gard, et auera lheire en garde fil foit deins age. Et fi de pleine age, il auera prinf feifin de 3. part virtute iftius claufule en le ftatut. Sauing al roy gard, primer feifin, liuery, et huiufmodi, per quod

Feffement de tout poft ftatute 32. H. 8.

Garde.
Primer feifin.

Vid 4. E. 6. 490

41. E. 3. 23. per Finch.

35. H. 8. 269.
37. H. 6. 10. per Danera.
26. H. 8. 8. cotr.

32. H. 8. ca. 1.
Ref. Willes. 2.

quod patet q̃ lentent del act eſt, que le roy
auera tant, cōe ſi le tenaunt vſt fait will et vſt
deuiſe ſeiſie. Tamen p omnes puis q̃ le roy eſt S. 36. H. 8. 287
ſerue de ſon duitie de ceo, le done ē bon al do- Vide H. 10. El.
nee vers lhr̄e, *B. Teſtament.* 24.

℃ Plus 1. E. 6. 377. 4. E. 6. 409. Plus.

Habend' puis
tiel leaſe ſine ou
neſt tiel leaſe.

395 ℃ Home leſſa pur ans, habēd poſt di-
miſſionem ind factā al J. N. ſinitā, & in veritie
J. N. nad leaſe en ceo, la le leas cōmence im-
mediat̄ per *Hales* Juſtice et plures alios. Et p Conc H. 1. M. 1
luy ſi prebend fait leaſe pur 21. ans per Inden-
ture, rendaunt le vſual rent, ceo liera le ſucceſſ. 23. H. 8. ca.
per le ſtatute de leaſes, Car ou leſtatute dit, en

Leaſe de pre-
bend'.

iure eccleſie, Et lentre pur prebend, eſt ſeiſitus
en iure prebende, vncore ceo liera per lequitie,

Equitie.

B. Leaſes. 62.

Reſtitution per
parliament.

396 ℃ Home eſt attaint de treaſon, le roy Vide 32. H. 8.
poet reſtore lheire al terre per ſon patent de 280.
graunt, Mes il ne poet faire le heire deſtr̄ hr̄e
de ſanke, Ne deſtre reſtore a ceo ſauns parliamēt, car ceo ē in preiudiciū aliorū *B. Reſtitution.* 37.

Part de aliens, &
part de denizēs.

397 ℃ Fuit agree en Curia *Scaccarii.* Ou
iury eſt agarde de medietate lingue, ou alien
eſt partie, et le pannel retourne que lun des de-
nyzens et lauter de aliens ſerra iures tanque ils
auer 6. denizens, et 6. aliens iures. Eadem lex
la ou le iurie remaine pur default de iurours, le

Tales.

Tales ſerra part denglois et parte daliens, et
hoc ſi le partie ceo pray. Mes ſil ne ceo pray,

Errour.

B. ſemble error niſi per leſtatute de Jeofailes 32. H. 8. ca.
32. H. 8. Et ſic par luy ou le pannel eſt par-
tie, le partie neſt arctable de prender le iurie
niſi 6. de lun, et 6. de lauter ſount iures, *B.*
Pannel 2. in fine.

An.

An. quarto Edwardi. 6.

Litt. 125. &
DS. 35.
& 9. E. 4. 33.
contr.

398 ❧ Vide per *Mountague* chiefe Juſtice & *Towneſend*, que per feoffement dun Manner, les ſeruyces paſſer ſauns attornement del franke tenauntes. Mes *B.* ſemble que les tenauntes doyent attorner, *B. Attornement.* 30.

Conc in caſu de Wimbiſh tēp. H. 8.
21. H. 7. 12.
21. E. 4. 5.
3. & 4. El. Com. 269.
St. 30. B.
3. H. 7. 12.
per Juſtic.
Vid St. 47. H.

399 ❧ Fuit agree que adire que le lieu ou &c. eſt 4 acres, q̄ eſt et fuit tempore capcioñ ſon franktenemēt, p q̄ il diſtraine & priſt les auers pur damage feſaunts, fuit bon auowre, *B. Auowre.* 122.

400 ❧ Burglarie ne ſerra adiudge niſi ou infreinder del meaſon eſt p noctē. Et p *Iuſtic.* ou le principal et acceſſoř ſont arraignes & le principal ad ſo clergie, ceo ne ſerueř lacceſſory, mes il ſerra arraine & pēd ou ambideux ſont troue culpable. *B. Corone.* 184.

401 ❧ Home eſt indict come acceſſorie al vn felony et acquit, & puis eſt indict de meſme le felony, come princ̄, il ſerra arraygne et pend non obſtaunt le acquitel come acceſſorie. Et ſic fuit Thomas Knightley primes indicte et arraygne come acceſſorie de J. S. et acquite, & puis fuit indict de m̄ le murder cōe princ̄ & arraygne de ceo arere. *B. Corone.* 185.

402 ❧ Fuit agree pro lege per lez *Iuſtices,* q̄ ſi home diſtraigne ſauns cauſe, le owner poet faire reſcous, Mes ſil eux empound, lhowner ne poet iuſtifier lenfreinder del pōud et eux prender horſe, car la ils ſont en Cuſtodia regis, *B. Diſtreſſe.* 74. *Reſcous* 12. in fine.

403 ❧ Si home done ou graunt omnia bona ſua, leaſe pur ans ne gard, ne paſſerout, car ſont

Seruices paſſe p feffemēt del manour ſans attornement.

Son frankt en auowry pur dam feſant.

Burglary.
Clergie le princ' ne ſerra lacceſſ.

Acquit come acc & puis arraigne come principal.

Pound infreint.

Que paſſa per graunt de omnia bona.

R　　　　ſont

ſont chattels reals. Et *B.* ſeble q̃ graunt de
prox. preſent eccleſie vnica vice eſt chattel & non
bona, car bona ſont biens mouables, vieſs &
morts, mes nemy chattels. *B. Graunts* 51.
Done 43.

Hijs ſimilia ẽ ac-
ction ſur le caſe.

404 ¶ Action ſur caſe pur appeale le pl̃
ſanx Juſtice del peace, vel hijs ſimilia, hec
verba (hijs ſimilia) fueř ord deſtre trahes horſe
del liuer per Curiam pur le incerteintie, *B.*
Action ſur le caſe 112.

Accio ſur le caſe
ſur trouer & co-
uerter in vſum
proprium.

405 ¶ Action ſur caſe cum queř poſſeſſiou
fuit de tielz bõs, vt d̃ proprijs, et illa perdidit,
et def. illa inuenit, et illa in vſum proprium
conuertit, Le def. dit que le pl̃ eux gagea a
luy pur 10. li. per quod ipſe ill detinet pro dict̃
10. li. prout ei bene licuit, abſque hoc quod
illa conuertebat en vſum ſuum propriũ prout
&c. Et bon ple p aliquos. Tñ p alios il plede
non culp̃ et donera ceſt matt̃ en euidence pur
le deteigne, *B. Action ſur le caſe.* 113.

Le conuerter al
oeps trauerſe.

Euidence.

Vide 33. H. 8.
198.

Deuiſee auera
fee ſans parolz,
heredibus, vel
imperpetuum.

406 ¶ Per opiñ in banco regis, ſi home
eduiſe ſon l̃re a W. N. ſoluend 10. li. a ſes
executors & deuie, le deuiſee ad ſee ſimple ratione del paiment, ſauns parols heredibus, vel
imperpetuũ, & ceo ſerra intende lentent d̃ deuiſor Eadem lex ſi hõe vẽd ſon terre a W. N.
pur 20. li. ceo ſerra entend vẽd en ſee ſimple
ſãs parols heires, car conſcience &c. et ẽ equum
et bonũ, q̃ eſt vn ground in cheſcun ley. *B.*
Eſtates. 78.

29. H. 8. 125.

Tẽp. H. 8. 358.
Poſt. 422.

Sans ceo que
riens auer.

407 ¶ Trñs, le def. dit q̃ J. N. fuit ſeiſie
en ſee, et luy leſſa pur 21. ans, & don colour,
le pl̃ dit que ſon pier fuit ſeiſie et deuie ſeiſie
&c. et il entra et fuit ſeiſie vſq̃ treſpas, abſque
hoc quod dictus J. N. aliquid habuit tempore
dimiſſionis,

18. H. 8. 326.
Tếp. E. 6. 442.

dimiſſionis, & male trauerſe, Mes dirr ſaũs ceo que J. N. fuit ſeiſie in fee mod & forma put &c. in cõmuni banco, *B. Trauers per* 372.

Caſus Cokes & Grene.

408 ¶ Aſſiſe, Le tenant fiſt barr per eſtraũger & done colour, le plaintife fiſt title per meſme ceſty per que le defendãt fiſt ſon barr. s. que J. S. fuit ſeiſie et done in taile a ſon pier que enfeffe W. N. que enfeffe le tenaunt, ſur q̃ A. B. enter & enfeffe le ayel le pleyntife que heire il ē en fee, que deuie ſeiſie, et le terre diſcend al plaintife & iſſint fuit eins en ſon remitter, quouſque per defendant diſſeiſie. Et in veritie A. B. ne vnq̃s enter, ne vnq̃s enfeſſe layel. Et vncore fuit tenus clerement, que le tenaunt en ſon barre al tytle ne poet trauers le feſſement de A. B. Mes doit trauers le murrãt ſeiſie del aile le plaintife que luy remit, car ceo lia lentre le tenaunt, & eſt le pluis notable choſe en le title. *B. Trauers per* 154.

Conc Hales & Whorwood.
2. E. 6. B. Surr 52. in. fine.

409 ¶ Home ad leaſe pur ans cõe executor J. S. et puys purchaſe le reuerſion del terre en fee, le leaſe eſt extinĉt. Mes vncor le leas ſerra v̄s lexecutor vn aſſets per *Whorwood* et *Hales* Juſtices. (*B. Extinguiſhment* 54. *Leaſes* 63. *Surrender.* 52.) Et ſil ſerr extinĉt *B.* ſeme dẽe vn deuaſtault ad vltimũ. *Extinguiſhmēt.* 57. in fine. Mes ou il ad ceo come executor, & ē vn meſne leaſe en reuerſion pur ans, & il purchaſe le reſſion en fee, le primer leaſe remaine ratione del meane remainder (*B. Leaſes* 63) Et per *Hales* ſi home leſſa a vn pur 10. ans, & puis leſſa meſme le terre a auter pur 20. ans, le prim̃ leſſee purchaſe le reuerſion en fee, vncore le primer leaſe nē extinĉt, pur ceo que le 2. leaſe que eſt pur 20. ans ē meſne

enter

Vid. 2. E. 6. 31.

Le meane conueiance en le tit ne ſerra trauerſe, ou le pl' en ſon title lie le def.

Remitter.

Executour ad terme & purchaſe le reuerſion in fee. Aſſets.

Deuaſtauit.

Diuerſitie.

Primer leſſee pur ans purchaſe le fee ſimple.

enter le primer leaſe, et le fee ſimple, que eſt
vn impediment del extinguiſhement. *B. Ex-*
tinguiſhment. 57.

Quare impedit
vers preſent roy
ſole.

410 ❡ Quare impedit p Marke Ogle vers
Harriſon Clerke incumbent, que fuit eins per
le preſẽtation le roy. Et ideo le briefe fuit port
Ꝑs luy ſole, & pend le briefe de Q. impedit, le
plaintife deuie puis le 6. mois paſſe que nauera
mes prox. preſentationem per grcount, ſon executors port auter Q. impedit per iournes ac-
compta, intend dauer ſaue le matter per les

14. H. 8. 3.
p. Fitziames.

Exec nauera bre
per iournes, per
mort lour teſta-
tour.

Journeys, Et per *Iuſticiarios* de communi banco
ou le plaintife deuie lexecutors nauera bȓ per
iourneys accompts (& *B.* ſemble que ou le
plaintif deuie, nul poet aͨ auter brief per iour-
neis accompts) Mes econtra en aſcuns caſes ou
le defendant deuie pend le bȓ (*B. Iourneys ac-*

Diuerſitie.

cõpts 23. *Quare impedit.* 158) Et nota per *B.*
ou le grauntee de proxiɱ preſentatioe port
Q. impedit vt deuaunt, et deuie puis les 6. moys
paſſe pend le briefe, & lexecutors port auter
Quare impedit per iourneys accompts, & priſteront general briefe, et count comẽt le grautͬ
fuit fait al teſtator, & il port Quare impedit &
deuie, & que ils port ceo briefe, & ea ratione
pertinet ad ipſos preſentare, & defendant ipſos
impeͩ, & donques ceo purport que ceo eſt dun
diſturbãce fait a eux meſmes puis le 6. mois
paſſ. & donques le briefe ne giſt, car tout doit

Briefe & count
ſpecial.
Briefe al epõ.

aͨ eſtre compriſe en le briefe, & count ſpecial-
ment, & demaundera bȓe al eueſque ſur le preſentation, & briefe le teſtator, & quia non, Ideo
male. Et nſhill inͩ venit in caſu predcã intͬ
Mark. Ogle & Harriſon p *B. Quare impedit.*
160.

411 ❡ Nota

411 ❡ Nota per *Bromley* chiefe iuftice, fi
hōe fait waft c̄ hedgerows que enuiron vn pafture, rien ferra recoſ, mes locum vaftatͬ. s. le
Circuit d̄ roote & nemy lētier paſ t̄, Et p luy
et *Hales* Juftices, le fuccider de keyns dage d̄
10. ou 8 ans eft waft, car eux poient eftre
timber en auant. Et q̄ ou eft bois in que ne
creſſ. nifi fubbois, le termor ne poet fuccider
tout. Contra del fubbois, ou keynes freynes,
et auters principaſ arbers crefcent enter eux,
car la il poet fuccider tout les fubboys. Et
termor poet prend keyns freynes & hm̄di q̄
font bien feifonable, que ont eſtr̄ vfe defte felſ
chefcun 20. ou 16. 14. ou 12 ans. Et per Aliquos a 26. ou 27. ou 30. anz fi font feifonable
boiz, que eft appelle *filua cedua*, *B. Waft.* 136.

Vide temp.
H. 8. 359. &
13. H. 7. 21.
per Brian.
Conc Finch.
48. E. 3. 25.
10. H. 7. 215.

VVaſt en
Hedgerowes.

Locus vaftat.

Ou l' termor
poet prender
tout les fubbois,
Et ecōtra.

Silua cedua.

❡ *Anno 5. Edwardi fexti.*

412 ❡ Dett fur efcape vers vicont, que dit
que deuant lefcape, le prifoner fuit condempñ
en le dit cōdemnation et en executiō, vt en
narratione, in temps vn former vicont que luy
fuffer defcape, et puis luy reprift & imprifon,
& fuit remoue, et cefty defend fuit fait vic̄, &
puys luy fuffer defcape iudg. fi de ceft 2. efcape
action deues aſ. Et bone plee, Car il ad confeſſe et auoyde le playnt. Car quaunt le
prifoner primes efcape, et le primer vic̄ luy reprift et imprifon, ceo 2. imprifonment neft execuc̄
pur le partie, mes le party ē mife a fon acc̄ pur
lefcape ꝑz le priñ vicont, *B. Efcape.* 45.

10. E. 4. 11.
per Billing.

Primer vic̄ fuf-
fer lefcape &
reprift & le ij.
vic luy fuffr
defcape arrer.

413 ❡ Nota per *Hales & Mountague* Juftices, fi feffees feifees al vfe deftate tayle font
aſſurance per bargaine & fale al W. S. et fes
heires

Conc Finch.
Juſt. temp.
H. 8. Et vide
361.

Feffement del
feffees feifie al
vfe del eftate
taile.

Vſe expreſſe.

heires ad vſū dict̄ W. S. et hered ſuorum expreſſe en le fait, la W. S. ſerra ſeiſie al ſon vſe
demeſne, et non al vſe de ceſty que vſe en
tayle, ne de ſes heires coment q̄ lachator auoyt

Notice.

notice del vſe del ſtate taile al temps d̄ le bargaine pur ceo que iuſe fuit expreſſe en le fait.
B. Feoffements al vſes 57.

Leaſe pur ans
deuant liuery
ſue.

414 ℂ Tenaunt le roy in capit̄ deuie &
lheire deuant liuery ſue· fait leaſe pur ans, ceſt
bone, ſi nul intruſion ſoit troue p office, & office
troue puis q̄ troue le morrant ſeiſie, & nul in-

Relation doffic'.

truſion, nad relation al mort le auncaſter niſi
pur les profits, & non pur defeter le leaſe, car

Ou le ſeme perdr
ſa dower.

le franktenement & inheritance remaine en
lh̄re. Mes ſi entruſion ſoyt troue, tunc nullum
accreſcit ei liberum tenemētum, et donques le
leaſe, et dower d̄l ſeme lh̄re ſōt voids. *B.
Leaſes,* 57.

Que ſerr dit px-
imo de ſanguine
de preder ladmi-
niſtration p leſ-
tatut.

415 ℂ Carolus Brādō dux Suff. auoit iſſue
fitz per vn venter, & file p auter venter, &
deuiſe biens all fits & deuie, & puis le fits deuie
enteſtat ſans feme & ſans iſſue, & le mier del
fits que fuit del ſecond vēter (car le file fuit del
primer venter) priſt ladminiſtration per leſtatute, que eſt que ladminiſtration ſerra committ
al prochein del kinne del inteſtate. Et ſur
graund argument en le ſpiritual court, tam per
legis peritos regni, quam per peritos legis Ciuilis
ladminiſtration fuit reuoke. Et ſic vide que
ladminiſtration poet eſtre reuoke, Et ſic fuit ſimiliter in caſu enter Browne & Shelton de bonis
willi Rawlin clici, que fuit commit a ſir Humfrey Browne que auer marie le ſoer le dit
Rawlins, & puiz viendrōt William S. & J. S.
fits le feme le dit ſir Henry (quel feme fuit le
mere

1. H. 7. 17.

33. H. 8. 205.

21. H. 8. ca. 5.
Raſt. Adminiſ-
traters. 1.

Tēp. H. 8. 330.

mere lez dits Sheltons per vn former barron) &
reuerſe le primer adminiſtration, & obtaine lad-
miniſtratyon a eux.   Et le dit Duke auoit iſſue
Fraunces p le frenche Queene, & puis cel feme
deuie, il marie le file de ſeignior Willoughby,
& auer iſſue p luy vn Henry & deuie, & puis
Henry deuie ſans iſſue & ſans feme, & le miere
heire priſt ladminiſtration, et puis le dit Fraunces feme le Marques de Dorſet ſua et reuerſe
ladminiſtration, & obtaine ladminiſtration a luy
meſme, coment que el ne fuit que ſoer de demie
ſanke al dit Henry, pur ceo que el eſt procheine
del kynne le dit Henry, eo que Henry nauer
aſcun children, car le mier neſt prochein del
kynne a ſo fitz demeſne in ceſt reſpeɗ de ceſt
matter : Car doit aler per deſcent, & nemy
paſcencion per le ley dengleterre, ne per ley
Ciuill, Et les children ſont de ſanguine patris
et matris, ſed pater & mater non ſunt ɗ ſanguine puerorum.   Et p Iſidorum, Pater &
mater, & puer ſunt vna caro, & ideo nul degree
eſt enter eux.   Contrary ē enter frere & ſoer,
Et le demy ſanke neſt impediment q̄it al biēs.
(*B. Adminiſtraters.* 47.)   Nota que in largu-
ment de ceo caſe fuit agree per *Iuſticiarios*, que
le roy neſt entitle al terre de ſon gard ſans
office, coment q̄ il nad in ceo niſi chattell. Tamen ceo viēt ratione tenure q̄ eſt ſeigniory &
franktenemēt en le roy.   *B. Office deuant.* 55.

416   ❡ Nota p *Hales* Juſtice clerement, q̄
clerke cōuiɗ perdra ſes biēs.   *B. Forfaiture.*
113.

417   ❡ Dicitur in banco regis ou briefe derrour port teſte demaunt le primer iudgement, et
le record ē certifie in ceo banke, que ceſt byen,
Et

Et vncore le briefe dit, quod ſi indicium redd   contr per
ſt, tunc record et proceſſ. habeatis &c.   *B.*   Aſhton.
Erruur. 76.   Vide 22. H.
6. 7.

Plus.   Plus 31. H. 8. 159. 32. H. 8. 177.

Anno 6. *Edwardi ſexti.*

Election de ſon
tenant.

418 ¶ Nota per *Iuſticiarios* in cõmuni banco, que in aſſiſe vers deux, hun priſt le tenaũcy
& plede nul tort, et launter priſt le tenancy,
ſauns ceo que launter rien ad, et plede en barre,
la le plaintiſe ſerra arɛ̃ deſtier ſon tenant a
ſon perill.   Cybien come ſi ambideux vſſent
plede en barre, et accept le tenancy ſeueral-
ment.   Et ſi ſoit troue q̄ il miſeleɛ̃ ſon tenant,
le bre abatera, mes il ne ſerr̄ barre.   Et la
quant le demaundaunt eleɛ̃ ſon tenant et il
plede, la ils ſerra a iſſu deuant que le tenancy
ſerra enquire, & donques le tenancy ſerra
primes enquire, et puis launter iſſue.   *B. Aſſiſe.*
384.

Burgage tenure.

419 ¶ Nota que par Burgage tenure del
roy, Home puyt alien ſauns lycence aſſets byen,
B. Alienations. 36.

Feme abiure.

420 ¶ Feme priſt Eſgliſe par felony, &
abiurauit regnum, *B. Corone.* 213.

Quel ioincture
ſerra barre de
dower & quel
nemy.

421 ¶ Nota per *Iuſticiarios*, per le ſtatute   27. H. 8. ca. 10.
ou home fait ſa feme ioynt purchaſor oue luy
puis le couerture daſcun eſtate de franktenement, niſi ſoyt a luy & ſa feme, & lour heires
in fee ſimple, ceſt bar̄ de dower, ſel agree al
ioynture poſt mortem viri, Contrary de fee

Deuiſe per ba-
ron al feme.

ſimple, car tiel iointure neſt parle in le ſtatute.
Ne deuiſe de terre p Baron al feme p teſtament
nẽ

nē barr̄ al dower, car ceo eſt beneuolence, et nemy iointure. *B. Dower.* 69.

422 ❡ Nota per *Iuſticiarios*, que ou deux iointenants ſount, lun alien touts ſon terres & tenements in D. poſt ſtatute de enrolments et deuant lenrolment lauter ioyntenaunt deuie, iſſint que ſon moytie ſuruiue al vendor, & puis le vendor deins le demy an enrolle le ſait, vncore ryens paſſa niſi le moitie, car lenrollement ad relation al ſeſans et deliuerie del ſait, iſſint que ceo donera ryen, mes ceo que ſuit vend per ceo tēpore deliberacoñ ſaɛti. Et p plures *Iuſticiarios*, ou home vende ſon terre per ſait endent al vn, & puis il ceo vend per autr̄ endēture al auter, & le darreigne ſait primes enrolle, & puis le primer ſait eſt enrolle deins l̄ demie an, la le primer vendee auera le terre, car ceo ad relac. de ſaire ceo le ſait del vendor, & de paſſer le terre ab deliberatione ſaɛti, Car le ſtatute eſt que franktenement ne vſe de ceo, ne paſſa, ne chaungera de lū al auter p bargaine & vend tantum, niſi ſit per ſait endent & enrolle deins le demy an, Ergo ſi ſoit p ſait endēt, & enrol̄ infra demy an c̄ paſſ. Cōe luſe poet paſſ. al cōmen ley per vend de t̄re q̃ ſuit mainteñt ſur le vend. *B. Faits enrolle.* 9.

423. ❡ Nota per plures, ſi home ſait ſeſſement en ſee deuant leſtatut de vſes, ou puis ceſt ſtatut al vſe de W. & ſes heirez tāque A. paie 40. li. al dit W. et tunc ad vſum diɛti. A. & hered̄ ſuorū, et puis vient leſtatut de vſes & execute leſtat̄ in W. et puis A. paie al W. le 40 li. La A. eſt ſeiſie en ſee, ſil enter, Tamen per aliquos A. ne ſerra ſeiſie en ſee per le dit payment, ſi non que les ſeoffees enter, *B.*

s   doubta

27. H. 8. ca. 16.

Tēp. H. 8. 368.
Supra 406.

27. H. 8. ca. 10.
7. E. 6. 435.

Relation dun enrolment.

Vſe de alter le franktenement del vn al auter per ſtatut.

Entre.

Quære.

doubta inde. Et ideo luy ſeble eſtre ſur dentre
en le noſme del feffees et en noſme de luy, et
donꝗs lun voie ou lauter, lentre ſerra bone &
fra A. deſtre ſeiſie en fee. Et auxi vide per *B.*
que home a ceſt iour poet faire feffemēt al vſe,
Ex poſt facto. & que luſe chāgera de vn in auter per act ex
poſt facto per circumſtance. Cibien que il
ſerra deuant le dit eſtatute, *B. Feſments al*
vſes 30.

Fine in hamlet.   424 ¶ Conceſſum fuit que fine poet eſtre   7. E. 6. 435.
leuie in hamlet, car ſi ſcire facias giſt ſur fine
in hamlet, (come appiert 8. E. 4. ꝗ il fait)   8. E. 4. 6.
ideo fine eſt bien leuie la. *B. Fines leuies.* 93.   per Curiam.

Briefe de garde   ·425 ¶ Fuit agree pur ley in le commen   7. E. 6. 430.
ſans ſeiſin infra bāke, que ſi le ſeignior nad. eſtre ſeiſie del
tempus memor. homage infra tempus memorie, mez ad eſtre
ſeiſie del rent, ceo ſuffiſt dauer briefe de gard,
& de counter que il deuie in ſon homage, car
la eſt ſeiſin daſcun choſe, coment que ne ſoit
del entier ſeruices, & pur cel cauſe, et auxi eo
Tenure trauer- que le ſeiſin neſt trauerſable mes le tenure, ideo
fable. laccion giſt ſans ſeiſin del homage, *B. Garde.*
122. in fine.

Copyhold.   426 ¶ Nota quod videtur clare, que le   32. H. 8. ca. 2.
nouel limitation, & auxi launcient limitation   Limitac 3.
extend al copyhold, cibien come a freehold, car
le nouel ſtatute eſt, que il ne ſerra preſcriptiō
title, ne claime &c. Et ceux ꝗ clayme per copie
font preſcription, title et claime &c. Et auxi les
plaintes ſont en natura et form̄ br̄is dn̄i regis ad
cōmunem legem &c. Et ceux briefes que ore
ſont portes al comen ley, ſōt rules per le nouel
limitation, & ideo les plaints de copihold ſerr̄ de
meſme le nature & forme. *B. Lymitations.* 2.

Vend' ou il nad   427. ¶ Nota que ſur le ſtatute dachate les   32. H. 8. ca. 9.
eſtre ſeiſi per vn titles et de mainteiner que home nachater terre,
an. niſi

Vide H. 6. & 7.
E. 6. Com.
88. 89.

nisi le vendor ad estre en possession &c. per vn
an deuaunt, fuit agree per *Mountague* chiefe
Justice, et per toutes de serieants Inne in
Fleeteftrete, que si home morgage son terre, et
ceo redeme, il poet vend son terre infra vnum
annum proxim &c. sans dauger del statute
auaunt dit, car sic est lentendement del statute,
Car les auncient statutz sont que nul maintener,
& vncore home poit mainteine son cosin, & sic
de consimilibus, car ne pas entend, mes de illoyal maintenance, Et sic de pretensed title, et
non de ceo q est clere title. *B. Mayntenance.* 38.

Statut expound.

428 ¶ Si home lessa pur ans redant rent al
Mich. & auters couenants, sil soyt oblige in
obligation de payer le rent precise, la il que-
rera le lessor, Mes sil soit oblige de perform
les couenats &c.   Le tender sur le terr suffist,
quia la le payment est del nature del rent reser-
ue, Contrar in primo casu. *B. Tender.* 20.

Tender fur le tre
& econtra.

2. M. 1. 464.
Et sic fuit ad-
iudge M. 4.
M. 1.
St. 38. B.

429 ¶ Fuit agrec q pur misprision de treason, ou si home sciant counterseit money &
emport ceo ext hibernia in Angl, et vtl ceo en
payment, vel huiusmodi, home perdera ses bies
imperpetuum, & les profits de son Pre pur sa
vie, & serra emprison pur terme de vie.   *B.*
Treason. 19. in fine.

Forfeiture pur
misprision de
treason.

Anno 7. *Edwardi fexti.*

6. E. 6. 425.

430 ¶ Fuit tenus per les *Justices* dambideux bakes, q ou home tient per rent et seruice
de chiualer, et le seigniour & ses auncestours
ount estre semper seisie del rent, mes nemy del
homage, escuage, ne dl gard, vncore si garde
chief, il auera le gard del heire, car le seisin del
rent suffist pur estre seisie del tenure, quaunt a

Nul feifin & vn-
core gard.

a

ceſt purpoſe. Tamen aliter *B.* ſemble de falſ
auowry. *B. Auowry.* 96. in fine *Gard.* 69.

431 ❡ Nota ſi home ad iſſue 3. fitz, &
deuiſe ſon ꝑres. s. vn parte al. 2. de fitz in taile,
et auter parte al 3. fits in taile, et que nul de
eux vend aſcun parte, mes q̃ cheſcū ſerra heire
al auter, et deuie, que in ceſt caſe, ſi vn deuie
ſans iſſue, ſon part ne reuert al eigne fitz, mes
remaiū al auꝉ fitz, car ceux parols (que cheſcun
ſerra heire al auter) emplie vn remainder, pur
ceo que eſt vn volunt, que ſerꝛ entend et
adiudge ſolonque lentent del deuiſour. *B.
Deuiſe.* 38. Done 44.

Deuiſe q cheſcun ſerra heire al auter.

Parols de faire rem.

432 ❡ Home deuiſe ſon terre a vn auter
pur doner, vend, ou faire de ceo a ſon wil &
pleaſure, ceo eſt fee ſimple, car ſon entēt ſerꝛ
priſe a doñ fee ſimple. *B. Deuiſe.* 38.

Deuiſe pur fair a ſon pleaſure.

19. H. 8. 9.
p. Norwich
Fitzh & More.

433 ❡ Nota per *Browne, Hales & Cooke*
Juſtices, ſi ſont ſeignior & tenant per fealtie &
rent, le tenaunt eſt diſſeiſi & deuie ſans heire,
le ſeigniour accept le rēt per maines le dit
ſeiſor, vncore il poet enꝉ pur eſcheat Ou auer bꝛe
deſcheat, & le reſceit del rēt nul barre, Car le
diſſeiſor eſt eins per tort. Auterment ſil vſt
auow pur c̃ in Court de recorde, Ou vſt priſe
corporal ſeruice come homage &c. Iſſint dac-
ceptaunce de rēt per maines le heire le diſſeiſor,
Ou de ſon feffee, queux ſont eins per title. *B.
Eſcheat.* 18.

*Briefe deſchete ou le tenaunt ne deuie ſeiſie.
Droit dentrie eſcheate.*

*Acceptance.
Diſſeiſor.*

*Diuerſitie.
Acceptance.*

Alienee.

Fitz. 144. C.

Conc Fitzh.
144. N.

434 ❡ Home plead pardon le roy in lex-
chequer pur alienac̃ ſãs licence ou le terre neſt
tenus del roy in Capite, ceo eſt eſtoppel a luy
adire en apres que il ne tient in Capite *B. Eſtoppel,* 222.

Eſtopp per pdon pled'.

435 ❡ Nota que fuit agree per Juſticiarios
que

6. E. 6. 424.

que fine poet bien eftre leuie in hamel, et hoc non obftante q̃ touts les meafons font decayes p̃l vn. Idem de briefe de dower, Et eadē lex de ceo que ad eftre ville & ore eft decaye, vncore le nofme del ville remaine, come old Salefbury, q̃ ad a ceo ioure burgeffes de parliament & huiufmodi, *B. Fines leuies.* 91.

Fine in hamlet ou ville decay.

Briefe de dower.

8. E. 4. 6. per Cur.

436 ¶ Formed fur done en fee, al vfe del feffor, & lheires de fon corps, que eft executed per le ftatut de vfes 27. H. 8. & puis le feffor aliē & deuie, fon iffue auera formedon quod les feffees dederunt tenementa prediɛ̃ta al pier le demaundant & difcendit i⁹ &c. Car ne poet eftr̃ fuppofe q̃ le feffor done a cefty que vfe que fuit luy mefme, Car home ne poet doner a luy mefme. Et ferra efpeciall declaratyon fur le feoffement all vfe le taile, Mes ou A. fayt feoffemēt en fee al 3. al vfe dune eftrange & lheires de fon corps q̃ eft executed per leftatut auauntdit, & puis cefty que fuit cefty que vfe, alien en fee et deuie, la fon iffue auera formedon, et dira que le feffor, done al fon pier & nemy q̃ les feffees done, Et ferra fpecial declaration, *B. Formedon* 46. *General briefe* 14.

Formedō fur vfe General bre, & fpecial declaration.

4. E. 6. Com. 59. p Mountegue cap.

4. E. 6. C. 59.

2. E. 6. 389.

Diuerfitie.

437 ¶ Home poffeffe de leafe pur terme de 40. ans, graunt tant d̃ ceux a J. N. que ferra arrere tempore mortis fue, et tenetur void per *Hales* Juftice et alios pur le incerteyntie eo que ne appiert quant ferra arrere tempore mortis fue, Car le grauntor poet viuer touts les 40. ans, et dōq̃ rien ferra arrere a fō mort, quere. (*B. Graūts* 154. *Leafes* 66.) Mes tiel deuife per teftament eft bone, (*B. Graūts.* 154.) Et nē feble ou hōe leffa terre pur terme de vie, & 4. ans oufter, ceo eft certaine que fes executors

Graunt void pur incerteintie.

Diuerfitie inter graunt & deuife.

Quære.

Leafe pur vie, & 4. ans oufter.

Conc Finch. 46. E. 3. 31. 11. H. 4. 34. per Hank.

executors auera 4. ans puis ſon mort (*B. Leaſes.* 66.) Et auxy ſi home leſſa ſon terre habend a morte ſua pur 40. ans, ceſt bone, car ceo eſt certayne, Et il ad aucthoritye de charger ſon terre demeſne *B. Grauts.* 154.

Graunt de terr, & tenements.

438 ¶ Home graunt omnia terras et tenementa ſua in Dale, leaſe pur ans ne paſſe. 37. H. 8. 301.

Que paſſa per graunt de oēs firmas. Eiectione firme.

Cōtrary ſil graūt omnes firmas ſuas, la per ceo leaſe pur ans paſſera, Car de ceo Eiectione firme giſt, & p ceo il recouera le ſme, Et ideo eſt bōe parol de graūt. *B. Graunts* 155.

Information.

439 ¶ Dicitur ſi informatyon ſoit miſe per ſubiect pur le Roy in Scaccario, Et le def. pleade barre et trauers le informac̄, le roy poit trauers le matter del barre ſil voet, et nē tenus de maintener le matter q̄ eſt conteyne in le abſque hoc. *B. Prærogatiue* 65. in fine. Vide 38. H. 8. 327. contr.

Br. Trauerſe p 207.

Que eſtate de particuler eſtate.

440 ¶ Nota que fuit agree per les Juſtices que home ne poet conuey intereſt per vn Que eſtate, de particuler eſtate, come tayle, pur vye ou pur ans, ſauns monſtre coment il ad ſo eſtate, ſoit ceo del part le pleintiſe, ou defendaunt. *B. Que eſtates.* 31.

Oblig pur Vſury. Concluſion.

¶ Nota que en det ſur obligation fait pur vſury, et le def. pled c̄ matter, il conclud et iſſint obligation eſt voids, Judgement ſi action, et ne cōcludera nō eſt factum. *B. Non eſt factum* 14. in fine.

Cogn; ſee purchaſe, & cogniſor repurchaſe.

441 ¶ *Concordatur* pur clere ley in Cuſ Cancellaſ, ſi home acknowledge vn ſtatut ſtaple, & puis infeſſe le recogniſee, & il fait feſſemt ouſtr, ore le terre eſt diſcharge, car le feſſee neſt q̄ eſtraunger. Mes ſi le cogniſor repurchaſe le ſre, il ſerra miſe en execution, & vncore fuit vn foitz, diſcharge *B. Recogniſance* 9. in fine. Vide 36. H. 8. 293. 5. H. 7. 25. per Towneſend.

442 ¶ Nota

3. M. 1. Com. 169.

442 ❧ Nota q̃ bois fuit mife deuant pafture in pleint daſſife, et exception ent prife, & vncore bone, coment que foet contra al Regifter B. *Faux latin et forme* 66.

4. E. 6. 407.

☞ Trefpas, le defendant dit q̃ J. fuit feifi & luy infeffe, & done colour, le pl' poit dire que H. fuit feifi, & leſſa a J. a volũt, q̃ done al defend, et R. reentre & infeffe le pl. Il doit dire, fãz ceo q̃ J. fuit feifi in fee mod & forma prout &c. B. *Trauerfe* per 217. in fine.

29. H. 8. 111.

443 ❧ Fuit tenu per plures in Cancellaria ſi rec̃ foit ewe in q̃ cefti q̃ vfe in taile eſt vouch, & le dd rec. donques ceo liera Hſſue. B. *Feffements* al vfes 56. in fine.

Vide 5. M. 1. 491.

☞ Si Alien nee purch. le Roy ceo auera. Mes le purch. doit eftr̃ troue per office. Et fic fuit in cafu Alani Kinge. Et B. femble que informatiõ in Lefchequer ne feruera en ceo cafe. B. *Denizen* 17. in fine.

☞ Brent del Comitaī Somerfet q̃ fuit prefēt pur Ideot, potuit fcribere litteras & acquietanc, et hm̃odi, & ideo fuit adiudg vnthrift, mez nul Ideot. B. *Ideot* 4. in fine.

Plus.

Plus tẽp̃ H. 8. 332. 4. M. 1. 480.

Ann̄ primo Mariæ primæ.

444 ❧ Nota per *Bromeley* chiefe Juſtice que le demaūd (in cafu numero 389) poet declar̃ generalm̃t ſil voit. Et ſi le t̃ pled ne dona pas, le demaund poit reply & mr̃e lefpecial matī, vt patet la, & cõclud & iſſint dona &c. Et biē. B. *Formedon* 49. in fine.

32. H. 8. ca. 3. Limitac. 3.

☞ Nota q̃ fuit agree, q̃ a cē iour p le limitation de 32. H. 8. Lauowrie ferra fait geſtalm̃t

Bois deuant paſ-tur ē pleint daſſ.

Seifin en fee trauerfe.

Rec de lier taile in vfe.

Alien purchafe.

Office.

Information.

Ideot & vnthrift diuerfitie.

General count en formedon.

Limitation en Auowrie.

ſtalm̄t ſicut vtebatur prius.* Et ſi ne fait ſeiſin
puis cē limitation, donq̄z le pl̄ in barre del
auowrie poet alledge c̄, & traūs le ſeiſin puis

Seiſin trauerſe en auowrie.

le limitac. (*B. Auowrie* 107) Auxi ou hōe port
actiō real ou mixt ou fait auowry ou conuſas,
& iſſue ē priſe ſur le ſeiſin infr̄ tēpus ſtatuti, &
ē troue contra le dd̄, pl. ou auowant, ceſt
pemptorie p m̄ leſtatut. *B. Peremptorie* 78.

Feme entitle al appell' de mort viri priſt auter baron, el perdera ſon appell'.

445 ℂ Nota ſi fēe q̄ ad title dappel de mort
viri priſt auter baron, il et le feme nauerōt
Appelle, car le feme doit auer c̄ ſole, Car le
cauſe de appel eſt que el fault ſon barō, & le
reaſon eſt eo q̄ le feme carens viro, neſt cibien
able de viuer, & ideo quant el ad aut̆ baron,
lappel eſt determine et le cauſe ceſſa, Et
ceſſante cauſa ceſſet effectus, (*B. Appel* 109.)

Quarentine.

Cōe ou fēe ad quarentine & el marie infra le
40. iours, el pdera ſon quarentine. *B. Appelle*
109. *Dower.* 101.

Fine leuy deuant ludge de nō ſane memorie, & done doffic p luy diuerſitie.

446. ℂ Nota ſi Judge ou Juſtice ſoit de non
ſane memorie, vncore lez fines, iudgements, &
auters records que ſont deuant luy, ſerra bon.
Mez ecōtra del dōe doffice vel huiuſmodi p
luy, car ceo eſt matt̆ in fait, & laut̆z ſot matt̆z
de record. Car matt̆s en fait potiēt eſtr̄ auoid p
non ſane memorie. Contra de matter de recorde, *B. Dum non fuit compos mentis* 7:

Vicount & Eſcheator.

447 ℂ Nota que le vicont & Leſcheator
voidront lour office per dimiſe le roy, car ils
ſont faits per patentz, que ſont come commiſſion eſt, & ideo ē vſe al dimiſe le roy pur ſuer
hors nouel patents vt fuit hoc An. *B. Officer*
25. in fine.

Verba poſt, In cuius rei.

☞ Nota que fuit agree per les Juſtic. q̄
ceſt clauſe que vient puis ceux pois, In cuius
rei

Conc per Juſt.
de banco Regis
M. 2. M. 1.
St. 59. B.
Vid. 21. E. 4.
73. per Huſſey.

rei &c. Sigillū appoſui &c. neſt aſcun parte del
fayt cōmt q̄ fuit eſcrie deuant le ſealer et deliuerie. *B. Faits* 72.

1. H. 7. 1. &
1. E. 3. 3.

448 ❡ Affirmaī p lege q̄ ſuerty d peace ē   Mort Regis.
diſcharge p mortē regis car ē de obſerſ le
peace illi⁹ regis, & quāt il eſt mort, il nē ſō
peace. *B. Suerty* 20.

Vid St. fo. 1. E.
& fo. 2. H. & fo.
6. A.

449 ❡ Nota quod appiert per diuers re-   Compaſſe ou
cordes et preſidents que ceux parols (cōpas,   Imagine.
ou imagin le mort le roy) ſont large parols,
car ceſty que maliciouſe deuiſe cōmt le roy
veigña al mort p parols, ou autermīt, & fayt
act de explañ c̄, Come in aſſaiant de harnes   Que ſerra dit
mittant, de letter meſſage, vel hm̄odi, cē trea-   treaſon.
ſon. Et cēy q̄ entēd pur depriſ le roy, en ceo
ē entend le mort le roy, Quere del depriū.   depriue.
Car p *B.* home poet depriū, et vnc. entend nul   Quære.
mort. Et pur cē cauſe vn ſtatut fuit ent fait

1. E. 6. 12.
Raſt. Treaſō 18

tēpore H. 8. & E. 6. Et le deteigñ d caſtel,
fortreſſe vel hm̄oi vers le roy eſt leuiant de
guerre Ƿs luy, toutes q̄ux parols (leſſ de guerre,
& alia ſupra) ſōt en le ſtaī de 25. E. 3. Et
adherent al enemies le roy ibm̄ eux aidāt ou
cōfort. *B. Treaſō* 24.

St. 1. S.

450 ❡ Dic. p. Juſt. q̄ br̄e de couenant giſt   Couenant ſans
ſur indeī ſans cē parol, couēnt & graunt pur   parols de coue-
luy ſes heires & executors. *B. Couenant* 38. in   nant pro ſe, ſes
fine.   hres & executs.

Plus.

❡ Plus 1. E. 6. 395.

451 ❡ Nota p lege, ou trm̄s de baterie,   Jurors preigne
biens importz, ou eſcript enfreint, q̄ ſont trāſi-   Conuſance et
tory, ſoit fait in vn countie, vncore acē poit eē   notice de choſe
port ē auſ cōm. (*B. Attaint* 104.) Et ſic con-   en auter Com.
cord fuit in trm̄s in Lōd d debruſer doble a D.
in Lond, ou in fait D. fuit in cōm E. car ceux

T   ne

ne ſot local. (*B. Lieu* 65.) Et ideo in trñs   24. H. 8. 232.
tranſitoř le lieu ne ſerra iſſue, ne nē traũſable.
Nient pluis q̃ in trñs ſur le caſe de aſſũption,

& ceux poient eſtre continue (*B. Trauerſe per*   39. H. 6. 8.
283) Et en ceux caſez le iury dauſ coũtie poit   per Aſhton.
prɇder ent conuſance, mes neſt tenus &c̃, Sed   9. E. 4. 45.
ſil p̃ign̄ conuſ, attaint ne giſt. Cōtř de trñs   per Choke.
darbřz ſcies, ou herbz puez, q̃ux ſot local, &
ſerra port in p̃prio coñ. (*B. Attaint* 104.
Iurors 50.)

452 ¶ Fuit dit q̃ ſi leſſor port det Ᵽs ſo   23. H. 8. ca. 15.
leſſee pur ans del rent, & le pł eſt nonſuit, Ou   Raſt. Dam. 6.
ſi lenqueſt paſſe, Ᵽs luy, il rendra coſtes al def.
p leſtatut. Car leaſe pur ans rendāt rēt eſt vn

contraɥ *B. Coſtes* 23.

453 ¶ Noť p *Bromley* chiefe Juſt. & alios,
ou hōe deuiſſe ſo ťř a vn eſtrange pur ł'me dās,
le rem̃ a ſo fits in fee et deuy, le fits poit
wayuer le deuiſe, & claim̃ p diſcent, & unɥ il

ne auoideř le ł'me. Niēt pluis q̃ ou hōe leſſe
pur ans & deuy, le leaſe eſt bon. Et vncore le
murrāt ſeiſi eſt bō auxi de toller lenť. *B. Deuiſe*
41. Et *B.* ſeble ou le pier deuiſe a ſon fils &
heire in fee, q̃ le heire poit waiũ le deuiſe et
luy prender al diſcēt. (*B. Diſcent* 4.) Contra

ou le pier deuiſe a ſon fitz in taile, le rem̃ al
vn eſtranger in fee, la lheire ne claimeř eins in
fee, ne waiuera le deuiſe pur le parde &
p̃iudice de cēy in le rem̃ in fee. *B. Deuiſe* 41.

454 ¶ Accompt ne giſt verz diſſeiſors, car
donq̃z le diſſeiſie auoideř le diſcents a ſon pleaſure. Et auxy le def. ne fuit vnq̃z, ſon receuier

pur accōpt renđ, Car c̄ ne poet eſtre ſauns
priuity in ley ou in fait, Cōe p aſſignem̃t, ou
cōe gardein, ou hm̃odi, Ou per pretence le def.

al

al vſe le pł & ou le defend claiɱ a ſon vſe
demeſn car la ł ple ē voier, ne vnq̚ ſo receiū
ſon baíly pur accōpt rēder. *B. Accōpt* 89.

Pledinge.

455 ⚓ Dictū fuit, p lege q̄ cuſtōe poet eē
alledge ou eſt nul pſo q̄ poet preſcriber. Cōe
inhabitãts ne poíēt preſcriber. Mes ilz poíēt
alł cuſtoɱ q̄ les ínhabitãts poíēt comen in D.
Car lun va oue le líeu, Et lauł oue le perſon,
quel perſon doít eſtre able de preſcriber, car
aliter nihil valet. *B. Preſcription* 100. in fine.

Cuſtome ſeruera
ou preſcription
ne voet ſeruer.

455 ⚓ Fuit tenus per le *Capitall Juſtice*,
que lenrac̄ de nouel frame q̄ ne vnq̄ fuit coūt
neſt waſt, Mes fuit agree, que ſi meaſon ſoit
ruinouz pur default daſcun couerture tēpore
mortiz del leſſor, et puis le tenãt ſuffer ceo
deſtre plus ruinous, que de cel nouel ruine
lheire aūa aꝗion de waſte, car ceo eſt waſte,
que contynue, car de le putritude que vient en
temp̄ hered lheire aūa acc. de waſt, Et econtra
de ceo q̄ fuit in le vie ſon pere. *B. Waſt* 117.
in fine.

VVaſt pur non
couerture, de
nouel frame, &
meaſon.

VVaſt per
lheire.

42. E. 3. 22.
per Finch.

456 ⚓ Si aꝗ ſoit fait felony per eſtatute,
come hunting vel huiuſmodi, et puis vn home
in ceo offende, et puis laꝗ eſt repeale p ſtatute,
la le hūting ē diſpuniſhable, car la ley p que il
ſerra puniſhe eſt repele. Tamen ou treſpas eſt
fait ſur termor, & puis le terme expire, le
treſpas eſt puniſhable, car la intereſt expire,
mez nemy le ley. Et ſic vide diuerſitie, ou
lintereſt expire, et le ley remayne, et ou le ley
eſt repell et ne remayne. *B. Corone* 202.

Diuerſiti ou in-
tereſt expire, Et
ou la ley.

Treſpas p ter-
mor puis le tme
expir.

457 ⚓ *Tenetur in communi banco per Pro-
thonatorios* ſi proteꝗion ſoit gette al iour de niſi
pri⁹, et les Juſtices priſterōt le Jurie de bene
eſſe, & al jour in bāk le proteꝗion eſt allowe,
ore

Enqueſt priſe de
bene eſſe.

Enqueſt recharge puis verdict.

ore comēt, que le primer priſel eſt voyd, Uncore lēqueſt ne ſerra recharge p reſumons, Car quāt lenqueſt eſt vn foitz jure, & done verdit, ilz ne ſerr̄ vnqz iure arrere ſur cē iſſue. *B. Enqueſt* 86.

Ou briefe de heretico comburēdo iſſera, Et ou nemy.

458 ¶ Nota que fuit agree per omnes *Juſticiarios*, et per *Baker* peritum in lege, et *Cancellarium* Scaccarii, et per *Hare* peritum in lege, et *Magiſtrum Rotulorum* Cancellarie, que per ſtatute de heritikes & lollardes, que ſi heretike ſoit conuict in preſence del vicōt, le ordinarie poet luy committer al meſm̄ le vicoūt, et il doit luy arſer ſauns auer briefe *de Heretico comburendo.* Mes ſi le vicoūt ſoit abſent, ou ſi lheretike ſerra arſe in auter county in que il neſt conuicte, donques in ceux caſes le briefe de heretico comburendo ſerra agard a ceſty vicōt, ou Officer q̄ ſerr̄ lexecution. Et le dit ſtatut in fine voet, *que le vicount ſerra preſent al conuiction ſi Leueſque luy require.* Et ideo le vſe ē q̄ lordinary appellera le vic. deſtre preſent al conuiction. Et vide in le briefe de heretico comburendo in nouel Natura breuiū, q̄ Larcheueſq̄, & ſon prouince en lour conuocatiō puiſſoient & vſont d̄ cōuicl̄ heretikes per le comen ley, & eux miſter a les layes maines. Et donquez le vicont per briefe de *Heretico comburendo* eux arſera. Mes pur ceo que ceo fuit trobleſome de appeller le conuocation de tout le prouince, Il fuit ordeigne p leſtatute auāt dit *Que cheſcū Eueſq̄ in ſō dioceſſe poet cōuicter heritike, et puis abiuration ſur relaps luy miſter a lay gents deſtre arſe.* Et *B.* ſemble que ſi lheritike ne voet abiurer al primer conuictiō, q̄ il poet eſtre arſe al priūſ conuictiō ſūs abiurac̄, Et ecōt ſil voet abiurer, car doqz il ne ſerra arſe

Abiuration.

arſe le priṁ tēps, Mes ſur relapz il ſerra arſe. Diuerſitie.
B. *Hereſie.*

459 ❧ Fuit determine in Parliament que　Tender de fine
impriſonmēt *Fere in omnibus caſibus* neſt mes de　per loffender.
reteiner loffender tanque il ad fait fine, et ideo
ſil offer ſon fine, il doit eſtre deliuer maintenaunt,
Et le roy ne poet luy iuſtṁt retaiñ in priſon puis
le fine tend. B. *Impriſonment* 100. in fine.

Vide 32. H. 8. 460 ❧ In waſt iſſue fuit priſe ſi le defendaunt　Iſſue en waſt.
190. ſuccide 20. querkes, la ſi le Jurie troue 10. et
non le reſt, le pleyntiſe recouera pur le 10. &　Amerciament.
ſerra amercy pur le reſt. B. *Iſſues Ioynes* 80.
in medio.

T. 13. El. Com 461 ❧ Nota per *Bromeley* chiſe Juſtice que　Iudgement done
394. contr. iudgement, ou eſt nul original, eſt voide, (Come　ſans original.
17. Aſſ. 17. en aſſiſe le plaintiſe appeare et aꝑs fiſt retraxit,
& puis les Juſtiē de laſſ. recorde vn agrement
inter eux in nature dū fine, ceo eſt voyde, et
coram non Judice, & ne ſerra execute rōne que　Retraxit deter-
nul original fuit pendāt, mes fuit determyne　mine loriginal.
deuaunt per le retraxit.) Car ſans original ilz
nōt cōmiſſ. de teigſi plee, & donques ils ne ſont
iudges de ceſt cauſe. B. *Judgement* 114.

3. M. 1. 468. 462 ❧ Nota per *Bromley* & auterz *Iuſtices,*　Leaſe tanq 100.
contra. ſi ieo leſſe terre a W. N. Habend tanqᵦ 100.　li. ſont pay.
li ſoit pay, & ſās liuery, donꝗz neſt ꝗ leaſe
a volūt pur le incerteintie. Mes ſil fait liſiry,　Diuerſitie.
le leſſee ē aſſa pur vie ſur cōdiē implie de ceſſ.
ſur ī 100. li. leuie. B. *Leaſes.* 67.

Vide 37. H. 6. 463 ❧ Dicitur ꝗ Eueſquez in tempore E. 6.　Leaſe p Eueſque
26. ne fuerount ſacres, & ideo ne fueront Eueſques,　nient ſacre Et p
& ideo leas pur anz p tiels, & confirme per le　Eueſque depriue
Deane & chapł, ne liera le ſucceſſor. Car tyels　diuerſitie.
ne vnques fuerount Eueſques, Contra de Eueſ-　Confirmation.
que depriue ꝗ fuyt Eueſque in fait tēpore dimiſſionis, & confirmaē fact. B. *Leaſes* 68.

464 ❧ Con-

Fine pur mifprifion de treafon.

464. ¶ Concordatū fuit in parliamento q̃ de mifprif. de treafon le fine foloyt deftre le forfeyture de toutes fes biens et les profites de tout fon terre pur fa vie, & fon corps a prifon ad voluntatem regis, car mifprifion ē finable. *B. Treafon.* 25. in fine.

6. E. 6. 429.

Condic q leftate ceffera.

Trial de Euefque.

465 ¶ Si home leffa terre pur term̃ de vie fur condition q̃ fil ne ala a Rome p tiel iour, q̃ fō eftate ferra void, & le leffor graūt le reuerc. ouftr̃ le t̃ attorna, et puys il ne ala pas, vncore il neft void tanq̃ vn entrie, p *Bromley* chiefe Juft. (*B. Côdition* 245 in fine.) ☞ Nota q̃ vn Euefq̃ eft pier del Realme, & ferra trie p parez fuos fur arrainm̃t de vn crime, Et iffint mife in vfe, Ideo chiualrz ferr̃ del iury, & finō le panel ferra quafh, Tñ vid 27. H. 8. q̃ le Euefq̃ d̃ Rochefter ne fuit trie per piers. *B. Trials* 142 in fine. ¶ Plus de hoc An. 6. H. 8. 1. 32. H. 8. 177. 1. M. 1. 445. 38 H. 8. 313.

21. H. 7. 12. contr per Frowike.
6. E. 6. Com 135.
1. M. 1. Com 142.
Vide 2. M. 1. Com. 117.
27. H. 8. hic 88.

Plus.

Anno Tertio Mariæ 1.

Damages ēcreafe puis iffue, & verdict fur ceo.

466 ¶ Tenetur per *Prothonotorios* de cō-muni banco in trñs de baterie q̃ de tiel matters q̃ gifont in conufās des Juftices, ils poiēt ēcreafer dāmages puis verdict fur iffue. Auterm̃t de tiel matter q̃ ne gift in lour conufans, Come arbres coupz. Mes vncore la ils poyent encrefe coftes. *B. Abridgement* 36. in fine.

3. H. 4. 4. per Rede.

34. H. 8. 238.
3. H. 4. 4. per Thirñ.
19. H. 6. 42.

Coftes.

Leafe pur vie, & graunt de reuerfion per ans, de cōmence puis.

467 ¶ Nota fi home leffe meafon et 200. acres de t̃re pur t̃me de vie, et puis graunt le reuerfion del dyt meafon & t̃re a auter, Habend̃ predict̃ meafō, t̃re & tent̃ a fefto f. Michaelis proximo poft mortem, vel determinationem intereffe de t̃ pur vie pur 21. ans tūc proximo
fequet̃,

Cafus Throckmerton & Tracie, de repl' in communi bāco Com 145. & 152.

sequēt, Le ĩ pur vie deuie deuaunt attornement,
vncore le graunt del reuerſion eſt bone, eo que
les parols ē le hēnð del meaſon et terre eſt entend deſtre vn leaſe, et rent fuit auxi reſerue
ſur ceo, et iſſint bone leaſe ſans attornement,
per opinionem *Browne, Saunders & Stampforde*
Juſtices. Tamē per *Brooke* chiefe Juſtice il neſt
q̄ graūt de reuerſion, & nul leaſe, mes vnc. le

Vide 2. E. 6.
379.
4. E. 3. 18. per
Scot.

grant eſt bōn jās attornemt, pur ceo q̄ ceo ē de
cōmencer puis le mort le ĩ pur vie, iſſint q̄ le
ĩ pur vie ne ſerra attendant al graūt, Nec il
ne fra auowrie ſur luy, Ne nauera acc. de waſt
nec alia &c. Per Judiciū Cur. *B. Attornemt* 60.
Leaſes 73.

2. M. 1. 462.
contra.
14. H. 8. 14.
per Brudnel.

468 ❡ Fuit tenus per omnes, ſi home leſſa
terre a vn auter tanque le leſſee ad leuy 20. li
que ceſt bone leaſe, non obſtaunt le incertaintie.
B. Leaſes 67. in fine.

Leaſe tanque il
ad leuy xx. li.

3. M. 1. Co. 163
10. El. ibm 342

468 ❡ Dictum fuit p lege q̄ aſiment nē
neceſſarie in auowrie. ſ. et hoc paraĩ eſt verificare, car ē in lieu de declaration, et le auowaunt
eſt actor *B. Auerment* 81.

Auerment ſur
auowry.

469 ❡ Nota q̄ deuiſe per teſtamt fuit priſe
deſtre vn alienac̄.   *B. Alienations* 37.

Deuiſe eſt aliena.

470 ❡ Si couenaunt ſoit per indenture q̄ le
fits A. marie le file C. pur que C. done al A.
100. li. & pur ceo A. couenant oue C. que ſi le
mariage ne prendra effect, que A. & ſes heires
ſerra ſeiſies del 150. acres in D. al vſe C. et ſes
heires quouſque A. ſes heires ou executors repay
le 100. li. et puis C. ad iſſue deins age & deuie,
et puis le mariage ne priſt effect, p q̄ leſtaĩ eſt
executed in lheire C. per leſtatute de vſes fait

Vſe veſt in lheire
come heire ſon
pier ou le pier
fuit mort deuant
que luſe vient.

27. H. 8. ca. 10.
Raſt. vſes 9.

Anno 27. H. 8. non obſtaunt que C. fuyt mort
deuaunt le refuſel del mariage. car ore luſe &
poſſeſſion

Relac.

poſſeſſion veſt in lheſr C. eo que lendentures et couenants auera relation al ſeſauns de lendenture, car ceux indentures lyont le terre oue le vſe, queux indentures fueront in vie C. Mes per *B.* quere ſi lheſr C. ſerra in gard al ſeigū, car il ē heire, & vnē purchaſor vt vydetur. *B.* *Feoffements al vſes* 59.

Quære.
Gard.

Done de charter al vſe.

471 ❡ Done de terre pur ans ou dun leaſe pur ans a vn vſe eſt bone, non obſtaunt le ſtatut, car le ſtatute eſt entende dauoyder dones de chattelles al vſes pur defrauder creditours tantum, et ſic eſt le preamble et entēt del ceſt eſtaī. *B. Feoffements al vſes.* 60.

3. H. 7. ca. 4.
Raſt. Vſes. 6.

Statut expound.

472 ❡ Fuit conceſſū in caſu Ben. Smithe ſuper ſtatuī de Anū 2. E. 6. ca. 24. de felonie in vn counte & acceſſorie in auter countie, Que les Juſtices de bāke le roy ſont Juſti. de Oyer et ter. de felonie, treaſōs et huiuſmody per le commen ley, et cuſtome del realme *B.* *Oier et ter.* 8.

Banc Reg. ad ſē per Inſt. de oyer & terminer.

473 ❡ Nota ou home leſſe terre pur terme dans le remainder ouſter pur vye, le rem͂ ouſter en fee, Ou reſeruant le reuerſion, la ceſty en remainder pur terme de vye poyt ſurrender a ceſtye en reuerſion ou a ceſtie in remainder in fee, & leſtate pur terme dans neſt impediment, car com͂t q̄ ē ne poit done le poſſeſſiō del lᵗre, vncore ceo done le poſſeſſion del frankī q̄ eſt in le choſe q̄ fuit ſurrēder. *B. Surrender.* 55.

Park. 115. H.

Ceſty in rem ſurrendr ou eſt leaſe pur ans in poſſ.

474 ❡ Nota p vener de commiſſion de Oyer & ter. le commiſſion de gaile deliuery neſt poynt delͫmyne, car lun eſtoiet oue lauter. Et econͭ, ou lun commiſſion eſt contrarye all auter. Come de commiſſ. del peace, ou e vn former cōmiſſ. inͩ al auterz, ceſt contrary que cheſcun de eux ſerra

Ou vn commiſſ. determinera ou voydra auter, Et econtra.

ra

ra commiſſioners dun meſme choſe & ambideux in force. Et le commiſ. del gaile deliuer eſt tantum pur deliuer le gaiole. Commiſſ. doyer et terminer, ad parols, ad enquirend, audiend & determinand. Mes plus communement les Juſtic. del gaile del ſont auxi en le commiſſ. del peac̄, et per ceo ils enditer, & puis deliuer le gaiole, cibien del eux come del auters. Et nota q̄ les Juſtices doyer et terminer ne poient p ce̅ aucthoritie arraigne nul priſoners, mes ceux que ſont indits deua̅t eux. Mes co̅trary ſils ont co̅miſſ. de gaiole deliuery auxi, car ceux amb. poient eſte exec. ſimul & ſemel. *B. Commiſſ.* 24.

Diuerſitie inter co̅miſſ. del Gaile deliuery, & Oier & terminer.

475 ❡ In action de det vers vn heire ſur oblig. ſon aunc. que plede riens p diſcent, & troue fuit que l̃re luy diſced̄, mes nemy aſſets, Fuit adiudge que le pl̃ aſſa exec. de touts ſes l̃res, ſibien de l̃re purchaſe, co̅e de terr̃ diſcend̄. Et *B.* ſemble le reaſon deſte pur ſon faux plee. *B. Aſſetes per diſcent.* 5. in fine

Iudgement ſur aſſets troue.

Faux plee.

477 ❡ Jurie priſt ſcrowe del pl̃ q̃ ne fuit a eux liuer e̅ court, & paſſa pur le pl̃, et pur ceo q̃ ceo matter apparuſt al court per examination, ideo le pl̃ nauera iudgement. *B. Iurors* 8.

Iury priſt ſcrowe nient deliu̅ a eux en court.

☞ Nota que in Regiſtro enter breuia de treſpas, ſont plures breuez de treſpas quare vi et armis equu̅ ſuu̅ apud D. inuentum cepit & effugauit &c. Et ſic vide que ſi ils ſount priſe en vn comen, Ou auter terr̃ q̃ neſt al owner del beſts, vncore il auera treſpas vi et arm̃, ſed non quar̃ clauſ. fregit. *B. Tenants* 421.

Quar vi & armis de priſe in auter ſoile.

Comen.

❡ Plus de hoc An. 19. H. 6. & 33. H. 8. 198.

34. H. 6. 22. co̅t p Wangf. 40. E. 3. 15. per Belk.

M. 11. H. 4. 18.

34. H. 6. 28. 12. H. 8. 2. per Brooke.

Plus.

Anno quarto Mariæ 1.

Age de Perſon, prebend' &c.

478 ❡ Nota fuit in maner agree per omnes *Iuſtic.* in coī banco, que ſi perſon, prebēd, vel hm̄odi ſoit deins age de 21. ans, et fait leaſe de ſon benefice deins age, que vnc̄ ceo luy liera, Car ou il eſt admit per le ley de ſeint eſgliſe de ceo prender deyns age: Iſſint le commen ley luy fayt able pur dimiſer ſon benefice deins age. *B. Age* 80.

Information.

479 ❡ Nota dicitur que ſur information fait per le roy, que paſſ. ſur iſſue trie, le roy, ne lenform̄ nauera attaint, car le inform̄ nē pleinment party. Et quaunt le defendaunt ad reſpond, lattorney le roy replye pur le roy, et nul plus menc̄ eſt puis del inform̄, et ideo lun ne lauter nauera attaynt. *B. Attaint* 127.

Vid 20. H. 7. 5.

Com 2.
Vide 7. E. 6.
439.

Pluſors hūndreds.

480 ❡ Nota p leſchequer & amb. bāks, lou pties ſont a iſſue in ple de terre, ou le terre giſt in 3. ou 4. hundreds, la ſi le Juror ad terre in aſcun del hundreds, Ou demurre in aſcun des hundreds, ceo ſuffiſt. *B. Challenge* 216.

Conc tempore
E. 6.

Accuſation in caſe de treaſon & miſpriſion.

481 ❡ Nota que fuit agre per toutes les *Iuſtices* al ſerieāts Inne in Chauncery lane 25. Oc̄t 1556. quant al trial de treaſon & miſpriſion de treaſon, que per leſtatutes, 2. accuſors ou teſtes doient eſtr̄ al inditemēt or the ſayings & accuſatiōs in eſcript de ſouth lour maynes, vel le teſtimonie des auters de meſme le accuſac. que ſerra lye al Jurie al Indiƈtment. Et ſi les accuſours ſount mortes al temps del inditement, vncore il ſuffiſt ſi laccuſatyon ſoyt la teſtmoygne, car donques il y fueroūt deux Accuſours. Mes pur aſcun Treaſon de Anno 25. E. 3. la ne beſoygne

5. & 6. E. 6. ca. 11

Raſt. Treaſ. 23.
St. 9. A. beſoygne accuſours all tryall, pur ceo que eſt Trial de treaſon per comen ley.
enaſt per leſtatute de 2. M. 1. cap. 10. *Que*
toutes trials de treaſons, ſerra per lorder del com-
men ley tantum, et non aliter, Et le comen triall
del commen ley eſt per le Jurie, et per wytneſſe,
et per nuls accuſours. Et eadem lex de treaſon
de coyninge que accuſors ne beſoigne al ar-
raygnement, Mes al indytement vt ſupra, tantum. Mes pur touts treaſons faites per le dyt
aſte de 2. M. 1. doyent eſtre witneſſes, vel accuſors cybyen al Inditement come al arraygne-
ment, accordāt al vn article contaygne in le dyt
ſtatute in fine. Et pur myſpryſyon de Treaſon
doyent eſtre witneſſes, vel accuſors cybyen ſur
Raſt. Treaſ. 18. lendytement, come ſur larraignment, per leſtatute de 1. E. 6. capitulo 12. in fine, Car le dyt
ſtatute de Roygne Marie ne reſtraygne accu-
ſours al tryall, mes tantum en caſes de Treaſon, Trial de petit treaſon.
et non pur myſpriſion. Et ſuyt agree que petie
treaſon doit eſtre trie come high treaſon, ceſtaſ-
ſauoir, per Accuſors per indiſtment, Mes al
trial ne beſoigne accuſours. Et a ceſt reſolution
fueront ſir William *Portman* chiefe Juſtice,
Maiſter *Hare* maſter del Rolles, ſir Robert
Brooke, Sir Dauid *Brooke*, Sir Humfreye *Browne*,
Sir John *Whyddon*, Sir Edward *Saunders*, Sir
William *Stampforde*, & maſter *Dalyſon* Juſtices,
Dyer Seriaunt, & *Griffine*, & *Cordell* Attorney
& Soliciter. Et fuit agree que counſelors que
done euidence vers traitours ne ſont accuſors.
Et per le ley ciuel accuſors ſont come parties Ciuyl ley.
et nemy witneſſes, car witneſſes doiēt eſtre in- Teſtmoignes et
different, Et ne veigne tāque ils ſont appelles, Accuſors diuer-
Mes accuſors offre eux meſmes daccuſer, car ſitie.
eſt bone challenge al witneſſes, adire q̄ il ſuit Challenge.

Challẽge pemptory en treafon.

vn de ſon accuſors (*B. Corone* 219.) Et nota q̃ p ſtat d̃ 33. H. 8. pēptory chalt eſt ouſte ē caſe d̃ hault treaſo̅, Tamen per le dit ſtatut de roygne M. eſt enaɛt que toutz trials de treaſon ſerra ſolonque le order del comē ley et non aliter. Et ideo videt̃ que il poet auer challenge peremptory, vt al cōmen ley. ſ. 35. Jurors. *B. Challenge* 217. *Trials* 151. in fine.

Deuiſe tolle diſcent & voile remitter.

482 ℂ Tenaunt en taile de terre deuiſable diſcontynue en fee, et repriſt en fee, et deuiſe al eſtraunge en fee, et deuie, liſſue en taile neſt remitte, car rien eſt a luy diſcend rōne del deuiſe que tolle le diſcent, Sino̅ q̃ le deuiſee ceo waiuer. *B. Deuiſe* 49. *Remitter* 52.

waiue deuiſe.

Ent per purchaſor dun reuerſion per condition.

483 ℂ Nota que eſt rule en le Seriaunts caſe que ou comen perſon leſſa t̃r pur ans, rendāt rent oue clauſe de reentre, et puis graunt le reuerſion ouſter, le tenaunt attorne, le grauntee poet reenter pur condition enfreint per leſtatute p expreſſe parols. Et eadem lex del grauntees del roy E. 6. et touts auters heires al roy H. 8. per lequitie del dit eſtatut, que prouide remedy pur les patentees del roy H. 8. Et pur graūtees de common perſons. (*B. Entre Congeable* 139.) Et nota que en le dit Seriauntes caſe, fuit agree que ou home leſſa terre pur ans rendant rent, & pur default del payment, vn reentre, il ſuffiſt pur le leſſee de tend̃ le rent ſur le t̃re le darraigne hour̃ del darraine iour del mois, ſi le argēt poet eſtr̃ numbred in ceſt temps. Et iſſint il ſuffiſt pur le leſſor pur dd̃er ceo meſm̃ le hour̃. *B. Tender* 41. Fuit auxi rule en le dit ſeriants caſe, q̃ ſi home leſſe terre 4. Januar̃, hend̃ p 40. ans, Reddendum annuatim ad Mich, & Paſc. 20. ſ. le t̃ paiera al Paſc. et

Equitie.

Condition de reentre pur nō paiment.

Quaunt & a quel tēpſ l' leſſee doit faire tender.

Ou lun feaſt eſt miſe deuant lauter en vn leaſe.

4. M. 1. Com. 175.

32. H. 8. cap. 34. Raſt. Condic 1. 4. E. 6. Com 34. 4. M. 1. Com 177.

4. M. 1. Co. 172. 36. H. 8. 275. contra. 6. H. 7. 3.

4. & 5. E. 6. Com 70. 4. M. 1. Co. 172. 4. M. 1. Com 171.

al

al Miͨ p equales porciones, & le leſſor ne perdra le rent al Paſc̄.　*B. Leaſes* 65.

484 ❡ Nota q̖ patebat p Scrutinium recor-
dorum de coĩ banco, q̃ les Juſtices del banke
potent prender & recorder recogñ, cybien extra
t̃minum come infra terminum.　Et cybien in
aſcun counte Dengl, c̄oe a weſtm̃.　*B. Recogniſance* 20.

Vide 5. M. 1. 496.

485 ❡ Nota que ſi home leſſa maner pur ans,
in q̃ ſont copyholds, et puis copyholder deuie,
le t̃mor del maner grant le terre p copy pur 3.
vies, ceſt bone, car le cuſtome p tout Engl ē,
que le ſūr pur le temps eſteāt poet dimitter p
copy &c.　Et hoc non obſtant q̃ il nad niſi durant bū placiſt, vel a volunt.　*B. T. per copy*
27.

486 ❡ Nota qd fuit adiudge intr̃ Umpton
& Hyde que lexplanation del ſtatute de willes
neſt de prendr̃ effeͨt tantum a tempore explanation Mes le primer ſtatute que eſt explane
ſerr̃ iſſint priſe ab initio.　Iſſint que les willes
de Umpton, Gainsforde & auters que ſont except in lexplanatyon ſerra pryſe bone per le
32. H. 8. ca. 1.
Raſt. Willes 2.
ſtatute de 32. H. 8. de willes, que fuyt explane.
B. Teſtament. 26.

487 ❡ Nota que ſi alien nee de pais, que eſt
in amitie et peace oue ceſt realme, veigne in le
realme oue traitors Anglois & leuie guerre, cē
treaſon in tout.　Contrarye ſi pays lalien fuit
in guerre vers Angl, car donq̖ laliē poet eſte
occide p Marſhal ley.　*B. Treaſon* 32.

Plus.
❡ Plus de hoc.　An. 32. H. 8. 182. 33. H. 8
204. 35. H. 8. 258. 6. E. 6. 429.

❡ *Anno*

Recognſaunce deſtre recorde per Iuſtices extra termin. Lieu.

Ou tenant a voluate, ou termor del manor grāt copyholde pur vie.

Explanation des willes per ſtatut 34. & 35. H. 8.

Aliē fait treaſon

Diuerſitie.

❡ *Anno quinto Mariæ.* 1.

Deuant que battaile ferra fait et trie.

488 ❡ Dicitur que fi appelle de murder foit port in banco regis, le def. ioyne battaile, ceo ferra trie denāt les Juftices de bāco regis, et nō deuant le Conftable et Marfhall. *B. Battaile* 16. in fine.

Abiure pur treafon. Quære.

489 ❡ Fuit dit pur ley que home ne poet abiure pur haut treaf. Quere de petit treafon car patet in vn cronid tēp. H. 6. q̃ femme que tua fon miftreffe abiura le realme. *B. Corone* 180. in fine. St. 116.

490 ❡ Manningt̃ & aut̃ fuer̃ endits de felony in le hault chimin in Comitatu Bedf. pur robbery dum Edward Keble clerke oue dagges et lenditement & le corpz fueront remoue en banco regis, et la ils fueront arraignes, et plede non culp̃ ad' patriam, et fueront tries. Mes puis vn briefe fuit maund oue le corps ē le pais oue nifi prius de luy trier in Comitatu Bedf. Et hoc eft comen courfe de iffint remoue le corps & le record extra banco regis al pais arrere. *B. Corone* 230.

Trial de felony. Remouer de prifoner extra banc reg. al pais.

491 ❡ Dictum fuit en parliamento q̃ fi alien nee obtaine leafe pur ans, que le roy ceo auera, car il ne poet auer terre en ceft realme de nul eftate. *B. Denizen* 22. Vide temp. E. 6. 443.

Roy auera leafe pur ans purchafe per alien.

492 ❡ Fuit agree in cōmuni banco, que fi home pur maryage fon file affume de paier 20. li. ann. al Pafche pur 4. ans. & faile deux ans, que le pleintife poet auer action fur le cafe fur le affumpfion pur le non paiment del 2. ans, coment que lauter 2. ans ne font vncore venus, car ceo eft in'naī de couenant. *B. Acc. fur le cafe* 108. in fine.

Action fur le cafe pur non paiment de mariage mony

Couenant.

❡ 493 Ou

493 ¶ Ou recognifaunce eſt conus in London deuant vn Juſt. d̃ communi banco, et certifie en banco, et la ingroſſe, Scire faĉ ſerra
port la direĉt al vic̄ de London, et non vic̄
Midd ou le banke eſt, per touts les Preigno-
thories del comen bāke. *B. Lieu* 85.

Scire fac' ſur re-
cognaiſance.

494 ¶ Nota per *B.* que Leueſque de Ely
dit a luy que il veie vn preſentation temp. E.
3. fait per le dyt roy, que il preſent al vn benefice pro illa vice que fuit dauter patroñ, per hec
verba, ratione prerogatiue ſue, quel benefice
void ratione que le roy auoit fait lencumbent de
ceo vn Eueſque que fuit ſacre, iſſint q̃ quaunt
benefice veigne void per ſeſans dun incumbent
Eueſque, le roy preſenťa a toutes ſes pꝛim̄ benefices pro illa vice, quecunq̃ q̃ ſoit patrone de ceo,
B. Preſentation 61.

Poſt. 498.
Cõc 41. E. 3. 5.
Vide 11. H. 4.
37. cõt p Hill.

Roy preſenter al
autr benefice per
ſõ progat rõne
que lencumb. eſt
fait Eueſque.

495 ¶ Nota que in banco regis ils ont diuers
preſidents, q̃ en bꝛe derror ſur fine, le rec. in̄ ſerꝛ
certifie iſſint que nul plures proclam̄ ſerra faytes,
car ſi rien ſoyt remoue niſi tranſcript ils poient
proceder in cõmuni banco nient obſtaunt ceo,
Et ſil ſoit reuerſe, ceo fait fine de tout. Mes
ſil ſoit affirme, donques le recorde ſerra maunde
in cõmuni bāco p mittimus deſtre proclaime &
engroſſe. *B. Record* 49.

1. H. 7. 20. cõtr
Com. 265.

Ou le record m̄
ſerra remoue p
briefe derr.

44. E. 3. 37.
per Kniuet.

Mittimus.

496 ¶ Tenet̃ q̃ tiel ɨ dun maɲnor en le caſe
N. 485. eſpecifie, ne poet dimiť̃ reſeruant meind
rent q̃ laūc. rent. Mes doit reſerue laūc. rēt
ou plus. *B. Tenaunt per copy* 27, in fine.

Dimiſ. rend.
laūc' rent ou
pluis.

497 ¶ Nota que fuit decl' p les Docťs del
ciuil ley que ou heire ou auter eſt marie infra
añ nubiles, et puis diſſaſſent al age de diſcreſ.
ou puis, denaunt aſſent al mariage que ceo
ſuffiſt, et le partye poet marier a auter ſans deuorce

Aſſent et diſaſ-
ſēt al mariage.

Deuorce.
Ordinarie.

uorce ou teſtm̄ de ceo deuaunt lordinary. Mes lordinarye poet ceo punier per arbitrium iudic. Mes le 2. eſpouſels eſt bone tam p legem regni, quā per legem eccleſie, *B. Gards* 124.

Iuſtic del cōmen banke ſait Iuſtic in banco Regis.

498 ¶ Si Juſtice del comon bāke ſoit ſait Juſtice del bāke le roy, comēt q̃ ceo ne ſoit poynt intende niſi pro illa vice. Cōe fuit de ſir James *Dyer* hoc Anno, vnc. ceo del̄minera ſon patent del comen banke, comt q̃ il ſurrendr̄ le patent del bāke le roy lendemain. Car le bāke le roy

Banc' Regis.
Errour.

eſt le pluis hault court. Et ſi le comē bāke err̄, ceo ſerr̄ cōtrol p le banke le roy. Et ideo home ne poet eſte iudge de lun banke & lauſ ſimul & ſemel de reuerſe ſon iudg. dem̄. Et ſi toſt cōe Juſtice del comen bāke ē ſait iuſtice de banco regis (cōe ad eē vieu ſepe) le cōmiſſ. del cōmen banke per ceo ō determine, car lun court

Iuſtice del commen bāke chiefe baron del Exchequer, Ou doier & termin. Ou Gaile deliuery.

eſt deins le controlm̄t de lauſ Mes home poet eſte iuſtice del comen banke & chiefe baron del Exch. ſimul & ſemel. Et poet eſte Juſtice de commē bāke, et iuſtice in oier et term̄, Ou de gaole deliuery ſimul et ſemel, car nul de ceux courts ad cōtrolm̄t del auſ. Et ſi encūb. del

Idem admittitur.
1. H. 7. 10.

Voydance per creation en Eueſque.

bn̄ifice ſoit ſait Eueſq̃, le prim̄ beneſice eſt voide, Car ceſty que ad loffice del ſoueraintie ne poet auer loffice del inferior per aſcun des Juſtices.

D S. 127.
29. H. 8. 116.
Supra 494.

Quære.
Oyer.
Oyer & term.
Peace.
Gaile deliuery.

Tū *B.* dubitat, Car iuſtice de banco regis poet eſtre iuſtice in oyer, Ou de oyer & term̄. Ou del peace, Ou gaole deliuere, Et vnc̄ ſi ils err̄

Errour en plees, Proces, ou vtlag.

en lour plees in le oyer, Ou oyer & terminer, Ou en lour pces, ou vt l' deuaunt iuſtice del peace, br̄e derrour ent giſt deuant le roy in ſon banke. Mes les plees in banco regis ſount tenus coram Rege vbicunq̃ fuerit in Anglia, et iſſynt le bāke le roy eſt court remouable. Et

per

Magna chart
ca. 11. Raſt.
Comen plees 1.

per leſtatut lez comen plees teneant[r] in loco
certo, donqz eſt contrarye del ſerement del Juſtice
de lun court et lauter, car lun eſt certeine, &
lauter eſt incerteyne. *B. Commiſſions.* 25.

14. H. 6. 2.

499 ❡ Nota ſi Duches, ou aut̃ tiel ſtate
marie oue gent̃ ou ſquire, el per ceo perdra ſon
dignity & noſm̃ per q̃ el fuit appelle deuaunt,
Ut en caſu domine Powes et Duciſſe Suff. lun
eſpouſe R. Hawarde, et laut̃. 2. le Duches,
Adrian Stokes. Et ideo briefes fuer̃ abates en
lour caſes, Car per le liſt de harolds, quando
mulier nobilis nupſerit ignobili, deſinit eſſe nobilis. *B. Briefs* 546. *Noſme* 69.

Feme perdr
noſm

Plus.

❡ Plus 36. H. 8. 284.

❡ Aliquot caſus ex quibuſdam

Lectur. temp. H. 8. & H. 7. cum paucis
aliis caſibus & regulis.

VVhorewoode
An. 35. H. 8.

500 ❡ Si l̃re diſcēd al file deins age, &
puis el ē diſſ. le diſſ. deuie & ſo heire enter,
et puis fits ē nee, il nee auoydera le diſcēt, car
il ne clayme cōe heire al ſoer ne il ne fuit en
eſſe tempore diſcenſus. *B. Diſcent* 40.

Diſcent al heire
in ventre matris.

Pl[9] de hac Lectura 35. H. 8. 257.

Plus.
Martin Juſtice
ſur leſtatute
de Parnor de
profits.
Temp. H. 8.

501 ❡ Hōe ne poet auerre vn aut̃ parnor
de profits des auters choſes, queux ne ſont in
dd̃. *B. Parnor* 4. in medio.

Parnour.

1. R. 2. ca. 9.
Raſt. Fefmts 1.
Vid 24. H. 8. 62

502 ❡ Nota q̃ p leſtat̃ de 1. R. 2. ou diſſeiſor fait feoffemēt pur maintenance et priſt les
profits, le feffemt̃ ē void p leſtatute al touts
entents. *B. Feffements* 19.

Feffement
voyde per ſta-
tute.

x　　　　　　*T. Frowike*

T. Frowike ſur leſtatute de Prærogatiua Regis.

Gard' & mariage

503 ❡ Garde & mariage ē p le cōmon ley. Et le pere aſſa le garde de ſon Fitz, ou file & heire apparāt deuant le roy ou auter ſn̄r. Et

Tenure.

ſocage tenure p 20. ans, & chiualrie apres. *B. Garde* 120. in fine.

Notice de reſignation ſerr done per lordinary.

504 ❡ Le patrō prendra notice de cheſcun voydāce de auowſon pretr̄ reſignatione, Et de ceo Lordinary donera a luy notice. *B. Notice.* 27.

Ou le Roy ſeiſera ſans office, Et ou econtra.

505 ❡ Nota q̄ de chattell le roy ē en poſſeſſiō ſans office. Et econtra de tr̄ & de frakt, niſi de termiñ, Et aliquando il ſerra en poſſeſſion denheritās ſans office, vncore le roy nauera le terr̄ de ſon garde ſans office coment q̄ il nad en ceo niſi chattel, car le garde vyent roñe tenure q̄ eſt ſn̄r et frankt̄ en le roy, & ideo dr̄e enter ceo, & leaſe pur ans de ceſty q̄ eſt vtlage. Car ſi

Vtlag.

hōe ad terme pur ans, ou garde, & eſt vtlage, ceo eſt en le roy ſans office. *B. Office deuant Eſcheter* 60.

Petition & trauerſe.

506 ❡ Nota q̄ petitiō fuit al coēn ley, mes Trauers eſt per ſtatute (*B. Peticion.* 41. *Trauers doffice* 54.) Et q̄ le nonſuit ou relinquiſhe dun trauerſe eſt pemptory, Contr̄ de nonſuit en pe

Nonſuit ē traūſe & petition diēſ.

Iudgement en trauerſe.

tition, Et le iudgement dū Trauerſe neſt auſ, ſed quod man⁹ dn̄i regis amoueantur, & q̄d poſſeſſio reſtituatur a ceſty q̄ trauerſe. *B. Trauerſe doffice.* 54.

507 ❡ Lage

507 ¶ Lage d̄ teſtmoigñ en *Etate Probanda* eſt 42. anz. *B. Teſtmoignes.* 30. in fine.

Age d' teſmoign en Etate probād'

508 ¶ Le roy naſra le villein dun auf̃ en garde, Et vnc. ſi ſoit ideot il aſsa le villeine dauter que eſt iſſint ideot (quere) Et le roy aſsa le pquiſit del villein dauter ſil luy ad come ideot. *B. Villenage* 71.

Ou le Roy auera le villeine eſteāt in gard, vel alit. Quære.

36. H. 8. 295. Marrow Seriāt in enter Tēpl' ſur leſtatute de peace.

509 ¶ Ou Juſtice de peace eſt fait Chiualer, ou priſt auter dignytie, vncore ſon aucthoritye remainera. Et ſic Juſtice del comen banke eſt fait chiualer ſon commiſſion remaine in force & Añ 1. E. 6. ca. 7. (*B. Commiſſions* 4.)

Iuſtice de peace fait chiualer puis le commiſſ.

☞ Si le roy grāt a Maior & Cōminaltie et lour Succeſſ. deſtr̄ Juſtices del peace in lour ville, & puys fait commiſſion del peace al auter la, Uncore le primer commiſſyon remaynera in force, pur ceo que eſt graunt a eux & lour Succeſſors, et iſſynt neſt reuocable, Come commiſſion eſt. (*B. Commiſſion* 5.) Si nouel commiſſion del peace ſoit proclaime, ou lie in pleyne cōm, launcient commiſſion del peace eſt determine. Et *Toutes les Iuſtices* doyent prender notyce, Et ſils ſeont per launcient Commiſſion, tout que ils ſot eſt voide. Et ſi cōmiſſion ſoit direct al A. & B. q̄ ne ſot in rerū natura, Ou ſont morts tēpore teſte &c. le auncient commiſſion rem̄ in force, car ceſt nouel commiſſion eſt voide, Si commiſſion ſoit direct al N. pro hac vice, ceo determinera launcyent commiſſiō del ceux matters. Et vncore le nouell commiſſioner ne poet ſeer niſi vnica vice. (*B. Commiſſion* 6) Si commiſſ. ſoit direct de Oyer et terminer feloniez, ceo determinera le auncient commiſſion del peace quāt al felonies, mes nemy quāt al peace. Et iſſint determyne in parte et in

Graunt & commiſſ. diuerſitie.

Commiſſ. lie, ou proclaime.

Notice.

Nul tiel in rerum natura.

Commiſſion vnica vice.

Commiſſ. determine in parte.

in parte nemy. (*B. Commiſſions* 7.) Commiſ-ſion in eyer eſt fait al cōm de N. & proclamaͨ la, ceo determynera le cōmiſſion del peace. (*B. Commiſſion* 8.) Commiſſion del peace eſt en le cōm de N. & le banke le Roy vient la, ceo ne determinera le commiſſion del peace, Con-trary ſilz ſont proclam del vener del bāke le Roy. (*B. Commiſſions* 9.) Commiſſion del peace eſt fait al 4. in le cōm de N. et puis le Roy fait J. S. Juſtice de peace la pur terme de ſon vie, le primer commiſſion eſt determyne. (*B. Commiſſions* 10.) Si Juſtices ſeont per commiſſion et ne ceo adiourne, le commiſſion eſt determine. Et vide vn Statut ou nouels Cōmiſſionerz de gaole deliueries poyent ſeer ſur lez records del auncient commiſſion del gaole que eſt determine. Et quāt cōmiſſion de Oier & determiner eſt determine, les recordes de ceo ſerra miſe in Banco regis, Mes recordes del Juſtices del gaole deliuerie remainera oue le Cuſtos rotulorum del Countie. Et les pro-chein Juſt. del gaol deliuery procedera ſur eux. *Sur Iudgement del mort* per le dyt ſtatute. *Quære* ſils procedera per ceux parols al allower del Clergie, ou Sanctuarie, Videtur ita per le-quitie (*B. Commiſſions.* 11.)

510 ❡ Nota que Riot eſt ou tres vel plures font illoial act in fait, et ceo execute, Come de bater home, Enter ſur poſſ. vel huiuſmodi. Illoial aſſemble eſt, ou home aſſemble gentes de faire illoyal act et ne ceo fait, ne execute in fait. Et tout eſt ou plurez eux aſſemble pur lour quarel demeſn̄, ceo eſt Rout & coūter le ley, comēt que ne ſoit execute, Come inhabitants
dū

Commiſſ. in Eire

Banke le Roy.
Diuerſitie.

Iuſtice pur terme de vie.
Commiſſion de-termine pur def. de aiournement.

Ou le recordes remainera.

Difference inter ryot, rout, & aſ-ſemble.

1. E. 6. ca. 7.

Ante. 369.

dū vilt, pur debrufer hey, mure, vel hm̄odi daſt cōen la, ou de baſt hōe q̃ ad fait a eux cōen diſpleaſure vel hm̄odi. *B. Riots.* 5.

Lectur S.

511 ❡ Nota q̃ le roy meſme ne poet prender Recogniſance, car il ne poet eſtr̃ iudge luy meſme, mes doit aſt vn iudge de ſouth luy de c̃ prend. Et nul poet prender recogniſaunce mes Juſtice de record ou per commiſſio. Come Juſtic. de 2. bankes, Juſtice del peace, & hm̄odi, Car cōſeruator del peace q̃ eſt p le cuſtome del realme, ne poet prend ſuertie del peace per recogniſance mes per obligation, Eadem lex de conſtable, *B. Recogniſance.* 14.

Roy ne poet prĕder recogniſāce.

Qui poet prĕder recogn.

Conſtable.

Vid Fitz. Juſt. de peace fo. 157 Sir John Fitz Iames.

512 ❡ Deuant leſtatut de Quia emptores terrarum, Si le ſeignior vſt purch. parcel del terre tenus de luy, ſon entier rent fuit extinct, coment que fuit ſeuerable, Tn̄ ore per le dit ſtatute ceo ſerr̃ apporcion, ſoyt ceo purch. per le ſeignior, ou p auter, Mes ceo ne aida rēt charge, Quia leſī eſt tm̄ pur le pard del chiefe ſūr Mes de rent ſeruice ſur recouerie de parcel, Ou diſcent del parcel et hm̄odi, que ſont lactes de Dieu, ou del loy, y fuit apporcionm̄t al cōmon ley, Contrary de ſon proper act come purch. Quia deuant leſtatut auant-dit il fuit de rent ſeruice, Come eſt a ceſt iour de rent charge, que per purch. de parcel del terr̃, lentier rent fuit extinct. *B. Apporciõ.* 28.

Ou rent ſeruice ſerra apporcioned, Et ou nemy.

32. H. 8. 183.

Rec ou diſcent de parcell.

Rent charge.

513 ❡ Le prerogatiue le roye eſt treatiſe del cōmen ley, & non ſtatute, ne declaration per parliamēt. Et myne de ore ou argent eſt al owner del ſoyle. (*Quere*) *B. Prærogatiue,* 134.

Prærogatiua Regis.

Myne.

Tēp. H. 7.

514 ❡ Appele de mort poet eſtre commence deuant

Vide St. 64. A.

Coroner et fon power.

deuant le Coroner, & agarde proces tanq, al exig. Mes le plee ne ferra termine deuant luy. *B. Appeale.* 62. in fine. *Corone.* 82.

Home prift efgl' & ne voet abiur.

Lectura W. N. temp. H. 7.

515 ¶ Home prift efgl. et le Coroner vient a luy, & dd de luy pur quel caufe il prift lefglife, que dyt que il voile eftre auife per 40. iours, deuaunt que il voet decl. fon caufe, le Coroner poet luy trahe hors maintenant, Mes fil voet confeffe a luy felony, il poet rem la per

Efglife ferue pur 40. iours.

40. iours deuaunt que il abiure. Econt ou il prift fanct come Weftm, Knol, & hmodi, car ceo poet luy tener pur terme de vie, nifi in cafu ou ftatute ceo chage. (*B. Corone.* 180. *Sanc-*

Abiuration & iour de ceo fair.

tuarie. 11.) Mes fil voet abiure deins les 40. iours, le Coroner donera a luy iour certeine de ceo faire. (*B. Corone fupra*) Nul prendra priui-

Sanctuary pro vita hominis.

ledge del efgt fi non que il foit in ieoperdie de fon vie. (*B. Cor.* 181.) Ne nul auera le priuiledge de Sanctuarie nifi foit in periculo vite, Et nota q fanctuarie ne poet auer loyal comencemt nifi pro vita hominis, coe pur treafon,

Graunt ou prefcription dauer fanctuary pur det bon, & ou nemy.

Felony & hmodi, Et no pur det, Ideo ou gr, ou prefcr eft dafl fanct pur det, ceo ne vault, car eft encounter la ley. Mes fi fon corps fuit in exec & il efcape & vient al fanct ordeigne pur fauegard de vie de hom, il enioyer ceo, car p long imprifonment fon vie poet eftre in ieo-

Efglife fufpend'.

pardye. Et fi lefgt foit fufp pur bloodfhed, vncore ceftuy que prife lefgt pur felony, enioyer ceo per 40. iours. (*B. Sanctuarie fupra*) Sont 2. maners de Sanct. f. priuate, come

Efglife & fanctuary.

Weftm, Knoll, et hmodi. Et general fanct come chefcun efgt. (*B. Corone.* 181. in fine)

Abiurac difch. felony.

Abiuration pur felony, difch. touts felonyes faits deuant le abiuratio. Home ne poet
abiurer

abiurer pur petit larcenye, mes pur tiels felonies pur q̃ il ſuffra mort (*B. Corone* 182.)

Abiure pur petit larceny.

☞ Hõe ẽ endicte de felonia de bõ ad valenc. 20. đ. & ẽ troue culp̃, mes q̃ les biẽs ne valent que xi.đ. il ſerra punie p̃ diſcrec. des Juſtices, Mes naſta ſon clergy niſi fuerit p̃ felonia, pur q̃ il ſuffra mort. (*B. Corone.* 183.)

Felony de xi. d. p eſpec verdit.

Clergie pur petit larceny.

516 ❡ Nul auera ſon clergie niſi ou ſõ vie eſt en leoperdie. Et Leueſque ẽ ordinary, touts prieſts Abbes & auťs inferiors a luy que dd clergie, ou ont clergie, Et ſi Leueſq̃, ad ſon clergie, le Metrop̃ luy gardera cõe ſõ orđ, Et ſi le Metrop̃ offend & ad ſon clergie, le Roy luy aſia & luy garđ. Iđ ẽ de lapſ. *B. Clerg.* 19.

Eueſque ou Metropolitan ad ſon clergie.

Laps pur lord' le Metrop & le Roy.

Cafus.

1. E. 6. ca. 12. Clergie 21.

517 ❡ Nota que a ceo iour Bigamus aſia ſon clergie per leſtaṫ, Mes home attaint de hereſye nauera ſon clergie, Cõtrary de hõe excommẽge, Et Jewe, ne Turke nauera lour clergie, & Greake & Romayne que ne vſe noſtre letters, auerount lour clergie, & targeront tanque liuer de letters de lour pais viẽt. (*B. Clergie* 20.) ☞ Et ſi home que eſt *Captus oculis* pria ſon clergie, il auera ceo ſil poet parler latin congruemẽt. *Quære*, car il ne poet eſtre prieſt, ne il ne poet miniſter. (*B. Clergie.* 21.)

Bigamus. Heretike. Excom. Iewe. Turke. Greeke. Romayne.

Cecus.

Quære.

☞ Baſtard aſia ſon clergie, car il poet eſťr prieſt p̃ licẽce. *B. Clergie.* 22.

Baſtarde.

518 ❡ Per *Hales & Mountague* ſi home leſſa a N. ſon terre dem̃, per fayt indent, lendenture

Quamdiu leaſe pur ans de ſon

terre demefne ferra eftoppel.

denture neft eftoppel mes tantū durant le leas, et non poftea. *B. Eftoppel.* 221.

519 ¶ Home leffe terre pur vie, le remaynder al W. en tayle, et eftr̄ port br̄e dentre en le poft vers auter eftraunge que rien nad en le terre, & il vouche cefty en remainder, que enter & vouche le comen voucher, que ne poet barre le demaund per que le dd rec̄, & cefty in remainder deuie, fō iffue fauxera le rec. p *Hals* Juftice. Et il vouche de ceo 12. et 13. E. 4. *B. Fauxifier.* 55.

Faux. de rec eo q le tenant nauera riē en le tr temp recuper.

3. E. 4. 14. per Grenef. contra.

520 ¶ Sir Robert *Brudnel* nuper capital. Juftic̄ de cōmuni b̄aco deuife vn garr̄ que eft ore vfe, ceft affauoir que le garrantor pur luy & fes heires warrantizabit contra ipfum & heredes fuos, et per ceo le feoffee rebutt̄a, mes ne vouchera. *B. Garranties.* 30. in fine.

Garrantie de rebutter, mes nemy de voucher.

521 ¶ Per *Fitzherbert* Juftice, vn iuftice de record poet eftre indicte de prife de money et auter tiel fauxitie, Mes nemy de ceo que va in fauxim ou defefauns del recorde. Come adire que il alter le record de trūs in felony et hm̄odi, que faux. le recorde. *B. Indictment* 50. in fine.

Iuftice indict.

Fitz. 243. E.

Diuerfitie.

Alter trefpas en felony.

522 ¶ Si ftate foit fayt a plufors & al heires lun, et ceftuy que ad le fee deuie fon heire deins age, il ferra in gard per leftatute de willes, non obftāt que lauters furuiue que font tenauntes per le commen ley. *B. Gard.* 100.

2. Ioint et heire lun en garde viuant lauter.

32. H. 8. ca. 1. Raft. Willes 1.

523 ¶ Si lheire cefty que vfe foyt de plein age tēpore mortis anteceff. le roy nauera primer feifin, car ceo neft done per leftatute, mes tm̄ le garde de terre et corps. Et fi vol. fuit decl. per ceftuy que vfe que neft performe dur̄ le nonage lheire, la le roy nauera le terr̄, mez lheire

Primer feifin de cefty vfe.

Conc Moūtag. 27. H. 8. 4.

Volunt nient perform.

4. H. 7. ca. 17. Raft. Wards 20

Iheire a plein age, prouera ſon age, & alera
quite per experientiam in Scaccario. *B. Liuery*
77. in medio.

524 ❡ Precipe quod redd vers tenaunt pur   Count vers te-
vie, que pria aide de ceſtuy in reuerſion, que   nãt et le prie en
appiert gratis, & ioyne in ayde, & le dd count   aide.
de nouel vers le tenaunt et le prie, et ils vouche
le commen voucher & ſuffer recouery pur aſſurance. Et vncoȓ dicitur q̃ le prie nauera que
oyer del count. 22. H. 7. *B. Coũt.* 87.

Regulæ.

525 ❡ Nota q̃ color doit eſtȓ matť in ley,   Matter en ley.
ou doubtful al lay gents, Et ſerȓ dõe al pl. Et   Al pl'.
nei al vn q̃ ē meſne en le cõueſace, Et ne ſerra   Al vn meſne.
dõe al eſtȓ q̃ enfeffe le pl.* Ne ſerȓ done al   Al def.
def.* Et ne ſerȓ done p poſſ. deťm̃. s. ou ap-   Poſſ. determ.
piert in plediag q̃ le poſſ. ē determ̃* Mes ſerȓ
dõe p eſtať defete* Et ou le def. lie le droit le   Poſſ. defeat.
pl. per feffement oue garȓ, Releaſe, Fine, Re-   Feſſ. Releaſ.
                                      Fine Rec'.
coſſy, Diſſeiſin & Reentre, & huiuſmodi, la ne   Diſſ. & Reent'.
beſoigne aſcun colour. Et cēy q̃ claime nul   Propertie.
propertie in le choſe, mes priſt ceo come diſtreſſe et hm̃odi, ne done color, Color ne ſerra
dõe mes ſur plee in barre. *B. Colour.* 64.   Sur barre.
Colour ne ſerra done, mes p cēy per q̃ vous   Per vn meſne.
commence vȓe title, Et nient per vn meſne in
le conueiance. Ceſty que plede al briefe ne   Briefe.
donera colour. Couïēt que coulour ſoit tiel,
iſſint que ſi ceo ſoit verie, que de tyel poſſ. le
pleintiſe ou dd purront auer lour action. Cēy   Iuſtifie come
que iuſtify cõe ſeruaunt et conuey tytle a ſon   ſeruant.
                                        Poſſ. en ley.
maſter doſta col'. Col. p poſſ. en ley eſt bo*.   Attaint.
526 ❡ In ceux caſes, home ne fra atturney,   Præmunire.
         Y   niſi

Appel.
Per que feruicia.
Quid iuris claim.
Quem redd'.
Error.
Contempt.
Ceffauit.
Refceit.
Affife.
Attachment.
Fine.
Caufe & lieu.
Dadiornement.
Demurr.
Dub. Verdit.
Foreine plee,
Certific'.

nifi in fpec. cafu. s. attaynt Premunire,† Appele, Per q̄ feruic. Quid iur̃ cl. Quē redd̃
reddit, Ne en affigner de errour, ne al plur̃ in
cafe de contempt, Ne le t̃ in Ceffauit fur tender
de arrerages. Ne le pray defte refc. en Pr̃ qd̃
redd̃. Ne en aff.* Ne in attachem̃t. Nec
contra finē leuat, Ne in afcun cas ou le def.
ferra imprif. *B. Attorney.* 82.

† Regifter. 9.

* Regifter. 9.

527 ¶ Les Juftices daff. poēt adiourñ laff.
fur chefcun demurre. Et fur chefcun dubious
plee, Ou Ꝑdiⱪ, Et fur chefcun forein plea, Et
al q̄l lieu q̄ ils voil. Et adiourñ poet efte fur
certific. daff. Cybien cōe fur affife *B. Ad-
iournement.* 28.

Iudgemēt de vie & member eft felony.

528 ¶ Nota q̄ ceux polz (*Qd' pd' vitā & membra*) in ftatuī font intend felony, fans parol de fel. en ceo *B. Corone* 203.

Vide St. 36. C.

Diuerfitie inter difcont & parol fans iour.

529 ¶ Nota que vn difconī mift le partie al nouel original, Mes ou le parol eft fans iour, ceo poet efte reuiue per vn refūmōs ou reattach. car le original rem̃. *B. Difcontinuance de proces.* 43.

De except le darr bond'.

530 ¶ Ou homes enter in arbitrement, & chefcū eft lie al auter in obl. Vel auters tiels couenantes, & font oblige de ceo performer, Et eft ag. que chefcun releas a auꝑ toutes aⱪions et huiufmodi, la il doyt efte expreffe touts actions deuaunt tyel iour que ferra deuant le date del oblig. car auterment les obligations del award, Ou les darreine obliga. de performer les couenātz ferr̃ auxy ret. *B. Affurances.* 4.

Vide 21. H. 7.
28. p Brudnel.

Deins lan.

531 ¶ Nota per leftatute, le partie que fua aⱪion populer doyt fuer ceo infra annum poft offenc fayt & non poftea, et hoc tam de offenc. faits contra ftatutū tunc editū, quā contra ftatuī
im-

7. H. 8. ca. 3.

impofterum edenđ, fic vide q̃ il va a ftatut poftea facĩ. *B. Aĩion Populer.* 6.

532 ❡ Vide que ceftuy q̃ plede fait ou reĩ.
Ou q̃ declar̃ fur vn fayt ou reĩ a luy appertient
de mr̃e ceo, Car oyer de ceux ē femper deë ewe
per cefty que eft charge per ceo *B. Monftrance.*
165. *Oyer de recordes* 15. in fine.

Diuerfitie inter
monftrance &
oyer Recordes.

533 ❡ Nota que en les comen recoueries
per fufferance pur affurances, le tenant tenđ
iffue, le dđant poet imparle al vn iour in mefme
le terme, Et donques le tenaunt eft demaundant et retreit, et iudgement eft done pur le
dđant vers luy, Et poftea le tenaunt oufter in
value fur vouchee &c. 22. H. 7. *B. Continuances.* 69.

Imparle al iour
in m le term en
comen recoũy.

FINIS.

Le Table.

Faits

Mifnofmer

FINIS.

z

⁋ Imprinted at London
in Fleeteſtreete within Temple
Barre at the ſigne of the Hand
and Starre by Ry-
chard Tottyl.
the xv. of October.
1578.

SOME
NEW CASES
OF THE
Years and time of King *Hen.* 8.
Edw. 6. and Qu: *Mary*;

Written out of the Great

Abridgement,

Compofed by
Sir ROBERT BROOK,
KNIGHT, &c.
There difperfed in the Titles,
but here collected under years.

And now Tranflated into Englifh by JOHN
MARCH *of* Grays-Inn, *Barrifter.*

All which faid Cafes are by the Tranflator
Methodifed, and reduced Alphabetically
under their proper Heads and Titles.

With an exact Table of the principall
Matter contained therein.

London, Printed by *T. N.* for *Richard Beft*,
and *John Place*, and are to be fold at
Grays-Inn gate, and *Furnivals
Inn-gate* in *Holborn*, 1651.

To the Reader.

READER,

WHEN I confidered what great care our *Parliament* had taken of the *publick* good; in enacting our Laws to be tranflated into Englifh, then which, certainly nothing more equall, that the people might in fome meafure inftruct themfelves in that to which they are bound to obedience; and of which by the Law it felfe, they cannot, nor muft not plead ignorance. And when I had likewife confidered the excellent, and moft ufefull Law that is contained in this little volume called *Petty Brook*; I thought it a labour fervicable to the publick to Tranflate it, which I here prefent you in your own Language: make ufe of it, and you will finde *Magnum in parvo*, great benefit in this little work; and I doubt not give him thanks for it, who is ambitious of nothing more then to be yours, and the Common wealths

moſt Faithfull

Servant,

Jo: MARCH:

Abridgment.

HOlden by the *Prothonatories* of the *Common Bench* in Trespass of Battery; That of such matters which lie in Conusance of the Justices; they may increase dammages after a Verdict upon Issue; otherwise of such matter which lies not in their Conusance; as Trees cut. But yet there they may increase costs. 3. *Mar.* 1. *B. Abridgement*, 36 the end.

3 H. 4. 4. by Reda.

34 H. 8. 238.
3. H. 4. 4. by Thirn.
19. H. 6. 42.

Acceptance.

Note, By *Fitzjames* and *Englefield*, Justices: if Tenant in Dower Leases for years, rendring rent, and dies, the Lease is void; and acceptance by the Heir of the Rent will not make the lease good, for twas void before: otherwise of voidable Leases. 22. *H.* 8. *B. Acceptance*, 14.

24. H. 8. 54.
See Tit. Leases.

If Tenant in Taill Leases his land for twenty years, rendring rent, and dies, and the Lessee leases to another for ten yeares, and the issue accepts the rent of the second Lessee, this is no affirmance of
the

the Leaſe : for there is no privity between the ſecond Leſſee and him ; contrary, if he paies it as Bayliff of the firſt Leſſee ; and *B.* ſeems if the firſt Leſſee had Leaſed over all his Term in parcel of the land let, and this Aſſignee paies the rent to the iſſue in tail, that this affirms the entire Leaſe : for Rent upon a Leaſe for years, is not apportionable. 32. *H.* 8. *B. Acceptance.* 13.

Tenant in Tail, the Remainder over Leaſes for years, rendering Rent, and dies without iſſue, he in the Remainder accepts the rent : this ſhal not binde him ; becauſe that when the tail is determind, all that is compriſed within it is determined, and ſo the Leaſe void, and he in the Remainder claims not by the Leſſor. 1. *E.* 6. *B.* *Acceptance* 19.

Biſhop Leaſes Land of his Biſhoprick for years, rendering Rent, and dies ; the Succeſſour accepts the Rent ; this ſhall binde him ; for the Biſhop hath a Fee-ſimple, and may have a Writ of Entry See Tit. Leaſes. *Sine aſſenſu capituli :* otherwiſe in caſe of a Parſon or Prebend, who can have but a *Juris utrum.* 2. *E.* 6. *B. Acceptance.* 20.

Jay accords 11. H. 7. 17. 34. H. 6. 18. by Briſot, 19. E. 4. 1. by Cateſby.

If a man be bound in an obligation to pay ten pound to the Obligee at *Paris* beyond Sea at a certain day, if the Obligor pay at another place, and the ſame day in *England,* and the other accepts it, tis good clearly. 38. *H.* 8. *B. Conditions.* 206.

Acceptance of Rent by the Lord from the diſſeiſor of the Tenant, ſhall not bar him of his eſcheat : otherwiſe if he had avowed for it in Court of Record, *&c.* See *Tit. Eſcheat.*

Action popular.

7 H. 8. c. 3.

Note, By the Statute the party which ſues an Action Popular, ought to ſue it within the year after
the

the offence done, and not after : and this as well of offences done against the Statute then made, as against Statutes after to be made ; so see that it goes to a Statute after made. *B. Action Popular.* 6.

Action upon the Case.

If I have a Mill in *B.* and another makes another Mill there by which I lose my Toll by going of divers to it, yet no Action lies : otherwise, if the Mill disturb the water from coming to my Mill ; there I shall have an Action upon my Case. 24. *H.* 8. *B. Action upon the Case.* 42. the end. Agrees Newton 22. H. 6. 15. 11. H. 4. 47. by Hank.

In an Action upon the Case where the Plaintiff delivers goods to the Defendant, and the Defendant for ten shillings promises to keep them safe, and does not, to the dammage, &c. And by *Fitzherbert* and *Shelly* Justices, *Non habuit ex deliberac'*, is a good Plea. 26. *H.* 8. *B. Action upon the Case.* 103.

Note, in an Action upon the Case betwixt *Awsten* Plaintiff, and *Thomas Lewis* Defendant, for calling him false and perjured ; he justifies, because that the Plaintiff was perjured in the *Starchamber* in such a matter, &c., and a good Plea by the Court. 28. *H.* 8. *B. Action upon the Case.* 3. more of this in the next. 30. H. 8. 127. 27. H. 8. 22. Petty Br.

Action upon the Case for calling the Plaintiff false perjured man ; the Defendant justifies that such a day and year in the *Starchamber* the Plaintiff was perjured, and pleaded certain in what, &c. for which he called him false perjured man, as afore, as twas lawful for him : and a good Plea by the Court in the *Common Bench.* Wherefore the Plaintiff said of his own wrong, without that he swore in manner and form, &c. 30. *H.* 8. *B. Action upon the Case.* 104. 28. H. 8. 85.

If a man bring debt of 10. l. the Defendant wages his Law : and after the Plaintiff brings an Action upon the Case against the same Defendant, that he promised to pay the 10. l. &c. The Defendant may plead that for the same summ the Plaintiff brought before an Action of Debt, in which the Defendant waged his Law, Judgement, if Action. And a good Plea, for he was once barred of the same summ. And in Action upon the Case, that the Defendant promised to pay 10. l. to the Plaintiff, which he ought to him for a Horse, and a Cow, the Defendant may say, That he promised to pay 10. l. to the Plaintiff, which he did ow to him for a horse, which he bought of him, which summ he hath paid to the Plaintiff without that that he promised to pay 10. l. which he did ow to the Plaintiff for one Horse, and one Cow, as &c. Or without that that he did ow to the Plaintiff 10. l. for a Horse and a Cow, as &c. 33. *H.* 8. *B. Action upon the Case.* 105.

3. M. 1. agrees.   Action upon the Case, for that the Defendant found the Goods of the Plaintiff, and delivered them to persons unknown there ; that he did not deliver them in manner and form, is no plea, without saying not guilty where the thing rests in doing. And if the Action were, That whereas the Plaintiff was possessed, &c. as of his proper goods, and the Defendant found them, and converted them to his proper use, tis no Plea that the Plaintiff was not possessed as of his proper Goods, but he shall say not guilty to the misdemeanour, and shall give in evidence that they were not the goods of the Plaintiff : and yet tis true, not guilty against him. 33. *H.* 8. *B. Action upon the Case.* 109.

In an Action upon the Case, that the Goods of
the

the Plaintiff came to the hands of the Defendant, and he wafted them, the Defendant faies that they came not to his hands, &c. and a good Plea, and gives in evidence that they were not the proper goods of the Plaintiff. 34. *H.* 8. *B. Action upon the Cafe.* 103. the end.

2. E. 6. and fee 4. E. 6. after under this title.

Action upon the Cafe was brought in *London* by *A. B.* that whereas he was poffeffed of certain wine and other ftuff (and fhews in certain) in fuch a fhip, to the value, &c. and doth not fhew the place certain where he was thereof poffeffed, and yet good. And alledged that the Defendant fuch a day, year, and place in *London*, promifed for 10. l. That if the faid fhip and Goods did not come fafe to *London*, and put upon the Land, that then he would fatisfie to the Plaintiff 100. L and that after the fhip was robbed upon the Trade on the Sea, for which he brought the action for not fatisfying: and the truth was, that the bargain was made beyond fea, and not in *London*. But in an action upon the Cafe upon an Affumpfit and the like, wch is not local, the place is not material (no more then in debt) for he alledged that the faid goods in the parifh of 8. *Dunftons* in the Eaft *London*, before they were fet to land, or &c. were carried away by perfons unknown, &c. and the action lies well in *London*, though they were perifhed upon the high fea. 34. *H.* 8. *B. Action upon the Cafe.* 107.

See 33. H. 8. before.

2. Mar. 1. 451. Time, H. 8. 366. Petty Br.

'Twas agreed, That an Action upon the Cafe doth not lie againft the Executors, upon the Affumpfit of the Teftator, though they have affets. 37. *H.* 8. *B. Action upon the Cafe.* 4. the end.

5. M. 1. Com. 182. 9. Rep. 87. &c. Pinchons cafe cont.

In an Action upon the Cafe for a thing which lies in Feafans, as for burning of Goods or Deeds, and the like, not guilty is a good plea: contrary, for

See 33. H. 8. before.

for *non Feafans* of a thing which he ought to do ; as to make or repair a Bridge, Houfe, Park, Pale, fcouring a Ditch, and the like, and doth it not, there not guilty is no plea. 2. *E*. 6. *B*. *Action upon the Cafe*. 111.

Action upon the Cafe for calling the Plaintiff falfe Juftice of Peace, *vel his fimilia*, thefe words (*his fimilia*) were ordered to be ftruck out of the book by the Court, for the incertainty. 4. *E*. 6. *B*. *Action upon the cafe*. 112.

Action upon the Cafe whereas the Plaintiff was poffeffed of fuch Goods, as of his proper Goods, and loft them, and the Defendant found them, and converted them to his own ufe : the Defendant faid, That the Plaintiff pledged them to him for 10. l. by reafon of which he detains them for the faid 10. l. as tis lawfull for him, without that that he converted them to his own ufe, as &c. and a good plea by fome. By others he muft plead not guilty, and

See 33. H. 8. before.

give this matter in evidence for the Detainer. 4. *E*. 6. *B*. *Action upon the Cafe*. 113.

Twas agreed in the *Common-Bench*, That if a man for marriage of his Daughter, affumes to pay 20. l. a year at *Eafter*, for four years, and fails two years, that the Plaintiff may have an Action upon the Cafe upon the Promife for the *non payment* of the two years, though the other two years are not yet come ; for this is in nature of Covenant. 4. *M*. 1. *B*. *Action upon the Cafe*. 108. the end.

Action upon the Statute.

See 24. H. 8. after.

In an Action upon the Statute of 8. *H*. 6. of forcible entry. Or in Trefpas upon 5. *R*. 2, *Vbi ingreffus non datur per legem, Non ingreffus eft contra formam*

formam ſtatuti, is a good plea : but his Free-hold is
no plea, as tis ſaid by *Sherwood* and others. 23. *H.*
8. *B. Action upon the ſtatute.* 40.

In Treſpaſs upon 5. *R.* 2. to ſay that the place,
&c. is the Free-hold of *I. N.* and hee by his commandment entred, is no plea : for the action is given
by the Statute, and therefore ought to have a ſpecial
anſwer, and not as in a general Writ of Treſpaſs.
24. *H.* 8. *B. Action upon the ſtatute.* 15.

See by *Fitz.* Juſtice, That a man may avow upon   21. *H.* 8. c.
the Land by the new Statute, and then the Tenant
ſhall not diſclaim : contrary, if he avow by the
Common Law, and relinquiſh the ſtatute, 28. *H.* 8.
B. Action upon the Statute. 6.

'Twas ſaid for Law, That tis no plea in Treſpaſs   See 27. *H.* 8.
upon the Statute of 5. *R.* 2. for the Defendant to   26. & 2. *E.* 4.
ſay, That the place where is twenty acres which is   6.
parcel of the Mannour of *B.* is his Free-hold. For
the Defendant ought to entitle him to a Lawfull
entry : for a Diſſeiſor hath a Free-hold, and yet
ingreſſus eſt, ubi ingreſſus non datur per legem, in the
time of *H.* 8. *B. Action upon the ſtatute.* 27.

Account.

Account lies not againſt Diſſeiſors, for then the
Diſſeiſee ſhall avoid the diſcents at his pleaſure :
and alſo the Defendant was never his Receiver for
to render account, for this cannot be without privity
in Law, or in Deed : as by Aſſignment, or as Guardian, or the like : or by pretence the Defendant to
the uſe of the Plaintiff, and where the Defendant
claims to his own uſe, there the plea is true ; neither
his Receiver, nor his Baily, to render account : 2.
Mar. 1. *B. Account* 89.

Adjournment.

Adjournment.

The Juſtices of Aſſiſe may adjourn the Aſſiſes upon every demurrer, and upon every dubious plea or Verdict ; and upon every foraign plea, and to what place they will ; and adjournment may be upon Certificate of the Aſſiſes, as well as upon the aſſiſe. B. *Adjournment.* 28.

Adminiſtrators.

31. E. 3. ca.
11. Raſt. Adminiſt. 1. 21.
H. 8. ca'. 5.
Raſt. Probat of Teſt. 3.

Debt is brought againſt the Ordinary, who pending the Writ, commits the adminiſtration to *J. S.* the firſt Writ ſhal abate : for the Ordinary is compellable to commit the Adminiſtration, by Statute, 34. *H.* 8 B. *Adminiſtrators* 39.

Nota, per omnes legis peritos, and by thoſe of the Arches, that at the time of vacation of an Archbiſhoprick, or Biſhoprick, the Dean and Chapter ſhall commit the adminiſtration, 36. *H.* 8. *B. adminiſtrators* 46.

27. H. 8. 26.
by Fitz.
4. H. 7. 14.
by Trema. See
5. E. 6. after.

Nota, where the Ordinary commits the adminiſtration, he may revoke it, and commit it to another (but mean acts done by the firſt adminiſtrator ſhall ſtand) and ſo 'twas put in ure between *Brown* and *Shelton,* for the goods of *Rawlins ;* the adminiſtration was committed to *Brown,* and revoked and committed to *Shelton :* for 'tis not an intereſt, but a power or authority ; and powers and authorities may be revoked ; *contra* of an intereſt certain. In the time of *H.* 8. *B. adminiſtrators* 33. the end.

Charles Brandon Duke of Suffolk, had iſſue ſonn by one *Venter,* and daughter by another *Venter,* and deviſed goods to the ſon, and dyes, and after
the

the ſon dyes inteſtate, without Wife and Iſſue; and the mother of the ſon who was of the ſecond *Venter* (for the daughter was of the firſt *Venter*) took the adminiſtration by the Statute; which is, That the adminiſtration ſhall be committed to the next of kinn of the inteſtate.   And upon great argument in the Spirituall Court, *Tam per legis peritos regni, quam per peritos legis civilis,* the adminiſtration was revoked.   And ſo ſee that the adminiſtration may be revoked; and ſo 'twas likewiſe in the caſe of *Brown* and *Shelton* before, of the goods of *W. Rawlin* Clerk, which was committed to Sir *H. Brown,* who marryed the ſiſter of the ſaid *Rawlins,* and after came W. S. and J. S. ſon of the Wife of the ſaid Sir *H.* (which Wife was the mother of the ſaid *Shelton* by a former Huſband) and reverſed the firſt adminiſtration, and obtained the adminiſtration to them.   And the ſaid Duke had iſſue *Frances* by the French Queen; and after this Wife dyed, he marryed the daughter of the Lord *Willoughby,* and had iſſue by her one *Henry,* and dyed; and after *Henry* dyed without iſſue, and without Wife, and the mother of the Heir took the Adminiſtration; and after the ſaid *Frances* Wife of the Marqueſs of *Dorſet* ſued, and reverſed the adminiſtration, and obtained the adminiſtration to her ſelf, though ſhe were but ſiſter of the half blood to the ſaid *Henry,* becauſe that ſhe is next of kinn to the ſaid *Henry,* for that *Henry* had not any Children; for the mother is not next of kinn to her own ſon in this reſpect of this matter; for it ought to goe by diſcent, and not by aſcenſion, by the Law of England, nor by the Law civill.   And the children are *de ſanguine patris & matris, ſed frater & mater non ſunt de ſanguine puerorum.*   And by Iſidore, *Pater &*

21. H. 8. c. 5. Raſt. Adminiſt. 1.

& mater & puer ſunt una caro; and therefore no degree is betwixt them; contrary between brother & ſiſter; and the half blood is no impediment as to goods (*B. adminiſtrators* 47.)

Note, that in the argument of this caſe, 'twas agreed by the Juſtices, that the King is not intitled to the land of his Ward, without office, though he hath but a Chattel in it, yet it comes *ratione tenuræ*, which is the Seigniory and Freehold in the King, 5 E. 6. B. *Office before, &c.* 55.

3. Eliz. Com. 229.

Age.

A man recovers Rent and arrearages by *aſſiſe*; Or if he recovers an annuity and arrearages of it in a Writ of annuity, the Defendant dyes, the Plaintiff brings a *Scire facias* againſt the heir, he ſhall not have his age of the arrearages, for they are reall, and parcell of the rent or annuity. But if the Judgment be of arrearages and dammages, there he ſhall have his age (*B. age* 50.) And where he recovers in a Writ of annuity, or *aſſiſe*, as before: Or hath avowed for a Rent, which is Freehold, and recovers the arrearages without coſts and damages, he ſhall not have an action of Debt of that, but a *Scire facias*, for tis real. But where he hath Judgement of it, with coſts and dammages which go together, ſo that that tis mixt with the perſonality, then lies a Writ of Debt againſt the Heir, of the arrearages and dammages (and this B. thinks in default of Execution) *per curiam*, 23. *H.* 8. B. *Debt*, 212. *& age* 50.

Kirton agrees 43. E. 3. 2. 15.

Note, That of the Land of the *Duchy* of *Lancaſter*, and other Lands which the King hath as Duke, or the like, his age is material, and he may have

4. El. Com. 213. 121. Cont.

have his age as another common perfon may; for he hath them as Duke, not as King (*B. Age* 52. & 78.) As if the King alien Land, parcel of his *Dutchy* of *Lancafter* within age, there he may avoid it for *Non-age* for the reafon aforefaid: otherwife of Land which he hath as King, for the King cannot be difabled by *Non-age*, as a common perfon fhall (*B. Prerogative.* 132.) Yet by the *Statute* of 1. *E.* 4. (which is a private act not printed, but inrolled in the *Dutchy Chamber*, by which King *H.* 6. was attainted of Treafon, and that all the Lands of the faid *Dutchy* fhould be forfeited, and fhould be a *Dutchy* feparated and incorporated, &c.) tis annexed to the Crown: but by another private act, 1. *H.* 7. tis difannexed, and made as in the time of *H.* 4. 1. *E.* 6. *B. Age.* 52.

Note, twas in a manner granted by all the Juftices in the *Common Bench*, That if a Parfon, Prebend, or the like be within age of 21 years, and makes a Leafe of his Benefice within age, that yet this fhall binde him: for where he is admitted by the Law of holy Church to take it within age, fo the Common Law inables him to Demife his Benefice within age. 4. *Mar.* 1. *B. Age.* 80.

Margin: Com. ibid. See the Stat. Com. 218.

Margin: How feperated, See Com. 219. & 220. See this Act, Com. 214.

Alienations.

If the Tenant of the King alien in Fee without licence, and die, his Heir within age, the King fhall not have the Ward, becaufe that nothing is difcended to him, and that the Alienation is good, fave the Trefpafs to the King, which is but a Fine by Seifer. *B. Alienations* 29. *Gard* 85. But otherwife if the Alienor were Tenant in Tail; and if the Alienation without licence be found by office, the

Margin: See 29. H. 8.

Margin: See 33. H. 8. 8. E. 4. 4. by Coke, Stp. 84.

King

King ſhall have the Iſſues of the Land from the time of the Inquiſition taken, and not before. (*B. Alienations* 26. *in medio.*) But where the Tenant dies, and his Heir enters upon an office found for the King, of the dying ſeiſed of the Anceſtor, there the heir ſhall anſwer the profits taken by him before. 26. *H. 8. B. Intruſion* 18. *the end.*

8. E. 4. 4. by Choke.

See 29. H. 8.

Tis ſaid for Law, That a fine for alienation is one years value of the land aliened: and the ſame Law of a Fine for intruſion upon the King. But the Fine to have licence to alien, is but the third part of the yearly value of the land which ſhall be aliened: and for licence to alien in *Mortmain*, the Fine is the value of the Land for three years. 31. *H. 8 B. Alienations.* 29. *the end.*

46. E. 3. 45. by Perſay.

If a man obtain licence to alien the Mannor of D. and all his Lands & Tenements in D. he cannot alien by Fine: for the Fine ſhall be certain: ſo many acres of Land, ſo many of Meddow, ſo many of Paſture, and the like: and the alienation ought not to vary from the Licence. Yet by B. tis otherwiſe uſed with an averment, that all is one. 32. *H. 8. B. Alienations.* 30.

40. E. 3. 41. By Thorp.

Note, if there be two Joynt-tenants who hold of the King *in Capite*, and one releaſes to the other all his right, this is no alienation; nor doth he need Licence, or pardon of it: for he to whom the Releaſe is made, is in by the firſt feoffor, and not by him that Releaſed: nor ſhall he Fine for ſuch releaſe: and ſo tis uſed in the *Chequer*, that tis no alienation. But if three Joynt tenants are, and the one Releaſes to one of the others, there he is in of it by him that releaſes: *Contra*, if he had releaſed to all his compagnions: and where a man Releaſes by Fine to the Tenant of the King, this is no alienation.

Stp. 30. cont. 33. H. 6. 5. by Wangf. Lit. 68.

tion. Otherwife of a Fine *Sur Conufans de droit Com ceo*, &c. for this is an eftate made by Conclufion. 37. *H.* 8. *B. Alienations* 31.

Tenant of the King *in Capite* cannot alien for term of life without Licence : for it alters the Free-hold. *Time H.* 8. *B. alienations* 22. the end. 45. E. 3. 6.

Note, That for Burgage Tenure of the King, a man may alien without licence well enough. 6. *E.* 6. *B. Alienations* 36.

Note, That a Devife by Teftament was taken to be an alienation. 3. Mar. 1. *B. alienations* 37.

Alien. See Tit. Denizen.

Note, by the whole Court in the *Kings Bench* an alien may bring an action perfonal, and fhall be an-fwered without being difabled, becaufe he is an alien born : otherwife in an action real (and the fame B. feems in an action mixt.) and he may have a pro-perty, and buy and fell. 38. *H.* 8. *B. Denizen* 10. *Nonability* 40. See 1. E. 6. next after. See Dyer the beginning.

Twas faid in the *Kings Bench*, That to fay that the Plaintiff is an alien born, Judgement ; if he fhall be anfwered, is no plea in an action perfonal, other-wife in an action real. Yet this hath been in quef-tion after this time in the fame Court : and twas faid that an alien born is no plea in Trefpafs, if he doth not fay further, That the Plaintiff is of allegiance of one fuch a one, enemy to the King : for tis no plea in an action perfonal againft an alien that he is of the allegiance of fuch a Prince, which is of amity with the King. 1. *E.* 6. *B. Nonability* 62. See 38. H. 8. before.

If an alien born purchafe, the King fhall have it : but the purchafe ought to be found by office : and fo twas in the cafe of *Alien* King : and B. feems that See 5. Mar. 1. after. See Coke upon Lit.

an

an information in the *Chequer*, will not ſerve in this caſe. *Time*, E. 6. B. *Denizen* 17. the end.

See before.
See Coke upon Litt. Twas ſaid in Parliament, That if an alien born obtain a Leaſe for years, that the King ſhall have it; for he cannot have Land in this Realm, of no eſtate. 4. *Mar.* 1. B. *Denizen* 22.

Amendment.

See 24. H. 8. after. By *Fitzherbert*, and the Court; where a Writ of Error was ſued to remove a Record out of the *Common Bench*, into the *Kings Bench*, betwixt an Abbot and I. N. the Warrant of Attorney varied in the Roll in the name of the Abbot, and twas amended after Judgement: and if they had not amended it, they ſaid, that thoſe of the *Kings Bench* would have amended it. 23. H. 8. B. *Amendment* 85. the end.

See before 23. H. 8. Note, That where a Warrant of Attorney varied from the name of the Corporation of the party, and a Writ of Error was brought to thoſe of the *Common Bench*, they amended it preſently: and they ſaid that thoſe of the *Kings Bench* would have done the like. 24. H. 8. B. *Amendment* 47.

1. E. 5. 7. by Vaviſor & Cateſby.
See 6. & 7. E. 6. Com. 85.
See 33. H. 8. Tit. Parliament. Note, twas agreed by the Kings learned Councel, That the King may amend his Declaration in another Term, in omiſſion, and the like: as where an information miſrecites the Statute, this may be amended; for miſrecital is the cauſe of Demurrer: for if it be miſrecited, then there is no ſuch Statute: but he cannot alter the matter, and change it utterly; yet the ſame Term he may. 4 *Eliz. Com.* 243. by *Weſton.* 30. H. 8. B. Amendment 80.

Appeal.

Appeal.

Note, by the Juftices of both Benches, a man fhall
not have the plea in an appeal; That the dead
affaulted him, and that he killed him in his defence,
but fhall plead not guilty in manner and form, and
fhall give this matter in evidence: and the Jurie is
bound to take notice of it; and if they finde it, he
fhall go acquitted in form aforefaid. Nor he fhall
not have this for plea with a traverfe of the murther:
for the matter of the plea is murther. Nor murther
cannot be juftified; and when the matter of the plea
is worth nothing, there a traverfe the like: (*B. Appeal*, 122. *Corone*. 1.) the end. And where the Jury
acquits the Defendant upon an Indiɗment before the
Coroners, they ought to finde that he killed the man;
and there they may fay, That the fame Defendant
killed him *fe defendendo*: but upon an Indiɗment
before other Juftices, it fuffices to fay, not guilty
only, without more. 37. *H.* 8. *B.* Appeal, 122.

1. M. 1. Com.
101.

4. E. 6. Com.
12. 14. H. 7.
2. by Fineux 13.
E. 4. 3. St.
181. B.

The Heir of a man killed fhall have an appeal, as
well of Homicide of his anceftor, as of Murther. 2.
E. 6. *B. Appeal* 124.

Note, if a woman who hath Title of an appeal of
the death of her hufband, takes another hufband; he
and the wife fhall not have an appeal; for the woman
ought to have it fole: for the caufe of an appeal is,
that fhe wants her hufband; and the reafon is, becaufe the wife wanting a hufband, is not fo well able
to live: and therefore when fhee hath another hufband, the appeal is determined: for the caufe ceafing,
the effeɗ ceafes. (*B. Appeal*, 109.) as where a woman
hath a *Quarentine*, and fhe marries within the 40.
daies, fhee lofes her *Quarentine*. 1. *Mar.* 1. *B. Appeal.* 109. *Dower*, 101.

M. 2. M. 1.
by the Juftices
accord. St. 59.
B. See 21. E. 4.
73. By Huffey.

Appeal

Time H. 7.

See St. 64. A.

Appeal of death may be commenced before the Coroner, and Proces awarded to the Exigent: but the plea ſhall not be determined before him. Reading 113. *B. Appeal* 62. the end. *Corone* 82.

Apportionment.

See 24. H. 8.
Tit. Contr.

Tis ſaid that if I ſell my Horſe, and the Horſe of W. N. to A. for ten pound, and W. N. retakes his Horſe, that A. ſhall render to me the entire ten pound: becauſe a Chattel cannot upon a contract be apportioned. 30 *H.* 8. *B. apportionment.* 7.

If the Kings Tenant of four acres, alien one to the King: Or if he hath two Daughters, and dies: and the one aliens to the King, the Rent ſhall be apportioned if it be ſeverable: and this by the Common

See after.

Law, by ſome. *Quære,* for the reading of *Fitzjames* is otherwiſe, 32. *H.* 8. *B. apportionment* 23.

Sir John Fitz.
James.

Before the Statute of *Quia emptores terrarum,* if the Lord had purchaſed parcel of the land holden of him, his entire Rent was extinct, though twas ſeverable: Yet now by the ſaid Statute it ſhall be apportioned, be it purchaſed by the Lord, or by another: But this doth not help a Rent Charge: becauſe the Statute is onely for the loſs of the chief Lord. But of a Rent ſervice upon recovery of parcel, or of a diſcent of parcel, and the like, which are the acts of God, or of the Law, there was an apportionment at the Common Law, contrary of his proper act, as purchaſe: becauſe before the Stat. aforeſaid, it was of a rent ſervice, as tis at this day of a Rent charge, which is extinct by purchaſe of parcel of the Land, Reading *B. Apportionment.* 28.

Arbitrement.

Arbitrement.

Debt upon an Obligation : the Defendant pleads
the Condition : if he fhall ftand to the award of I.
and N. fo that the award be made before fuch a day,
and faies, that the award was not made by the day :
the Plaintiff may fay, That they made fuch an award
before the day, which the Defendant in fuch a point 8. H. 6. 18. by
(and fhew in certain in what) hath broken : for he Newton B.
muft fhew the breach in fome point certain : other- Arbitrement
wife the action lies not. 31. *H.* 8. *B. Arbitrement* 18.
42.

Affets inter maines.
Affets in their hands. See Tit.
Extinguifhment.

Note, if Executors plead fully adminiftred in an 21. E. 4. 21.
action of Debt, and give in evidence payment of by Choke &
Legacies, the Plaintiff may demur upon it ; for fuch Nele. Perk.
adminiftration is not allowable in Law, before debts 94. E. 190.
paid. 33. *H.* 8. *B. Affets inter maines* 10. E. D. S. 79.
37. H. 6. 30.
Where a perquifite of a Villain fhall be Affets : by Prifot.
See Tit. Villeinage. 2. H. 6. 16.
per curiam.

Affets per difcent.
Affets by difcent.

In an action of Debt againft an Heir upon an 34. H. 6. 22.
obligation of his anceftor, who pleaded nothing by contra by
difcent ; and twas found that Land difcended to Wangf.
him, but not affets ; twas adjudged that the Plaintiff 40. E. 3. 15.
fhould have Execution of all his Lands, as well of by Belk.
Land purchafed, as of Land difcended : and *B.*
feems

ſeems the reaſon to be for his falſe plea. 3. *Mar.* 1. B. *Aſſets per diſcent* 5. in the end.

Aſſignee.

A man Leaſes a houſe and Land for years; and the Leſſee Covenants that he and his Aſſignes will repair the houſe; and after the Leſſee grants over his Term, and the aſſignee doth not repair, an action of Covenant lies againſt the aſſignee; for this is a Covenant which runs with the land: (*B. Covenant* 32. *Deputy* 16.) and alſo it lies clearly againſt the Leſſee after that he hath aſſigned over his Term: and *B.* ſeems that if he bring ſeveral Writs of Covenant againſt both, that there is no remedy till he takes execution againſt the one: and then it ſeems to him, that if he ſues againſt the other, he ſhall have an *Audita Querela.* 25. *H.* 8. *B. Covenant* 32.

Aſſiſe.

Aſſiſe: the Tenant pleads not attached by fifteen daies; the Bayliff was examined, who ſaid that he attached him by the horſe of a Farmor which was a Termor to the Tenant of the land in plaint, which matter was recorded: and *B.* ſeems that tis no good attachment; for the Tenant cannot forfeit the beaſts of his Farmor: and an attachment ought to be made of ſuch things which the Tenant may forfeit by Outlary. Note, between *Dudly* and *Leveſon,* for the Mannor of *Parton,* in the County of *Stafford.* 31. *H.* 8. *B. Aſſiſe* 480.

27. H. 6. 21.

Note, by the Juſtices in the Common Bench, That in an aſſiſe againſt two, the one takes the Tenancy and pleads no wrong, and the other takes the Tenancy

nancy without that, that the other hath any thing, and pleads in Bar : there the Plaintiff ſhall be compelled to chuſe his Tenant at his peril, as well as if both had pleaded in Bar, and accepted the Tenancy ſeverally : and if it be found that he miſ-elects his Tenant, the Writ ſhall abate, but he ſhall not be barred. And there when the Demandant elects his Tenant, and he pleads, there they ſhall be at iſſue, before that the Tenancy ſhall be inquired, and then the Tenancy ſhall be inquired firſt, and after the other iſſue. 6. *E.* 6. *B. Affife* 384.

Affurances.

Note, that Tenant in Tail who levies a Fine with Proclamation, ſhall be bound, and his Heirs of his body alſo after the Proclamation made, and not before : ſo that if the Tenant in Tail die before all the Proclamations made, this ſhall not binde the iſſue in Tail ; and the Proclamation cannot be made in ſhorter time then in four Terms (*B. Fine Levies* 109. *affurances* 6.) But Tenant in Tail who is not party to the Fine, ſhal not be ſo bound after the Proclamations, but that he ſhall have five years to make his claim : and if he fails of them, and dies, his iſſue ſhall have other five years by the equity of the Statute of W. 2. *Quod non habeat poteſtatem alienandi.* Yet tis ſaid, if the firſt Iſſue neglect the five years, by which ·he is barrable, and dies, his iſſue ſhall not have other five years ; for if the iſſue be once barrable by ·the Fine, the Tail is by this bound for ever : (*Quære*) And the Statute ſaies, That it ſhall binde parties and privies : and therefore where Tenant in Tail is party to the Fine, with Proclamation, and his iſſue claims *Per formam doni*, the iſſue is privy : .

Weſtm. 2. c. 1.

c c   for

for he cannot convey to him*felf* as heir in tail, but as
of the body of his Father, which is privity. But
a Fine with Proclamation, may be confe*ff*ed and
avoided ; and then it *fh*all not binde : for the Statute
is intended *De finibus ritè levatis.* And therefore he
may *f*ay, that the partie*s* to the Fine had nothing
tempore finis, &c. For if none of the Parties had
nothing *tempore finis,* then tis a Fine by conclu*f*ion
betwixt the parties : but all *f*trangers may avoid it
by the averment as afore. (*B. Fines, Levies,* 109.)

See Tit. Fines
Levied.
Fitz. 142. A.

And by the Statute of 32. *H.* 8. Fine with Proclamation by *Ceftui que ufe* in Tail, *fh*all binde him and
his heirs after Proclamation made : and a Fine with
Proclamation, the Rever*f*ion or Remainder in the
King, and the Conu*f*or die*s*, the Proclamation made
tis no Bar, nor di*f*continuance ; becau*f*e that the Rever*f*ion or Remainder in the King, cannot be di*f*continued : therefore there the i*ff*ue in Tail may enter
after the death of the Tenant in Tail. (*B. Bar* 97.

32. H. 8. c. 26.
Raft. Fines 9.
4. H. 7. cap. 24.

Affurances 6.) And *B.* *f*eems, that neither the Statute of 32. *H.* 8. nor 4. *H.* 7. *fh*all not binde the
i*ff*ue in Tail, nor the Rever*f*ion to the King by Fine
with Proclamation, though that the Proclamation be
made : and yet the Statute of 4. *H.* 7. wils that
after Proclamation made, it *fh*all be a final end, and
*fh*all conclude as well privies, as *f*trangers, except infants, Fem Coverts, and the like, *&c :* And the i*ff*ue
in Tail is privy. Yet *B.* thinks that the intent of

See Cokes 1.
Book.

the Statute was not that the i*ff*ue in Tail, the Rever-
*f*ion to the King *fh*ould be bound : for by him after
this Statute, this was taken to be no di*f*continuance :
and therefore it *f*eems to him that it *fh*all not binde
the I*ff*ue in Tail, the Rever*f*ion in the King. (*B.*

32. H. c. 36.

Fines, Levies 121.) Yet *Quære,* for the Statute of
32. *H.* 8. which wils that the heir in Tail *fh*all be
barred

barred by Fine with Proclamation after the Proclamation made, hath an exception of thoſe, of which
the Reverſion, or Remainder, is in the King, ſo that
it ſhall not binde ſuch iſſue in Tail. *B. aſſurances* 6.
the end.

But otherwiſe tis of a recovery, and Execution had
by writ of entry in the *Poſt*, with voucher by the
Common Law : for though that the Reverſion, or
Remainder be in the King, ſuch recovery ſhall binde,
and was a bar againſt the Tenant in Tail, and his
iſſue preſently ; but not againſt the King. But at
this day by the Statute of 34. & 35. *H.* 8. Recovery
againſt Tenant in Tail ; the Remainder, or Reverſion in the King ſhall not binde the iſſue in Tail, but
that he may enter after the Death of Tenant in Tail.
30. *H.* 8. *B. Bar* 97. the end. *Aſſurances* 6.

See 32. H. 8.
Tit. diſcontinu-
ance after.

Note, That for aſſurance of land, that the heir
ſhould not ſell, twas deviſed, That a man ſhould
make a Feoffment in Fee to two, to the uſe of himſelf for Term of life without impeachment of waſt,
and after to the uſe of his ſon, and his heirs, until
the ſon ſhould aſſent and conclude to alien it, or any
part of it ; or to charge or incumber it, and after
imediately upon ſuch conſent and concluſion to the
uſe of *A.* and his heirs, until as afore, and then &c.
to the uſe of *B.* and his Heirs, until, &c. and ſo of
more, &c. and by ſuch aſſent and concluſion by the
Statute of uſes. *Anno,* 27. *H.* 8. *c.* 10. the other
ſhall be in poſſeſſion, *&c.* 38. *H.* 8. *B. Aſſurances* 1.

Where men enter into an arbitrement, and every
one is bound to the other in an obligation, or other
ſuch Covenants, and are bound to perform it : and
tis awarded that every one ſhould releaſe to the other
all actions, & the like : there it ought to be expreſſed
all actions before ſuch a day, which ſhall be before
the

See 21. H. 7.
28. by Brudnel.

the date of the Obligation for otherwiſe the Obligation of the award, or the laſt Obligations to perform the Covenants, ſhall be alſo releaſed. *Regulæ B. Aſſurances* 4.

Attaint.

Caveatur in every action triable by Jury, of the quantity of the land, as where a man demands 200. acres, where they are but a hundred ſixty or the like : and the title is for the demand, there if the Jury finde that he deſeiſed him of 200 acres, or the like, this is matter of Attaint. And ſo where they finde him guilty in treſpaſs or the like, of more treſpaſſes then he did, or of exceſſive dammage, and the like. 24. *H.* 8. *B. Attaint* 96.

Quære by B. if an Attaint doth not lie upon a Verdict in an appeal of *Maihem* at this day, by the Statute of 23. *H.* 8. *cap.* 4. For this year twas doubted. 38. *H.* 8. *B. Attaint* 10. the end.

Aſſiſe is brought againſt Tenant by Statute Merchant, and againſt the Conuſor Tenant of the Freehold, and the *Aſſiſe* acquits the Tenant by Statute Merchant, and attaints the other of diſſeiſen : the Tenant by Statute Merchant ſhall not have an Attaint, nor the Lord where Land is recovered againſt him, and the heir, where he hath the heir in Ward ; nor the Termor, where land is recovered againſt him, and the Leſſor, becauſe they loſe not any Free-hold : and becauſe that they are acquitted by *W. Whorewood* the Kings Attorney. Yet by B. tis not reaſonable where they are named, and loſe their intereſt : yet it ſeems to him, that he that is acquitted ſhall not have an attaint ; but if they are found diſſeiſors, they ſhall have an attaint by him. *Time, H.* 8. *B. Attaint* 82. the end.

Note ;

1. E. 5. 6. by Sullard. 1. R. 3. 3. by Huſſey.

43. Aſſ. 41.

Note; For Law, where Trefpafs of battery, goods carried away, or a writing broken (which are tranfitory) is done in one County, yet an action may be brought in an other. (*B. Attaint* 104. And fo twas agreed in Trefpafs in *London*, of breaking of at D. in *London*, where indeed D. was in the County of E. for thefe are not local. *B. Lieu.* 65.) And therefore in Trefpafs tranfitory, the place is not iffuable, nor traverfable. No more then in Trefpafs upon the cafe, upon a promife; and thefe may be continued. (*B. Traverfe, &c.* 283.) — See 24. H. 8. Tit. Action upon the cafe.

And in thofe cafes, the Jury of another County may take Conufance thereof, but is not bound to it: but if they take Conufance, attaint lies not. Otherwife of Trefpafs of Trees cut, or Grafs trod, which are local, and fhall be brought in the proper County. 2. *Mar.* 1. *B. Attaint* 104. *Jurors* 50. — 39. H. 6. 8. by Afhton. 9. E. 4. 45. by Choke.

Note; Tis faid that upon an Information for the King, which paffes upon the iffue tried, the King nor the informer fhall not have an attaint: for the informer is not fully party. And when the Defendant hath anfwered, the Kings Attorney replies for the King; and after, no further mention of the informer: and therefore neither the one, nor the other fhall have an attaint. 4 *Mar.* 1. *B. Attaint.* 127. — See 20. H. 7. 5. Com. 2. See 7. E. 6.

Where an attaint lies, where not. See *Tit. Dammages.* And *Tit. Fauxifier.*

Attornment.

Note; That Attornment may be made by Tenants, to the Lord in his Court: to the Steward in abfence of the Lord, or purchafor. But Attornment to the fervant of the purchafor out of Court, and in abfence — See my Lord Cokes Rep.

fence of the Purchafor, is not good : but by payment of one penny for every Tenant to the fervant of the Purchafor ; and in his abfence, in name of Seifen of their feveral Rents, is a good attornment : for a fervant may receive Rent for his Mafter.

Quære. If no Rent then is due, nor the rent day come. 28. *H.* 8. *B. Attornment* 40.

Conc. Lit. 39.
H. 6. 24. c. 16.
Raft. Inrolments. 2. c. 10.
Raft. Ufes 9.
Twas agreed, That where Land is fold by Deed, indented and inrolled according to the Statute of 27. *H.* 8 *c.* 10. there becaufe the ufe is changed by the bargain and fale, by the faid Statute, and the buyer in poffeffion ; and hath no means to compel the Tenant to attorn ; there he may diftrain, and avow without attornment. Otherwife upon a grant by

Lit. 230.
Fine ; for there he may have a Writ of *Per quæ fervitia.* 30. *H.* 8. *B. attornment* 29. the end.

Abr. of Aff. 22.
Note, That if a man hath Common of Pafture to a certain number ; or Common of Eftovers to a certain number of Carts and will Grant them over ; they pafs without attornment ; becaufe they are not to be taken by the hands of the Tenant, but by the

See 2. E. 6. after.
mouth of beafts, and by cutting, and carrying. So fee that when no attendancy nor payment is to be made by the Tenant, there the thing paffes without attornment. 31. *H.* 8. *B. Attornment.* 59.

See 2. E. 6.
Com. 379.
See by *Wherewood* the Kings Attorney ; where a man Leafes for forty years, and after Leafes the fame Land to another, to have from the end of the firft Term for twenty years, this needs no attornment : otherwife where he grants the Reverfion as

See Tit. Leafes
See after.
afore, there ought to be attornment. (*Quære,* and fee after.)

And if a man Leafes for ten years, and after Leafes to another for twenty years, this is good for ten years without Attornment : otherwife if there

were

were a word of Reverſion. 37. *H.* 8. *B. attorn-*
ment. 41.

A man Leaſes Land for twenty years, the Leſſee
Leaſes over for ten years, rendring Rent, and after
grants the Reverſion of the Term, and Rent to a
ſtranger, this ſhall not paſs without attornment, by
reaſon of the attendancie of the Rent: otherwiſe, if
no Rent were reſerved upon the ſecond Leaſe for
ten years, for then there is no attendancie to be
made, nor action of Waſte, nor the like to be   See 31. H. 8.
brought. For as B. ſeems, attornment is not neceſ- before.
ſary; but to have avowry, or an action of Waſte.
2. *E.* 6. *B. attornment.* 45.

See by *Mountague,* chief Juſtice, and *Townſend,*   Lit. 125. & D.
That by a Feoffment of a Mannor, the ſervices paſs   S. 35. & 9. E.
without attornment of the Free-holders. But B.   4. 33. contra.
ſeems that the Tenants ought to attorn. 4. *E.* 6.
B. attornment 30.

Note; If a man let a houſe, and 200 acres of
Land for Term of life: and after grant the Re- Com. 145. &
verſion to another, to have the ſaid Houſe, Land,   152.
and Tenements, *a Feſto Sancti* Michaelis *prox poſt*
mortem vel determinationem intereſſe of Tenant for
life for twenty one years then next following: the
Tenant for life dies before attornment, yet the grant   See 37. H. 8.
of the Reverſion is good, becauſe that the words in   before.
the *Habendum* of the houſe and land, is intended to
be a Leaſe; and a Rent was alſo reſerved upon it,
and ſo a good Leaſe without attornment: By *Brown,*
Sanders, and *Stamphord,* Juſtices: Yet by B. Chief
Juſtice, tis but a Grant of a Reverſion, and no
Leaſe: but yet the grant is good without attornment; becauſe that tis to Commence after the death
of Tenant for life, ſo that the Tenant for life ſhall
not be attending to the Grantee; nor ſhall he avow
upon

upon him, nor have an action of Waſte, or the like: by judgment of the Court. 3. *Mar.* 1. *B. Attornment* 60. *Leaſes* 73.

Attorney.

In theſe Caſes a man ſhall not make an Attorney, except in ſpecial caſe, *viz.* Attaint, Premuniri, Appeal, *Per quæ ſervitia. Quid juris clam. Quem redd. reddit.* Nor in aſſigning of Errors: nor at the *Plures* in caſe of contempt: nor the Tenant in a *Ceſſavit* upon tender of arrearages. Nor the pray' to be received in a *Pr. quod redd.* Nor in an aſſiſe; nor in an attachment. *Nec contra finem levat:* nor in any caſe where the Defendant ſhall be impriſoned.

Regiſter 9. — margin (line 2)
Regiſter 9. — margin (line 8)

Audita querela.

A man ſeiſed of 20. acres, is bound in a Statute Marchant; and makes a Feoffment of 15. to ſeveral perſons, and Execution is ſued againſt one of them, he ſhall have an *Audita querela* upon his ſurmiſe, to have the other Feoffees to be contributory with him. But if execution be ſued againſt the Conuſor himſelf, he ſhall not have ſuch contribution: for this is upon his own act. *B. Audita querela* 39.

Yet if the Conuſor dies, and the Conuſee ſues Execution againſt the heir, he ſhall have Contribution of the Feoffee. So every of them ſhall have of the heir. 25. *H.* 8. *B. Audita querela* 44. the end.

Margin note beside *Audita querela*:
45. E. 3. 17. 13.
H. 7. 22. by
Rede. 16. H. 7.
6. by Keble.
5. E. 6. Com.
72. 9. H. 4. 4.
by Gaſc. 36. H.
8. B. Audita
querela 2. the
end. 48. E. 3.
5. by Finch.
17. E. 2. B.
Suit 13. econt.
See Cokes Rep.

Averments. See Tit. Pleadings.

Note, Where a man pleads a recovery by a ſtrange name of the thing demanded (*B. Averments* 42.)

42.) as if a *Precipe quod redd.* be brought of the Mannor of B. or the like, the Tenant pleads a Fine, Recovery, or the like, of the Mannor of G. he ought to aver that the one and the other, are one and the fame Mannor, not divers : contrary, if he pleads a Fine, or recovery *de predict. Manerio de* B. for this word (*predict.*) is in effect an averment that all is one. (*B. Pleadings* 143.)

And where a man pleads a Recovery by a ftrange name of the parties, he ought to aver that the firft perfon, and this perfon, are all one, and not divers. Otherwife B. feems where he pleads it by this word *predict.* 33. *H.* 8. B. *Averments* 24.

Twas faid for Law, That an averment is not neceffary in an avowry. *viz. & hoc. parat eft verificare;* for tis in lieu of a Declaration ; and the avowant is actor. 3 *M.* 1. B. *averment* 81.

21. E. 4. 52.

3. M. 1. Com. 150.

3. M. 1. Com. 163. 10. Eliz. ibid. 342.

Avowry.

Lord and Tenant by Fealty & 3 pence Rent, the Lord dies, his wife is endowed of the Seigniory ; fhe may diftrain for 1 peny, & the Heir for 2 pence, & fo now the Land is charged with two diftreffes, where it was charged but with one before : but this is not inconvenient : for he fhall pay no more Rent then before. The fame Law where the Lordfhip is divided by partition, between Heirs Females, and the like. 24. *H.* 8. B. *Diftreffe* 59. *Avowry* 139.

If two Copartners make partition, and give notice to the Lord, he ought to make feveral avowries. And if a man fell his land by Deed indented, inrolled within the half year according to the Statute, the avowry is not changed, *&c.* without notice, no more then upon a Fine. Yet B. doubts of a

27. H. 8. c. 10.

Perk 131. 39. H. 6. 25. by Prifot.

D D   *Conufans*

Conufans de Droit com. Ceo. &c. but if a man recover againſt the Tenant, or if the Tenant is defeiſed, the diſſeiſor dies feiſed, and his heir is in by diſcent, ſo that the entry of the diſſeiſee is taken away, the avowry ſhall be changed without notice.   The ſame

law, if the Tenant make a Feoffment, and dies, the Lord ſhall change his avowry without notice ; for nothing is diſcended to the heir of the Feoffor. And where notice is neceſſary, it ſhall be done upon the Land holden, with tender of the arrearages ; for otherwiſe the Lord ſhall loſe his arrearages, if he

avows or accepts ſervice of the Feoffee, *&c.* before the arrearages paid, *Ideo caveatur inde.* 29. *H.* 8. *B. avowry* 111. 146.

In a Replevin, if the Defendant avows becauſe that A. was Lord, and was feiſed by the hands of B. then Tenant, *&c.* of ſuch ſerviſes, he may con-vey the eſtate of the ſaid B. in the Tenancy to the

Plaintiff in the Replevin, by a *que eſtate,* without ſhewing how, but he cannot convey to himſelf of the ſaid A. in the Seigniory by a *que eſtate,* without ſhewing how ; for the Seigniory is there in demand, and not the Tenancy. 34. *H.* 8. *B. avowry* 7. *que eſtate* 2. the end.

Note, That he which avows upon the Land, as within his Fee or Seigniory, by the Statute ſhall aleadge a ſeiſen, as in other avowry ; and then ſhall conclude his avowry upon the land, as within his Fee and Seigniory: and in ſuch avowry, every Plaintiff in the Replevin (be he Termor or other) may have every anſwer to the avowry ; as to tra-verſe the Seiſen, the Tenure, and the like, which are a good anſwer in an avowry : or plead a releaſe, or the like, as Tenant of the Freehold ſhall, though he be a ſtranger to the avowry ; for ſuch avowry is

not

not made upon any perſon certain ; therefore every
one is a ſtranger to this avowry : and ſo the Plaintiff may have every anſwer which is ſufficient 34.
H. 8. *B. Avowry* 113.

Twas agreed that to ſay, That the place where,
&c. is 4. acres, which is, and was the time of the
caption his Freehold, for which he diſtrained, and
took the beaſts for dammage Feaſent, was a good
avowrie. 4. *E.* 6. *B. avowrie* 122. Wimbiſhes Caſe, Time H. 8. Com. 21. H. 7. 12. 21. E. 4. 5. Com. 269.

'Twas holden by the Juſtices of both Benches,
That where a man holds by Rent and Knights ſervice, and the Lord and his anceſtors have been
alwaies ſeiſed of the Rent, but not of the homage,
eſcuage, nor of ward, yet if a ward falls, he ſhall
have the Wardſhip of the heir, for the ſeiſen of the
rent ſuffices to be ſeiſed of the Tenure, as to this
purpoſe, yet otherwiſe B. ſeems to make avowry.
7. *E.* 6. *B. avowrie.* 96. the end. Ward, 69. See 6. E. 6. Tit. Ward.

Note, That 'twas agreed that at this day by the
limitation of 32. *H.* 8. the avowry ſhall be made
generally, as was uſed before : and if there were not
ſeiſin after this limitation, then the Plaintiff in bar
of the avowry may alleage it, and traverſe the ſeiſin
after the limitation (*B. avowry* 107.) Alſo where a
man brings an action real, or mixt ; or makes
avowry, or Conuſance, and iſſue is taken upon the
ſeiſin *infra tempus Statuti,* and tis found againſt the
Demandant, Plaintiff, or Avowant ; this is peremptory by the ſame Statute. 1. *M.* 1. *B. Peremptory*
78. 32. H. 8. c. 3. Limitation 3.

Averment is not neceſſary in an Avowry. See
Tit. *Averment.*

Barre.

Barre.

WHERE a Fine with Proclamation, or a Recovery ſhall bar an eſtate tail; where not, and where the Reverſion is in the King, with other good matter concerning Fines. See Tit. *aſſurances.*

Baſtardie.

Note, That twas taken by the Commons houſe of Parliament, if a man marry his Coſin within the degrees of Marriage, who have iſſue, and are divorced in their lives, by this the eſpouſals are avoided, and the iſſue is a Baſtard. Otherwiſe, if the one die before divorce, there divorce had after ſhal not make the iſſue a baſtard; for the eſpouſals are determined by death before, and not by the divorce. And a dead perſon cannot bring in his proofs; for divorce after the death of the parties, is but *ex officio*, to inquire *de peccatis*, for a dead perſon cannot be cited nor ſummoned to it. 24 *H.* 8. *B. baſtardie.* 44. *D'arraignement* 11.

[margin: 39. E. 3. 31. by Thorp.]

Battel.

Tis ſaid that if an appeal of Murther be brought in the *Kings Bench*, the Defendant joyns battel, it ſhall be before the Juſtices of the *Kings Bench*, and not before the Conſtable, and Marſhal. 5. *M.* 1. *B. battail.* the end 16.

Bill.

Bill.

'Twas faid, That a *Premunire* fhall be maintainable by Bil in the *Kings Bench*, though that the party be not *in cuftodia marefcalli.* (*B. Bill.* 1.) And 'twas common that many Clerks were compelled to anfwer to bills there, who were not *in Cuftodia marefcalli.* 22. *H.* 8. *B. Premunire* 1.

27. H. 6. 5. econtra.

Cerciorari.

'TWAS agreed in *Chancery*, That there is no *Certiorari* in the *Regifter* to remove a Record out of a Court into the *Common Bench* immediatly, but it fhall be certified in the *Chancery* by Surmife, then to be fent into the *Common Bench* by *Mittimus.* And indi&ments may be removed out of the Countrey by *Cerciorari* to the Chancery, and may be fent to the Juftices of the *Kings Bench* by *Mittimus*, and then they fhall proceed upon it. 36. *H.* 8. *B. Certiorari* 20. the end.

44. E. 3. 28. accord.

Certificate of the Bifhop.

'Twas holden that if the Bifhop certifies that fuch a perfon paid not his Tenths, according to the form of the Statute, which wills, That *ipfo fa&o*, the Benefice fhall be void ; that in this cafe a man fhall not have an averment contrary to the certificate. *Time H.* 8. *B. Certificate devefque* 31. the end.

Time E. 6. accords 26. H. 8. c.

Challenge.

Note by the *Exchequer*, and both *Benches*, where the parties are at iffue in a plea of land, where the

land

Time E. 6. accord.

land lies in three or four hundreds, there if the Juror hath land in any of the hundreds, or dwells in any of the hundreds, it fuffices. 4. *M.* 1. b. *Challenge* 216.

In Treafon tis a good challenge to witneffes, to fay that he was one of his accufers (b. *Corone* 219.)

See Coke upon Litt.

And note, that by the Statute of 33. *H.* 8. a peremptory challenge is oufted in cafe of high Treafon: yet by the faid Statute *Queen Mary*, tis enacted, That all tryals of Treafon fhall be according to the order of the Common Law, and not otherwife. And therefore it feems that he may have a challenge peremptory, as at Common Law. S. 35. Jurors. 4. *M.* 1. B. *Challenge* 217. *Trials* 151. the end.

Charge.

Where a Grant of the Bifhop, or charge by him, with the affent of the Dean and Chapter, fhall binde the fucceffor, and where not? See Tit. *Confirmation*.

Charters of Pardon.

Note that thefe words (executiome eorundem) are neceffary, 6. E. 4. 4. by Choke. See my Lord Coke.

Note, if a man be attainted of murther, or Felony by Outlawry or otherwife, and the King pardons him all Felonies, Murthers, and Executions *eorundem*, and Outlawries, and Waivings; and *Sectam pacis*. And a pardon and releafe of all Forfeitures of Lands and Tenements; and of Goods and Chattels, fhall ferve but for the life; and for the land, if no Office be thereof found. But it fhall not ferve for the goods without reftitution or gift. For the King is intitled to them by the Outlawry, without Office: but the King is not intituled to the Land, till Office found.

See 30. H. 8. after.

And if an Office be found after, yet the pardon fhall ferve; for it fhall have relation

to

to the judgement, and then the mean pardon ferves well; contrary, where an Office is found before the pardon granted; for then the King is feifed by the Office, and there a releafe or pardon cannot give it; but there ought to be a Gift or Grant. 29. *H*. 8. *B. Charters of Pardon* 52.

Note, if alienation without licence be pardoned by Act of Parliament, the party may enter without *Oufter l'main,* or *amoveas manum.* Otherwife by another pardon, by letters Pattents. 29. *H.* 8. *B. Charters of Pardon* 53.

If intrufion by the heir, *poft mortem anteceforis* be found by Office, and after the King pardons it by act of Parliament, or by letters Pattents, yet the heir fhall fue Livery: for this is not reftored to him by a pardon: but if the pardon were granted before Office found, and at the making of the pardon, the heir is of full age, he fhall retain the land, and the Office found after the pardon fhall not hurt him. 30. *H.* 8. *B. Charters of Pardon* 54.

Filpot 16. E. 4. 1. accord. See 29. H. 8. before & 33. H. 8. Tit. Intrufion.

Chattels.

If Leffee for years devife his Term, or other his Chattel or Goods, by Teftament, to one for term of his life, the Remainder over to another, and dies, and the Devifee enters, and aliens not the Term, nor gives, or fels the Chattel, and dies, there he in Remainder fhall have it: but if the firft Devifee had aliened, given, or fold it, there he in the Remainder had been without remedie for it (*B. Chattels* 23. *Done* 57.) And fo B. feems if they be forfeit in his life, he in remainder hath no remedy. 33. *H.* 8. *B. Done.* 57. the end.

See Time H. 8. Tit. devife & Cokes Rep.

Choice

Chofe in Action.
Thing in Action.

See 32. H. 8.
after, & Cokes
Rep. 4. M. 1.
Com. 173.

Note, where the Statute of 31. *H.* 8. gives to the King the poffeffions of Abbies, and all rights of Entries, Actions, Conditions, and the like, which the Abbies might have had ; and that he fhall be in poffeffion without office, and that he fhall be adjudged in actual and real poffeffion of them, in fuch plight and fort as they were at the time of making of the Statute. Yet if an *Abbot* were diffeifed of 4 acres of land, the King cannot grant it over before entry made by him in it, becaufe tis a thing in action real, and not like to a thing in action perfonal or mixt, as debt ward, and the like, by fome. And fome *è contra*, by reafon of thefe words, *That the King fhall be in poffeffion.* Yet by B. this feems, that he fhall be in fuch poffeffion as the *Abbot* was. S. of a thing of which the *Abbot* had poffeffion, the King hath of this actual poffeffion : & of fuch of which the *Abbot* had but a caufe of entry, or right in action ; of thefe the King fhall be vefted of a Title of Entry ; and Title of action. But the thing to which he hath fuch caufe of entry, or of action, is not for this in him in poffeffion : and therefore cannot pafs from the King by general words ; but *B.* feems, if the King recites the difeifen, and how the right and action thereof is given to him by the Statute, and grants it fpecially that tis good. 33. *H.* 8. B. *Chofe in Action* 14.

See 33. H. 8.
before, 2. H. 7.
8. by Huffey.
See Cokes Rep.

'Twas faid for Law, That the King may grant a thing in action, which is perfonal ; as debt, and dammages, and the like, or a thing mixt ; as the ward of body : but not a thing real, as an action of land,

land, and the like, as Rights, Entries, Actions, and
the like, which *Abbots* might have. (And that the
King fhall have thefe by the Statute of diffolution
of *Abbies.* 31. *H.* 8.) Thefe things in action the
King cannot grant. Yet by B. fee if there be not
words in this Statute, to put the King in poffeffion,
though the *Abbot* were put to his action. 33. *H.* 8.
B. *Pattents* 98.

Clergy.

No man fhall have his Clergy but where his life
is in jeopardie : and therefore not in petty larceny.
And the *Bifhop* is Ordinary : all *Priefts*, *Abbots*, and
others inferior to him, which demand Clergy, or have
Clergy : and if the *Bifhop* hath his Clergy, the
Metropolitan fhall keep him, as his Ordinary : and
if the Metropolitan offend, and hath his Clergy, the
King fhall have him and keep him : the fame is of
Laps. *Reading B. Clergy* 19. *Corone* 183.

Note, That at this day *Bigamus* fhall have his
Clergy by the Statute : but a man attainted of Herefie fhall not : otherwife of a man excommunicated :
and a *Jew*, nor *Turk* fhall not have their Clergy :
and a Greek and Roman, who ufe not our letters
fhall have their Clergy, and fhall ftay till a book of
letters of their countrey comes. (*B. Clergie* 20.)

1. E. 6. c. 12.
Clergy 21.

And if a man who is *captus oculis* prayes his
Clergy, he fhall have it if he can fpeak latine con-
gruoufly. *Quære*, for he cannot be a Prieft, nor he
cannot Minifter. *Cafus B. clergie* 21.

A Baftard fhall have his Clergy ; for he may be
a Prieft by licence. *Cafus B. clergie* 22.

Colour.

Colour.

See Cokes
Book.

Note, That Colour ought to be matter in law, or doubtful to the lay people; and ſhall be given to the Plaintiff, and not to one who is mean in the conveyance: and ſhall not be given to a ſtranger who infeoffed the Plaintiff: nor ſhall be given to the Defendant: and ſhall not be given by a poſſeſſion determined. S. where it appears in the pleading, that the poſſeſſion is determined: but ſhall be given by an eſtate defeated: and where the Defendant bindes the right of the Plaintiff by Feoffment with Warranty, Releaſe, Fine, Recovery, Diſſeiſin, and Reentry, and the like, there needs not any colour. And he which claims no property in the thing, but takes it as a diſtreſs, and the like, ſhall not give colour. Colour ſhall not be given but upon a plea in bar. *B. colour* 64. Colour ſhall not be given but by him, by whom you commence your Title, and not by a mean in the conveyance. He which pleads to the Writ, ſhall not give Colour. It behoves that colour be ſuch, ſo that if it be true, that of ſuch poſſeſſion, the Plaintiff or Demandant may have their action. He which juſtifies as ſervant, and conveys Title to his Maſter, ſhall give colour: colour by poſſeſſion in law, is good. *Regula.*

Commiſſion.

35. H. 8. accord. See after.
See Tit. Officer.

Note, for Law, That where a Commiſſion of the peace iſſues to I. N. and others; and after I. N. is made Knight, yet the Commiſſion remains for him. (Yet *Anno primo, E.* 6. cap. 7. is a Statute made, That making of the Plaintiff Knight, ſhall not abate
the

the action, nor the Commiſſion in which ſuch perſon is named.)

And where a man learned in the ſame Law is put in Commiſſion, and after is made Serjeant at Law, yet he remains in authority by the ſame Commiſſion. And when a Juſtice of the Bench is made Knight, yet he remains Juſtice, and this Commiſſion ſhall ſerve him. 36. *H.* 8. *B. Commiſſions* 22.

Note, by comming of a Commiſſion of *Oyer* and *Terminer*, the Commiſſion of Gaole Delivery is not determined; for the one ſtands with the other. Otherwiſe, where the one Commiſſion is contrary to the other.   See Tit. Officer.

As of a Commiſſion of the Peace where there is a former Commiſſion thereof to others, this is contrary that every of them ſhould be Commiſſioners of one and the ſame thing, and both in force. And the Commiſſion of Gaole Delivery, is onely to deliver the Gaole. Commiſſion of *Oyer* and *Terminer*, hath words *ad inquirendum audiendum, & determinandum.* But moſt commonly the Juſtices of Gaol delivery are alſo in the Commiſſion of the Peace, and by this they indict, and after deliver the Gaol as well of them, as of others.

And note, That the Juſtices of *Oyer* and *Terminer*, cannot by this authority arraign no Priſoners, but thoſe which are indicted before them: but contrary, if they have Commiſſion of Gaol delivery alſo, for theſe both may be executed *ſimul & ſemel* 3. *M.* 1. *B. Commiſſion* 24.

If a Juſtice of the Common Bench be made Juſtice of the Kings Bench, though that it be intended but *Pro illa vice:* as twas of Sir *James Dier* this year; yet this ſhall determine his patent of the Common Bench, though he ſurrenders the Pattent of the

Kings

Kings Bench the next day : for the Kings Bench is the higheſt Court : and if the Common Bench erre, this ſhall be controlled by the Kings Bench. And therefore a man cannot be Judge of the one Bench, and the other together to reverſe his own judgement. And as often as a Juſtice of the Common Bench, is made Juſtice of the Kings Bench (as it hath been often ſeen) the Commiſſion of the Common Bench by this is determined : for the one Court is within the controlment of the other : but a man may be a Juſtice of the Common Bench, & chief Baron of the *Exchequer* together, & may be Juſtice of the Common Bench, & Juſtice in *Oyer*, and *Terminer*, or of Gaol delivery together : for none of theſe Courts hath controlment of the other. And if an Incumbent of a Benefice be made a Biſhop, the firſt Benefice is void : for he which hath the office of Soveraignty, cannot have the office of inferiour, by ſome of the Juſtices. Yet B. doubts ; for a Juſtice *de banco regis*, may be a Juſtice in *Oyer*, or of *Oyer* and *Terminer*, or of Peace, or of Gaol delivery ; and yet if they err in their pleas in the *Oyer*, or *Oyer* and *Terminer*, or in their Proces, or outlawry before Juſtice of Peace, Writ of Error lies thereof before the King in his Bench. But the Pleas in the *Kings Bench* are holden *coram rege ubicunque fuerit in Anglia,* and ſo the *Kings Bench*, is a Court removable : and by the Statute the *Common Pleas teneatur in loco certo*, then tis contrary of the Oath of the Juſtice of the one Court, and the other ; for the one is certain, and the other incertain. 5. *M*. 1. *B. Commiſſions* 25.

Where a Juſtice of Peace is made Knight, or takes other dignity, yet his authority ſhall remain. And ſo of a Juſtice of the *Common Bench* made Knight, his Commiſſion remains in force. 1. *E.* 6. c. 7. *B. Commiſſion* 4.   If

---

The ſame admitted. 1. H. 7. 10.

D. S. 127. 29. H. 8. 116. Petty Br. See before.

Magna-Charta. c. 11. Raſt. Common-Pleas. 1.

36. H. 8. accord. before. Marrow Serjeant in the Inner-Temple upon the Stat. of Peace.

If the King grant to a Major and Commonalty, and their fucceffors to be Juftices of Peace in their Town, and after makes a Commiffion of the Peace to another there, yet the firft Commiffion fhall remain in force ; becaufe that tis a grant to them, and their fucceffors, and fo not revocable as a Commiffion is. (*B.* Commiffion 5.)

If a new Commiffion of the Peace be proclaimed, or read in full County, the ancient Commiffion of the Peace is determined. And all the Juftices ought to take notice, and if they fit by the ancient Commiffion, all they do is void. And if a Commiffion be directed to *A.* and *B.* who are not in *rerum natura*, or are dead at the time of the Tefte, *&c.* The ancient Commiffion remains in Force, for this new Commiffion is void.

If a Commiffion be directed to N. *pro hac vice*, this fhall determine the ancient Commiffion of thefe matters. And yet the new Commiffioners cannot fit but *Vnica vice.* (*B. Commiffion* 6.) If a commiffion be directed to hear and determine Felonies, this fhall determine the ancient commiffion of the Peace, as to Felonies, but not as to the Peace ; and fo determined in part, in part not, (*B. Commiffion* 7.) commiffion in *Eyer* is made to the county of N. and Proclamationt here, this determines the Commiffion of the Peace. (*B. Commiffion* 8.) Commiffion of the Peace is in the county of N. and the *Kings Bench* comes there, this fhall not determine the Commiffion of the Peace : contrary, if they make Proclamation of the coming of the *Kings Bench* (*B. commiffion* 9.) Commiffion of the peace is made to 4. in the County of N. and after the King makes I. S. Juftice of Peace there for term of his life ; the firft Commiffion is determined. (*B. Commiffion* 10.)

If

1. E. 6. c. 7.
See after
1. E. 6. Tit.
Corone.

If Juſtices ſit by Commiſſion, and do not adjourn it, the Commiſſion is determined. And ſee a Statute where new Commiſſioners of Gaol delivery, may ſit upon the Records of the ancient Commiſſion of the Gaol, which is determined.

And when a Commiſſion of *Oyer* and *Terminer* is determined, the Records of that ſhall be ſent into the *Kings Bench;* but Records of the Juſtices of Gaol delivery, ſhall remain with the *Cuſtos rotulorum* of the County. And the next Juſtices of Gaol delivery ſhall proceed upon them, upon judgement of death by the ſaid Statute. *Quære,* if they ſhould proceed by the words to allowance of Clergie, or Sanctuary, it ſeems ſo, by the equity. *B. Commiſ-ſions* 11.

Conditions.

See after
33. H. 8. &
37. H. 8.

Debt upon an Obligation, with a condition to perform all covenants contained in certain Indentures; the defendant cannot plead the condition, and reherſe the covenants, and ſay generally that he hath performed all the covenants, without ſhewing how, by the *Prothonotaries,* 20. *H.* 8. *B. conditions* 2.

If a man deviſe 20.*l.* to W. S. to be paid in four years after his death, and dies, and after the Deviſee dies within the four years, yet the Executor of the Deviſee ſhall have the Money, or the reſt of it by ſuit before the Ordinary in the court Spiritual; for tis a duty by the Teſtament, or deviſe. 24. *H.* 8. *B. Deviſe* 27. 45. *conditions* 187.

Fineux agrees,
11. H. 7. 12. &
12, H. 7. 18.

By *Fitz.* if a man before the Statute of Tenures had made a gift of Land to one in Fee, for to repair a Bridge, or for to keep ſuch a caſtle, or for to marry yearly a poor virgine of *S.* this is a Tenure, and not a condition; and the Donor may diftrain, and make avowrie.

But if a woman give land to a man for to marry her, this is a condition in effect, and no Tenure, which no bodie denied. 24. *H.* 8. *B. condition* 188. *tenures* 53.

14. H. 8. 10. by Brudnel Fitz. 205.

If a man Mortgage his land to W. N. upon condition that if the Mortgager, and I. S. repay 100 l. by *fuch* a day, that he *fhall* re-enter, and he dies before the day, but I. S. paies by the day, the condition is performed; and this by reafon of the death of the Mortgager, notwithftanding that the payment were in the copulative; otherwife, if it were not in the cafe of death, 30. *H.* 8. *B. conditions* 109.

Accord. 15. H. 7. 2. & 13.

By many, if a man make a Feoffment in Fee, *ad intentionem,* to perform his will, this is no condition, but a Declaration of the purpofe and will of the Feoffer, and the heir cannot enter for *non performance.* 31. *H.* 8. *B. conditions.* 191.

D. S. 123. See 27. H. 8. 15. by Knightly.

If a man be bound in a bond to pay 20 l. the Obligor in whofe difcharge the condition goes, ought to be ready at the place, *&c.* all the day, and the Obligee may come any time of the day. 32. *H.* 8. *B. conditions* 192.

6. H. 7. by Bryan Cont.

A man gives land in Tail, or Leafes it for life, or for years, rendring rent, with a condition of re-entry for default of payment, there if he Leafes part of the land to the Donor, or Leffor, or if the Donor or Leffor enter in part of the land, he cannot re-enter for the rent arrear after; for the condition is wholly *fufpended*; for a condition cannot be apportioned nor divided. 33. *H.* 8. *B. Extinguifhment* 49. *conditions* 193.

Perk. 163. C. See Cokes Rep. Knights cafe. Lillingftons. c. Damports. c.

Debt upon an obligation, to perform all covenants contained in certain Indentures, tis no plea that he

hath

20 H. 8. 9.
26. H. 8. 5.
by Engelf. 6. E.
4. 5. by Rogers.
27. H. 8. 1. 27.
See before
20. H. 8. Plead-
ing of Cove-
nants per-
formed.

hath performed all the covenants generally, S. *Quod performavit omnes & fingulas conventiones in indentura pred. fpecificat. ex parte fua perimplend.* if they be in the affirmative; but muſt ſhew in certain in every point how he hath performed them, (*B. conditions* 198. *covenant* 35.) And where in a Covenant the Defendant ſaies, that the covenants are that he ſhall pay 10 l. by ſuch a day, and infeoff him by the ſame day *quas quidem conventiones idem defenfor bene perimplevit,* this is no good plea; for he muſt ſhew in certain how he hath performed it. 33. *H.* 8. *B. covenants* 35. *the end.*

See Cokes Rep.

Note for Law, That *Provifo femper* put on the part of the Leſſee upon the words of *Habendum,* makes a condition; otherwiſe of a *Provifo* of the part of the Leſſor, as tis covenanted in the Indenture, That the Leſſee ſhall make the reparations; *Provifo femper,* That the Leſſor ſhall finde the great Timber, this is no condition.

Nor by ſome tis no condition when it comes amongſt other covenants on the part of the Leſſee, as tis covenanted after the *Habendum,* and after the *Reddendum,* That the Leſſee ſhall ſcowre the ditches, or the like: *Provifo femper,* That the Leſſee ſhall carry the Dung from it to ſuch a field; this is no condition to forfeit the Leaſe for not doing of it: contrary, if ſuch *provifo* be put imediately after the *habendum,* which makes the eſtate; or after the *red-dendum. Quære,* by *B. conditions* 195. 35 *H.* 8.

Quære.

If a man Mortgage his land upon defeiſance of repayment to re-enter, and the bargain to be void: and the vendee Leaſes the Land to the vendor for ten years by Indenture of defeiſance; and further grants to him, That if he paies 100 l. *infra terminum dict.* 10. *annorum,* that then the ſale ſhall be void,

void, &c. and the Leffee furrenders the Term, yet
the tender of the 100 l. is good within the ten years;
becaufe that the ten years is certain, though the
leafe is furrendred or forfeited. Otherwife, if it were
to repay *infra terminum predict.* without thefe words,
ten years; for in the one cafe the Term, S. the Leafe
is the limitation of payment, and in the other cafe
the ten years, by *Whorewood* in his Reading in the
Lent. (*B. conditions* 203. *Defeafans* 18.) The fame
law if B. holds certain land for term of ten years of
A. and tis covenanted betwixt A. and B. That if
B. pay 100 l. to A. within the faid ten years, that
then he fhall be feifed to the ufe of B. in Fee, and
B. furrenders his term to A. and after payes him
100 l. within the ten years, there B. fhall have Fee;
for the years are certain: otherwife, where tis covenanted, That if he payes 100 l. *infra terminum pre-*
dict. and he furrenders, and after payes the 100 l.
this is nothing worth; for the Term is determined:
but in the other cafe the ten years remain, notwithftanding the furrender. 35. *H.* 8. *B. Expofition,* 44.

Twas holden clear in the *Kings Bench* that where
M. and other two are bound to ftand to the award
of I. N. fo that it be made and delivered by the
Arbitrators in writing to the parties before Michaelmas, they make the award, and deliver it to one by
Michaelmas, and cannot finde the other by the day,
this fhall not binde the others to whom twas not
delivered. And the reafon B. feems; becaufe that
in this cafe they might have made 3 parties, and
have delivered to every party one. 37. *H.* 8. *B.*
conditions 46. the end.

Tis faid by the Court in the Kings Bench: in
Debt upon an obligation to keep without dammage,
S. harmlefs, where the Defend. pleads that he hath

F F faved

See my Lord Coke Ched-
dingtons. c.

See Coke lib. 8.
97. 98. Bafpoles
cafe Dyer fol.
216. b. See 38.
H. 8. after. 4.
H. 7. 12. by
Keble. 22. E. 4.
43. by Catefby
35. H. 6. 11.
per cur. 40. E.
3. 20. M. 35.
H. 8. B. cond.
18. the end 38.

H. 8. 31. 6. H. 7.6. by Huffey. Admitted 18. E. 4. 27. See before Jay accords 11. H. 7. 17. 34. H. 6. 18. by Prifot. 19. E. 4. 1. by Catefby. See before 37. H. 8.

faved him harmlefs, tis no plea without fhewing how; for he which pleads a difcharge, or faving harmlefs, ought to plead it certain when he pleads in the affirmative. Otherwife, where he pleads in the negative; for if the Plaintiff be not dempnified, he may plead *quod non damnificatus eft* generally. 37. *H.* 8. *B. conditions* 16. 198. *in finibus.*

If a man be bound in an Obligation to pay 10*l.* to the obligee at *Paris* beyond Sea, at a certain day, if the Obligor pay at another place, and the fame day in *England*, and the other accepts it, tis good clearly. (*B. conditions* 206.) And tis faid in debt upon an obligation to acquit & fave without damage, *quod non damnificatus eft*, is a good plea, for tis in the negative, and therefore good without fhewing how, but where he pleads, that he hath kept him without dammage in the affirmative, he fhall fhew how. 38. *H.* 8. *B. Conditions.* 93. the end.

21. H. 7. 12. cont. by Frowick. 6. E. 6. Com. 135. 1. M. 1. Com. 142. See Coke Penants cafe.

If a man let land for term of life upon condition, that if he doth not go to *Rome* by fuch a day, that his eftate fhall be void, and the leffor grants the reverfion over, the Tenant attorns, and after he doth not go, yet tis not void till entrie, by *Bromley* chief Juftice: 2. *M.* 1. *B. Conditions.* 245. the end.

Confefs, and avoid.

Replevin, the defendant faid that *B.* was feifed in fee and leafed to *E.* for 40 years, which *E.* granted his intereft to the defendant. 38 *H.* 8. by which he was poffeffed, and diftrained for damage feafant, the plaintiff faid that the fame *E.* 28. *H.* 8. granted his intereft to him, he fhall not traverfe the Grant. 38. for hee hath confeffed and avoided it, by the eldeft grant obtained. 2. *E.* 6. *B. Confefs and avoid.* 65.

Con-

Confirmation.

Bifhop charges, or grants an office with the affent of the Deane and Chapter, and dyes, this is worth nothing, by fome, for it ought to be confirmed by the Dean and Chapter ; And this fell out in the grant of the Stewardfhip of the Bifhop of *London,* betwixt *Aldred Fitzjames,* and *John Edmunds* of the middle Temple, where the Bifhop granted the Stewardfhip of his lands to *A. F.* by the affent of the Dean and Chapter, and died, by which the grantee loft the office, as tis faid, becaufe the Dean and Chapter had not confirmed it, yet more was in the grant of the Bifhop, as Mifnofmer, and the like, for the faid *A. F.* was named *Etheldredus,* where it fhould be *Aldredus,* and fo he was mifnamed. Alfo there was a default in the Seale (*B. Charge* 58. *Confirmation.* 30.) And alfo the Deed was *Quod figillum noftrum appofuimus,* which may bee referred to the Bifhop onely, and not to the Bifhop, Dean and Chapter: And therefore by more, to this day the grant was avoided for thefe caufes, and not for the other caufe ; and fo a grant with affent of the Dean and Chapter, with all perfections is good. 33. *H.* 8. *B.* Confirmation. 30. the end.

If the bifhop be patron, and the parfon makes a leafe or grant by deed, there the Bifhop patron, and the ordinary, and the dean and chapter ought to confirm, if the grant or leafe fhall be fure ; otherwife where a lay man is patron in fee, and he and the ordinary confirmes, this fuffices without the dean and chapter, for in the firft cafe, the Bifhop patron hath an intereft in inheritance to the Bifhoprick. But in the other cafe, he hath but a judicial power, therefore

Cafus Hill for the Parfonage & glebe of Stoke, fuper Derne in Com. Salop. where the Parfon, Patron, Dean & Chapter made the affurance B. Charg 40. the end.

therefore it fuffices that he who hath the power at the time, &c. confirmes, for tis a judicial act. But in the other cafe, it bindes the inheritance, which he hath in *jure Ecclefiæ* which he cannot do againft his fuccefſor, without confirmation by the dean and chapter. (33. *H.* 8. *B. Confirmation.* 21. *Charge.* 40. *Leafes.* 64.) *Patet hic* that the patron ought to have a fee fimple, and this *juri proprio*, becaufe of the dean and chapter, to be joyned with the Bifhop, where he is patron. *B. Charge* 40.

See Tit. Leafes.

Note, that if the King for him and his heires grants *Catallafelonum & fugitivorum*, or the like, which lie in grant, and dies, the grantee needs no confirmation of the new King. But if it be a fair, or market, or the like, and tis abufed or mifufed, as it may be, or if it be a judicial, or minifterial office or power, as to be a Juftice of peace, Efcheator, or the like, there he ought to have a confirmation of the new King (*B. Confirmation.* 19. & 29.) yet *B.* feems that the grant of a thing which lies in grant, is good clearly, without thefe words, for him and his heires; But of warranty, covenant, Annuity, or the like, there he ought to make it for him and his heirs. 33. *H.* 8. *B. Confirmation.* 19.

1. R. 3. 4. See Cokes Rep.

Confcience.

If a man buyes land, and the vendor executes an eftate to the vendee, *Habendum fibi imperpetuum*, without words of heires, where the intent of the bargain is to pafs a fee fimple, and the vender upon requeft refufes to make other affurance, there lies a writ of *Subpœna.* 32. *H.* 8. *B. Confcience* 25.

See Time. H. 8. after. 7. & 8. E. Com. 302.

Audely, Chancellor of *England* held clearly that if a man fell his land before the Statute of Ufes, this fhall

See 4. E. 6. Tit. Eftates. & 6. E.

shall change the ufe of the fee fimple. And the
fame Law of a fale by Indenture, by the Statute of
27. *H.* 8. without words heires. *Time H.* 8. *B.* Confcience. 25. the end.

6. Faits inrolle
27. H. 8. cap.
16. Raft. Inrol-
menta.

Continuances.

Note, that in the common recoveries by fufferance,
for affurances, the Tenant tenders iffue, the demandant may imparle to a day in the fame terme,
and then the Tenant is demandant, and retracts, and
judgement is given for the demand : againft him, and
after the Tenant over in value upon the vouchee,
&c. Regula. 22. *H.* 7. *B. Continuances* 69.

Contract.

A man fells a leafe of land, and certain cloath for
10*l.* the contract is intire, and if the one of thefe
were by defeafible Title, yet the vendor fhall have
the intire fumme, though the one part were devefted
from the vendee, for contract cannot be fevered. 24.
H. 8. *B. Contract.* 35.

See 30. H. 8.
Tit. Apportion-
ment. & 12. H.
8. 18.

If a man be indebted to me upon contract, and
after makes to me an obligation for the fame debt,
the contract by this is determined, for in debt upon
the contract, tis a good plea, that he hath an obligation for the fame debt. So if the obligation be
made for parcell of the contract, which is intire.
3. *H.* 4. 17. But if a ftranger makes an obligation
to me, for the fame debt, yet the contract remains,
becaufe that tis by another perfon, and both are now
debtors. 29 *H.* 8. *B. Contract* 29.

See 33. H. 8.
Tit. Prefcrip-
tion. 18. H. 7.
21. 24. Fitz.
121. M. 9. E.
4. 25. by Genny
& Choke 50.
1. H. 6. 8. by
Babing. 22. H.
6. 56. by
Choke. 20.
H. 6. 21. by
Newton 28. H.
6. 4. 21. H. 7.
5. by Cutler.

Corone,

Corone, Crown.

Note, if a felon hath a pardon to plead, and
pleads not guilty, he ſhall loſe the advantage of his
pardon, and ſhall not plead it after.   18 *H.* 8. *B.
Corone.* 199.

A man pleads
M. 3. M. 1.
cont. 11. H. 4.
41. by Huls &
Firwith accord.
St. 34. C. ſee 9.
E. 4. 28. by
Neele.

Note, that at the Seſſions at Newgate, a man
was judged to be hanged, and delivered to the
Sheriff to make execution, and after eſcapes, and
flees to the Church : and had the priviledg of it.
22. *H.* 8. *B. Corone.* 110. the end.

Note, twas holden by all in the houſe of Parliament, that if a man kill one who is attainted by
Premunire, this is no felony, for he is out of the
protection of the King, which is, as if he were out
of the Kingdom, and power of the King.   Otherwiſe of him who is attainted of felony, and judged
to death, the killing of him is felony.   24. *H.* 8. *B.
Corone.* 196.

St. 13. D. See
Coke upon Lit.
S. D. S. 134.
35. H. 6. 58.
St. 13. C.
St. 198. C. 23.
Aff. 2.

Tis ſaid, where a woman is arraigned, and adjudged to be hanged, or burnt, according to the
Crime, and becauſe that ſhe is with childe, Execution is reſpited untill ſhee bee delivered, and now
ſhe is with childe again, becauſe that once execution
was ſpared for the ſame cauſe, now execution ſhall
be commanded to be done : and the Gaoler ſhall not
be puniſhed.   28. *H.* 8. *B. Corone.* 97.

12. Aff. 11.

A man ſteals goods in one County, and flees with
them into another, he may be indicted, or appealed
in any of the Counties, for tis felony in every of the
Counties, for felony alters not the property.   34. *H.*
8. *B. Corone.* 170.

4. H. 7. 5. by
Frowick. B.
Corone. 139.
St. 182. C.

Note, that if 12 come for to do robbery, affray,
riot, or the like, which are unlawful acts, one of
them enters into the houſe, and kills a man, or doth
                                                 other

1. M. 1. Com.
98. See Coke.
Lib.

other unlawful act, all the others which came with
him to do the unlawfull act are principals. The
same Law in the case of *Fines* Lord *Dacres*, one
of his company killed a man in hunting in a Forrest,
and the Lord *Dacres* and the other hunters, as *Mantel*; and others were principals, and were all hanged.
34. *H. 8. B. Corone.* 171.

See 33. H. 8.
Tit. Triall.

A man shall not plead that the dead assaulted
him, and in his own defence, &c. but not guilty in
an appeal, and give it in evidence, and murder cannot be justified. See *Tit. Appeal.*

Note, by the Justices, that tis felony to kill a
man in Justing, or where men play at sword and
buckler, and the one kills the other, and the like
notwithstanding the commandement of the King, for
twas against Law. *Time. H. 8 B. Corone.* 228.

11. H. 7. 20.
accord. by
Fineux.

Note, by all the Justices, that if a man be indicted
of felony, in the time of *H.* 8. the King dies, he
shall be arraigned for it in the time of *E.* 6. But
by some this indictment shall be removed by *Cerciorari* from the antient *custos Rotulorum*, and put to
the new commissioners. 1. *E.* 6. *B. Corone.* 177.

1. E. 3. 4. by
Borous.

Note, that Indictments and Records, which are
taken before Justices of *Oyer* and *Terminer*, and
not determined before their commission be ended,
these shall be put into the Kings Bench to arraign
the parties there. *S.* by *Cerciorari* out of the
Chancerie, which shall be to commissioners of *Oyer*
and *Terminer*, and after shall be sent into the
Kings Bench by *Mittimus* (*B. Corone.* 178. *Oyer*
and *Terminer.* 2.) But indictments taken before
Justices of Gaol delivery, and not determined, shall
be delivered to the Clerk of the peace, or shall
remain with the *custos rotulorum* of the County,
where, &c. and when other Justices of Gaol delivery

See 38. H. 8.
Tit. Oyer &
Terminer.
44. E. 3. 43.
accord.

See Tit. Com-
mission the end.

come

1. E. 6. cap. 7. come there, they may proceed upon them upon judgement of death, and this by Statute. And *B.* seems that they ſhall proceed by the equity of the words, to allowance of Clergy or Sanctuary; and Clergy.
Sanctuary. the like. 1. *E.* 6. *B. Corone.* 178.

See Tit. Com-
miſſion the end.
See Cokes Rep. Note, that twas holden, that where a ſtable is near a houſe inheritable, as parcell of the houſe, and a man breaks it by night, to the intent to rob in it, tis felony, though he takes nothing, for tis burglary. 2 *E.* 6. *B. Corone.* 179.

Burglary ſhall not be judged, but where there is breaking of a houſe by night. And by the Juſtices, St. 30. B. 3.
H. 7. 12. by
Juſtices. See
St. 47. H. &
Cokes 4. Book. where the principall and acceſſarie are arraigned, and the principall hath his Clergie, this ſhall not ſerve the acceſſarie, but he ſhall be arraigned and hanged, where both are found guilty. 4. *E.* 6. *B. Corone.* 184.

A man is indicted as acceſſary to a felony, and acquitted, and after is indicted of the ſame felony, as principall, he ſhall be arraigned and hanged, notwithſtanding the acquittal as acceſſary. And ſo was *Thomas Knightly* firſt indicted and arraigned as acceſſary of *I. S.* and acquitted, and after was indicted of the ſame murder as principal, and arraigned of it again. 4. *E.* 6. *B. Corone.* 185.

? A woman took the Church for felony, and abjured the Kingdome. 6. *E.* 6. *B. Corone.* 213.

5. & 6. E. 6.
cap. 11. Note, that 'twas agreed by all the Juſtices at *Serjeants* Inn in *Chancery* Lane 25 *Octob.* 1556. as to the Trial of Treaſon, and miſpriſion of Treaſon, that by the Statutes, 2 accuſers or teſtes ought to be at the indictment, or the ſayings and accuſations in writing under their hands, or the teſtimony of others of the ſame accuſation, which ſhall be read to the Jury at the indictment; and if the accuſers are dead

at

at the time of the indictment, yet it suffices if the Raft. Treafon 23. St. 9. A. accufation be there teftifying it, for then there were two accufers. But for any Treafon *de Anno* 25. *E*. 3. there needs no accufers at the trial, becaufe that 'tis enacted by the Statute of 2. *M*. 1. *cap*. 10. That all trials of Treafons, fhall be by the order of the common Law onely, *& non aliter*. And the common trial by common Law, is by Jurie, and by witnefs, and by no accufers. And the fame Law of Treafon of coyning, that accufers need not at the arraignment, but at the indictment *ut fupra* onely. But for all treafons done by the faid Act of 2. *M*. 1. there ought to be witneffes, or accufers, as well at the indictment, as at the arraignment, according to an Article contained in the faid Statute, in Fine. And for mifprifion of treafon there ought to be wit- Raft. Treafon 18. neffes, or accufers, as well upon the indictment, as upon the arraignment, by the Statute of 1. *E*. 6. *cap*. 12. the end, for the faid Statute of *Q*. *Mary*, doth not reftrain accufers at the trial, but only in cafes of treafon, and not for mifprifion. And twas agreed that petty treafon ought to be tried as high treafon, S. by accufers by indictment; But at the trial there needs not accufers, And at this refolution, were Sir *William Portman* chief Juftice, Mr. *Hare* Mafter of the Rolls, Sir *Robert Brook*, Sir David Brook, Sir *Humfrey Brown*, Sir *John Whiddon*, Sir *Edward Saunders*, Sir *William Stampforde*, and Maf-ter *Dalyfon*, Juftices, *Dyer* Serjant, and *Griffine*, and *Cordell* Attorney and Soliciter. And twas agreed, that Counfellers who give evidence againft Traytors, are not accufers. And by the Civill Law, accufers are as parties, and not witneffes, for witneffes ought to be indifferent, and not come till they are called, but accufers offer themfelves to accufe, for tis a good

G G   challenge

challenge to witnesses, to say, that he was one of his accusers. 4. *M.* 1. *B. Corone.* 219.

St. 116.

'Twas said for Law, that a man cannot abjure for high treason. Quære of petty treason, for tis manifest in a Chronicle in the time of *H.* 6. that a woman that killed her Mistress abjured the Realm. 5. *M.* 1. *B. Corone.* 180. the end.

Manningť. and another were indicted of felony in the high way in the County of *Bedford,* for robbery of one *Edward Keble* Clerk with daggs, & the indictment and the body were removed into the Kings Bench, and there they were arraigned, and pleaded not guilty to the countrey, and were tried. But after a writ was sent with the body into the countrey with *Nisi prius* to trie them in the county of *Bedford.* And this is a common course, so to remove the body and the Record out of the Kings Bench to the countrey again. 4. *M.* 1. *B. Corone.* 230.

Lectura. W. N.
Time. H. 7.

A man takes Church, and the Coroner comes to him, and demands of him for what cause he does it, who said that he would be advised by 40. days before that he would declare his cause, the Coroner may draw him out presently; but if he will confess to him felony, he may remain there by 40 days, before that he abjures. Otherwise where he takes Sanctuary, as *Westm. Knoll,* and the like, for this may hold him for term of life, except in case where a Statute changes it (*B. Corone* 180. *Sanctuary.* 11.) But if he will abjure within the 40 days, the Coroner shall give him a certaine day to doe it. (*B. Corone supra.*) None shall take priviledg of the church, except that he be in danger of his life. (*B. Corone.* 181.) Nor none shall have the priviledg of Sanctuary except he be in *periculo vitæ.* And note that

that Sanctuary cannot have a lawful commencement, }
Nifi pro vita hominis, as for treafon, felony, or the }
like ; and not for debt, therefore where a grant, or
prefcription is to have Sanctuary for debt, tis worth
nothing, for tis againft the Law. But if his body
were in execution, and he efcapes, and comes to a
Sanctuary ordained for fafeguard of the life of a
man, he fhall enjoy it, for by long imprifonment his
life may be in jeopardy. And if the church be
fufpended for bloodfhed, yet he which takes the
church for felony, fhall enjoy it by 40 daies (*B.
Sanctuary fupra.*) There are two manner of Sanc-
tuaries. *S.* private, as *Weftminfter Knoll,* and the
like. And general fanctuaries, as every church (*B.
Corone.* 181. the end.) Abjuration for felony, dif-
charges all felonies done before the abjuration. A
man cannot abjure for petty larceny, but for fuch
felonies for which he fhall fuffer death. *Lecture B.
Corone.* 182.

Note, that thefe words (*Quod pred. vitam &*   See St. 6. C.
membra) in a. Statute, are intended felony, without
the word of felony in it. *Regula* (*B. Corone.* 203.)

Corporations.

Note, that the Juftices of the common bench ac-   1. E. 4. 7.
cords in cafe of a corporation, that known by the   Mark. accord.
one and the other, in a fuite by a name known, is
no plea for the plaintiff, for he ought to acknowledge   21. H. 6. 4. by
his proper name. But if the defendant be named   Newton. See
by the plaintiff by a name known, though the defen-   20. H. 6. 29.
dant be corporate, it fuffices. Yet Quære, if there
be not a diverfity betwixt an action real, and an
action perfonal. 25. *H.* 8. *B. Corporations.* 82.

By *Fitz.* if the Abbot and Convent fel all the
lands

See 10. H. 8.
10. See Coke
lib.
lands and the Abby, yet the Corporation remains Quære by B. of what he ſhall be Abbot, for there is no church nor monaſtery. And by him Quære if the Abbot die, if they S. the Covent, may chuſe another, the houſe being diſſolved. 32. *H.* 8. *B. Corporations.* 78. See *Tit. Extinguiſhment.*

See 2. H. 7. 13.
by Keble.
The King makes a Duke or Earl, and gives to him 20. *l.* of land, or the like, by the ſame name, ſo that the creation and the grant, is all by one and the ſame patent, yet tis good. And the ſame Law of making a corporation and giving to them land by the ſame patent, and name. 2. *E.* 6. *B. Corporations.* 89.

Coſtes.

9. H. 6. 32. by
Newton. 27.
H. 6. 10.
Note, by *Spilman* Juſtice, that at common Law, a man ſhall recover coſts in a *Quare impedit :* but otherwiſe, after the Statute of *Weſtm.* 2. cap. 5. becauſe the Statute gives great dammages in a *Quare impedit.* 22. *H.* 8. *B. coſtes.* 25.

T. 4. M. 1.
accord.
Note, where an action penal is given by Statute, to recover a great ſumm by action of Debt for ingroſſing, or the like, there the Plaintiff ſhall not recover coſts nor dammages in this action of Debt. 35. *H.* 8. *B. Dammages* 200. *coſts* 32.

23. H. 8. c. 15.
Raſt. dam. 6.
Twas ſaid, That if a Leſſor brings Debt againſt his Leſſee for years, for Rent, and the Plaintiff is *nonſuit,* or if the inqueſt paſs againſt him, he ſhall render coſts to the Defendant by the Stat. for a Leaſe for years rendring rent, is a contract. 2. *M.* 1. *B. coſts* 23.

Covenant.

Where an aſſignee ſhall be charged with the Covenant of his Grantor. See *Tit. Aſſignee.*

Plea

Plea of Covenants perform generally, without ſhewing how, is no good plea. See *Tit. conditions.*

Tis ſaid by the Juſtices, That a Writ of Cove- nant lies upon an Indenture, without this word Covenant and grant for him, his heirs and executors. 1 *M.* 1. *B. covenant* 38. the end.

Stat. 1. 8.

Coverture.

Note, that a Statute Staple, nor Deed enrolled, ſhall not be accepted of a Fem Covert, by the Common Law: contrary, by the cuſtom in *London* of a Deed enrolled; for this ſhall binde in *London* as a Fine at Common law, (*B. coverture* 59. 76. the end.)

Nor a Fine, Statute, nor Deed enrolled, ſhall not be ſuffered by an Infant. 32. *H.* 8. *B. coverture* 59. the end.

19. H. 8. 19. See Coke L 19. Mary Porting- toes caſe. 29. H. 8. See 30. H. 8. Tit. Fines.

Count.

Precipe quod reddat againſt Tenant for life, who prays in aid of him in reverſion, who appears *gratis*, and joyns in aid; and the Demandant counts *de Novo* againſt the Tenant, and the Prayee, and they vouch the common Voucher, and ſuffer recovery for aſſurance. And yet tis ſaid, That the Praiee ſhall not have *Oyer*, but of the Count. *Caſus* 22. *H.* 7. *B. count* 87.

Court Baron.

Twas ſaid that the Lord of a Mannor cannot hold Court, nor do juſtice without two Suitors: and if they die, or if that there be but one ſuitor, the mannor is determined; for tis not a Mannor without Suitors. 23. *H.* 8. *B. Court baron* 22. the end.

See 33. H. 8. Tit. Mannor.

If

If an underſteward holds a Court Baron, and grants Copy-holds to the Tenants by Copy of Court Roll, without authority of the Lord, or high Steward, this is a good grant.; for *in plena curia.* Contrary if he doth it out of Court, without ſuch authority. Yet the high Steward may demiſe cuſtomary land by copy out of Court by ſome. *Quære* thereof by B. if he hath not a ſpecial authority from the Lord to demiſe. 2. *E.* 6. *B. Court baron* 22. *Tenant by copie,* 26.

Cuſtoms.

Information in the *Exchequer* againſt a Merchant for lading Wine in a ſtrange Ship; the Defendant pleads the licence of the King made to I. S. to do it, which I. S. had granted his authority thereof to the Defendant *& quod habetur conſuetudo inter mercatores per totam Angliam :* that one may aſſigne ſuch a licence over to another, and that the aſſignee ſhall enjoy it, *&c.* to which twas demurred in law : and twas agreed for law, That a man cannot preſcribe a cuſtom *per totam Angliam :* for if it be *per totam Angliam,* this is the Common law, and not a Cuſtom : contrary, if the cuſtom had been pleaded to be in ſuch a City or County, as *Gavelkinde, Borrow-Engliſh, Gloceſt. Fee,* and the like. 35. *H.* 8. *B. Cuſtomes* 59.

Dammages.

19. H. 6. 10.
27. H. 8. 2.
contra. 3. M. 1.
See tit. Abridg-

NOTE in Treſpaſs local, That upon an inqueſt of Office to enquire of Dammages, the Court may abridge, or increaſe them. But otherwiſe upon the Principall, S. upon iſſue tryed betwixt party

and

and party, (but there it may encreaſe coſts.) For
the party is at his attaint: but upon an inqueſt of
Office he cannot have an attaint. 34. *H. 8. B. dammages* 144. See *Tit. coſts.*

ment. 34. H.
6. 12. by Moyle.

Default.

If a woman be received in default of her Huſband,
and after ſhee makes default, judgement ſhall be
given upon default of the huſband; and no mention
ſhall be made of the receit. *Time H. 8. B. default* 85.

22. H. 6. 14.
per cur.

Demurrer.

Inquiſition found that I. S. held certain land of
the King, *ut de honore ſuo Glouceſter,* which is not in
Capite, upon which proces iſſued againſt W. S. who
had intruded, *&c.* and to ſue Livery: and becauſe
that this Tenure is not in *capite,* and therefore Livery
not due; the party demurred upon the record; for
tis no cauſe of Livery. And where a man declares
upon a Statute, and recites it otherwiſe then tis, or
pleads it otherwiſe then tis, the other may demur
upon it; for no ſuch Law if it be miſrecited. 32 *H.
8. B. Demurrer in Law* 25.

See Tit. Livery.

See 33. H. 8.
Tit. Parliam.

Denizen. See Tit. Alien.

Note, for Law, That where an Alien born comes
into *England,* and brings his ſon with him who was
born beyond Sea, and is an Alien as his Father is,
there the King by his Letters pattents cannot make
the ſon Heir to his Father, nor to any other: for he
cannot alter his law by his letters Pattents, nor otherwiſe, but by Parliament; for he cannot diſinherit the
right

See Tit. Reſtitu-
tion. and Coke
upon Lit. the
beginning.

right heir, nor difappoint the Lord of his efcheat:
and the fon of an Alien, which fon is born in *England*, he is Englifh, and not an Alien, 36. *H*. 8. *B.
Denizen* 9.

Deputie.

Tis faid that a Deputation of an Office which lies
in grant, ought to be by Deed, and not by word,
28. *H*. 8. *B. Deputy* 17.

Detinue.

27. H. 8. 13.   By *Shelley* and others, if a man meddle with goods,
cont. by Fitz.   as by trover of them, he fhall be thereof charged,
though that he deliver them over before action
brought, 32. *H*. 8. *B. Detinue de biens* 1. The
end.

Debt.

Where Debt lies, and where a *Scire facias?* See
Tit. *Age.*

Debt upon Indentures of Covenants: where the
Defendant had Covenanted to do many things, and
the Plaintiff the like, to do many other things, *ad
quas quidem conventiones perimplendas uterque obligatur alteri* in one hundred pound, and the one breaks
Covenant, by which the other brings Debt, and the
Defendant pleads payment of ten pound to *D.* which
was all to which he was bound: judgement if action,
Curia.   and no plea *per curiam*, becaufe he did not fhew
45. E. 3. 5.   thereof a Deed, where the Plaintiff declared upon
Chetle accord.   the Indenture, which is a Deed.   And yet otherwife in pleading of payment of Rent referved upon
a Leafe for years, made by Indentures: For there
he

he may levy it by diſtreſs, and therefore an averment may come in ure.

But otherwiſe where all riſes by ſpecialty, where it lies in payment. 25. *H.* 8. *B. Debt* 173.

Debt upon an obligation with Condition, where the condition is not broken, by which he is barred, he ſhall never ſue this obligation again: for once barred *eſt pro imperpetuo,* 29. *H.* 8. *B. Debt* 174. **B. debt 126. the end accord.**

Adminiſtrator of a Lord brings an action of Debt for relief, which fell *tempore inteſtati,* and the Defendant pleaded in Bar, and traverſed the Tenure, and ſo at iſſue. **See Coke L. & his Lit.**

And therefore B. ſeems that the action lies clearly for him: for the Defend. did not demur: ſo if it be brought by an Executor of the Lord for relief due to the Teſtator, *Rot.* 529: in the Common Bench. 32. *H.* 8. *B. debt* 193. *Relief* 11. the ends. **9. H. 61. 13. by Rolfe.**

Deviſe.

Note, that a Fem Covert with aſſent and will of her huſband, may make her Teſtament, and deviſe the goods of her Huſband, yet if the Huſband prohibit the probat of the Teſtament of the Wife after her death, then all is void: For the huſband may countermand it: *B. deviſe* 34. the end. *Teſtament* 21. the end. **The ſame caſe 34. H. 8. at S. Albons.**

And a Deviſe by the huſband to his Wife is good, though they are one and the ſame perſon in the Law; for the deviſe takes not effect till after the death of the huſband, and then they are not one perſon, 24. *H.* 8. *B. Deviſe* 34. **Lit. 37. N. B. 86.**

Twas agreed by all, that if a man wills that *I. S.* ſhall have in his Land in date after the death of his Wife, and dies, now the wife of the Deviſor by theſe **13. H. 7. 17. by Fineux, 3. M. 1. Com. 158.**

H H words

words ſhall have the Land for her life, by reaſon of
the intent of the Will. 29. *H.* 8. *B. devife* 48.

5. H. 7. 10.
D. S. 21.

Note. That in London a man may Deviſe by
Teſtament to a common perſon, though the Teſtament be not enrolled, but if he Deviſes in *Mortmain*

See 45. E. 3. 26.

he ought to be a Citizen, and a Freeman reſident :
and the Teſtament ought to be enrolled at the next
Huſtings. 30. *H.* 8. *B. devife* 28.

A man Deviſes to two & *heredibus eorum*, and
dies ; and after one of the Deviſees dies, and the
other ſurvives, he ſhall not have the intire by Sur-
vivor, but onely a moytie ; for this was the intent of
the Deviſor : by *Audley Chancellor* of *England*, *B.*

Perk. 106. G.

devife 29. and by B. there the end. If one deviſe
to another *in feodo fimplici*, the deviſee hath a Fee
ſimple. 30. *H.* 8.

A man wills that his land Deviſable ſhall be ſold
by his Executors, and makes four Executors, and
dies, all the Executors ought to ſell, for the truſt is

See Coke upon
Lit.

put joyntly in them. *Quære*, for B. ſeems, That if
one or two die, that the three or two which ſurvive,
may ſell ; for there is the plural number, Executors :
and death is the act of God (*B. Devife* 31.) and by
him where ſuch will is made, and ſome of the Exe-

21. H. 8. c. 4.
Raft. Probat.
of Teſt. 3.

cutors refuſe, and the other prove the Teſtament,
thoſe, or he which proves the Teſtament may ſell
by the Statute, (*B. devife* 29. 31.) where tis expreſſed
that twas doubted at Common Law, if the ſale by
one executor were good, or not (*B. Devife* 31.)

See Coke upon
Lit.

And by ſome, where a man wills that the Land
ſhall be ſold *poſt mortem I. S.* by his Executors, and
makes four Executors, and dies, and after two of the
Executors dies, and after *I. S.* dies, there the two
Executors that ſurvive may ſel, for the time is not
com til now, 30. *H.* 8. *B. Devife* 31.

Twas

'Twas said that *Baldwin, Shelley,* and *Montague,* Justices, determined for Law, That where a man hath Feoffees to his use before the Statute of uses made 27. *H.* 8. and after the same Statute; and also after the Statute of 32. *H.* 8. of Wills, he wills that his Feoffees shall make an estate to W. N. and his heirs of his body, and dies, that this is a good Will and devise *ratione intentionis,* &c. 38. *H.* 8. *B. Devise* 48. the end.

If a man devises his land to be sold by his Executors, and dies, the heir enters, and after is deseised, yet the Executors may sell, and the Vendee may enter, *B. Devise* 36. *Entre congeable.* 134. the same Law if the heir suffer a Recovery or levies a Fine. And the same law by some, where a man disseises the heir, & dies seised, and his heir enters, the Executors shall sell, and by the vendee may enter; for he hath no right, nor no action is given to him: for he hath but a Title of entry by the sale, and therefore he may enter, for otherwise he hath not any remedy, by *Hales* Justice 1. *E.* 6. *B. Devise* 36. *See Coke upon Lit. & Tit. Mortmain.*

Agreed for good Law, that the occupation of a Chattel may be devised by way of Remainder, but if the thing it self were devised to use, the Remainder is void; for a gift or devise of a Chattel for an hour, is for ever; and the donee, or devisee may give, sel, and dispose it, & the remainder depending upon it, is void, *Time H.* 8. *B. Devise* 13. the middle. Where a man devises that W. O. shal have the occupation of his plate for term of his life, and if he dies, that it shal remain to I. S. this is a good remainder: For the first hath but the occupation, & the other after him shal have the property, 2. *E.* 6. *B. Devise* 13. the end. Note if a man hath issue 3. sons, and devises his Lands: S. one part to the *See 2. E. 6. after. & Tit. Chattels.*

See before & Tit. chat.

the two of his Sons in Tail, and another part to the third ſon in Tail, and that none of them ſell any part, but that every one ſhal be heir to the other, & dies, that in this caſe if one dies without iſſue his part ſhall not revert to the eldeſt ſon ; but ſhall remain to the other ſon : for theſe words (*That every one ſhall be heir to the other*) implies a Remainder ; becauſe that tis a Will, which ſhal be intended and adjudged according to the intent of the Deviſor. 7. *E*. 6. *B. deviſe* 38. *Done* 44.

19. H. 8. 9. by Norwich. Fitz. & More. See Coke upon Lit. A man Deviſes his Land to another, for to give, ſell, or to do with it at his pleaſure ; this is a Feeſimple : for his intent ſhall be taken to give a Feeſimple. 7. *E*. 6. *B. Deviſe* 38.

Note, by *Bromley* Chief Juſtice, and others ; where a man Deviſes his land to a ſtranger for Term of years, the Remainder to his ſon in Fee, and dies ; the ſon may waive the Deviſe, and claim by diſcent, and yet he ſhall not avoid the Term : No more then where a man Leaſes for years, and dies, the Leaſe is good : and yet the dying ſeiſed is good alſo to toll the entry, *B. deviſe* 41. And *B.* ſeems where the Father deviſes to his ſon and heir in Fee, that the heir may waive the Deviſe, and take himſelf to the diſcent, (*B. Diſcent* 4.) Contrary, where the Father Deviſes to his ſon in Tail, the remainder to a ſtranger in Fee, there the Heir ſhall not claim in Fee, nor waive the Deviſe, for the loſs and prejudice of him in remainder in Fee. 2. *M.* 1. *B. Deviſe* 41.

Tenant in Tail of Land Deviſable, diſcontinues in Fee, and retakes in Fee, and Deviſes to a ſtranger in Fee, and dies, the iſſue in Tail is remitted ; for nothing is diſcended to him by reaſon of the Deviſe, which Tolls the diſcent, except that the Deviſee waives it. 4. *M.* 1. *B. Deviſe* 49. *Remitter* 52.

Divorce.

Divorce.

What divorce may Baſtardize the iſſue ? what not ?
See Title Baſtardie.

Note, for Law, That where the huſband and wife
are divorced where ſhee is an Inheritrix ; yet mean
acts executed ſhall not be reverſed by the divorce ;
as waſte, receit of Rents, taking of Ward, preſentment to a Benefice, gift of goods of the wife ; otherwiſe of inheritance, as if the huſband had diſcontinued, or charged the land of his wife, *cui ante
Divorcium* lies. The ſame of a releaſe of the huſband, or Manumiſſion of villains, or the like. And
if the huſband and wife purchaſe joyntly, and are
diſſeiſed, the huſband releaſes, and after are divorced,
the wife ſhall have the Moytie, though there were
not Moyties before the divorce ; for the divorce converts it into Moyties. 32. *H.* 8. *B. Deraignment* 18.

See Coke upon Lit.

Diſcent.

If Land be given for Term of life, the Remainder
to the right heirs of W. N. which W. N. is attainted
of Felony, and dies, and after the Tenant for life
dies, the Remainder ſhall not take effect, nor none
ſhall have the Land ; for he hath not heir *ratione
attincturæ.* And though all be a name of purchaſe,
yet none can take it, but he which is heir, (*B. Diſcent* 59. *Done* 42.) And where Land in *Gavelkinde*
is given to one for life, or in tail, the Remainder to
the right heirs of W. N. who hath iſſue 4. ſons and
dies, and after the Tenant for life, or the Donee
dies, the eldeſt ſon ſhal have the land, for he is right
heir

38. H. 8. B. Diſcents 59. accord. vide infra.

heir at Common Law, & this is a name of purchafe, which fhall be ordered by the Common Law.

See 26. H. 8. 4.

But otherwife of difcents to heires in Gavilkinde, for then it fhall goe to all the fons.   37. *H. 8. B.*

B. Done. 61.

Difcents, & Done. 42. *Nofme.* 6.

See 32. H. 8.
Tit. Livery.

Note, that Sir *John Huffey* Knight, enfeoffed certain perfons in fee to the ufe of *Anne* his wife, for terme of her life, and after to the ufe of the heirs males of his body, and for default of fuch iffue, to the ufe of the heires males of the body of Sir *William Huffey* his father, and for default of fuch iffue, to the ufe of his right heires, and after had iffue *William Huffey* the elder ; and after Sir *John* was attainted of Treafon.   29. *H.* 8. and put to execution, and after *Anne* died, and the faid *William Huffey* the fon prayed an *Oufter l'main* of the King.   And by *Whorewood* the Kings Attorney he fhall have it, for this name heires males of the body, is but a name of

See Coke upon
Litt.

purchafe, and Sir W. H. fhall not have it as heir to Sir *John*, but as purchafer. (*B. Nofme.* 1. *Livery* 1. *Difcent.* 1.)   As if land is given to a man and his heires males of his body, and he hath iffue 2 fons, the eldeft hath iffue a daughter, and the father, and the eldeft fon dies, the younger brother fhal have the land, and yet he is not heir to his father.   And the

Litt. 5.

fame Law where land is given to a man, and to his heirs females of his body, and he hath a fon and

Litt. 169. 3. E.
Com. 237. c. 13.
Raft. Treafon.
12. W. 2. c. 1.

daughter, and dies, the daughter fhall have the land, and not the fon.   (*B. Nofme.* 1. 40.)   And fo where Tenant in tail is attainted of Treafon before the Statute of 26. *H.* 8. his fon fhall have the land, for he doth not claim onely as heir, but by the Statute and *per formam doni* (*B. Nofme.* 1.)   Yet fome were

9. H. 6. 24. by
Ellerker. See
Coke upon Litt.

of a contrary opinion, and took a Diverfity, where the gift is to the father himfelf, and where tis to the

heires

heires of his body by remainder (*B. Nofme.* 1. & 40.)
And therefore in 9. *H.* 6. if lands are given for term
of life, the remainder to the heires females of the
body of *I. S.* who is dead, and hath iffue a fon and
daughter, and after the Tenant for life dies, the
daughter fhal not have the land, for fhe is not heir :
for by *Hare* Mafter of the Rolls an antient apprentice, there is a difference betwixt a gift in poffeffion to a
man and his heires females, &c. and a gift to a
ftranger, the remainder to the heirs females of
another, for there he ought to be heir indeed when
the remainder falls, or otherwife the rem' is void for
ever. (*B. Done.* 61.) for though that the cafe holds
place in the two cafes put by *Whorewood*, this is becaufe that the gift was once vefted which was in the
father, and therefore good law there, otherwife in
the principall cafe, where the rem'. is not vefted. Yet
by fome the opinion of *Whorewood* is the better, for
where land is given to a man and his wife for term
of life, the rem'. to the heires males of the body of
the man, this remainder cannot be vefted in the life
of the wife, for tis not a tail in the man, by reafon
of the eftate of the wife ; yet, if he hath iffue 2 fons,
and the eldeft hath iffue a daughter and dies, the
father and mother dies, the younger fon fhall have
the land, as heir male, and yet he is not heir indeed ;
The fame Law, if fuch gift were, the rem' to the
heirs females of the body of the man, who hath a
fon and daughter and dies, the daughter fhall have
the land though fhe is not heir; The fame Law
where land is given to *W. N.* for life, the remainder
to *I. S.* for life, the remainder to the heires males of
the body of the faid *W. N.* who hath 2 fons, the
eldeft hath iffue a daughter and dies, *W. N.* and *I. S.*
die, the younger fon fhall have the land as heir
male,

See before. B.
Nofme. 1.
Whorwood. 35.
H. 8.

male, yet he is not heir indeed, but his Neece is heir to his father; for tis not matter of the firft vefting, nor of the remainder, for where the firft eftate for term of life is executed, the remainder over *ut fupra,* the remainder may depend in abeyance *quoufque, &c. ut fupra.* But otherwife of a remainder to the right heires, for none can have that, but he which fhall be heir indeed. (*B. Nofme.* 40.) and therefore twas agreed, that the 2 remainders to the right heires of Sir *John Huffey* was forfeited by the attainder. 37. *H.* 8. *B. Nofme.*

If land difcends to the daughter within age, and after fhe is diffeifed, the diffeifor dies and his heir enters, and after a fon is born, he born fhal avoid the difcent, for he claims not as heir to his fifter, nor was he in *effe* at the time of the difcent. *Lecture. B. Difcent.* 40.

Difcontinuance of Poffeffion.

See Tit. Af-
furances, &
Recovery in
value.

Recovery againft Tenant in tail, the reverfion or remainder in the King in fee, fhall binde the Tenant in tail, and the iffue in tail, but not the King. But now by the Statute it fhall not binde the iffue in tail, but that he may enter. 32. *H.* 8. *B. Difcontinuance of poffeffion.* 32.

The like was
agreed. 37. H.
8. B. Patents.
101. See Time
H. 8. Tit.
Patents.

Note, that twas agreed in the cafe betwixt the King and *Anthony Lee* Knight, if the King Tenant in tail of the gift of another makes a leafe for years, or for life, and hath iffue and dies, the iffue may make another grant without reciting them; for they are void by the death of the King Tenant in tail, who granted, and the heir of the King fhall avoid it, fo that this fhall not binde but during the life of the grantor, for a grant without warranty or livery, is no difcontinuance,

difcontinuance, and the King upon his grant doth not make livery. And alfo every difcontinuance is a wrong, which the King cannot do; the fame law if he had granted in fee, tis no difcontinuance; (*B. Patents.* 101. *Difcontinuance of Poffeffion.* 35. *Tail.* 39. *Leafes* 61.) And fo fee that the King may be Tenant in tail, for when a man gives to the King in tail, he cannot have a greater eftate then the donor will depart with to him. 38. *H. 8. B. Tail.* 39.

4. E. Com. 250. 2. I. B. Tail. 39. & 4. E. Com. M. 234.

Releafe no Difcontinuance.
See Tit. Releafes.
Difcontinuance of Proces.

Note, that a Difcontinuance puts the party to a new originall, but where the Parol is without day, this may be revived by a re-fummons or re-attachment, for the originall remains. *Regulæ. B. Difcontinuance of proces.* 43.

Difmes, Tythes.

Twas faid that if a Parfon demife his Glebe to a lay man, there he fhall pay Tythes; contrary of the Parfon himfelf, that referves them in his proper hands. And that land firft difcharged of Tythes, fhall be ever difcharged of them. Yet if he which hath purchafed a Mannor and Rectory, which is difcharged of Tythes, Leafes part of his demeanes, the leffor fhall have Tythes of that, becaufe that he hath the Parfonage. 32. *H. 8. B. Difmes* 17.

I I

Diffeifor.

Diſſeiſor.

T. 25. H. 8.
accord. Fitz.
179. G.
See Coke upon
Litt. Twas ſaid for Law, if *A.* leaſes the land of *I. N.* to me for years, rendring rent, the leſſee enters, and payes the rent to the leſſor, the leſſor is a deſſeiſor, for countervails a commandment to enter, and he which commands is a diſſeiſor, which note by his void leaſe. 23. *H.* 8. *B. Diſſeiſ'.* 77.

Diſtreſs.

Where land ſhall be charged with 2 diſtreſſes by Dower of part, and ſo of partition. See *Tit. Avowry.*

See 4. E. 6.
Com. 68. by
Mountague,
and Coke upon
Litt. Note, for Law, that he which diſtrains beaſts may put them into a cloſe houſe, if he will feed them; for the diſtreſs in pound overt, is but to 'the intent, that the owner may feed them. 33. *H.* 8. *B. Diſtreſs.* 66.

Twas agreed for Law by the Juſtices, that if a man diſtrain without cauſe, the owner may make reſcous, but if he impounds them, the owner cannot juſtifie the breaking of the pound, and taking them out, for they are in *Cuſtodia Legis.* 4. *E.* 6. *B. Diſtreſs.* 74. *Reſcous.* 12. the end.

Done, Gift.

See Tit. Grants. Deviſee for life of a Chattell, the remainder over, he for life gives the Chattell, whether this ſhall barr the remainder. See *Tit. Chattells.*

Tis ſaid for Law, that if a man gives *omnia terras & tenementa ſua* in *D* by this leaſes for years do not paſs, for theſe words lands and tenements ſhall be intended free-hold at leaſt. 37. *H.* 8. *B. Done.* 41.

The

The difference betwixt a gift in Remainder, *Heredibus mafculis de corpore & rectis Heredibus.* See *Tit. Difcent.*

Twas granted by *Shelly* Juftice, and others, that if the King give a Chattell without deed, and the donee takes it by his commandment, tis good. 2. *E.* 6. *B. Done.* 16 the middle.

See Tit. Prerogative. 37. H. 6. 10. by Davers. 26. H. 8. 8. cont.

If a man gives or grants *omnia bona fua*, leafes for years, nor award, fhall not pafs, for they are Chattels reals. And *B.* feems that a grant of *Prox' prefent. Ecclefiæ unica vice* is a Chattell, & *non bona*, for *bona* are goods moveable, living and dead, but not Chattels. 4. *E.* 6. *B. Grants.* 51. *Done.* 43.

Dower.

A woman fhall not be endowed of a rent referved upon a leafe of her hufband for term of life, for the rent is not an inheritance, and tis determinable upon the death of the Leffee, and yet the heir fhall have it, for tis incident to the reverfion. And where a man feifed in fee, leafes for years rendring rent, and afterwards takes wife and dies, the wife fhall have dower of the land, but fhall not have execution during the term of years, for elder title, &c. and fhe cannot be indowed of the rent for the caufe aforefaid. 1. *E.* 6. *B. Dower.* 89.

7. H. 6. 3. by Jane Perk. 68. See Coke upon Lit. Dower. Perk. 67. Perk. 69.

Note, by the Juftices, by the Statute where a man makes his wife joynt purchafer with him after the coverture, of any eftate of free-hold, except it be to him and his wife, and their heires in fee fimple, this is barr of Dower, if fhe agree to the joynture *poft mortem viri*, otherwife of fee fimple; for fuch joynture is not fpoken in the Statute. Nor a devife of land by the hufband to the wife by teftament, is no barr

27. H. 8. c. 10. See Vernons c. Coke. L

to

to Dower, for this is a benevolence, and not a joynture. 6. *E.* 6. *B. Dower.* 69.

Dum non fuit compos mentis.

See Coke Beverlies. c. lib. Note, that if a Judge or Justice be of *non sane memory*, yet the Fines, Judgements, & other records which are before him, shalbe good. But otherwise of the gift of an office or the like by him ; for this is matter in fact, and the others are matters of record ; for matters in fact may be avoided by *non sane memory*, otherwise of matter of record. 1. *M.* 1. *B. Dum non fuit compos mentis.* 7.

Ejectione Custod.

14. H. 8. 23. by Brudnel. TWAS said that a man shall have a Writ *de Ejectione custodie* of a rent, and this before seisin of it ; for seisin in Law shall be thereof adjudged, by reason that he cannot receive it before the rent day. Yet otherwise of land, for there he may enter. 23. *H.* 8. *B. Quare ejecit infra terminum.* 5.

Enquest.

See Tit. Tryall. Note, betwixt the King and the Bishop of *Rochester* for Treason, the Bishop shall not have Knights in his Jury, where Knights ought to be returned, when a Peer of the Realm, as a Bishop, and the like, is party, yet quære, if it were challenged. 27. *H.* 8. *B. Enquest.* 100.

Twas

Twas holden in the common Bench by the Prothonatories, if a protection be caſt at the day of *Niſi prius*, and the Juſtices take the Jury *de bene eſſe*, and at the day in bank, the protection is allowed, now though the firſt taking is void, yet the Inqueſt ſhall not be recharged by reſummons, for when the Inqueſt is once ſworn, and give verdict, they ſhall never be ſworn again upon this iſſue. 2. *M.* 1. *B. Enqueſt* 86.

35. H. 6. 59.
Moil accord.

Entre congeable : lawfull Entry.

Tenant for term of life aliens to B. to have to him and his heires for term of life, of Tenant for term of life, this is no forfeiture, for all is but the limitation of the eſtate. *B. Forfeiture of lands.* 87.) And if Tenant for terme of life ſuffers a recovery, he in reverſion cannot enter, but is put to his Writ of Entrie, *ad terminum qui preteriit*, or Writ of Right, and ſhall falſiſie the recovery in it, if he hath cauſe. (And if he will have it *ſure*, the Tenant for life ought to pray in aid of him in reverſion, and if he joynes in aid, and both vouch over, then well upon recovery had, &c. as betwixt *Corbet* and *Clifford* in the Countie of *Buck*' this year.) But if Tenant for life be impleaded, and prayes in aid of a ſtranger, he in Reverſion may enter, for this is a forfeiture. But if he doth not enter till the other hath recovered, then he cannot enter, but is put to his writ of Entrie, *ad terminum qui preteriit, vel ingres. ad communem legem*, and ſhall falſiſie the recovery there. 24. *H.* 8. *B. Entrecongeable.* 115. *Fauxiſier.* 44. *Forfeiture of Lands.* 87. the end.

See 21. H. 8. 1. Fitz. & Brook. accord. 12. H. 8. 7. N. B. 124. 4. H. 7. 2. 14. H. 7. 6. See Coke l. 23. H. 8. 39. 30. H. 8. 143. book at large. 1. H. 7. 22. 10. H. 7. 20. by Keble 25. H. 8. 70.

Ceſtuy que uſe in tail ſuffers a recovery againſt him upon a faint title before the Statute of Uſes, and dies,

See 20. H. 8. after. See Coke upon Litt.

dies, the Feoffees cannot falfifie it in an affife by way of entry, but fhall have a writ of entry, *ad terminum qui preteriit*, or a writ of right, and fhall falfifie it by this action. (*B. Entre congeable*, 123. *Fauxifier.* 49.) And if he *Leuies* a fine with proclamation, and dies, if a ftranger of his own head enters in name of the Feoffees, or to their ufe within the 5 years, this fhall avoid the Fine though the Feoffees did not command him ; for by this the freehold is in them till they difagree, or till another enters. 31. *H.* 8. *B. Entre congeable.* 123. the end.

See 29. H. 8.
111. the book
at large. and
antea. See
Coke upon Litt.
19. H. 8. 13.
See Fines levies.
W. 2. cap, 1.

Twas doubted, if a recovery had againft *ceftuy que ufe* in tail, fhall binde the heire. in tail. But by *Hales* Juft. by fuch recovery the entry of the Feoffees feifed to the ufe of the eftate taile is taken away, but after the death *ceftuy que ufe*, who fuffered the recovery, the Feoffees may have a writ of right, or writ of entrie, *ad terminum qui preteriit* in the poft, or the like. And by fome, there is no ufe in tail, but tis a fee fimple conditional at the common Law, as twas of a tail before the Statute of *W.* 2. And this Statute makes not mention but of gifts in tail, which is tails in poffeffion. And therfore quære, if the tail in ufe cannot be taken by the equity of it, yet twas doubted if the iffues and the Feoffees fhall be

1. R. 3. cap. 5.
See before. 32.
H. 8. cap. 36.

bound after the death of *ceftuy que ufe*, who fuffered the recovery, by reafon of thofe words in the Statute of 1. *R.* 3. which wills that the recovery fhall be good againft the vendor, and his heires, claiming only as heir, and againft all others, claiming onely to the ufe of the vendor and his heires, and this is intended by fome of a fee fimple, and in the cafe afore the iffue in tail, claims as heir in tail in ufe. (*B. Feoffements to ufes.* 56. the middle.) Yet fee the Statute of 32. *H.* 8. that a Fine with proclamation
levied,

levied, or to be levied by Tenant in tail in poffeffion, reverfion, remainder, or in ufe, after proclamation had, fhall binde thofe Tenants of thofe tails and their heires for ever. And fee that the fame Statute is as well *pro temporibus preteritis, quam futuris.* 30. *H.* 8. *B. Feoffements to ufes.* 57. the end.

G. *T.* Knight feifed in tail to him and the heires males of his body, difcontinues, and retakes to him and *E.* his wife, and to the heires of their two bodies, and had iffue, *T.* and *W.* and died, and after *E.* his wife furvived, and *T.* had iffue *E. nuptam T. W.* and died, and after *W.* by covin of *E.* his mother, Tenant in joynture, brings a *Formedon* upon the elder tail againft his mother, and fhe appeared the firft day, and *W.* recovered by *Nihil dicit,* and *T. W.* and *E.* his wife heir to G. enters by the Statute of 11. *H.* 7. and the entry adjudged lawfull by the fame Statute, which wills fuch difcontinuances, alienations, warranties, and recoveries fhall be void (*B. Entre congeable* 140. *Judgement.* 153.) And it need not to fay that the recovery was executed, for becaufe twas void, it fhal never be executed. And *E.* the heir averred that he is the fame perfon to whom the reverfion appertained, and fhewed not how heir to it, and yet good by *Molineux,* and *Hales* Juftices, *contra Brown* and *Mountague* chief Juftice of the Common Bench. But all agreed that twas a recovery by covin, notwithftanding twas upon a true title. And good, notwithftanding he did not fhew caufe of covin. 32. *H.* 8. *B. Entre congeable.* 140. *Collufion.* 47.

Agreed for Law, that if land efcheat to the King, which is in leafe for years, or charged with a rent charge, and office is found for the King of the efcheat (the leafe or grant not found in the office) the leffee cannot enter, nor the Grantee cannot diftrain, but if
the

The like cafe betwixt Villiers and Beamont was adjudged in the Commō bench. T. 4. M. 1. 4. E. 6. Com. 42. 11. H. 7. 20. Raft. Difcontinuance of proces. 1.

the King grant the land over, the leſſee may enter, and the grantee may diſtraine. But a man which claims freehold in the land, cannot enter without traverſe of the office, by *B.* 33. *H.* 8. *B. Entre congeable.* 124.

4. M. 1. Com. 175. 32. H. 8. cap. 34. Raſt. Com. 1. 4. E. 6. Com. 34. 4. M. 1. Com. 177. See Coke upon Litt.

Note, that tis ruled in the Serjeants caſe, that where a common perſon leaſes lands for years, rendring rent with a clauſe of reentry, and after grants the reverſion over, the tenant atturns, the grantee may reenter for condition broken, by the Statute by expreſs words. And the ſame Law of the grantees of the King. *E.* 6. and all others heires to King *H.* 8. by the equitie of the ſaid Statute, which provides remedy for the patentees of the King. *H.* 8. And for grantees of common perſons. 4. *M.* 1. *B. Entre congeable.* 139.

Twas ſaid that where the intereſt of the King is certain and determined, the party may enter, quære by *B. Time. H. B. Reſeiſer.* 36. the end.

Error.

'Twas ſaid in the Kings Bench, where a writ of Error beares *teſte* before the firſt Judgement, and the Record is certified in the Bench, that 'tis good ; and yet the Writ ſaith, *quod ſi judiciũ reddit. ſit, tunc Record. & proceſs. babeatis, &c.* 5 *E.* 6. *B. Errour.*

Eſcape.

Debt upon an Eſcape, againſt the Sheriffe, who ſaid That before the Eſcape the Priſoner was condemned in the ſaid condemnation, and in Execution, *ut in narratione,* in the time of a former Sheriffe, who ſuffered him to Eſcape, and after re-took and impriſoned him, and was removed, and this Defendant

dant was made Sheriffe, and after fuffered him to Efcape; judgement is, Of this fecond Efcape you ought to have your Action; and a good Plea, for he hath confeffed and avoided the Plaint; for when the Prifoner firft Efcaped, and the firft Sheriffe re-took and imprifoned him: This fecond Imprifonment is no Execution for the party, but the Party is put to his Action, for the Efcape againft the firft Sheriffe, 5. *E.* 6. *B. Efcape* 45.

10. E. 4. 11. by Billing, fee Cooke, lib. 3. Ridgways Cafe.

Efcheate.

Founderfhip cannot Efcheate by death without Heir, nor bee forfeited by attainder of Felony or Treafon; for 'tis a thing annexed to the blood, which cannot be divided, as 'twas faid after the augmentation Court took commencement; for a man who is Heir to another, cannot make another to be Heir, *Time: H.* 8. *B. Corodies* 5. *the end.*

Note, by *Brown, Hales & Cooke,* Juftices; if there bee Lord and Tenant by Fealty and Rent, the Tenant is diffeifed and dies without Heir, the Lord accepts the Rent by the hands of the faid diffeifor, yet hee may enter for the Efcheate, or have a Writ of Efcheate, and the receipt of the Rent no barre; for the Diffeifor is in by wrong: Otherwife if he had allowed for it in a court of Record, or had taken corporall fervice, as Homage, &c. So of acceptance of Rent by the hands of the Heir of the Diffeifor, or of his Feoffee, which are in by Title. 7 *E.* 6. *B. Efcheate* 18.

Fitz. 144. C. Fitz. 144. N. accord. fee Cooke upon Lit.

Effoign.

If the Tenant in a *Præcipe quod redd:* prayes the view by Attorney; his Attorney fhall bee Effoyned

K K

upon

upon the view : But if he himſelfe prayes the view
in proper perſon ; then *per plures*, none ſhall be
Eſſoyned upon the view but the Tenant himſelf ;
for after Proceſſe upon a Voucher, he himſelf ſhall
bee Eſſoyned, and by conſequence in like manner
ſhall be upon the view.   And note, That granting
of an Eſſoyn, whereon Eſſoyn lyes not, is not error.
Contrary of denying of Eſſoyn where it lyes, 33 *H.*
8. *B. Eſſoine* 116.

*So of ayde
prayer,* 5. *H.* 7.
8. & 9.

Eſtates.

The King gives Land to *J. S. & heredibus
maſculis ſuis ;* and 'twas adjudged by all the Juſtices
in the Exchequer Chamber, that the Grant is void ;
becauſe the King is deceived in his Grant ; for it
ſounds in Fee ſimple ; whereas it ſeems the King
intended but an eſtate tail, which is not ſo expreſſed ;
and therefore now he is but Tenant at will.   Otherwiſe in caſe of a common perſon, 18 *H.* 8. *B.
Patents* 104 *Eſtates* 84.

Raſt. 60. M. 9.
& 10. Eliz.
Com. 335. Lit.
6. & Cook
upon it. *Raſt.*
60. 27. H. 8.
27.

'Twas ſaid for Law, That if a Feoffment bee
made to *W. N.* during the life of *J. S.* theſe
words (during the life of *J. S.*) &c. ſhall be void ;
for they are contrary to a Fee.   Contrary of a
Feoffment in Fee ſo long as *Pauls* Steeple ſhall
ſtand, 21 *H.* 8. *B. Eſtates* 50.

27. H. 8. 29.
cont. ſee 24. H.
8. tit. *Entre
congeable :* &
Cook lib.

A man gives Land to two *& heredibus*, and doth
not ſay *ſuis :* This is no Fee-ſimple : And 'twas
ſaid that the reaſon is, becauſe that two are named
in the Deed ; and therefore 'tis incertain to which
of them *heredibus* ſhall bee referred.   But if there
were but one in the Deed, then it ſhall be referred
to the one only.   But in a Deviſe 'twas ſaid by
ſome, that the words afore are a Fee-ſimple.   Contrary

22. E. 4. 16.
by Genney.
4. E. 6. Com.
28. 20. H. 6.
36. by Porting.
See Cook lib.
& his Lit. fo.
8. b.

trary in a Gift and Feoffment; for the one fhall bee taken by intendment, the other not, 31 *H. 8. B. Eftates* 4.

A man gives land to a Hufband and Wife for terme of their Lives, *& diutius eorum vivent.* the remainder to the Heirs of their bodies, this is a taile executed, by reafon of the immediate remainder, notwithftanding the words of the Statute, *quod voluntas Donatoris in omnibus obfervetur,* by all the Juftices, 35 *H. 8. B. Eftates* 78.

Weftm. 2. c. 1. Raft. Tail. 1.

By opinion in the kings Bench, If a man devifeth his Land to *W. N. folvend* ten pound to his Executors, and dies, the Devifee hath a Fee-fimple, by reafon of the payment, without words, *Heredibus,* or *in perpetuum,* and this fhall be intended the intent of the Devifor: The fame Law if a man fell his Land to *W. N.* for twenty pound, this fhall be intended a fale in Fee-fimple, without words, *Heirs,* for Confcience &c. *& eft equum & bonum,* which is a ground in every Law, 4 *Ed. 6. B. Eftates* 78.

See 29. H. 8. Tit. Teftament & Cook upon Lit. &c. Tit. Confcience.

Eftoppell.

If a man hath Liberties, Rent, Common, or the like, by prefcription, and after takes a grant thereof of the King by Patent, or of another by Deede, this determines his prefcription by conclufion (*B. Prefcription.* 102. *Eftoppell* 210.) for Writing fhall determine Contracts and matter in Fait, 33 *H. 8. B. Prefcrip.* 102.

29. H. 8. See Tit. Contract.

'Twas agreed that a ftranger to a Fine or Recovery, fhall not pleade it for *Eftoppell; contra,* If hee claim the fame Land under the Fine or Record, by thofe which were parties, or claims the fame Eftate, or part of it, and that this eftate continues,

30. H. 6. 2. by Fortefcue accord. See Cooke upon Lit. Eftoppell.

for

for then he is privy in the *Per.* 36. *H.* 8. *B. Eſtoppell* 216. *the end.*

If two Joyn-Tenants are which hold of the King in chiefe, and the one releaſes to the other in Fee, and after both reſpit Homage in the Exchequer; by this, he which releaſed hath gained the moity by concluſion, as it ſhall be where two joyne in ſuite of livery out of the hands of the King, where the one hath nothing, by the opinion of ſome : And the ſame of Partition by two, where the one hath nothing, 37 *H.* 8. *B. Eſtoppell* 218.

Note that a man which Leaſes by Deede poll for yeeres, or by Parol, may avoid this Leaſe to ſay, That hee had nothing in the Land, *tempore dimiſ-ſionis :* Contrary, Upon a Leaſe by Indenture, for this is an *Eſtoppell* 38. *H.* 8. *B. Eſtoppell* 8.

If a man Indicted of Extortion, or Treſpaſſe, puts himſelf upon the grace of the King, and makes a Fine, and after the party ſues him for it, by Bill or Writ, and he pleades Not Guilty, hee ſhall have the Plea, and the making the Fine to the King ſhall not eſtop him; for there the Entry is, *quod petit ſe admitti per Finem,* and doth not confeſſe it preciſely, and therefore no *Eſtoppell :* Yet *B* ſeemes to make the Fine by proteſtation that hee is not guilty, and then 'tis all cleere, *Time. H.* 8. *Eſtop-pell* 82.

A man pleads a Pardon of the King, in the Exchequer, for alienation, without Licenſe, where the Land is not holden of the King *in capite :* This is an *Eſtoppell,* to him to ſay after that, He doth not hold *in capite,* 7 *Ed.* 6. *B. Eſtoppell* 222.

By *Hales* and *Montague,* If a man Leaſes to *N.* his own Land, by Deed intended; the Indenture is no *Eſtoppell,* but during the Leaſe ; and not after, *Caſus B. Eſtoppell* 221.   *Eſtranger.*

Side notes:

33. *H.* 6. 7. by Laken, D. 8. 33.

Lit. 12. ſee Cook, 34. *H.* 6. 48. Danby accord. ſee 5. *H.* 7. 19.

9. *H.* 6. 60. per Cur.

9. *H.* 6. 60. by Babington.

See 38. *H.* 8. before.

See Cook upon Lit. fo.

Eſtranger.

A. is bound to *B.* in a 100.l. and *B.* makes a Defeſance to *W. S.* That if *W. S.* payes 40.l. that the Obligation ſhall be void. This is worth nothing *per opinionem;* becauſe that *A.* that ſhould plead it, is a Stranger to the Deed: But where two are bound to me, and I make a Defeſance to one; this ſhall ſerve the other to plead, if he can ſhew it: as in Treſpas againſt two, a releaſe to one ſhall ſerve the other, if he can ſhew it. 34 *H.* 8. *B. Eſtranger al fait* 21.

Lit. 82. 14.
H. 8. 10. by
Brudnell. Huſ-
ſey accord.
22 E. 4. 7.

Eſtray.

If a man takes Beaſts as an Eſtray, and keeps them three quarters of a yeer, and after they ſtray from him, and another happens on them; the firſt Lord which kept them for three quarters, cannot take them again, becauſe that he had no property in them till hee had kept them a yeer and a day, and Proclamation paſſed in the two next Market Towns, and two Market dayes, the one in the one Town, and the other in the other; for the poſſeſſion of the ſecond Seizor is good againſt him who hath no property. 33 *H.* 8. *B. Eſtray* 11.

Eliot accord.
12. H. 8. 10.

Executions.

Note, by *Fitz.* and the Court, If a man recover in a Writ of Annuity, he ſhall have a *Fieri facias* of the Arrearages incurred within the yeer, and a *Scire fac.* after, as ſoon as the Annuity is Arrear, and never a Writ of Annuity again; for 'tis executory,

11. H. 4. 34.
by Thirning.
6. E. 6. Com.
137. 2. H. 6.
9. caſ. 6.

tory, and the *same* Law of an Action, and Judgement upon *composition,* which is executory *de tempore in tempus,* and the like. And in every *Scire fac.* in which he recovers after the first Judgement, he shall have execution of the Arrearages within the yeer, by *Fieri fac.* for every one is founded upon the Judgement, 23 *H.* 8. *B. Executions* 119. *Scire fac.* 213.

By the whole Court in the Common-Bench, If two are bound in an Obligation *conjunctim & divisim,* the Obligee impleads the one, and hath execution of his body; and after impleads the other, and condemns him, hee may have execution against him also; for the taking of the body is a good execution, but 'tis no satisfaction; and therefore hee may take the other also. But if the one satisfie the Plaintiff, hee shall not have execution after; and therefore this Order, That the Plaintiff upon an Obligation shall have but one execution, is intended such execution which is a satisfaction, and where both are impleaded by one originall, by severall *Precipes, &c.* 29 *H.* 8. *B. Execution* 132.

Scire fac. upon recovery of Debt and Damages; the Defendant said, that once the Plaintiff sued a *Capias ad satisfaciend.* by which the Sheriff had took his body, Judgement, &c. And there 'tis said, That a *Capias ad satisfaciend.* is not of Record before the retorn of it; therefore no Plea: Yet *B.* seems the Plea good by the taking of the Body, though no Writ bee returned, 37 *H.* 8. *B. Executions* 6.

(marginal note: 4. H. 7. 8. 45. E. 3. 4. by Thorpe.)

Executors.

(marginal note: 6. E. 4. 1. 7. E. 4. 9. by Choke.)

'Twas noted by *Fitz.* and others, That in an Action of Debt against an Executor, 34 *H.* 6 upon

an

an Obligation of his Teſtators, who pleaded not his Deed, and found againſt him, the Judgement by the Record was, That the Plaintiff ſhould recover of the Dead, if hee hath any; and for that, the book at large, *fol.* 24. is reported further in theſe words; and if he have not, then *de bonis proprijs*, which words are not in the Record; 'Twas comanded by them to mend the Book; for 'tis contrary to the Record, and ſo miſ-reported, 23 *H.* 8. *B. Executors* 22.

A man makes two Executors, and dyes; the one Executor makes an Executor, and the other ſurvives, and dyes inteſtate; the Executor of the Executor ſhall not meddle; for the power of his Teſtator was determined by his death, and by the ſurvivor of the other; ſo that now the Ordinary ſhall commit the Adminiſtration of the goods of the Executor which ſurvived, & *de bonis non Adminiſtratis* of the firſt Teſtator, 32 *H.* 8. *B. Executors* 149.
Moile and Aſhton accord. 39. *H.* 6. 45.

A man makes *A.* and *B.* his Executors, and wills that *B.* ſhall not meddle during the life of *A.* and good; for he doth not reſtrain his intire power; for he may make one Executor of his goods in *C.* and another Executor of his goods in *D.* and ſo he may divide the time *ut ſupra*, 32 *H.* 8. *B. Executors* 155.
19. *H.* 88. by Fitz. See Dyer, 19. *H.* 8.

A man hath a Leaſe for yeers as Executor *B.* and after purchaſes the reverſion of the Land in fee, the Leaſe is extinct. Bet yet the Leaſe ſhall be againſt the Executor aſſets by *Whorewood* and *Hales* Juſtices. (*B. Extinguiſhment* 54. *Leaſes* 63. *Surrender* 52.) And if it ſhall bee extinct, *B.* ſeems to be a *devaſtavit ad ultim.* 4 *E.* 6 *B. Extinguiſhment* 57. the end.
Hales and Whorewood accord. 2. *E. B.* Surr. 52. the end. See Cook upon Litt. Jo. See Tit. Extinguiſhment.

Expoſition.

Expofition.

The feverall expofition of *infra terminum* 10. *annorum & infra terminum prediƈt.* See Tit. Conditions.

Extinguifhment.

See 32. H. 8. Tit. Corporation.

If the Abbot and Convent give all their Lands and Poffeffions to another in fee, yet the corporation remains by *Fitz.* Juftice, 20 *H.* 8. *B. Extinguifhment* 35.

See 27. H. 8. Tit. Parliament.

Lord and Tenant; the Tenant is attainted of Treafon by Aƈt of Parliament, and to forfeit all his Lands; and after he is pardoned, and reftored, by another Parliament, *habend. fibi & heredibus,* as if no fuch attainder, nor former Aƈt had been. Or if the Heir of him who was attainted, be reftored by Parliament in fuch form; now the Seigniory which was extinguifhed, is revived, and he fhall hold of the common perfon as before; and yet once the tenure was extinƈt by the forfeiture of the Land to the King, 31 *H.* 8. *B. Extinguifhment* 47. *Revivings* 8. *Tenures* 70.

See Tit. Apportionment. Lit. 48. 11. H. 7. 13. by Davers accord. Perk. 16. C.

Lord and Tenant; The Tenant holds by third three Acres of Land, the Tenant infeoffs the Lord in fee, of one Acre; the Seigniory is extinƈt for the third part, and remains for the other two parts; but if the Tenant had let to the Lord one Acre for yeers, there the Seigniory is fufpended in the whole, during the term; for the Seigniory may be extinƈt in part, but not fufpended in part, but for the intire, 32 *H.* 8. *B. Extinguifhment* 48.

Where a Condition fhall not be apportioned, but extinƈt, See *Tit. Conditions.*

A

A man hath a Leaſe for yeers as Executor *B.* and after purchaſes the reverſion of the Land in fee, the Leaſe is extinct; but yet the Leaſe ſhall be againſt the Executor aſſets, by *Whorwood* and *Hales* Juſtices. (*B. Extinguiſhment* 54. *Leaſes* 63. *Surrender* 52.) And if it ſhall be extinct, *B.* ſeems to be a *devaſtavit ad ultimum, Extinguiſhment* 57 the end. But where he hath it as Executor, & there is a mean Leaſe in reverſion for years, and hee purchaſes the reverſion in fee; the firſt Leaſe remains by reaſon of the mean remainder. (*B. Leaſes* 63.) And by *Hales,* If a man Leaſes to another for ten years, and after Leaſes the ſame Land to another for twenty years; the firſt Leſſee purchaſes the reverſion in fee; yet the firſt Leaſe is not extinct, becauſe that the ſecond Leaſe, which is for twenty years, is mean betwixt the firſt Leaſe and the Fee ſimple, which is an impediment of the extinguiſhment, 4 *E.* 6. *Extinguiſhment* 57.

Where an Action by Entry and Feoffment ſhall be extinguiſhed, See *Tit. Reſtor. al primer action.*

2. E. 6. B. Surr. 52. the end. See Tit. Executors and Surrender.

Faits, Deeds.

NOTE, If an Action be ſued upon a Deed, bearing date at *Cane* in *Normandy,* 5 *Dat. apud Cane, &c.* That the Plaintiffe ſhall count that the Deed was made at *Cane* in *Com. Kanc.* and good; for the place is not traverſable (*B. Faits* 95. *the end*) And alſo where in truth it was written in *Cane,* 'tis ſuable in *England,* where it beares date at large, and at no place certaine: But if it bee

48. E. 3. per accord.

See 34. H. 8. Tit. Action upon the Caſe. 21 E. 4. 74. per Cur. ſee Cooke upon Lit. fo.

(*dat.*

(*dat. apud Cane in Normandy, &c.*) *quære* If the Action lyes, &c. *Time. H.* 8.

Note, That 'twas agreed by the Juſtices, that this clauſe which comes after theſe words, *In cujus rei, &c. Sigillum appoſui, &c.* is not any part of the Deede, though 'twere written before the ſealing and delivery, 1 *M.* 1. *B. Faits* 72.

Faits inroll: Deeds inrolled.

See 32. H. 8. Tit. coverture. 7. E. 4. 5. by Lit.

Note, That a Deed of Huſband and Wife ſhall not be inrolled in the common Bench, except for the Huſband only, and not for the Wife; by reaſon of coverture: Nor ſhe ſhall not be bound with her Huſband in a Statute-Marchant, nor the like : But if they make a Deed inrolled of Land in *London*, and acknowledge it before the Recorder and an Alderman, and the Wife examined ; this ſhall binde as a Fine at common-Law, by their cuſtome, and not only as a Deede, and it ſuffiſeth without Livery of Seiſin, 29 *H.* 8. *B. Faits inroll.* 14. & 15.

See Tit. Fines, Levies.

12. H. 4. 21. ſee 37. H. 6. 10. by Davers. 4. Eliz. Con. 213. & 242.

A man infeoffs the King by Deede, and makes Livery ; this is worth nothing, for the King ſhall not take but by matter of record : But if he inroll the Deed, then 'tis good to the King without Livery, for the King takes not by Livery, 29 *H.* 8. *B. Faits inroll.* 16. *Feoffments* 69.

27. H. 8. ca. 16.

Note, by the Juſtices, That where two Joyn-Tenants are, the one aliens all his Lands and Tenements in *D.* after the Statute of Inrollments, and before the Inrollment the other Joyn-Tenant dies, ſo that his moitie ſurvives to the Vendor, and after the Vendor, within the halfe yeere, inrolls the Deede ; yet nothing paſſes but the Moitie, for the Inrollment hath relation to the making and delivery

of

of the Deede, ſo that it ſhall give nothing but that which was ſold by it at the time of delivery of the Deede : And by more Juſtices, Where a man ſells his Land by Deede Indented to one, and after hee ſells it by another Indenture to another, and the laſt Deede is firſt Inrolled, and after the firſt Deed is Inrolled, within the halfe yeere, there the firſt Vendee ſhall have the Land, for it hath relation to make it the Deed of the Vendor, and to paſſe the Land *ab deliberatione faƈti;* for the Statute is, That a Free-hold, nor uſe of it ſhall not paſſe, nor change from one to another by bargain and ſale only, except it bee by Deed Indented and Inrolled within the halfe yeere ; *Ergo,* if it bee by Deede Indented and In-rolled within the halfe yeere it ſhall paſſe as the uſe might paſſe at common-Law, by ſale of the Land which was preſently upon the ſale, 6 *E.* 6. *B. Faits Inroll.* 9.

See Tit. Con-ſcience.

Fauxifier, Falſefying.

Where he in reverſion ſhall falſifie a recovery had againſt Tenant for term of life, where not, See Tit. *Entre Congeable.*

Where the Feoffees may falſifie a recovery ſuf-fered by *Ceſty que uſe* in tayl ; where not, See *Tit. Entre Congeable.*

'Twas holden that an attaint ſhall goe with the Land, as a Writ of Error ſhall, *Time. H.* 8. *B. Fauxifier* 50. the end.

Fitz. 21. L.

Faux Impriſonment, falſe Impriſonment.

'Tis ſaid, That a man, as Conſtable, cannot Arreſt another for an Affray, after that the affray is paſt, without Warrant : contrary, before the Affray,

Affray, and in the time of the Affray &c. And the fame Law of a Juftice of Peace, 38 *H.* 8. *B.* Faux *Imprifonment* 6. the end.

Faux Judgement, Falfe Judgement.

Note, by *Fitz.* for cleer Law, That in a Writ of falfe Judgement *in nullo eft erratum* is no Plea; for they joyn iffue upon fome matter *in fait* certain alledged by the party, and fhall bee tryed by the Country; for 'tis no Record, *contra,* in Error, 23 *H.* 8. *B. Faux Judgement* 17.

Fealtie.

Note, in the Chequer, That if Land defcend to me, which is holden of *J. S.* by homage, and I doe to him homage; and after other Land defcends to me by another Anceftor, holden of him by homage, I fhall doe fealty, but not homage again; for I became to him his man before. And if both the Tenements are holden of the King by homage, he fhall not refpit both the homages in the Exchequer; but one homage only, 24 *H.* 8. *B. Fealty* 8.

Note, in the Exchequer, That a Dean and Chapter, and other bodies politique, fhall nor doe homage; for this fhall be done in perfon: And a Corporation cannot appear in perfon, but by Attorney; and homage cannot be done by Attorney, but only in perfon, 33 *H.* 8. *B. Fealty* 15.

Feoffments.

9. E. 4. 32.
See 31. H. 8.
Tit. Leafes. 6.
& 7. E. 6. Com.

A man makes a Feoffment of a houfe *cum pertinentiis*, nothing paffes by thefe words *cum pertin.* but the Garden, the Curtilage, and Clofe adjoyning

to

to the houfe, and upon which the houfe is built, and no other Land, though other Land hath been occupied with the houfe, 23 *H.* 8. *B. Feoffments* 53.

Note, by *Fitz james* ch. Juftice, *Englefield* Juft. and divers others, where a Diffeizor makes a Feoffment for maintenance, and takes the profits, the Feoffment is void by the Stat. of 1 *R.* 2. *ca.* 9. as to a Stranger which fhall have an Action, for he fhall have it againft the *pernour* of the profits; but 'tis not betwixt the Feoffor and the Feoffee. And alfo a man who vouches by fuch Feoffment, one of the Feoffees, the Demandant, fhall counter-plead by the fame Stat. becaufe the Feoffment was void. And *B.* feems that fuch Feoffment fhall not be a remitter in prejudice of a third perfon, 24 *H.* 8. *B. Feoffments* 19.

If a man makes a Feoffment to four, and the one of the four makes a letter of Attorney to *J. N.* for to take livery for him and his companions, who doth it accordingly; nothing paffes, but to him who made the Letter of Attorney only, 27 *H.* 8. *B. Feoffments* 67.

'Twas faid for Law, That if a man Leafes Land for ten years, and the fame Leffee lets it over to another for four years; the Leffor makes a Feoffment to a Stranger by fufferance of the fecond Leffee, this is a good Feoffment without Attornment of the firft Leffee, 28 *H.* 8. *B. Feoffments* 68.

'Tis faid, That a Feoffment of a moity, is good, 31 *H.* 8. *B. Feoffments to ufes* 19.

If a man makes a feofmēt of a houfe, *ac omnia terras, tenementa et hereditamēta eidem meffuag. pertinen. aut cum eodem occupat. locat. aut dimiff. exiften.* by this the Land ufed with the houfe fhall paffe, 32 *H.* 8. *B. Feoffments* 53. the end.

Marginal notes:

36. by Hales Juft. 4. M. 1. Com. 171. 6. & 7. E. 6. Com. 85. 3. M. 1. Com. 168. 27. H. 6. 2.

27. H. 8. 23. by Fitz.

21. H. 6. Counter-plea of Voucher 3.

See Time. H. 8. after.

Lit. 67. 21. E. 4. 22. by Rede accord.

A

See 31. H. 8. Tit. Leafes.

A man makes a Deed of Feoffment to another, and delivers the Deed to him in the Land, or upon the Land; this is a good Feoffment by all the Juftices in the Common-Bench, 35 *H. 8. B. Feoffments* 74.

Accord. Frow. 9. H. 7. 25. & 7. E. 4. 20. 3. M. 1. Com. 154.

If a man bee feized of one acre of Land in Fee, and another is feized to his ufe in Fee of another acre, and hee makes a Feoffment of both acres, and Livery of the acre which he hath in poffeffion, by this the acre in ufe paffes not, though he made the Livery in the one in the name of both, for this is

1. R. 3. ca. 4.

not his acre; but the acre of the Feoffees, and the Stat. faies that his feofment fhall be good, but 'tis no Feoffment except hee makes Livery in the fame Land : Otherwife if Livery were made in the Land, in ufe, by reafon of the Stat. 37 *H. 8. B. Feoffments* 77. *Feoffments to ufes,* 55.

If a Feoffment be made within the view, when this is pleaded ; 'tis faid that expreffe mention fhall be made in the pleading, that the Land was within the view, *Time H. 8. B. Feoffments* 57. *the end.*

Feoffment is good of the Land by Deede, by Livery of the Deed within the view, fo that the Feoffee enters accordingly : But if the Feoffor dies before the Feoffee enters, then the Land is difcended to the Heir of the Feoffor, and the Feoffment fhall not take effect, *Time H. 8. B. Feoffments* 72.

10. E. 4. 1. by Choke. fee 27. H. 8. before. 40. E. 3. 41. by Finch. 18. E. 4. 12. by Collow & Townef.

A man makes a Feoffment by Deed to twenty, and delivers the Deed and Seifin to one in the name of all, this is good to all ; but if hee Infeoffs twenty without Deed, and delivers Seifin to one in the name of all, this is no feofment to any but to him who takes the Livery, *Time H. 8. B. Feoffments* 72.

1. R. 2. c. 9. Raft. Feoff-

Note, that by the Stat. of 1 *R.* 2. where a Dif-feizor makes a Feoffment, for maintenance, and takes

the

the profits; the Feoffment is void by the Stat. to all intents, *Lecture Whorwood* 35 *H.* 8. *B. Feoffments* 19.

menu 1. See 24. H. 8. before.

Feoffments to uses.

By *Shelly* Juft: Where the Father Infeoffs his Son and Heir apparent, to the intent to defraud the Lord of his Ward, this Feoffment was to the ufe of the Father, during his life, and hee takes the profits during his life, and fo fee that ufes were in antient times, 24 *H.* 8. *B. Feoffments to ufes* 20. *the end.*

See the next fect. prope fine. 33. H. 6. 16. by Prifot.

A man makes a Feoffment in Fee, to four, to his ufe, and the Feoffees make a gift in tayle without confideration, to a ftranger, who had not conufance of the firft ufe, *habend.* in tayle, to the ufe of *ceftuy que ufe,* and his Heirs; the tenant in tayle fhall not be Seifed to the firft ufe, but to his own ufe, for the Stat. of *Weftm.* 2 *cap.* 1. wills, *quod Voluntas Donatoris in omnibus obfervetur;* that a man ought to refer his Will to the Lawe, and not the Lawe to his Will: Alfo none can bee Seifed to the ufe of another, but hee which may execute an Eftate to *ceftuy que ufe,* which fhall bee perfect in Law, which tenant in tayle cannot doe; for if hee executes an Eftate, his Iffue fhall have a *Formedon;* And the beft opinion that an Abbot, Mayor and Commonalty, nor other Corporations fhall not bee feifed to a ufe, for their capacitie is only to take to their own ufe: And alfo if the Abbot execute an eftate, the fucceffor fhall have a writ of Entry *fine affenfu capituli:* and thofe that are in the *poft,* as by *Efcheate,* Mortmain, *Perquifite* of *Villeine,* Recovery, *Dower* by the courtefie, and the like, are feifed to their own ufe and to another ufe: And alfo the Stat. of 1 *R.* 3. is,
That

See Cook upon Lit.

Weft. 2. ca. 1. 27. H. 8. 10. by Montague. See Cook, lib. 1. Chudleighs cafe.

Of the Efcheat, 14. H. 8. 8. by Pollard: of the Recovery, 4. E. 6. Com. 54. by

Halles. 1. R. 3. ca. 5.

That all Gifts, Feoffments & Grants of *ceſtuy que uſe* ſhall be good againſt all, &c. ſaving to all perſons their rights and intereſts in tayl, as if this Stat. had not been made; and therefore Tenant in tayl ſhall not bee ſeized to a uſe. And 'twas agreed by the Court, That the words in the end of the Stat. of 1

See 29. H. 8. after. 14. H. 8. 8. by Br. Juſt. Perk. 103. C.

R. 3. ſaving ſuch right and intereſt to the Tenant in tayl, &c. is taken Tenant in tayl in poſſeſſion; and not Tenant in tayl in uſe : for *ceſtuy que uſe* in tayl hath no right nor intereſt. And alſo here there is a

Litt. 29. Perk. 103. D. ſee after.

Tenure betwixt the Donors and the Donees, which is a conſideration that the Tenant in tayl ſhall be ſeized to his own uſe : And the ſame Law of Tenant for term of yeers, and Tenant for life, their fealty is due; and where a rent is reſerved, there, though a uſe be expreſſed to the uſe of the Donor, or Leſſor;

See Dyer 5. M. fo. 155.

yet this is a conſideration that the Donee or Leſſee ſhall have it to his own uſe : And the ſame Law where a man ſells his Land for 20. l. by Indenture, and executes an Eſtate to his own uſe ; this is a void limitation of the uſe : for the Law by the conſideration of money, makes the Land to bee in the Vendee. *Et opinio fuit*, That a uſe was at Common-Law

Weſtm. 3. ca. 2. Raſt. Tenure 4. 45. E. 3. 15. by Finch. Perk. 103. B.

before the Stat. of *Quia emptores terrarum*, but uſes were not common before the ſame Stat.   For upon every Feofment before this Stat. there was a Tenure betwixt the Feoffors and the Feoffee; which was conſideration, that the Feoffee ſhall be ſeized to his own uſe ; but after this Stat. the Feoffee ſhall hold *de capitali domino*, and there is no conſideration betwixt the Feoffor and the Feoffee without mony paid, or other eſpeciall matter declared, for which the Feoffee ſhall be ſeized to his own uſe : For

Cap. 6. ſee before.

where the Stat. of *Marlebr.* is, that a Feofment by the father, Tenant in chivalry, made to his ſon by
covin,

covin, ſhall not toll the Lords Ward, &c. In theſe See Cook lib.
Caſes the Feoffor after ſuch Feofment takes the profits of the Land all his life. And the ſame Law by
Shelley of a Feofment made by a Woman to a Man
to marry her, the Woman takes the profits after the
eſpouſalls : *Quære inde;* for this is an expreſſe conſideration in it ſelf. And by *Norwich*, If a man
deliver money to *J. S.* to buy land for him, and he
buyes it for himſelf, & to his own uſe, this is to the
uſe of the buyer, and to the uſe of him who deli- 20. H. 6. 34.
vered the mony; and there is no other remedy but by Wangf.
an action of deceipt, 14 *H.* 8. *B. Feoffments to uſes* 40.

Note, if a Feofment be made to the uſe of *W. N.*
for term of his life, & after to the uſe of *J. S.* and
his Heirs, their *ceſtuy que uſe* in remainer or rever- 10. El. Com.
ſion, may ſell the remain or reverſion in the life of 350.
W. N. but hee cannot make a Feoffment till after
his death, 25 *H.* 8. *B. Feoffments to uſes* 44.

'Tis holden that if the Feoffees ſeiſed to the uſe See before
of an Eſtate taile, or other uſe, are impleaded, and Time. H. 8. &
ſuffer the common recovery againſt them upon bar- after, 30. H. 8.
gaine, this ſhall bind the Feoffees and their Heirs,
and *ceſtuy que uſe* and his Heirs, where the buyer
and recoveror hath not conuſance of the firſt uſe :
And by *Fitz.* it ſhall binde, though they had notice
of the uſe; for the Feoffees have the Feeſimple :
Et per plures, if *ceſtuy que uſe* in taile be vouched in
a recovery, and ſo the recovery paſſes, it ſhall bind
the tail in uſe *ſ. ceſtuy que uſe* and his Heirs ; and 1. R. 3. ca. 5.
otherwiſe not ; And this *B.* ſeems to be by the Stat. Raſt. Uſes, 4.
which excepts tenant in taile, which is intended
tenant in taile in poſſeſſion, and not *ceſtuy que uſe*
in taile, for *ceſtuy que uſe* in tail is not tenant in taile,
29 *H.* 8. *B. Recovery in value*, 20. *Feoffments to*
uſes, 56.

Feoffees

See before.

Feoffees in use make a leafe for yeers, rendring rent, to another who hath notice of the firſt uſe, yet the Leaſe ſhall be only to the uſe of the Leſſee him-

19. H. 8. 1. accord.

ſelfe : And the ſame Law *per plures* though no rent be reſerved : And if a man makes a Feofment, and annexes a Schedule to the Deed conteyning the uſe, hee cannot change the uſe after ; and ſo if hee ex-preſſes the uſe in the Deed of Feofment, but other-wiſe where hee declares the uſe by words of his

See 20. H. 7. 11..

Will ſ. I will that my Feoffees ſhall bee ſeized to ſuch a uſe, there he may change this uſe, becauſe by Will, &c. And that if a Feofment be made to the uſe of the Feoffor in tail, & after he execute an eſtate to him in fee, the uſe of the Eſtate taile is de-termined, 30 *H.* 8. *B. Feofments to uſes,* 47.

If *A.* Covenants with *B.* That when *A.* ſhall be Enfeoffed, by *B.* of three acres of Land in *D.* that then the ſaid *A.* and his Heirs, and all others ſeized of the Land of the ſaid *A.* in *S.* ſhall be thereof ſeiſed to the uſe of the ſaid *B.* and his Heirs ; there if *A.* makes a Feofment of his Land in *S.* and after *B.* Enfeofs *A.* of the ſaid three acres in *D.* there the Feoffees of *A.* ſhall bee ſeiſed to the uſe of *B.* not-withſtanding they had not notice of the uſe ; for the

14. H. 8. 9. by Pollard.

Land is and was bound with the uſe aforeſaid, to whoſe hands ſoever it ſhall come ; and 'tis not like where a Feoffe in uſe ſells the Land to one who had not notice of the firſt uſe ; for in this firſt Caſe the uſe had not being till the Feofment be made of the three acres, and then the uſe doth commence, 30 *H.* 8 *B. Feoffments to uſes* 50.

See 29. H. 8. before.

'Twas doubted if a Recovery had againſt *ceſtuy que uſe* in taile, ſhall binde the Heir in taile ; But by *Hales* Juſt. By ſuch Recovery the entry of the Feoffees ſeiſed to the uſe of the Eſtate taile is taken

away,

away, but after the death of *ceftuy que ufe* who fuffered the Recovery; the Feoffees may have a writ
of right, or writ of entry *ad terminum qui preteriit* in
the *poft*, or the like : And by fome there is no ufe
in taile, but 'tis a fee-fimple conditional at common
Law, as 'twas of the tafle before the Stat. of *W.* 2.
And this Stat. makes no mention but of gifts in
taile, which is taile in poffeffion ; and therefore
quære, if the taile in ufe cannot be taken by the
equity of it, yet 'twas doubted if the iffues and the
Feoffees fhall be bound after the death of *ceftuy que* 19. H. 8. 13.
ufe, who fuffered the Recovery, by reafon of thofe fee before.
words in the Stat. of 1 *R.* 3. which wills that the 1. 1. R. 3. ca.
Recovery fhall bee good againft the Vendor and his 5.
Heirs, clayming only as Heir, and againft all others
clayming only to the ufe of the Vendor and his
Heirs; and this is intended, by fome, of a Fee-
fimple : And in the cafe aforefaid the iffue in taile
claymeth as Heir in taile in ufe, (*B. Feofments to*
ufes 56, *the middle*) yet fee the Stat. of 32 *H.* 8. 32. H. 8. ca.
That a Fine with Proclamation, levyed or to be 36.
levyed by tenant in taile in poffeffion, Reverfion,
Remainer, or in Ufe, after Proclamation had, fhall
binde thofe tenants of thofe tayles and their Heirs See Tit. Fines.
for ever : And fee that the fame Stat. is as well for
the time paft, as to come, 30 *H.* 8. *B. Feofments to*
ufes, 57.

If Covenants and Agreements are conteined in
Indentures and not ufes ; and 'tis Covenanted by
the Indentures that *A.* fhall recover againft *B.* his
Land in *D.* to the ufe of the recoveror and his
Heirs, and to the ufes of the Covenants and Agree-
ments in the Indentures ; there if he recovers, the
recovery fhall be to the ufe of the recoveror and his
Heirs ; and not to the ufes of the Covenants and
Agreements

Agreements in the Indentures, where no uſes are in the Indentures. But otherwiſe, if uſes are conteined in the Indentures, and 'tis Covenanted, That *A.* ſhall recover to the uſe of *A.* and his Heirs, and to the uſes in the Indenture; there the recovery ſhall goe according, and ſhall be executed by the Stat. 32 *H.* 8. *B. Feoffments to uſes* 58.

27. H. 8. ca. 10. Raſt. Uſes, 9.

'Twas agreed by all the Juſtices, upon great deliberation, in the caſe of *Mantel* Eſq. of the County of *North.* who was attainted with the Lord *Dacres* of the South, for the death of a man (which ſee *Tit. Corone.*) that where he at his marriage 31 *H.* 8. after the Stat. of uſes made, 27 *H.* 8. Covenanted, That for a 100. l. and in conſideration of marriage, that hee and his Heirs, and all perſons ſeized of his Lands and Tenements in *H.* ſhall bee thereof ſeized to the uſe of his wife for term of her life, and after to the Heirs of his body by her ingendred, that this ſhall change the uſe well enough, and very good: And by this the Land was ſaved, and was not forfeited, 34 *H.* 8. *B. Feoffments to uſes* 16. the end.

A man purchaſes Land, and cauſes an Eſtate to bee made to him and his wife, and to three others in Fee, this ſhall bee taken to the uſe of the huſband only; and not to the uſe of the wife without ſpeciall matter to induce it. And ſo ſee a Woman may be ſeized to the uſe of her huſband, and by him ſuch Feofment was, 3. *H.* 7. and intended as aforeſaid, 34 *H.* 8. *B. Feoffments to uſes* 51.

See 4. E. 6. Com. 44.;

A man makes a Feofment in Fee to his uſe for term of Life; & that after his deceaſe *I. N.* ſhall take the profits; this makes a uſe in *I. N.* contrary if he ſaies, that after his death his Feoffees ſhall take the profits and deliver them to *I. N.* this doth not make a uſe in *I. N.* : for he hath them not but by

the

the hands of the Feoffees, 36 *H.* 8. *B. Feoffments to uses,* 52.

A man cannot fell Land to *I. S.* to the ufe of the Vendor, nor let Land to him rendring rent, *habend.* to the ufe of the Leffor, for this is contrary to Law and Reafon, for he hath recompence for it : And by *Hales,* a man cannot change a ufe by a covenant which is executed before, as to covenant to bee feifed to the ufe of *W. S.* becaufe that *W. S.* is his Cofin ; or becaufe that *W. S.* before gave to him twenty pound, except the twenty pound was given to have the fame Land. But otherwife of a confideration, prefent or future, for the fame purpofe, as for one hundred pounds paid for the Land *tempore conventionis,* or to bee paid at a future day, or for to·marry his daughter, or the like, 36 *H.* 8. *B. Feoffments to uses,* 54.

Note, a Recovery was fuffered by *Grafeley* of the County of *Stafford,* by advice of *Fitz Serjeant* and others, and he was only *ceftuy que ufe* in tail, and after he died without iffue, and his brother recovered the Land in the Chancery, for at this time 'twas taken that a Recovery againft *ceftuy que ufe* in taile, fhould not ferve but for term of his life, by which 'tis not but a grant of his eftate, *Time H.* 8. *B. Feoffments to uses* 48. *the end.*

By *Fitz* Juft. if the Feoffees to the ufe of an Eftate taile, fell the Land to him that hath notice of the firft ufe, yet the buyer fhall not be feifed to the firft ufe, but to his own ufe, by reafon of the bargaine and fale, for the Feoffees have the Fee fimple, and therfore their fale is good, *Time H.* 8. *B. Feoffments to uses* 57. *the middle.*

Note, *per plures,* If a man makes a Feofment in Fee before the Stat. of ufes, or after this Stat. to the ufe

See 24. *H.* 8. before. More held time M. 1. that a ufe may be well changed for a confid. paft. See T. 8. El. 309. cont.

See Mildmayes cafe, Cook, lib. 7. & 8. El Com. 302.

See 30. *H.* 8. before.

See 29. *H.* 8. & 5. E. 6. before.

17. *H.* 8. ca. 10. See Cook.

lib. 1. Chud-
leighs cafe.

ufe of *W.* and his Heirs, till *A.* pay fourty pound to the faid *W.* and then to the ufe of the faid *A.* and his Heirs, and after comes the Stat. of ufes and executes the Eftate in *W.* and after *A.* paies to *W.* the 40. l. there *A.* is feifed in Fee, if he enters; yet by fome *A.* fhall not be feized in Fee by the faid payment, except that the Feoffees enter: *B.* doubts thereof, and therefore it feems to him beft to enter in the name of the Feoffees, and in his name, and then the one way or the other the entry fhall be good, and fhall make *A.* to bee feifed in Fee; and alfo fee by *B.* that a man at this day may make a Feoffment to a ufe, and that the ufe fhall change from one to another by act *ex poft facto,* by circumftance, as well as it fhould before the faid Statute, 6 *E.* 6. *B. Feoffments to ufes* 30.

See before.

'Twas holden *per plures* in the Chancery; if a Recovery bee had, in which *ceftuy que ufe* in taile is vouched, and the demandant recovers, then this fhall bind the iffue, *Time E.* 6. *B. Feoffments to ufes* 56. *the end.*

If a Covenant bee by Indenture, that the fonne of *A.* fhall marry the daughter of *C.* for which *C.* gives to *A.* a hundred pound, and for this *A.* covenants with *C.* That if the marriage takes not effect, that *A.* and his Heirs fhall bee feifed of a hundred and fiftie acres in *D.* to the ufe of *C.* and his Heirs, *quoufque A.* his Heirs or Executors repaies the hundred pound, and after *C.* hath iffue within age and dies, and after the marriage takes not effect by which the State is executed in the Heir of *C.* by the Statute of ufes made 27 *H.* 8. notwithftanding that *C.* was dead before the refufall of the marriage, for now the ufe and poffeffion vefts in the Heirs of *C.* for that the Indentures and Covenants fhall have relation to the

27. H. 8. ca. 9.
Raft. ufes. 9.
See Cook lib.
1. Shellies cafe.

the making of the Indentures, for theſe Indentures binde the Land with the uſe, which Indentures were in the life of *C.* But by *B. quære* if the Heir of *C.* ſhall bee in Ward to the Lord, for hee is Heir, and yet a Purchaſor, as it ſeemes, 3 *M.* 1. *B. Feofments to uſes,* 59.

Gift of Land for yeeres, or of a Leaſe for yeeres to a uſe, is good, notwithſtanding the Statute; for the Statute is intended to avoide gifts of Chattells to uſes for to defraude Creditors only, and ſo is the preamble and intent of this Statute, 3 *M.* 1. *B. Feofments to uſes,* 60.

8. H. 7. ca. 4. Raſt. uſes. 6.

Fines levies, Fines levied.

Note, That 'twas Covenanted that *A.* ſhall make to *B.* his wife, daughter of *I. K.* a joynture by Fine, and the Writ was brought by *I. K.* againſt *A.* and *B.* his wife, and they offered to acknowledg to *I.* to the intent that *I.* ſhould render to them, for life of *B.*, and becauſe *B.* the wife, was within age, therefore ſhee was drawne out and rejected: And then becauſe that none can take the firſt eſtate by the Fine, but thoſe who ſhall be named in the Writ of Covenant (but every Stranger may take a remainder) therefore the Writ was made betweene *I.* and *A.* only by which *A.* acknowledged the Tenements to bee the right of *I. ut illa que, &c.,* and *I.* granted and rendred it to the ſaid *A.* for terme of his life, without impeachment of Waſte, the remainder to the ſaid *B.* his wife, for terme of her life, the remainder to the ſaid *A.* and his Heirs, 30 *H.* 8. *B. Fines, Levies,* 108.

Fine with proclamation to bind Tenant in tail

and

H. 38. H. 8. accord between W. Roch. and Radm. Latharne, &c. See Tit. Coverture.

and his iffue, the time for to make proclamation, &c.
See *Tit. Affurances.*

If *ceftuy que ufe* for term of life levies a Fine with
Proclamation ; there none need to enter nor make
claim within the five years, becaufe that 'tis but a
Grant of his Eftate, which is lawfull, and no forfeiture ; for hee hath nothing in the Land ; nor hee
cannot make a forfeiture of the ufe. The fame
Law of a Fine levyed by Tenant for life in poffeffion : Yet *B.* doubts thereof and thinks otherwife
if hee levy it in Fee (*B. Feoffments to ufes* 48. *Fines
levies* 107.) *Et per plures,* if it be levyed by *ceftuy
que ufe* in tail, it fhall bind him and his Heirs ; but
not *ceftuy que ufe* in the reverfion nor the Feoffees
after the death of the Conufor, for the Statute of 1
R. 3. is, That it fhall bind him and his heirs and
Feoffees clayming onely to the fame, which is not
fo here, *Quære inde ;* for *B.* feems by the fame
Statute, that tayl in poffeffion is remedied by this
Statute ; but not tayl in ufe : for this feems to him
to remain at Common-Law, as a Fee-fimple in ufe
conditionall ; for 'tis not a Gift of the Land ; yet
quære, for by him, by the equity of the Statute of
W. 2. of tayles, devifes in tayl are taken ; yet this
is in nature of a Gift ; yet not at this day by the
Statute of 32 *H.* 8. fine with Proclamation by
ceftuy que ufe in tayl, fhall bind the tayl after Proclamation, 30 *H.* 8. *B. Fines levyed* 107. the end.

Note, That a Deed inrolled in *London,* binds as
a Fine at Common-Law (but not as a Fine with
Proclamation ;) and there need not livery of Seifin
upon fuch Deed : And this is a difcontinuance without livery, becaufe that by the cuftome there (which
is referved by divers Parliaments) it fhall bind as a
Fine, 31 *H.* 8. *B. Fines Levies* 110.

'Twas

10. H. 7. 20.
by Keble.

27. H. 8. 20.
Fitz. accord.

1. R. 3. ca. 5.
Raft. ufes 4.
See Tit. Feoff-
ments to ufes.

W. 2. ca. 1.

32. H. 8. ca. 36.

See Tit. fair
inroll.

'Twas granted for Law, where two are of the
fame name (as if there bee two *R. B.*) and the one
levies a Fine of the others Land; there the other
fhall avoid it by Plea, *f.* to fay that there are two
of the name; and that the other *R. B.* levied the
Fine, and not this *R. B.* 33 *H.* 8. *B. Fines levies*
115. the end.

34. H. 6. 19.
by Danby.

Note that if the Writ of *Dedimus poteftatem*, to
levie a Fine doth not beare *tefte* after the writ of
Covenant, 'tis Error; for the *Dedimus poteftatem*
faies, *cum Breve noftrum de conventione pendet* betwixt *A. B.* and *C. D.*, &c. 35 *H.* 8. *B. Fines,*
Levies, 116.

Note, that 'twas devifed to have a Leafe for
yeeres to binde Tenant in taile, that the tenant in
taile and the Leffee fhould acknowledge the tenements to bee the right of one *A.* a ftranger, and that
A. fhould grant and render by the fame Fine to the
Leffee for fixtie yeeres, the remainder to the Leffor
and his Heirs, and 'twas with Proclamation, which
fhall binde the taile after proclamation made (And
fo fee that the Devife after will not ferve for taile,
but for Fee fimple, for hee which takes by Fine,
fhall not bee concluded if hee bee an Infant, or
Feme covert, or the iffue in tail of the Conufor:)
And in this cafe no rent can bee referved; for *A.*
was a ftranger to the Land, by which the Leffee
granted ten pound of rent, and *extra terra. illa.* with
a claufe of diftreffe during the yeeres or terme aforefaid to the Leffor, 36 *H.* 8. *B. Fines, Levies,* 118.

See Time. H.
8. after.

Leafe may be made by Fine for term of yeeres
rendring rent, and firft the leffee to acknowledg the
tenements to be the right of the Leffor *come ceo, &c.*
and then the other grant and render to him for terme
of fixtie yeeres, rendring therefore yeerely ten pound

See 36. H. 8.
before.

N N

per

per annum, &c. And with Claufe of Diftreffe, *Time, H.* 8. *B. Fines, Levies,* 106.

Fitz. 97. A. Note, by *Fitz* Juft : That a fine levyed by *A.* and *B.* his wife, where the name of the wife is *M.* fhall binde her by eftoppell, and the tenant may plead that fhee by the name of *B.* levyed the Fine, and fo 'twas in ure by him, and 'twas pleaded according, *Time H.* 8. *B. Fines, Levies,* 117.

Note, by *Bromeley* chiefe Juftice, and others, That a Writ of Error was brought in the Kings bench, becaufe a Fine was acknowledged by *Dedimus potef-tatem,* before one who was not a Judge, Abbot, Knight nor Sargeant : and for this caufe 'tis refufed to admit any which is taken by fuch ; for the Statute *de finibus & Attorn.* gives power to none except to Juftices, Abbot and Knight ; *quære,* by *B.* if a Sarjeant at Law, bee not taken as a Juftice by the equitie of the Statute, *Time H.* 8. *B. Fines, Levies,* 120.

'Twas granted that a Fine may be levyed in a Hamlet ; for if a *Scire fac.* lyes upon a Fine in a 8. E. 4. 6. per Cur. Hamlet (as it appears 8 *E.* 4. that it doth) therefore a Fine is well levyed there, 6 *E.* 6. *B. Fines Levies* 93.

See 6. E. 6. before. Note, that 'twas agreed by the Juftices, that a Fine may be well levyed in a Hamlet, and this, notwithftanding all the houfes are decayed but one. 8. E. 4. 6. per Cur. The fame of a Writ of Dower : And the fame Law of that which hath been a Ville and no wis decaid ; yet the name of the Ville remains, as old *Salifbury,* which hath at this day Burgeffes of Parliament, and the like, 7 *E.* 6. *B. Fines Levies* 91.

Forcible Entry.

Hee which hath been ſeized peaceably by three yeeres, may retaine with force : But if a Diſſeizor hath continued poſſeſſion three yeers peaceably, and after the Diſſeiſee re-enters (as he may lawfully) and after the Diſſeiſor re-enters, hee cannot deteine with force, becauſe that the firſt diſſeiſin is determined by the entry of the Diſſeiſee, and the Diſſeiſee by this remitted, and this Entry is a new Diſſeiſin : But if a man hath beene ſeiſed by good and juſt Title by three yeeres, and after is diſſeiſed by wrong, and after hee re-enters, hee may retaine with force ; for he is remitted, and in by his firſt Title, by which hee firſt continued peaceably by three yeeres, *per quoſdam :* for it ſeemes to them, by the *Proviſo* in the end of the Statute, that this is good Lawe in the laſt Caſe, and ſtands well with the Statute ; yet by ſome this is not Law, therefore *quære* 23 *H.* 8. *B. Forcible entry,* 22.

27. H. 6. 2.

22. H. 6. 18.

8. H. 6. ca. 9.

Forfeiture of Marriage.

'Twas ſaid, if a man brings a Writ of Intruſion *maritagio non ſatisfac.* for the ſingle value, and makes mention in the Writ of tender of marriage to the Heir, and that hee refuſed, &c. that the tender is not traverſable, *Time H.* 8. *B. Forfeiture of Marriage* 7. *Intruſion* 23. *in finibus.*

Fitz. 141. D.

Forfeiture de Terre, &c. Forfeiture of Land, &c.

What ſhall be a forfeiture of the Eſtate of Tenant for life, what not, See *Tit. Entry Congeable.*

Richard

Richard Fermor of *L.* was attainted in *Premunire*, and his Lands forfeited in Fee *in perpetuum*, and not only for term of life : And *fo fee* 'tis not only a forfeiture for life, as in an attaint ; for the one is by Statute, the other by the Common-Law, 34 *H.* 8. B. *Præmunire* 19. the end, *Forfeiture* 101.

4. H. 7. 11. by Townef.

Note, If a man bee attainted of Treafon by Parliament ; by this his Lands and goods are forfeited, without words of forfeiture of Lands or Goods in the Act, 35 *H.* 8. B. *Forfeiture* 99.

Founderfhip cannot Efcheate, nor be forfeited by attaindor of Felony or Treafon, See *Tit. Efcheate.*

St. 185. 20. E. 4. 5. by Billing. 40. E. 3. 42.

Note, by *Hales* Juftice cleerly, that a Cleark convict, fhall lofe his goods, 5 *E.* 6. B. *Forfeiture* 113.

Formedon.

See 24. H. 8. Tit. Tayl.

'Tis faid that if the iffue in taile bee barred by Judgement, by reafon of warranty and affets difcended, and after hee aliens the affets, and hath iffue and dies, the iffue of the iffue fhall not have a *Formedon* of the firft Land tayled ; but if fuch thing happens before hee bee barred by Judgement, the iffue of the iffue fhall have a *Formedon, Time H.* 8. B. *Formedon* 18.

This matter was in ure P. Rot. 505. in the Common Bench betwixt Jarveis Demandant & Brown Tenant. See 7. E. 6. after.

See 1. M. 1. after, & 7. E. 6.

Note, If the Feoffees are infeoffed to the ufe of the Feoffor, for terme of life, and after to the ufe of *A.* in taile, before the Statute of 27 *H.* 8. of ufes, and after the Eftates, in ufes are vefted in poffeffion by the fame Statute, and after the tenant for life dies, and the tenant in tayle enters, and difcontinues and dies, and the iffue brings a *Formedon*, upon this matter hee fhall fuppofe the Feoffor to be Donor, and not the Feoffees, and the Writ fhall bee generall *quod dedit, &c.* but the Declaration fhall bee fpeciall and

and declare the whole matter, That the Feoffor was
seised in fee, and enfeoffed the Feoffees to uses *ut
supra*, and shew the Execution of the Estates by the
Statute of uses made 27 *H.* 8. briefly and not at
large, and the seisin &c. and the death of tenant for
life and tenant in taile *& quod post mortem, &c.
discend. jus, &c.* 2 *E.* 6. B. *Formedon*, 49.

Formedon upon a gift in Fee to the use of the
Feoffor and the Heirs of his body, which is executed
by the Statute of uses 27 *H.* 8. and after the
Feoffor aliens and dies, his issue shall have a *Formedon* that the Feoffees *dederunt tenement. predict.* to
the father of the Demandant, *& discendit jus, &c.* for
it cannot be supposed that the Feoffor gave to *cestuy
que use* which was himselfe; for a man cannot give
to himselfe: and hee shall make a speciall Declaration upon the Feoffment to the use of the taile:
But where *A.* makes a Feoffment in Fee, to three,
to the use of a Stranger and the Heirs of his body,
which is exempted by the Statute aforesaid, and
after who was *cestuy que use* aliens in fee, and dyes;
there his issue shall have a *Formedon*, and shall say
that the Feoffor gave to his father, and not the
Feoffees gave, and shall make a speciall Declaration,
7 *E.* 6. B. *Formedon* 46. *Generall Briefe* 141

Note by *Bromley* chief Justice, That the Demandant (in the case 2 *E.* 6. before) may declare
generally if he will; and if the Tenant pleads *ne
dona pas*, the Demandant may reply and shew the
speciall matter, as appears there, and conclude, &
so he gave, &c. and good, 1 *M.* 1. B. *Formedon* 49.
the end.

4. E. 6. Com.
59. by Monta-
gue.

See 2. E. 6.
before.

Forme.

Note, that Wood was put before Pasture in a
Plaint

3. M. 1. Com. 169. See Cook. lib. Plaint of *Affize*, and exception thereof taken, and yet good, though it be contrary to the *Regifter*, *Time. E.* 6. *B. Faux Latin & Forme* 66.

Franke-marriage.

7. E. 4. 12. cont. by Molle and Fitz. 172. H. Litt. 4. accord. Perk. 48. E. Note, that 'twas faid for Law, that Land cannot bee given in Frank-marriage with a man who is Cofin to the Donor ; but it ought to be with a woman who is Cofin to the Donor, *Time. H.* 8. *B. Frank-marrige* 10.

See 4. E. 6. Com. 14. by Harris. Fitz. 136. B. of the acquittall. See Cook upon Litt. Note, 'tis faid for Law, that a Gift in Frank-marriage, the remainder to *J. N.* in Fee, is not Frank-marriage ; for warranty and acquittall is incident to Frank-marriage, by reafon of the Reverfion in the Donor, which cannot be where the Donor puts the remainder and Fee to a Stranger úpon the fame Gift, *Time. H.* 8. *B. Frank-marriage* 11.

Garde, Warde.

IF the Kings Tenant, Alien in Fee, without licence, and dyes, his Heire within age, the King fhall not have the Ward, becaufe that nothing is difcended to him ; and that the alienation is good, fave the Trefpafs to the King, which is but a Fine by Seifure : 26 *H.* 8. *B. Alienations* 29. *Garde* 85.

See Tit. Intrufion.

If the King hath an heir in Ward, which is a Woman, and marries her before the age of Fourteen years ; there fhe fhall be out of Ward at Fourteen years, and then may fue Livery, for the Two years to make Sixteen years are not given, but to

tender

tender to her marriage, therefore when ſhee is married ſooner, ſhee ſhall be out of cuſtody at Fourteen years, 28. *H. 8. B. Garde* 86. *Livery* 54.

A man makes a Feoffment before the Statute of execution of Uſes, to the uſe of himſelf for term of his life, the remainder to W. in Taile, the Remainder to the right Heires of the Feoffor, the Feoffor dyes, and W. dyes without iſſue, the right Heir of the Feoffor within Age, he ſhall be in Ward for the Fee diſcended; for the uſe of the Fee-ſimple, was never out of the Feoffor. And the ſame Law where a man gives in Taile, the Remainder to the right Heires of the Donor, the Fee is not out of him. Otherwiſe, where a man makes a Feoffment in Fee upon condition to re-infeoffe him, and the Feoffee gives to the Feoffor for life, the Remainder over in Taile, the Remainder to the right Heirs of the Feoffor, for there the Fee, and the uſe of it was out of the Feoffor ; & therefore he hath there a remainder and not a reverſion, 32. *H. 8. B. Garde* 93.

27. H. 8. c. 10. See Dyer H. 8. Bockinghams. c.

Where a man holds certain land of the King in Soccage in *Capite,* the King ſhall not have livery of more then the Soccage land. The ſame where he holds of the King in Knights ſervice, and not in *Capite,* the King ſhall not have more in ward, but onely that which is holden of him immediately, 32. *H. 8. B. Garde* 97.

Fitz. 256. c. See 38. H. 8. Tit. Livery. Stp. 10. 13.

Note by all the Juſtices of *England,* that a Lord in Knights ſervice, by non-age of the Heir, ſhall not ouſte the grantee of *Wreck,* or *de proxima preſentatione ;* nor the termors which are in by the father of the Heirs *B. Grants,* 85. *Garde* 66. *Leaſe* 31. in *finibus :* So of a Leaſe for term of life. 35. *H. 8. B. Garde* 61. the end.

5. H. 7. 37. See 36. H. 8. Tit. Leaſes. See Time. H. 8. after. 5. H. 7. 37. by all.

A

A man dyes feifed of lands holden in Knights fervice, his brother and Heir within age, the Lord feifes the ward, the wife of the Tenant privily with childe with a fon, and after the wife is delivered, the brother is out of ward. But if the Infant dye, the brother yet within age, there the brother fhall be in ward again. And the fame Law where a daughter is heire, and after a fon is born, the daughter is out of ward : And if the fon dies without iffue, the daughter within age, fhe fhall be in ward again ; fo fee that one and the fame perfon may be twice in ward by two feveral anceftors. But where the Lord feifes the fon for ward for land to him defcended from his Father, and grants the marriage of him to another, and after other land holden in Knights fervice, holden of the fame Lord defcends to the fame fon from his mother, there *B*, feems that the Lord fhall not have the ward again, becaufe he had him, and granted his marriage before, and the body is an intire thing. 35. *H.* 8. *B. Garde* 119.

See 35. H. 8. before.
11. H. 6. 7. by Babing.

'Tis granted by all the Juftices that the King fhal not oufte the termor of his tenant, becaufe he hath the heir of his tenant in ward by office found for him ; nor execution upon a Statute Merchant made againft his tenant ; nor a rent charge granted by his tenant, nor a grant *de prox. prefentatione* of an Advoufon. *Time H.* 8. *B. Garde* 44.

See 15. E. 4.
10. 6.
El. Com. 268.
côtra. And fee Cokes Books.

If the fon and heire of the Kings tenant, or of another Lord be made a Knight in the life of his Father, and after the Father dies, the heir fhall be in ward ; for otherwife the Anceftor may procure his fon within age to be made a Knight by collufion, to the intent to defraud the Lord of Ward, which fhal

ſhal not be ſuffered. And ſo it fell out of the Lord
Anth. *Brown* of *Surrey*, who was made Knight in
the time of his Father, who died, the ſon within
age, and twas holden he ſhould be in ward, notwithſtanding he was a Knight; wherefore he agreed
with the King for his marriage : Otherwiſe *B*. ſeemes
where hee is in ward, and is made Knight in ward,
this ſhall put him out of ward, and by him the Stat.
which is, *Poſtquam hæres fuerit in cuſtodiam cum ad*
ætatem pervenerit S. 21, *annorum*, *habeat hereditat.*
ſuam ſine relevio, *& ſine Fine* : *Ita tamen quod ſi ipſe*,
dum infra ætatem fuerit, *fiat miles*, *nibilominus terra*
ſua remaneat in cuſtodia dominorum uſque ad termi-
num ſupradict. is intended where he is made Knight
within age being in ward after the death of the
Anceſtor, and not where he is made Knight in the
life of the Anceſtor. 2. *E*. 6. *B*. *Garde* 42. & 72.

6. El. Con. 268.
Magna Cart. ca.
3. Raſt. ca. 1.

'Twas agreed for Law in the Common Bench,
that if the Lord hath not been ſeized of homage
within time of memory; but hath been ſeiſed of
rent, it ſuffices to have a Writ of Ward, and to
count that he died in his homage ; for there is ſeiſin
of ſomething, though it bee not of the intire ſervices :
And for this cauſe, and alſo for that the ſeizin is
not traverſable, but the Tenure ; therefore the
action lies without Seiſin of the Homage, 6. *E*. 6.
B. *Garde* 122. the end.

See Cokes
Books, & 7. E.
6. after.

Twas holden by the Juſtices of both benches,
That where a man holds by Rent and Knights
Service, and the Lord and his anceſtors have been
alwaies ſeiſed of the Rent, but not of the homage,
eſcuage, nor of Ward : yet if a Ward fall, he ſhall
have the ward of the heir, for the ſeiſin of the Rent
ſuffices to be ſeiſed of the Tenure, as to this pur-
See 6. E. 6. be-
fore.
See Coks
Books.
o o   poſe.

poſe. Yet otherwiſe *B.* ſeems to make avowry, 7. *E.* 6. *B. Avowry* 96. the end. *Garde* 69.

Where a uſe veſts in the heir, as heir of his Father, where the Father was dead before? Whether the heir ſhall be in ward, or not : Quære, See Tit. *Feoffments to uſes.* 3. *M.* 1.

Note that twas declared by the Doctors of the Civil Law, That where an heir or other is married *infra annos nubiles*, and after diſaſſents at the age of diſcretion, or after, before aſſent to the Marriage, that this ſuffices : and the party may marry to another without divorce, or witneſſing of it before the Ordinary : but the Ordinary may puniſh it *per arbitrium judicis*; but the ſecond eſpouſals is good, as wel by the Law of the Kingdom, as by the Law of the Church, 5. *M.* 1. *B. Garde* 124.

Frowlke Lect. upon the ſtat. de Prærogativa Reg. 55. 33. H. 6.

Ward and marriage is by the Common Law : and the Father ſhall have the Ward of his ſon or daughter, and heir apparent, before the King or other Lord ; and Soccage Tenure by 20 years, and Knight ſervice after. *B. Garde* 120. the end.

32. H. 8. ca. 1. Raſt. Wills 1.

If an eſtate be made to many and the heirs of one of them, and he which hath the Fee dies, his heir within age, he ſhall be in Ward by the Statute of Wills, notwithſtanding the others ſurvive which are Tenants by the Common Law. *Caſus B. Garde.* 100.

Garranties, *Warranties.*

If the huſband & wife alien land of which ſhe is dowable, there to have collateral warranty, tis good to have the Warranty of the Wife againſt her and her heirs ; and then if ſhe hath iſſue by the huſband, and ſhe and the huſband die, the Warranty ſhall be collateral

collateral to the iſſues, becauſe that the land came by the Father, and not by the Mother. 31. *H. 8. B. Garranties* 79.

Note if the huſband diſcontinues the right of his wife, and an anceſtor collaterall of the wife releaſes with Warranty and dies, to whom the Wife is heir, and after the huſband dies, the wife ſhall be barred in a *Cui in vita* by this Warranty, notwithſtanding the Coverture ; becauſe that ſhe is put to her action by the diſcontinuance ; for Coverture cannot avoid Warranty, but where the entry of the wife is lawful, which is not upon diſcontinuance. 33. *H. 8. B. Garranties* 84.

If a man ſaies in his Warranty, *Et ego tenementa prædict. cum pertinent. præfato* A. B. the Donee *Warrantizabo,* and doth not ſay, *ego & heredes mei,* he himſelfe ſhall warrant it, but his heir is not bound to warrant it ; becauſe that (heirs) are not expreſſed in the Warranty. 35. *H. 8. B. Garranties* 50. See Coke upon Lit.

Sir *Robert Brudnel,* late Chief Juſtice of the Common Bench, deviſed a Warranty now in uſe, *viz.* That the warrantor for him and his heirs *Warrantizabit contra ipſum & heredes ſuos,* and by this the Feoffee ſhall rebut, but not vouch. *Caſus B. Garranties* 30. the end.

General Writ.

Where upon a *Formedon* upon a uſe, there ſhall be a General Writ, and ſpecial Declaration ? See Tit. *Formedon.*

General iſſue.

In an Aſſiſe or Treſpaſs, if a man entitles a ſtranger, and juſtifies by his Commandment, this ought

ought to be pleaded; and not given in evidence upon *Nul tort.* or not guilty pleaded.

Of the Licence. 4. E. 6. com. 14. by Harris. So of Common Rent Service, Rent Charge, Licence, and the like, theſe ought to be pleaded and not given in evidence upon a general iſſue. Contrary of a Leaſe of Land for years upon not guilty pleaded, the Defendant may give it in evidence;
12. H. 8. 1. by Brook. (*B. General iſſue*, 81.) otherwiſe of a Leaſe at will; for this is as a Licence, which may be Countermanded, or determined at pleaſure.

And if a Villen plead Free, and of Free Eſtate he may give manumiſſion in evidence; for this is Manumiſſion indeed.

Lit. 45. See the Act of this preſent Parliament which inables to plead the general iſſue & to give the ſpecial matter in evidence. But where he is Manumitted by act in Law, as a ſuit taken againſt him by his Lord; or an Obligation made to him by his Lord, or a Leaſe for years, and the like, which are manumiſſions in Law, of which the Jury cannot diſcuſs, and therefore theſe ſhall be pleaded. 25 *H.* 8. *B. General iſſue* 82.

Debt upon an eſcape in the Exchequer againſt the Sheriffs of *London*, for leting a man arreſted by them by *capias ad ſatisfaciendum*, and in Execution to eſcape: the Defendandts cannot ſay that he did not eſcape, and give in evidence that he was not arreſted for the arreſt is confeſſed, if he ſaies that he did not eſcape. 34. *H.* 8. *B. General iſſue* 89.

Grants.

M. 5. E. 6. accord. See 34. H. 8. after. *Nota per plures Juſt. & alios legis peritos,* That where a man grants an office of Bayliff, Steward, Receiver, Parker, and the like; and a Fee certain for his labour onely, there the Grantor may expulſe ſuch Officers.

But they ſhall have their Fee, for tis but an Office of Charge. But

But where the Steward, & Parker have profits of Courts, Winde-Falls, Dear-skinnes, and the like casuall profits, tis said that they cannot be expulsed, and that of such Offices they may have an Assise.

And tis said that twas so taken in the time of *James Hobert* Attorney of King *HENRY* the 7. And the Officers may relinquish their Offices when they will, but then their Fee ceases.

And *Whorewood* Attorney of King *HENRY* the 8. granted the Cases aforesaid, 31.*H.* 8.*B.Grants,* 134.

Twas said for Law, That I may Ouste my Bayliff, Receiver, and the like, giving to them their Fee; for it rests in Charge, and no profit. See 31. H. 8. before.

B. doubts of the Steward, for an Assise lies of such Ousters, 34. *H.* 8. *B. Grants* 93. the end.

What shall pass by a Grant of *omnia bona sua.* See Tit. *Done.*

A man possessed of a Lease for term of fourty yeers, grants so many of them to *I. N.* which shall be arrear *tempore mortis suæ,* and held void by *Hales* Just. and others, for the incertainty, because it doth not appear how many shall be behinde at the time of his death: for the Granter may live all the 40 yeers, and then nothing shall be arrear at his death, *quære.* (*B. Grants* 154. *Leases* 66.) but such Devise by Testament is good, (*B. Grants* 154.) And 'tis not like where a man leases Land for term of life, and four yeers over: this is certain, that his Executors shall have four yeers after his death. (*B. Leases* 66.) And also, if a man leases his Land to have from his death for four yeers, 'tis good: for this is certain; and he hath authority to charge his own Land. 7. *E.* 6. *B. Grants* 155. See Coke Litt. and the Rector of Chedingtons case.

Accord. Finch 46. E. 3. 31. 11. H. 4. 54. by Hank.

A man grants *omnia terras & tenementa sua* in *D.*

a

See 37. H. 8.
Tit. Done.

a Leafe for yeers fhall not pafs. Contrary, if he grants *omnes firmas fuas*, there by this a Leafe fhall pafs: for of this an *ejeƈtione Firme* lies, and by this he fhall recover the Term; and therefore 'tis a good word of Grant. 7. *E.* 6. *B. Grants* 155.

Hariots.

D. S. 76. 8. H.
7. 10. 7. E. 6.
Com. 96.

TIS faid that for Hariot-cuftom a man fhall always feife; and if it be efloigned, he may have detinue. And for Hariot-fervice efloigned, he may diftrain, but not for Hariot-cuftom. *Time. H.* 8. *B. Hariots.* 6. *the end.*

Herefie.

2. H. 4. c. 15.
Raft. Herefie,
1.

Note, that 'twas agreed by all the Juftices, and by *Bake,* learned in the Law, and Chancellor of the Exchequer: and by *Hare,* learned in the Law, and Mafter of the Rolls, That by the Statute of Hereticks and Lollards, that if a Heretick be conviƈted in prefence of the Sheriff, the Ordinary may commit him to the fame Sheriff; and he ought to burn him, without having a Writ *de hæretico comburendo.* But if the Sheriff be abfent, or if the Heretick fhall be burnt in another County in which he is not conviƈted, then in thefe cafes the Writ *de hæret. comburend.* fhall be awarded to that Sheriff or Officer who fhall make execution. And the faid Statute in the end wills, *that the Sheriff fhall be prefent at the conviƈtion, if the Bifhop requires him.* And therefore the ufe is, that the Ordinary fhall call the Sheriff to be prefent at the conviƈtion. And fo in the Writ *de hæret. comburend.*

rend. in the *Nat. Brin.* that the Archbifhop and his Province in their Convocation might and ufed to convidt Hereticks by the Common Law, and to put them to lay hands: And then the Sheriffs by Writ *de bæret. comburend.* burnt them. But becaufe that this was troublefome, to call the Convocation of all the Province, 'twas ordained by the Statute afore-faid, *That every Bifhop in his Diocefs may convidt a heretick, and after abjuration upon relapfe, put him to lay hands to be burnt.* And *B.* feems that if the Heretick will not abjure at the firft Convidtion, that he may be burnt at the firft convidtion without abju-ration. Otherwife, if he will abjure: for then he fhall not be burnt the firft time, but upon relapfe he fhall be burnt. 2. *M.* 1. *B. Herefie.*

Homage.

See Tit. *Fealty.*

Ideot.

BRENT of the County of *Somerfet*, who was pre-fented for an Ideot, could write Letters and Acquittances, and the like; and therefore was ad-judged an Unthrift, but no Ideot. *Time. E.* 6. *Ideot* 4. *the end.*

Imprifonment.

'Twas determined in Parliament, that Imprifon-ment almoft in all cafes is but to retain the offender till he hath made a Fine; and therefore if he offers his Fine, he ought to be delivered prefently; and the
King

See 33. H. 8.
Tit. Mannor.
D. S. 11. 8. H.
7. 5. by Vavi-
four. 12. H. 7.
16. by Yaxley.
& 17. by Tre-
maile. 12. E. 4.
9. by Genny.
22. E. 4. 33.
by Suliard.
See Cokes
books.

King cannot retain him in prison after the Fine tendered. 2. *M.* 1. *B. Imprisonment* 100 *the end.*

Incident.

Court-Baron is incident to a Mannor, and Court of Pipowders to a Fayr; and 'twas *sed arguendo,* that therefore the Lord of the Mannor or Fayr cannot grant over the Court-Baron, nor the Court of Pipowders: or if they grant the Mannor with the Fayr, they cannot reserve such Courts, for they are incident, &c. 19. *H.* 8. *B. Incidents* 34.

39. H. 6. 25.
by Moile, & 44.
E. 3. 19. p.
Cur. & Perk.
24. cont. See
Cokes books.

'Twas said, that if a Seigniory rests in Homage, Fealty, and Rent, and a man recovers the Rent; by this is the Homage recovered: for a *Precipe* lies not of it. *Time. H.* 8. *B. Incidents* 24. *the end.*

Indictments.

St. 21. D.

An Indictment of Death ought to comprehend the day of the stroke, and day of the death; and the same Law of Poysoning; so that it may be known if he died of the same stroke or not. 24. *H.* 8. *B. Indictments* 41.

Fitz. 243.

By *Fitz* Just. a Justice of Record may be indicted of taking of money, and other such falsity, but not of that which goes in falsifying or defeating of the Record, as to say that he altered the Record from 'Trespass into Felony, and the like, which falsifies the Record. *Casus B. Indictment* 50. the end.

Intrusion.

See Tit. Garde,
& 33. H. 8.

Tenant in Tayl of Lands holden of the King, aliens without license, which is found by Office, the King

King fhall have the Iffues of the Land *à tempore in-* quifitionis capt. and not before. (*B. Alienations*, 26. *in medio.*) But where the tenant dies, and his heir enters, upon Office found for the King of the dying feifed of the anceftor; there the heir fhall anfwer the profits taken by him before. 26 *H.* 8. *B. Intru-* fion, 18. *the end.*

after. 8. E. 4. 4. by Choke. Stp. 84. See Tit. Leafes.

Note, where 'tis found by Office that *I. N.* tenant of the King was feized, and died feized, and that *W.* his heir intruded, and after by Act of Parliament the King pardons all Intrufions; in this cafe the entry and the offence is pardoned, but not the iffues and profits: for the efcheator fhall be charged of this by way of account, whether he hath received them or not: For when the office is of Record, he ought to receive them, except where 'tis found in the Office that fuch a man took the profits thereof. But where the King pardons, where no Office is found, the heir is difcharged as well of the iffues and profits, and alfo of Livery, as of Intrufion, by reafon of the pardon: for by this all is pardoned. And there though the Office comes after which findes the intrufion of the heir, yet all is gone by the Pardon; and this fhall ferve, becaufe all was pardoned before, to which the King was intitled of Record. 33. *H.* 8. *B. Charters de pardon,* 71. *Intrufion* 21. *Iffues returns* 22.

M. 4. M. 1. accord in cafu Mainwaring. See Tit. Leafes.

See 30. H. 8. Tit. Charters de Pardon.

Office fhall have relation to the death of the anceftor, as to Land defcended to the heir of the Kings tenant, and as to intrufion. (*B. Relation* 18. *the end.*) Otherwife, as to alienation made by the Kings tenant without Licenfe: this fhall not relate before the finding of it. (*B. Relation* 18. *Intru-* fion 19.) And fuch entry by purchafe is not called Intrufion, but a Trefpafs; and fo are the words of

See 26. H. 8. before. See Tit. Leafes.

P P · the

the pardon thereof, *quod pardonamus transgression' prædict. &c.* 33 *H.* 8. *B. Iutrusion* 19.

Joyntenants.

See Coke upon Litt. & Baldw. case, lib. 3.

If a Leafe be made to three of Land at Common Law, for term of life, or for yeers *habendum successive*, yet this is a joynt estate, and they shall hold in Joynture, and *successive* is void: But where the custom of Copie-holds is, that this word *successive* shall hold place, this is good there by the custom. 30 *H.* 8. *B. Joyntenants* 53.   *Leases* 54.

41. E. 3. 18. by Finch.

If a man infeoffs two, upon condition that they shall infeoff *W. N.* before *Michael'* and the one dies, the other sole makes the Feoffment; this is good. The same Law if two leafe Land rendring rent, and that if it be arrear by two months, and lawfully demanded by the said Lessors, that they may re-enter, the one dies, and the other that survives demands it, and 'tis not paid, he may re-enter. And the same Law if the Leafe were made to two, with words that if it be arrear, and demanded of them two, *&c.* and the one dies, and the Lessor demanded it of the other that survived, and he doth not pay, this is a good demand, and the Lessor may re-enter. 33 *H.* 8. *B. Joyntenants* 62.

Journeys accounts.

Grantee of a next presentation brings a *Q. impedit*, and dies after the six months past, and his Executors bring another *Q. impedit* by Journeys accounts, and by the Justices it will not lie. See Tit. *Q. impedit.*

Judgement.

Judgement.

A man recovers by default against an Infant, and the Infant brings a Writ of Errour, and reverses it for his non-age. Otherwise, if he had appeared, and loft by plea, or by voucher, he shall not reverse it for non-age. *B. 6. H. 8. Saver de default 50.*

2. M. 1. accord B. Judgment 147. the end.

If I have Title by Formedon, or *cui in vita*, and enter, and the other recovers against me, I am remitted to my first action: But if a man recovers against me by false Title, by Action tried, where I was in by good Title, I shall then have Error, or Attaint, or a Writ of Right. 23 *H.* 8. *B. Judgement* 111.

See after Tit. Restore al primer action.

Assise in Com. *B.* the tenant pleads in Bar a recovery by Assise by him against the Plaintiff of the same Tenements in Com. *O.* and this now Plaintiff then tenant pleaded in Bar by release of the anceftor of the Plaintiff with Warranty, which was void by non-age: and this found for the Plaintiff, by which he recovered against this Plaintiff judgement *fi*, where he accepts the Land to be in the County of *O.* now he shall be received to say, that it lies in the County of *B.* And 'twas said in the Common Bench, that though this Land were then put in view, the Plaintiff shall not be bound by the recovery: for it cannot be intended one and the same Land. 25 *H.* 8. *B. Judgement* 62.

Assize of Land in *N.* the Defendant said that once before he brought an assize of the same Land in *H.* against the same Plaintiff, and these Lands put in view: and this now Plaintiff then took the tenancie, and pleaded in Bar, and said that *H.* and *N.* are one and the same Ville, and known by the one

one name and the other; and that *A.* brought a
Formedon of thefe tenements, and pleaded certain,
&c. and recovered by Action tried, and the eftate
of the Plaintiff mean betwixt the title of
and his recovery, judgement *fi* of fuch an eftate affize,
&c. to whom the other faid, that every of the faid
H. and *N.* were Villes by themfelves, and fo at
iffue : and 'twas found that they were feveral Villes,
and the feifin and diffeifin ; by which 'twas awarded
that this tenant then Plaintiff fhould recover. And
becaufe that he hath recovered thefe fame Lands
againft the Plaintiff himfelf in *H.* judgement *fi* affife.
And *Shelly* Juft. held ftrongly, that this recovery of
Land in *H.* is no plea in an affife of Land in *N.*
and therefore the affife ought to be awarded ; and
fo it feems to *B.* 25 *H.* 8. *B. Judgement* 66.

44. E. 3. 45.
cont. 23. Afi'
16.

If *A.* infeoffs *B.* upon condition, *&c.* to re-enter,
there if a man impleads *B.* who vouches *A.* and fo
recovers ; or if *A.* re-enters upon *B.* without caufe,
and is impleaded and lofes ; there in the one cafe,
and the other, the condition is determined : for the
Land is recovered againft him who made the condition. 26 *H.* 8. *B. Judgement* 136.

Tr. 13. El. Com.
394. cont.

Note, by *Bromley* chief Juft. that a Judgement,
where there is no original, is void, (as in an affife
the Plaintiff appears, and after makes a *retraxit* ;
and after the Juftices of Affize record an agreement
betwixt them, in nature of a Fine : this is void, and
coram non Judice, and fhall not be executed, by reafon that no Original was pending, but was determined before by the *retraxit.*) For without Original
they have not Commiffion to hold Plea ; and then
they are not Judges of this caufe. 2 *M.* 1. *B. Judgement.* 114.

Iffues

Iſſues joyns, Iſſues joyned.

Treſpaſs upon the caſe, *quod def. aſſumpſit deli-
berat. quer.* 4 *pannos laneos,* and he pleads, *quod aſſumpſit liberare* 4 *pannos lineos,* without that *qd. aſſumpſit
modo & forma,* and ſo at iſſue.   And 'tis found that
he aſſumed to deliver 2 *pannos laneos, ſed non* 4 (ſo
ſee that this iſſue, though that it comes in a traverſe,
doth not amount but to the general iſſue) the Pl.
recovered dammages, for the 2, and was barred and
amercied for the reſt.   But otherwiſe 'tis if the iſſue
be ; If *A.* and *B.* infeoffed the tenant in a *Precipe
quod reddat, necne,* and 'tis found that *A.* infeoffed
him, but that *A.* and *B.* did not infeoff him, this is
found againſt the tenant in *toto,* or againſt him who
pleads ſuch Feoffment, which is ſo found, 32 *H.* 8. *B.
Iſſues joyns.* 80. *Verdict* 90.

See 2. M. 1.
after.

10. E. 4. 2. by
Litt.

Informed in the *Excheq.* againſt *A. B.* for buying
Wools betwixt ſhearing time and the Aſſumption,
ſuch a year of *C. D. contra formam Statuti,* where 'tis
not cloth, nor he did not make thereof cloth nor
yarn ; He ſees that he did not buy of *C. D. contra
formam Statut. propt. &c.*   And no iſſue, for 'tis not
material nor traverſable whether he bought of *C. D.*
or of *E. F.* or of another, but whether he bought
them *contra formam Statut. necne.*   And therefore the
Iſſue ſhall be that he did not buy *modo & forma, &c.*
33. *H.* 8. *B. Iſſues joyns.* 81. *Negativa pregnans.*
54. *Travers, per* 367.

24. H. 8. cap.

In waſte iſſue was taken if the defendant cut
twenty Oaks, there if the Jury finde ten and not
the reſt, the Plaintiff ſhall recover for the ten, and
ſhall be amercied for the reſt. 2 *M.* 1. *B. Iſſues joyns*
80. the middle.

See 32. H. 8.
before.

Iſſues

Iffues returns ; Iffues returned.
See Tit. Intrufion.

Jurifdiction.

If the Lord of a Mannor claim the Tythes of
fuch Lands in *D.* to finde a Chaplain in *D.* and the
Parochians claim them alfo for the fame purpofe,
'tis faid for Law, that the Lay Court fhall have
jurifdiction betwixt them, and not the Spiritual
Court. 25 *H.* 8. *B. Jurifdiction* 95.

Thorp accords, 'Twas faid where a man pleads a plea in *Banco*
41. E. 3. 4.   *ultra mare,* it fhall be condemned at this day, becaufe that it cannot be tried in *England.* 36 *H.* 8. *B.*
Jurifdiction 29.

Jurors.

Trial of a Peer of the Realm arraigned upon an
Indictment, and appeal diverfity. See Tit. *Trial,*
and Tit. *Enqueft.*

Where Jurors may take conufance and notice of a
thing in another County. See Tit. *Attaint.*

M. 11. H. 4. 18. Jury took a Scroll of the Plaintiff, which was not
delivered to them in Court, and paffed for the
Plaintiff : and becaufe that this matter appeared to
the Court by examination, therefore the Plaintiff
fhall not have Judgement. 3 *M.* 1. *B. Jurors* 8.

Leet.

Leet.

NOTE, for Law, if a pain be put upon a man in a Leet for to redreſs a Nuſance by a day *ſub pœna* 10. *l.* and after 'tis preſented that he did it not, and ſhall forfeit the pain ; this is a good preſentment, and the pain ſhall not be otherwiſe affeered. And the Lord ſhall have an Action of Debt clearly ; but he cannot diſtrain and make avowry, except by preſcription of uſage to diſtrain and make avowry. 23 *H.* 8. *B. Leet* 37.

Note, where the Statute of *Magna charta, cap.* 25. ſaith, *Et viſus de Franchi-plegio tunc fiat ad illum Terminum St. Michaelis, ſine occaſione* ; this is intended the Leet of the Tourne of the Sheriff, and not other Leets. 25 *H.* 8. *B. Leet* 23 *the end.*

10. *H.* 7. 4. by Keble. Vaviſour accord. 13. *H.* 7. 19. See Coke, Beechers Caſe.

Magna Chart. c. 15.

Leaſes.

By *Fitz-James* ch. Juſt. *Englefield* Juſt. and many others, if tenant for life leaſes Land for yeers, rendring rent, and dies, the Leaſe is void, and then the rent is determined. The ſame Law of a Parſon. And though the ſucceſſor receives the rent, the Leaſe is not good againſt him : for when 'tis void by the death of the Leſſor, it cannot be perfected by no acceptance. (*B. Leaſes* 19. *Debt* 122.) Otherwiſe *B.* ſeems of a Leaſe for life made by a Parſon rendring rent, and the ſucceſſor accepts the rent, this affirms the Leaſe for life. 24 *H.* 8. *B. Leaſes* 19.

A man leaſes for ten yeers, and the next day leaſes

22. *H.* 8. 16. 14. *H.* 8. 14. by Brudnel. 22. *E.* 4. 27. by Wood, 4. *E.* 6. Com. 30. 4. & 5. El. Com. 264. See 32. *H.* 8. after, & Coke lib. and Tit. Acceptance.

See 37. H. 8.
Tit. Attorn-
ment.

leafes the fame Land to another for twenty yeers :
this is a good Leafe for the laft ten yeers of the
fecond Leafe. 26 *H.* 8. *B. Leafes* 48.

Where a Leafe for 300 or 400 yeers fhall be
Mortmain. See Tit. *Mortmain.*

M. 3. M. 1. ac-
cord. 23. H. 8.
31. 3. M. 1.
Com. 168. See
6. & 7. E. 6.
Com. 85. See
2. M. 1. Com.
103.

A man leafes a houfe *cum pertin.* no Land fhall
pafs by thefe words *cum pert.* Contrary, if a man
leafes a houfe *cum omnibus terris eidem pertin.* there
the Lands to this ufed pafs : and many Grants are
de omnibus terris in D. nuper Monafterio de G. pertin.
and efpecially if he avers that it hath pertained *de
tempore, &c.* 31 *H.* 8. *B. Leafes* 55.

11. E. 3. Fitz.
Abbe g. See
before, and fee
tit. Acceptance,
and 38. H. 8.
after.

If a Parfon of a Church leafes for life, and dies,
the fucceffor accepts fealty ; he fhall be bound by
this during his life. *Contra* upon a Leafe for yeers
made by him ; this fhall not binde the fucceffor by
acceptance of the rent : for 'twas void by the death
of the Leffor. 32 *H.* 8. *B. Dean* 20. *Encumbent*
18. *Leafes* 52.

Where a confirmation fhall be by the Bifhop,
Dean and Chapt. of a Leafe made by the Parfon.
Et contra. See Tit. *Confirmation.*

See 37. H. 8.
after : and 35.
H. 8. tit. Garde.
Fitz. 142. C.
cont. Fitz. 198.
F. accord.

A man is a purchafer with his wife to them and
to the heirs of the hufband ; and after the hufband
leafes for years and dies, the wife enters, this fhall
avoid the Leafe for her life ; but if fhe dies during
the term, there the reft of the term is good to the
Leffee againft the heir of the hufband. And the
fame Law of a Rent-charge granted out of it : for
the hufband had the Fee-fimple *tempore,* &c. and
might well charge it. And note by all the Juftices,
that the Guardian in Knights fervice fhall not oufte
the termor of the anceftor of the heir. And the
fame Law of the Lord by Efcheat. 36 *H.* 8. *B.
Leafes* 58.

If

If a man leafes for life to *I. S.* and the next day leafes to *W. D.* for twenty yeers, the fecond Leafe is void, if it be not a grant of a Reverfion with Attornment : for in Law the Free-hold is more worthy and perdurable then a Leafe for yeers. Yet if the Leffee for life dies within the term, the Leafe for yeers is good for the reft of the yeers to come. 37 *H.* 8. *B. Leafes* 48. *the end.* H. 1. E. 6. accord. See before.

See 36. H. 8. before.

'Twas agreed *per plures,* that where *I. N. convenit & conceffit* to *W. S.* that he fhall have 28 acres in *D.* for 20 yeers, that this was a good Leafe : for this word *conceffit* is as ftrong as *dimifit vel locavit.* 37 *H.* 8. *B. Leafes* 60. Admitted P. 1. E. 6. in Chancery.

King tenant in Tayl makes a Leafe for yeers, or life, his iffue may avoid it. See Tit. *Difcontinuance in poffeffion.*

If a Parfon lets Land for term of yeers rendring rent, and dies, the fucceffor receives the rent, the Leafe is not good againft him, for he hath not Fee-fimple. Nor he cannot have a Writ of Right but *Juris utrum,* therefore the receipt of the rent by his fucceffor, doth not affirm the Leafe ; for this was void by the death of the Parfon who leafed. 38 *H.* 8. *B. Leafes* 18. *the end.* See 32. H. 8. before, and Tit. Acceptance. 44. E. 3. 11. plur. Fitz. 5. contr. Lit. 144.

'Twas holden by *Bromley* Juft. and others, that if a man leafes for 20 yeers, and the next day leafes for 40 yeers, the fecond Leafe fhall take effect for 40 yeers, *f.* after the twenty yeers paft. *Time. H.* 8. *B. Leafes* 35. *the end.* See 26. H. 8. and 37. H. 8. before.

'Twas agreed for Law in the Chancery by the Juftices, that if a Leafe for yeers be made by a Bifhop, that 'tis not void, but voidable ; for he had a Fee-fimple. Otherwife of fuch a Leafe by a Parfon ; this is void by his death : for he hath not the Fee-fimple, but 'tis in abeyance. And the Bifhop Goofan Abbot. 14. H. 8. 12. by Carel. & 21. H. 7. 38. by Lee.

Q Q   may

may have a Writ of Right, or a Writ of Entry *fine affenfu capituli*, where a Parfon fhall have but a *Juris utrum*. And therefore if the fucceffor of a Bifhop, Dean, Prebend, and the like, who have a Fee and Leafe, and die, accepts the Rent, this affirms the Leafe to be good. And otherwife of such acceptance by the fucceffor of a Parfon who made fuch Leafe: for this Leafe is void prefently. But if a Chantry Prieft makes a Leafe, his fucceffor fhall avoid it, notwithftanding the predeceffor had a Fee, becaufe that 'tis donative, or prefentative, and then fuch Leafe is not perdurable, except it be confirmed by the Patron in the one cafe, and by the Patron and Ordinary in the other cafe. 2 *E.* 6. *B. Leafes* 33. *the end.*

A man leafes for yeers, *habendum poft dimiffionem in faĉā* to *I. N. finitā*, and in truth *I. N.* hath no Leafe in it, there the Leafe commences immediately, by *Hales* Juft. and many others. And by him if a Prebend makes a Leafe for 21 yeers by Indenture rendring the ufual rent, this fhall binde the fucceffor by the Statute of Leafes: for where the Statute faith, *in Jure Ecclefiæ*, and the entry for a Prebend *eft feifitus in jure Prebende*, yet it fhal bind by the equity. 3 *E.* 6. *B. Leafes* 62.

An Executor hath a term and purchafes the reverfion in Fee, whether the term be extinĉt, or no. See Tit. *Extinguifhment.*

Tenant of the King in *Capite* dies, and the heir before Livery fued, makes a Leafe for yeers, 'tis good, if no intrufion be found by Office, and an Office found after, which findes the dying feized, and no intrufion, hath not relation to the death of the anceftor, but for the profits, and not to defeat the Leafe: for the Free-hold and Inheritance remain

in

See before, and Tit. Acceptance.

See Coke upon Lit.

H. 1. M. 1. accord. See Coke upon Lit.

23. H. 8. ca.

1. H. 7. 17. See Tit. Intrufion.

· in the heir. But if intrufion be found, *tunc nullum accrefcit ei liberum tenementum*, and then the Leafe, and dower of the wife of the heir, are void. 5 *E*. 6. B. *Leafes* 57.

A man poffeffed of a Leafe for 40 yeers, grants fo many of them as fhall be behind at his death, 'tis void. See Tit. *Grants.*

Note, by *Bromley* and others Juftices, if I let Land to *W. N. habendum* till 100 *l.* be paid, and without Livery; then 'tis but a Leafe at will for the incertainty. But if he makes Livery, the Leffee fhall have it for life upon condition implied to ceafe upon the 100 *l.* levied. 2 *M.* 1. B. *Leafes* 67. *See 3. M. 1. after: contra. See Coke upon Litt.*

'Tis faid that Bifhops in the time of *E.* 6 were not facred, and therefore were not Bifhops, and therefore a Leafe for yeers by fuch, and confirmed by the Dean and Chapter, fhall not binde the fucceffor: for fuch never were Bifhops. Contra of a Bifhop deprived who was Bifhop indeed at the time of the demife, and confirmation made. 2 *M.* 1. B. *Leafes* 68. *See 37. H. 6. 26.*

What fhall be faid to be a Leafe in reverfion, and what a grant of reverfion? fee Tit. *Attornment.*

'Twas holden by all, if a man Leafes Land to another till the Leffee hath levyed 20 *l.* that 'tis a good Leafe, notwithftanding the incertainty. 3. *M.* 1. B. *Leafes* 67. the end. *See 2. M. 1. before, contra. 14. H. 8. 14. by Brudnel.*

'Twas ruled in the Serjants cafe, that if a man let Land 4. *Jan. habend.* for forty years, *Reddend. annuatim* at *Mich.* and *Eafter* 20.*s.* the tenant fhall pay at *Eafter* and at *Mich.* I. *equales porciones,* and the Leffor fhall not lofe the rent at *Eafter.* 4. *M.* 1. B. *Leafes* 65. *4 & 5. E. 6. Com. 70. 4. M. 1. Com. 171. 172.*

Ley

Ley gager, Law wager.

Detinue of a Deed indented, where an obligation of a Leafe for term of years, the defendant fhall not wage his Law, for this concerns Land, and a Chattel real. And fo 'twas late adjudged in the Kings-Bench. 34. *H.* 8. *B. Ley gager* 97.

8. H. 5. Fitz.
Ley 66.

'Twas faid for Law, that a man fhall not wage his Law in a *Quo minus*. 35. *H.* 8. *B. Ley* 102. *Quo minus* 5. *in finibus*.

Licenfes.

Twas agreed, that if a Bifhop, Dean and Chapter give their Land in Fee without Licenfe of the King, who is Founder, and is found fo by Office, the King fhall have the Land. And another Founder may have a *contra formam collationis*. And if he aliens *fine affenfu*

Litt. 145.

Decani & Capituli, then lies the Writ *de ingreffu fine affenfu Capituli*. 36. *H.* 8. *B. Licenfes* 21.

Lieu, Place.

Place is not material in actions tranfitory. See Tit. *Attaint*.

Where a Recognizance is acknowledged in *London* before a Juftice of the Common Bench, and certified *in banco*, and there ingroffed, a *Scire facias* fhall be brought there directed to the Sheriff of *London*, and not to the Sheriff of *Middlefex* where the Bench is, by all the Prothonotaries of the Common Bench. 4. *M.* 1. *B. Lieu* 85.

Limitations.

Limitations.

Note, that it feems cleer, that the new Limitation, and alfo the ancient Limitation extends to Copie-hold, as well as to Free-hold : for the Statute is, that he fhall not make prefcription, title, nor claim, &c. And thofe who claim by Copie, make prefcription, title, and claim, &c. And alfo the plaints are *in natura & forma Brevis Domini Regis ad communem Legem*, &c. And thofe Writs which now are brought at Common Law, are ruled by the new Limitation, and therefore the plaints of Copie-hold fhall be of the fame nature and form. 6. *E.* 6. *B. Limitations* 2.

32. H. 8. ca. 2.
Limitation. 3.

Livery.

Note, if the King hath a Ward becaufe of Ward, and the firft Ward comes to full age, and fues Livery, the other Ward being within age, there the Ward fhall not fue Livery, but *oufter le maine;* for now the Seigniory of his Land is revived by the Livery, fo that he holds not of the King as afore, but of his immediate Lord. But if the Ward becaufe of Ward had been of full age before the firft Ward, he fhould fue Livery. 25. *H.* 8. *B. Livery* 47.

See 13. E. 4. 10.

28. H. 6. 11.
Stp. 18.

Where a woman out of Ward by Marriage fhall fue Livery at fourteen yeers. See Tit. *Garde.*

He which holds Land within the County Palatine of *Lancafter* of the King in Knight fervice, *ut de Ducatu Lancaftr.* fhall fue Livery. *Contra* of him who holds Land which lies out of the County Palatine of the King in Knight-fervice, &c. 28. *H.* 8. *B. Livery* 55.

Time. H. 8.
after contra.
28. H. 6. 11.

Note, that general Livery cannot be, but upon
Office

Office found: but ſpecial Livery may be without Office, and without probation of age, but there he ſhall be bound to a rate and ſum certain to be paid to the King. (*B. Livery* 56.) And by *B. ibidem* 31. this cannot be claimed by the Common Law, as general Livery may, but is at the will of the King. 28. *H.* 8.

If the King purchaſes a Mannor of which *I. S.* held in Knight ſervice, the tenant ſhall hold as he held before, and he ſhall not render Livery nor primer ſeiſin: for he holds not in *Capite*, but holds, *ut de manerio:* And if his heir be in Ward by reaſon of that, he ſhall have an *ouſter le maine* at full age. And 'tis ſaid, if the King after grant the Mannor to *W. N.* in fee, excepting the ſervices of *I. S.* now *I. S.* holds of the King, as of the perſon of the King, and yet he ſhall not hold in Capite, but ſhall hold as he held before, for the act of the King ſhall not prejudice the tenant. But if the King give Land to me in fee, *tenend. mihi & heredibus meis* of the King, *&c.* and expreſſes no certain ſervices, I ſhall hold in Capite, for 'tis of the perſon of the King. And note that tenure in Capite, is of the perſon of the King. 29. *H.* 8. *B. Livery* 57. *Tenures* 61.

Extent of livery is the value of the Land by half a year. But if he intrudes and enters without livery, he ſhall pay the yearly value by experience of the *Exchequer*. And where *ceſtuy que* uſe is attainted of Treaſon, and 'tis enacted by Parliament, That he ſhall forfeit his Land in poſſeſſion, and in uſe, that there the King is but a purchaſer, and therefore thoſe who hold of him that was attainted, ſhall not ſue livery. *Quære,* If it be enacted that he ſhall forfeit it to the King, his heirs and ſucceſſors. *Econtra,* if he had been ſole ſeiſed, and had been attainted

by

See after.

See 33. H. 8. Tit. Tenures. and 3. El. Com. 241.

33. H. 6. 7. by Briſot.

8. H. 7. 13. 13. H. 7. 11. by Davers.

See 30. H. 8. Tit. Office devant. &c. 3. El Com. 243. by Carus.

See 31. H. 8. Tit. Alienation. & 32. H. 8. after.

by the Common Law, for there the King hath the Land as King, and there thofe who held, *&c.* fhall fue livery. And yet the Statute is, *Si quis tenuerit de nobis de aliqua efchaeta, ut de honore* Wallingford Bofen, *&c. non faciet aliud fervicium quam fecit preantea.* And therefore this is intended of a common efcheat. And alfo fome Honours are in *Capite,* as part of *Peverel,* and others. 29 *H.* 8. *B. Livery* 58.

Magna Charta. cap. 31. Raft. Tenures.

The Kings tenant leafes for years and dies, the heir fhall fue livery notwithftanding the Leafe indures. And the fame where the Father declares his will of the Land for yeers and dies. 30 *H.* 8. *B. Livery* 59.

Stp. 13.

If a man holds of the King before the Statute of ufes, and infeoffs others to his for term of life, the rem' over in tail, the rem' to his right heirs, and dies, and after the tenant in tail dies without iffue, the heir of the Feoffer fhall fue livery, for the fee fimple was never out of him, and therefore it defcends to his heir, and if he hath it by defcent, he fhall fue livery. And the fame Law and for the fame reafon, if at this day a man gives in tail, the rem' to his right heirs. Otherwife *B.* 2. feems where a man makes a Feoffment in fee in poffeffion, and difmiffes himfelf of all, and retakes for term of life, the rem' in tail, the rem' to his right heirs, and dies, and after the tenant in tail dies without iffue, there the heir, who is right heir is a purchafer. And if the King feifes, he fhall fue oufter le main, and fhall not be compelled to fue livery; But if the tenant in tail had dyed without iffue in the life of tenant for life, and after the tenant for life dies, there his heir fhall fue livery, for the fee fimple was vefted in the tenant for life, by extinguifhment of the mean rem', and therefore the fee fimple defcends. And note, livery

See 37. H. 8. Tit. difcent, Sir John Huffeys cafe.

is

is that the King ſhall have the value of the land by half a year. And ouſter le main is a Writ to ouſte the King of the Land without any profit given to the King, 32 *H. 8 B. Livery* 61.

Where a man holds certain Land of the King in Soccage in Capite, the King ſhall not have liberty of more then the Soccage-Land, 32 *H. 8. B. Garde* 97.

He which holds of the King in Knight ſervice and not in Capite, ſhall not ſue livery, becauſe he holds not in Capite, and there when the heir comes to full age, he ſhall have an ouſter le main, for none can enter upon the King. But if he be of full age at the time of the death of his anceſtor, then he ſhall render relief to the King and goe quite, as if he had holden of a common perſon. *Contra, of Tenure in Capite.* 32 *H. 8. B. Livery* 62.

Note, that the heir of him who holds of the King in Capite in Soccage ſhall not render *primer ſeiſin* to the King for all his Lands, but onely for thoſe Lands holden in Soccage in Capite. Contrary of him who holds in Knight ſervice in Capite, by the experience of the *Exchequer.* And the heir which ſues Livery ſhall have in every County a ſeveral livery. And note that livery is where the heir hath been in Ward, and comes to full age, he ſhall have livery *extra manus Regis.* And primer ſeiſin is, where the heir is of full age at the time of the death of his anceſtor, or where his tenant holds in Soccage in Capite, and dies, there the King ſhall have primer ſeiſin of the Land, which amounts to the like charge to the heir, as the livery is. 38 *H. 8. B. Livery* 60.

Note that a man cannot ſue livery in the *Chancery* for Land in *Wales,* Nor in a County Palatine by experience. *Time H. 8. B. Livery* 63.

If

See 29. H. 8. before, and 38. H. 8. after.

F. N. B. 256. C. See 38. H. 8. after.

See 33. H. 8. Tit. Fenuces.

Stp. 13. See 32. H. 8. Tit. Demurrer in Law.

Stp. 13. 2. M. 1. Com. 109. 2. El. Com. 204. See 32. H. 8. before.

Stp. 13. 44. E. 3. 12. Fitz. 257. L. See the extent of it. 32. H. 8. before, and 29. H. 8.

28. H. 8. before, contra.

If the heir of *ceſtuy que uſe* be of full age at the time of the death of his anceſtor, the King ſhall not have primer ſeiſin, for 'tis not given by the Stat. but onely the ward of Land and body. And if a will were declared by *ceſtuy que uſe*, which is not performed during the nonage of the heir, there the King ſhall not have the Land, but the heir at full age, ſhall prove his age, and ſhall goe quite by experience in the Exchequer. *Caſus B. Livery* 77. the middle.

27. H. 8. 4. Mountague accord. 4. H. 7. c. 17. Raſt. Wards. 20.

Mainpriſe.

IF a man be arreſted in *London*, and finds ſureties to the Plaintiff there, and after is diſmiſſed in *banco* by Writ of priviledge, and after a Procedendo comes in the ſame ſuit to the court of *London*, this ſhall not revive the firſt mainpriſe, or ſuretiſhip, for once diſmiſſed, and always diſmiſſed. And 'tis ſaid that after a man hath found mainpriſe to a Bill in the Kings Bench, and after is at iſſue or demurrer, and after is awarded to replead, and to make a new declaration, the Mainpriſe is by this diſcharged. Contrary, where they *manuceperunt uſque ad finem pliti*, and where the original remains. 32. *H.* 8. *B. Mainpriſe.* 96.

See 31. H. 8. Tit. Procedendo cont.

If a man be convicted of Felony, and remains in priſon, and after the King pardons him, there the Juſtices of Gaol-delivery may bail him till the next Seſſions of Gaol-delivery, ſo that he may then come with his Pardon, and plead it. 2. *E.* 6. *B. Mainpriſe.* 94.

Maintenance.

19. E. 4. 3.
Afcue & Mark-
ham accord. 21.
H. 6. 16. 14.
H. 7. 2. by Rede.
See H. 6. & 7.
E. 6. 33.
Note, by all, where Tenant in Tayl, or for term of Life, is impleaded, he in rem' or reverfion, may maintain, and give of his proper money to maintain for fafeguard of his intereft: for 'twas agreed that he who hath an intereft in the Land, may maintain to fave it. 1 *E.* 6. *B. Maintenance.* 53.

32. H. 8. ca. 9.
See H. 6. & 7.
E. 6.
Com. 88. 89.
Note, that upon the Statute of buying Titles, and to maintain that a man fhall not buy Land, except the vendor hath been in poffeffion, &c. by a yeer before, 'twas agreed by *Mountague* chief Juftice, and by all of Serjeants Inne in Fleet-ftreet, that if a man morgages his Land, and redeems it, he may fell his Land *infra unum annum prox.* &c. without danger of the State aforefaid: for fo is the intendment of the Statute: for the ancient Statutes are, That none fhall maintain; and yet a man may maintain his Coufin, and fo of the like: for 'tis not intended, but of unlawful maintenance; and fo of a pretenfed Title, and not of that which is clear Title. 6. *E.* 6. *B. Maintenance.* 38.

Mannor.

See 35. H. 8.
Tit. Tenures.
A man cannot make a Mannor at this day, notwithftanding that he gives Land to many feverally in Tayl, to hold of him by Services, and fuit of his Court: for he may make a Tenure, but not a Court: for a Court cannot be but by continuance
See 23. H. 8. tit.
Court-Baron, &
Time H. 8. Tit.
Suitor.
cujus contrarium memoria hominum non exfiftit. And 'tis faid for Law, that if a Mannor be, and all the Free-tenures efcheat to the Lord, but one, or if he purchafes all but one, there after this the Mannor

is

is extinct : for there cannot be a Mannor, except there be a Court-Baron to it. And a Court-Baron cannot be holden but before Suitors, and not before one Suitor : therefore one Free-holder onely cannot make a Mannor. 33. *H.* 8. *B. Comprife* 31. *Mannor.* 5.

Mifnofmer, Mifnamer.

A Statute was acknowledged by a man in the name of *I. S. de D. in Com' E. Butcher,* and he was taken upon Procefs, and faid in avoydance of the Statute, that he was always dwelling at *S.* and not at *D.* and was a Husbandman, and not a Butcher ; and that *I. S.* of *D.* acknowledged the Statute without this, that he is the fame perfon that acknowledged it : which Plea was refufed, for a great inconvenience that might fall upon it. 36. *H.* 8. *B. Mifnofmer.* 34. *the end.*

Monftrans de faits. Shewing of Deeds.

See that he which pleads a Deed or Record, or which declares upon a Deed or Record, it behoves him to fhew it : for Oyer of thofe is always to be had by him which is charged by it. *Regulæ B. Monftrans.* 165. *Oyer de Recordes.* 15. *the end.*

See Cokes books.

Mortdaunceftor.

By the beft opinion in the Common Bench, if two purchafe jointly to them and to the heires of one, and he which hath the Fee dies, and after the other dies, the heir of the firft fhall not have a

See Cokes Rep.

Mort-

Mortdaunceflor (and *B.* feems the reafon to be, becaufe the Fee was not executed in Poffeffion, by
reafon of the furvivor of the other, and 'tis in effect
now but the difcent of a reverfion) and the wife of
him who had the Fee, fhall not have Dower, and
yet he might have forfeited the Fee fimple or given
it by Feoffement, but not by grant of the Reverfion.
12. *E.* 4. 2. and joyn the Mife in a Writ of Right,
for he in Reverfion, and the Tenant for life may do
it. *Quære*, if he may releafe it. 29. *H.* 8. *B.*
Mortdaunceflor. 59.

Mortmain.

Lord and Tenant, the Tenant leafes for life to
I. S. the remainder to an Abbot and his fucceffors,
the Lord need not to make claim, till the Tenant
for life be dead ; for if he will wave the Remainder
'tis not Mortmain. But of a grant of a Reverfion
with Attornment, 'tis otherwife. And if the
Tenant makes a Feoffment in Fee, to the ufe of *A.*
for life, and after to the ufe of an Abbot and his
fucceffors, there 'tis not Mortmain, till the Tenant
for life in ufe dies, and he in Remainder takes the
profits. Note that appropriation of an advowfon
without licence is Mortmain. 25. *H.* 8. *B. Mort-*
main. 37.

8. H. 4 15. B.
Mortmain. 11.

6. El. Com.
273.

If a man leafes to an Abbot and his fucceffors, or
to another Religious perfon for a 100 years, and fo
from a 100. years to a 100 years, until 300 years
be incurred, this is one Leafe, and fuch Leafe is
Mortmain by the words of the Statute *de religiofis.*
7. *E.* 1. *S. colore termini,* for the faid Statute is, *quod*
nullus emeret, vel fub colore donationis aut termini, aut
ratione alterius tituli ab aliquo reciperi, aut arte vel
ingenio

ingenio fibi appropriare prefumat, &c. And the fame Law of a Leafe for 400 years, or the like, Contrary, if a man leafes for a 100 years, or the like, and covenants that he or his heirs at the end of a 100 years, will make another Leafe for another 100 years, and fo further, this is not Mortmain, for 'tis but one Leafe for a 100 years, and the reft is but a Covenant, but in the firft cafe, for that is for 300 years at firft in effect, and all by one and the fame Deed, (*B. Mortmain.* 30. *Leafes.* 49.) And 99 years is not Mortmain. And alfo a Leafe for a 100 years is not Mortmain by *B.* for tis a ufual term. 29. *H.* 8. *B. Mortmain.* 30.

3. E. 4. 13. by Nele accord.

3. E. 4. 13. by Nele contra. 47. E. 3. 11. fee 1. B. 6. Tit. Devife.

By *Br.* if an alienation in *Mortmain* be, and the alienee is diffeifed, and the diffeifor dies feifed, his heir is in by difcent, yet the Lord may enter within the year, for he hath but onely a Title of Entry, and cannot have an Action. But otherwife of him who hath right of Entry, and may have an Action. 1. *E.* 6. *B. Mortmain.* 6. the end.

Negativa preignans;
fee Tit. Iffues joyns.

Non-ability.

WHERE, and in what Cafe an Alien is difabled from bringing of an Action, what not? See *Tit. Alien.*

Non eſt Faƈtum.

See Cokes Rep. Whelpdales cafe.

Note, that in Debt upon an obligation made for Uſury, and the Defendant pleads this matter, he ſhall conclude, and ſo the obligation is void, Judgement *ſi aƈtion*, and ſhall not conclude *non eſt faƈtum*. 7. *E.* 6. *B. Non eſt faƈtum.* 14. the end.

Nonſuit.

Note, that the King cannot be nonſuited ; yet *B.* ſeems that he who *tam pro Domino rege, quam pro ſcipſo ſequitur* may be nonſuited. 25. *H.* 8. *B. Nonſuit.* 68.

Entries ?

14. H. 8. 24. per Cur. 28. H. 6. 8. & 4. E. 4. 24. accord.

Note, when the parties in an Aƈtion have demurred in judgement, and have a day over, there at that day the Plaintiff may be demanded, and may be nonſuited, as well as at a day given after iſſue joyned. 38. *H.* 8. *B. Nonſuit.* 67.

Nontenure.

See 20. H. 8. after.

Where a man is barred by a falſe verdiƈt, and brings an attaint againſt the firſt Tenant, *nontenure* is no plea, for he is privy ; contrary of a ſtranger, as where the Tenant infeoffs a ſtranger after. 19. *H.* 8. *B. Nontenure.* 6.

29. H. 8. 2. fee 19. H. 8. before.

In an attaint *Nontenure* is no plea for a privy to the firſt aƈtion : *contra* for a ſtranger to the firſt Aƈtion (*B. Nontenure.* 16.) And tis ſaid that 'tis no plea in an attaint, to ſay that the Plaintiff in the Attaint hath entered after the laſt continuance. 20. *H.* 8. *B. Nontenure.* 22.

Nontenure is no plea in Waſte. See Tit. *Waſte. Noſme.*

Nofme. Name.

What fhall be a good name of Purchafe. See Tit. *Difcent.*

Note, if a Dutchefs, or other fuch ftate marries with a Gentleman or an Efquire, fhe by this fhal lofe her dignity and name by which fhe was called before as in the cafe of the Lady *Powes,* and Dutches of *Suffolk,* the one efpoufed *R. Howard,* and the other *S.* the Dutches, *Adrian Stokes;* and therefore Writs were abated in their Cafes; For by the book of Heralds; *quando mulier nobilis nupferit ignobili, definit effe nobilis.* 4. *M.* 1. *B. Brief.* 546. *Nofme.* 69.

14. H. 6. 2. See Cokes Rep. the Countefs of Rutlands Cafe: noble, by marriage lofes her dignitie: in fuch cafe not noble by difcent.

Notice.

The Patron fhall take notice of every voidance of an Advowfon, except refignation, and of this the ordinary fhall give him notice. *Lecture Frowick. B. Notice.* 27.

Fitz. 35. H.

Office devant, &c.

Office before, &c.

NOTE, by thofe of the Exchequer; where a man is attainted by Parliament, and all his Lands to be forfeited; and doth not fay that they fhall be in the King without Office, there they are not in feifure of the King without Office, for *non confat* of Record what Lands they are. 27. *H.* 8. *B. Office devant.* 17.

See 35. H. 8. Tit. Forfeiture. St. 54.

If

18. H. 6. cap.
6.

If the King grant Land for term of life, & after the Patentee dies, yet the King cannot grant it over till the death be found by office, & this by reaſon of the Stat. that a grant before office ſhall be void. 29. *H. 8. B. Office devant.* 56.

If an Office finde the death of the Kings Tenant, and that his heir is of full age, and doth not ſay when, there it ſhall be intended that he is of full age, *tempore captionis inquiſitionis*, but that he was within age *tempore mortis tenentis*, and therefore it ought to be expreſſed certain when he was of full age. 29. *H. 8. B. Office devant.* 58.

See 13. H. 7.
11.

Note, that 'tis an antient courſe in the Exchequer, that if it be found by Office that *I. S.* was ſeiſed in Fee and died, *ſed de quo vel de quibus tenementa tenentur, ignorant*, that a Commiſſion ſhall iſſue to enquire of it certainly, *de quo &c.* and if it be found that of *W. N.* then the party ſhall have *Ouſter l'main*

Kings & Fineux
accord. 13. H.
7. 5. & 9. 26.
H. 8. 9. by
Bromley ſee
29. H. 8. Tit.
Livery. 2. E. 6.
cap. 8.

of the King. But if an Office be found, *quod tenetur de Rege, ſed per que ſervitia ignoratur*, this is good for the King, and it ſhall be intended to be holden in *Capite per ſervitium Militare*, for the beſt ſhall be taken for the King. But now in theſe caſes, a *Melius inquirendum* ſhall be awarded by the Statute. 30. *H. 8. B. Office devant.* 59.

3. E. Com. 229.
See after.

Land was given by the King *pro erectione Collegii Cardinalis Eborum*, and the Colledg was not erected, and upon office found thereof, the King ſeiſed. *Time. H. 8. B.* Office. 4. the end.

See 5. E. 6.
before.

Twas agreed by the Juſtices, that the King is not intitled to the land of his ward without office, though he hath in it but a Chattell, yet it comes *ratione tenure*, which is a ſeigniory and freehold in the King. 5. *E. 6. B. Office devant.* 55.

Note, that of a Chattell the King is in poſſeſſion
without

without office. And *contra* of land and of freehold, except of a term; And sometimes he shall be in possession of inheritance without office; yet the King shall not have the land of his ward without office, though he hath in it but a Chattel; for the ward comes by reason of the tenure, which is a seigniory and freehold in the King, and therefore a difference betwixt this, and a lease for years of a man outlawed. For if a man hath a term for years, or a ward, and is outlawed, this is in the King without office. *Lecture.* B. *Office devant.* 60.

Officer.

Note, for Law, if a man hath a fee of a Lord, and after is made Justice, this fee is not void by the Law, but after the making of him Justice, he is not to take any fee, but of the King; and the same law of him who hath an office of Steward, and after is made Justice. *Et per plures* where a man is a Baily of a Mannor by patent, and after is made Steward of the same Mannor by another patent, both patents are good; For the Suitors are Judges, and not the Baily. But *per plures* if a man be a Forrester by patent, and after is made Justice of the same Forrest, the first patent is void. As where a man is made a Bishop, the Parsonage is void, for he cannot be ordinary of himself, nor punish himself. And *B* accords that a man cannot be Keeper of a Forrest, and Justice of the Forrest, for the killing of the Deer by the Keeper, and the like, is a forfeiture of his office, which shall be adjudged by the Justices of the Forrest, and he cannot judge himself. But a man may be a Steward of a Forrest by patent, and Justice of the same Forrest by another patent, and both good,

39. H. 6. 5. by Prisot. See 5. M. 1. Tit. Commission.

10. H. 7. 7. by Vavisor. 15. E. 4. 3. by Brian.

s s

for

for both are judicial. And Juftices of the Forreſt may make a Steward of the Forreſt. 29. *H.* 8. *B. Officer.* 47.

See Coke Rep. Cafe of Difcontinuance. Note, that the Sheriff and Eſcheator void their office by demiſe of the King, for they are made by patents, which are as a commiſſion is, and therefore 'tis uſed at the demiſe of the King for to ſue out new patents, as 'twas this year. 1. *M.* 1. *B. Officer.* 25. the end.

Obligation.

See Billing 2. E. 4. 2. If *A.* be bound to *B.* in 40. *s. ad uſum I. S.* there *I. S.* may releaſe the obligation, becauſe that (*ad uſum*) is expreſſed in the obligation. *Et econtra* if this did not appear in the obligation. 36. *H.* 8. *B. Obligation.* 72.

Oyer of Records, &c. ſee Tit. Monſtrans de faits.

Oyer & Terminer.

Tis ſaid that if a Commiſſion of *Oyer* and *Terminer* expire or diſcontinue, then the indictments and record ſhall be ſent into the King's Bench, and there they ſhall be finiſhed (ſee how *Tit. Corone.*) 38. *H. B. Oyer & Terminer.* 1. the end.

Twas granted in the caſe of *Ben. Smith* upon the Statute of 2. *E.* 6. *cap.* 24. of Felony in one County, and acceſſary in another County; that the Juſtices of the King's Bench are Juſtices of *Oyer* and *Terminer* of Felony, Treaſons, and the like, by the Common Law, and Cuſtom of the Realm, 3. *M.* 1. *B. Oyer & Terminer.* 8.

Pain.

Pain.

T'WAS adjudged in *Curia hospitii Domini Regis*   See St. 38. C.
apud Greenwich *verfus* Edmundum Knivet
militem, that he should be disinherited, imprisoned,
for ever, and his hands cut off, *quia percussit quen-
dam hominem ibidem*, the King being there in his
Court. 33. *H. 8. B. Pain.* 16. the end.

Panell.

Twas agreed in the Exchequer where a jury is
awarded *de medietate lingue*, where an alien is party,
and the panel returned, that the one of the denizens
and the other of aliens shall be sworn, till they have
6 denizens, and 6 aliens sworn. The fame Law   See Coke upon
there, where the jury remains for default of jurors,   Lit. & Dyer
there a Tail shall be part of English, and part of   econtra. 32. H.
aliens, and this if the party prayes it. But if he   8. cap.
doth not pray it, *B.* feems 'tis error, except by the
Statute of *Jeofails* it be holpen. 32. *H.* 8. and fo by
him where the panel is party, the party is not compellable to take the jury, except 6 of the one, and 6
of the other are sworn. 4. *E.* 6. *B. Panel.* 2. the end.

Parliament.

If the King be intitled to the land of *I. S.* by   See 31. H. 8.
forfeiture of Treason, or Felony, by act of Parlia-   Tit. Extinguish-
ment or office, by this all tenures are determined, as   ment.
well of the King, as of all others. And there, if
this

this land after be given to another, by another Act of Parliament saving to all others all their Rights, Interests, Titles, Rent-service, and the like, as if no such Act had been, there the Seigniories and the like shall not be revived, for no Seigniorie was in *esse* at the time of the second Act made.   And here are not words of Gift, nor Reviving, but words of Saving, which serves not but to save that which in *esse* at the time of the Saving, &c.   But such *Proviso* in the first Act would serve; for this comes with the Act which Intitles the King.   And where the King is Intitled to Land by Office for Escheat, and after 'tis enacted by Parliament that the King shall enjoy it, saving to all others their Seigniories, and the like, there such Saving will not serve (for the reason aforesaid) for all was extinct before by the Office, and nothing was in *esse* at the time of the Saving (which was in ure between the King and *Keckwich* in the County of *Essex*, where *R.* lost his Seigniory) But there ought to be words affirmative, that the Lords shall have their Seigniories. 27. *H.* 8. *B. Parliament.* 77.

35. H. 6. 34. Danby accord.

See 34. H. 8. Tit. Remitter. & Dyer.

Note by *Englefield* Justice, in the Case between *Button* and *Savage*, that where a man hath Title to Land by a Tail, and after the same Land is given to him by Parliament, that his Heirs shall not be remitted; for by the Act of Parliament all other Titles are excluded for ever; for this is a Judgement of the Parliament: And where the Land is given expresly to any person by name, by Act of Parliament, he, nor his Heirs shall not have other Estate then is given by the Act, but that that onely shall stand. (*B. Parliament.* 73. *Remitter.* 49. the end.) And the same Law where the King had Title in Tail, and the Land is given to him by Parliament

in

in Fee, the Tail is determined. So that the Heir
ſhall not avoid Leaſes made by his Father, nor
Charges, and the like; for the laſt Statute bindes
all former Titles and Eſtates not excepted. 29. *H.*
8. *B. Parliament.* 73.

If divers Seſſions are in one and the ſame Parliament, and the King ſignes not a Bill till at laſt, there
all is but one and the ſame day, and all ſhall have
relation to the firſt day of the firſt Seſſions, and the
firſt day and the laſt, all is but one and the ſame
Parliament, and one and the ſame day in Law,
except ſpecial mention be made in the Act when it
ſhall take force. But every Seſſions in which the
King ſignes the Bills, is a day by it ſelf, and a
Parliament by it ſelf, and ſhall not have other relation but to the ſame Seſſions. 33. *H.* 8. *B. Parliament.* 86. *Relation.* 35.

Note, if a man in an Action, or pleading alledges
a Statute, and miſ-recites it in matter, or in year,
day, or place; the other may demurr generally, for
there is no ſuch Statute, and then there is no ſuch
Law, for every one that meddles with it, ought to
ſhew the Law truly. But in caſe of the King it
may be amended, and this in another Term; Contrary for a common perſon. 33. *H.* 8. *B. Parliament.* 87.

Memorandum, that at the Parliament holden by
adjournment *H.* this year, 'twas admitted by the
King's Writ, and ſo accepted, that if one Burgeſs
be made Major of a Town which hath judicial juriſ-
diction, and another is ſick, that theſe are ſufficient
cauſes to elect new ones, wherefore they did ſo by
the King's Writ out of the Chancery, compriſing
this matter, which was admitted and accepted in the
Commons Houſe of Parliament. 38. *H.* 8. *B. Parliament.* 7.

An

H. 6. & 7. E. 6.
Com. 79. per
Juſticiarios.

H. 6. & 7. E.
6. Com. 79.
by Hales Juſt.

See 32. H. 8.
Tit. Demurrer
in Law. 6. & 7.
E. 6. Com. 79.
84.

Parnour, Taker of the profits.

27. H. 8. cap.
10. Raft. Ufes.
9. 4. E. 4. 24.
26. H. 8. 3. 8.
13. H. 7. 15.
Vavifor accord.

An Office is found after the death of *Ceftuy que ufe* that he died *feifed,* and the heir is in ward of the King, and after a Recovery is had againft the Heir during the poffeffion of the King as againft the Pernour of the profits, before the Statute of Ufes 27. *H.* 8. the Feoffees traverfe the office, or *fue* an *Oufter l'main,* this Recovery *fhall* binde the heir, but the Recoverer cannot enter during the Poffeffion of the King. 29. *H.* 8. *B. Pernour.* 32.

A man cannot aver another Pernour of the Profits of other things, which are not in demand. *B. Pernour.* 4. the middle.

Patents.

The King gives Land to *I. S. Et heredibus mafculis fuis,* the grant is void. See *Tit. Efates.*

See Stp. 31.

If the King Licences his Tenant to alien his Mannor of *D.* and he aliens it except one acre, the licence *fhall* not *ferve* it, for the King is not affertained of his Tenant of all. And if I have a Licence to impark 200 acres, and do it according, and after increafe by other 10 acres, there this is not a Park. 23. *H.* 8. *B.* Patents. 76.

If the King grants *omnia terras & tenementa fua* in *D.* this is a good grant by thefe general words. 30. *H.* 8. *B. Patents.* 95.

The King gave to the Earl of *Rutland* in Tail, and after intended to give to him in Fee *fimple,* and to extinct the Tail, and 'twas doubted that the furrender of the Letters Patents of the Tail, and the cancelling of them, and of the Inrollment and Bill

affigned,

affigned, will not extinct the Tail, for the Tail executed may be averred without fhewing the Patent. And a *Formedon* lies after the Tail executed, without fhewing the Patent. And 'twas taken that 'twas not a good furety for the King, for his fervices to give the reverfion, to hold the reverfion by fuch fervices when it vefts, and to except the firft fervices during the Tail, for when the reverfion is gone, the Rent and Services referved upon the Tail, are gone as wel in cafe of the King, as a common perfon. And therefore the devife was, that the King by a new Patent, reciting the firft Patent, fhall give the Reverfion, and the first Rent and Services to have in Fee, to hold by fuch Services, and rendring fuch Rent, and by this the King fhall have the new Tenur prefently, and the Grantee fhal not be charged with double Services and Rents during the Tail, and 'twas agreed for Law, that if a man lofes his Letters Patents, he fhall have a *Conftat* of the Letters Patents out of the Inrolment, and Bill affigned, which remains in the Chancery: And therefore *B.* feems that the Inrolment fhall not be cancelled (*B. Patents.* 97.) And 'twas agreed by *Whorewood* the Kings Attorney, *& optimos legis peritos*, that if Tenant in Tail of the Gift of the King furrenders his Letters Patents, this fhal not extinct the Tail, for the Inrolment remains of Record, out of which the iffue in Tail may have a *Conftat*, and recover the Land, wherefore they made the Devife aforefaid, *viz.* that the King fhall grant to the faid Earl Tenant in Tail the Fee fimple alfo, and then a Recovery againft him will barr the Tail. Otherwife the Reverfion being in the King (*B. Surrenders.* 51.) And 'tis faid for Law, if the King gives in Fee, or in Tail, or for life, the Patentee Leafes for years, or grants, Leafes,

or

4. E. 6. Com.
5. econtra.

See 35. H. 8. Tit. Tail. contra.

See 12. H. 7.
12. by Fifher.

See 32. H. 8. Tit. Difcontinuance de poffeffion.

or gives part of the Land or of the Interest to another, and after surrenders his Patent, by which 'tis cancelled, this shall not prejudice the third person, that he shall lose his interest by it: for he may have a *Constat* out of the enrolment which shall serve him. *Quære inde*, because a Statute is made of it. And Quære if the Common Law shall not serve: for it appears in the book of Entries so. that a man pleaded a *Constat*, 32. *H. 8. B. Pattents.* 79. the end. *Surrender.* 51.

4. E. 6. c. 4.

What thing in action the King may grant, what not? See *Tit. Chose in action.*

If the King grant a Baliwick, or sheriffwick to *I. S. absque compoto reddend.* the word *absque compot.* is worth nothing: for 'tis contrary to the Nature of the thing granted, 36. *H. 8. B. pattents.* 99.

If Conusance of plea be granted by the King, he ought to shew where; as in *Guild-hall*, or the like; and before whom, as before his Steward, &c. And the King may grant Toll, Fair, Market, and the like: but not to have Assise of Fresh force, nor Toll traverse, nor Through Toll, nor that the Land shall be Devisable, Borrough-English Gavelkinde, nor the like: for these are by Custom, which cannot commence at this day by grant: for the King cannot make a Law by his grant: and that by grant of Conusance of pleas, he shall not hold plea of an assise, nor of a certificate of assise.

2. H. 7. 13. by Keble. 37. H. 6. 27. by Litt. Abr' of the Aff. 56. 9. H. 6. 27. by Martin. 44. E. 3. 18. by Thorp. Fitz. accord. 26. H. 8. 1. & 21. E. 4. by Huffey. 3. H. 7. 6. 11. E. 41. by Litt. See Coke Rep. Altonwoods cafe. Time E. 6. accord.

And 'tis said for Law, That a false consideration in Letters patents shal not avoid them: as where the King for ten pound to him paid, gave such Land, and the ten pound is not paid, the patent is not void, nor shall not be repealed: Contrary of a patent granted upon a false surmise: as to falsifie that the land came to the King by attainder of *I. S.* which is

not

not true, or the like. Quære, the diverſity, 37. *H.* 8 *B. patents.* 100.

See 38. H. 8. Tit. Diſcontinuance de poſſeſſion. & Cokes Rep.

Where the King, Tenant in Tail, cannot diſcontinue, or charge by grant, by patent. See *Tit. Diſcontinuance de poſſeſſion.*

Note, that 'twas agreed, That where the King grants Land which is in Leaſe for tearm of years, of one who was attainted, or of an Abby, and the like, that the grant is good without recital of the Leaſe of him who was attainted, or of the Abby : for he ſhall not recite any Leaſe but Leaſes of Record. *Time H. 8. B. patents.* 93.

'Twas granted in the caſe of *Thomas Inglefield,* Knight, where the King Recites, *quod cum A. B. tenet manerium de B. pro termino vitæ ſuæ de conceſſione noſtra,* &c. *Sciatis nos conceſſiſſe C. S. reverſionem manerii prediƈt,* &c. *Habendum,* &c. that this is a good Grant. Therefor *B.* ſeems that if the King miſ-recites the date of the firſt Letters Patents, or the like, yet if he well recites the eſtate and the thing, and the name of the Leſſee, that then the Grant of the Reverſion is good. For where the King takes notice of his Tenant for term of life, and of his eſtate, and grants the Reverſion, he is not deceived in his Grant, for he takes upon him notice of the former Intereſt for life, and then the date of the firſt Patent is not material. *Time H. 8. B. Patents.* 96.

38. H. 6. 37. by Danby.

By *Mervin* Juſtice, a *Conſtat* is pleadable ; contrary of an *Inſpeximus,* for in the one caſe the Patent remains, and in the other 'tis loſt, And by *B.* in the Book of entries a *Conſtat* was pleaded, and aid granted of the King upon it. 1. *E.* 6. *B. Patents.* 97. the end.

See 32. H. 8. before.

Peace.

Peace.

A man is bound to the peace, and procures another to break the peace, this is a forfeiture of his Bond, as 'twas said. *Time H.* 8. *B. Peace.* 20.

Peremptorie.

8. E. 4. 15. by Danby.

A man recovers debt or damages and after brings thereof a *Scire Fac'* the firft return of *Nihil* againft the Defendant is peremptory if he makes default. 24. *H.* 8. *B. Peremptorie* 63.

Where a man brings an Action real or mixt, or makes an avowry or conufans, and iffue is taken upon the feifin *infra tempus ftatuti*, and 'tis found againft the demandant Plaintiff, or avowant, this is peremptory by the fame Statute. 1. *M.* 1. *B. Peremptorie.* 78.

Petition.

3. H. 7. 3. by Keble 3. E. 4. 25. & 4. E. 4. 25. See Cokes Rep. Communalty of Saddlers Cafe & Tit. Traverfe &c. 10. H. 6. 15. 4. E. 4. 25.

'Tis held for Law, if the King be Intitled by double matter of Record, as 'tis enacted by Parliament, that *I. S.* fhal be attainted of Treafon, or Felony, and fhall forfeit all his Lands, and alfo an Office is found thereof, there the party who hath right, cannot traverfe, but is put to petition. And the fame Law if the King grant it over after the double matter of Record found. 33. *H.* 8. *B. Petition.* 35. *Trovers de office.* 51.

Note, That Petition was at Common Law, but Traverfe is by Statute, *Lecture. B. Petition.* 41. *Travers de office.* 54. See Tit. *Travers de Office.*

Pledges.

Pledges.

A man gages his goods in pledge for 40.*l.* bor- | 22. E. 4. 11.
rowed, and after the Debtor is convicted in 100.*l.* in | accord.
debt to another, thefe goods fhall not be taken in
Execution till the 40.*l.* be paid : for the Creditor
hath an intereſt in them : and alfo goods taken for
Diſtreſs, cannot be taken in Execution, 34. *H.* 8. *B.*
pledges. 28.

Pleadings.

Note that it is faid for Law, That he which | 22. E. 4. 32.
pleads a Recovery by default, ought to aver his Title | by Brian.
of his Writ. And alfo that the Defendant in the
Recovery was Tenant of the Free-hold *die brevis :*
but if the recovery were by action tried, he needs
not to take the one averment or the other. Yet
'twas faid, that in a *quod ei deforceat* he that pleads
the recovery by defalt, need not aver the party
tenant of the Freehold *tempore brevis fui*, for 'tis
proved that he was Tenant *tempore*, &c. by the uſe
of the *Quod ei deforceat*, for this is the effect of this
action; becauſe that the Demandant in this action,
loſt by default in the firſt action : yet he fhall aver
the Title of his Writ :

And he which pleads a Recovery in a Writ of | 36. H. 6. 29.
Waſte by default, needs not to aver the party Tenant;
for Non Tenure in this action is no Plea. 24. *H.* 8.
B. Pleadings. 6.

He which pleads an entry for to defeat a Col- | 3. H. 7. 2. 4.
lateral Warranty, ought to aver that he entred in | E. 6. Com. 46.
the life of the Anceſtor. And in Dowre if the
Tenant pleads a diſſeiſin by the huſband, and the
wife

wife pleads a Feoffment by *I. N.* to the hufband, who after infeoffed the Tenant, and after diffeifed him, fhe fhal fay that the Feoffment of *I.* and the feifin of the hufband, were during the coverture; and he which derives an interest by Leafe from Tenant for life, or in Tail, ought to aver the life of the Tenant for life, or in Tail, 26. *H.* 8. *B. pleadings.* 147.

19. H. 6. 74.
13. H. 8. 15.
by Wilby.

Where a man ought to aver that, the one and the other are one, and not divers, See Tit. *Averments.*

Where a ftranger to a Deed may plead it, where not? See Tit. *Eftranger.*

See Tit. Titles.

Note, for Law, That 'tis good pleading to fay, that *I. N.* and *W. N.* were feifed *in Dominico fuo ut de Feodo ad ufum T. P.* and his Heirs, without fhewing the Commencement of the ufe; as to fay, that *A.* was feifed in Fee, and infeoffed *I. N.* and *W. N. ad ufum T. P.* &c. But a man cannot plead that *A. B.* was feifed in Tail without fhewing the gift; for the one is a particular eftate, and not the other, 36. *H.* 8. *B. Pleadings.* 160.

Plenartie.

See 13. H. 8.
fo. 13. by Newd.
& fo. 14. by
Brud. 33. H.
6. 12.

Note, when there is no Patron, as where the Patron is a Prieft and is admitted to this Benifice himfelfe. Or where my Advowfon is aliened in Mortmain, and appropriated to a Houfe of Religion, and the like; in thefe cafes *I.* may have a *Quare impedit,* and there Plenarty by *fix* Months is no plea, 6 *H.* 8. *B. Plenartie.* 10.

Premunire.

See Cand. 44.
E. 3. 32. & D.
S. 57. 104.

Premunire by Bil in the Kings bench, See Tit. *Bill.*

A

A Prohibition lies often where a Premunire lies not; as of great Trees, *vel pro decimis, de septima parte,* prohibition lies, and not a Premunire; for the nature of the action belongs to the Spiritual Court, but not the cause in this form. But where 'tis of a lay thing which never appertained to the Spiritual Court, of this a Premunire lies, as of Debt against Executors upon a simple contract, or *pro lefione fidei,* upon a promise to pay 10.*l.* by such a day, 24. *H.* 8. *B. Premunire.* 16.

44. E. 3. 36. accord. See D. S. 106. & 8. E. 4. 13. by Catefby that a prohibition lies.

Where a man attainted in a Premunire shall forfeit his Lands in Fee *imperpetuum,* See Tit. *Forfeiture de terre,* &c.

Prerogative.

A man hath land in ufe; of which, part is holden of *A.* by prioritie, and the reft of the King by Pofterity in Knights fervice, and dies, the King fhal have the ward of the body by his prerogative, and by the Statute of 4. *H.* 7. which gives the ward of *Ceftuy que ufe* where no will is declared; and *per prerogativam regis:* Yet otherwife 'tis faid of land in ufe holden of a common perfon; for the Tenant in ufe dyed not feifed, and therefore out of the cafe of Prerogative for the Land, 21. *H.* 8. *B. Prerogative.* 29.

See 3. El. com. 240.

4. H. 7. ca. 17. Pre. Re. ca. 2. Stp. 9. & 4. E. 6. Com. 59. by Montague contra.

Note, by *Whorewood* the Kings Attorney, and others: where an information is in the Exchequer upon a penal Statute, and the Defendant makes a bar, and traverfes the Plea, that the King is bound to ftand to the firft traverfe, which tenders an iffue, and cannot waive fuch iffue tendered, and traverfe the former matter of the Plea, as he may upon a traverfe of an office, and the like where the King is fole

See 38. H. 8. Tit. traverfe.

See 6. & 7. E. 6. Com. 85. & 3. El. com. 263. 13. E. 4. 3. Stp. 65.

ſole party, and intitled by matter of Record; for upon the information there is no office found before: and alſo a ſubjeᶜt is party with the King for to recover the moytie or the like, 34. *H.* 8. *B. Preroᵃgative.* 116.

See 2. E. 6. Tit. Done.

Shelley Juſt. was preciſe that a gift of the King is good of Chattels moveables without writing; as of a horſe, and the like, 35. *H.* 8. *B. Prærogat:* 60. and 71. the ends.

Note by ſome, the King ſhall not have a *Precipe quod redd.* (as a Writ of Eſcheat) but his Title ſhall be found by Office. *Time. H.* 8. *B. Prærogative.* 119.

Where the King ſhall have his age? where not? See *Tit. Age.*

34. H. 8. beᵃfore & 38. H. 8. Tit. Travers per &c. è contra. Br. Traverſe per 207.

'Tis ſaid if an information be by a ſubject for the King in the Exchequer, and the Defendant pleads a Bar, and traverſes the information, the King may traverſe the matter of the Bar if he will, and is not bound to maintain the matter which is contained in the *abſque hoc* 7. *E.* 6. *B. Prærogative.* 65. the end.

Prærogativa Reg.

The Prerogative of the King is a Treatiſe of the Common Law, and not Statute nor Declaration by Parliament. And a Mine of *Ore*, or *Argent* is to the owner of the ſoil. *Quære, Lecture. B. Prærog.* 134.

Where the Incumbent is made a Biſhop, the King ſhall preſent by his Prerogative. See Tit. *Preſentation.*

Preſcription.

Where preſcription ſhall be gone by acceptance of a grant of the thing, See Tit. *Eſtopel.*

'Twas

'Twas faid for Law, that a cuftome may be alledged where there is no perfon that can prefcribe: as inhabitants cannot prefcribe: but they may alleadge a cuftom that the inhabitants may Common in *D.* for the one goes with the place, and the other with the perfon, which perfon ought to be able to prefcribe; for otherwife 'tis worth nothing, 2. *M.* 1. *B. Prefcription,* 100. the end. See Coke upon Lit.

Note, by the Juftices, that if a man grants *prox. prefentationem* to *A.* and after before avoidance grants *prox. prefentationem ejufdem Ecclefiæ* to *B.* the fecond grant is void: for this was granted over by the Grantor before: and he fhall not have the fecond prefentation, for the grant doth not import it, 20. *H.* 8. *B. Prefentation.* 52. 15. H. 7. 7. contra per curiam, as I take it. See 33. H. 8. after. & Dyer.

A man grants *prox. prefentationem,* and hath a wife and dies, the Grantee fhall have the firft prefentation, the heir the fecond, and the wife for Dowre the third, 33. *H.* 8. *B. Prefentation.* 55. See 20. H. 8. before. & Dyer.

Note, by *B.* That the Bifhop of Ely faid to him, that he faw a prefentation in the time of *E.* 3. made by the faid King. That he prefented to a Benefice *pro illa vice,* which was of another patronage, by thefe words, *ratione prærogative fue,* which Benefice voided by reafon that the King had made the incumbent of it a Bifhop, who was confecrated: fo that when a Benefice becomes void by making of an incumbent a Bifhop, the King fhall prefent to all his former benefices *pro illa vice,* whofoever is Patron of them, 4. *M.* 1. *B. Prefentation.* 61. See 4. M. 1. Tit. commiffions. 41. E. 35. accord. See 11. H. 4. 37. contra by Hill.

Priviledge.

Note, when a Record is removed out of a Court of Record, as *London,* &c. into the Kings Bench,
or

or into Common Bench, there they ſhall not proceed
upon the Original which was in *London* : but in the
Kings Bench the party may aid himſelfe by Bill of
Midd. brought there againſt the party upon his ap-
pearance : and in the Common Bench to bring an
Original retornable the ſame day. 36. *H.* 8. *B. priviledge.* 48.

Procedendo.

If a man arreſted in a *Franchiſe,* ſues a Writ of
Priviledge and removes the body and the cauſe, and
after comes not to prove his cauſe of Priviledge, the
Plaintiff in the Franchiſe may have a *Procedendo.*
And therefore *B.* ſeems that there the firſt ſureties
remain : otherwiſe if it had been diſmiſſed by allowance of the priviledge, for then his Sureties are diſcharged. Yet it ſeems to him, that when they remove the body and the cauſe, they remove no
ſuerties : but then there is not any Record againſt
them ; and then it ſeems that the priviledge being
allowed, the ſureties are diſcharged. Otherwiſe
where the priviledge is not allowed ; for then the
Priſoner and the cauſe was alwaies remaining in the
cuſtodie of thoſe of the Franchiſe. 31. *H.* 8. *B.*
Procedendo. 13. *Sureties.* 28.

See 32. H. 8.
Tit. Mainprize
contra.

Proclamation.

Note, that none can make Proclamation but by
authority of the King, or Majors and the like, who
have priviledge in Cities and Boroughs to do it, or
have uſed it by cuſtom. And Sir *Edmund Knightly,*
Executor to Sir *William Spencer,* made Proclamation in certain market Towns, That the Creditors
ſhould

ſhould come by a certain day, and claim and prove their Debts, &c. due by the Teſtator ; and becauſe that he did it without authority, he was committed to the Fleet, and put to a Fine. 22. *H*. 8. *B. Proclam.* 10.

Prohibition.

'Tis agreed, That if a man be ſued in the Spiritual Court, for Tythes of ſeaſonable wood, the partie grieved may make a ſuggeſtion in Chancerie, or in the Kings Bench, that he is ſued in the Spiritual Court for Tythes of great Trees, which paſſ the age of 20. years, by the name of *Sylva Cædua*, which is ſeaſonable wood uſed to be cut, where indeed 'tis great Trees, and pray a Prohibition, and have it. And the ſame Law where a man is ſued in *curia Admiral'* for a thing done upon the ſea, where indeed 'twas done upon the land, there upon a ſurmiſe that it was done upon the land, he ſhall have a prohibition. 31. *H*. 8. *B. Prohibition.* 17.

Fitz. accord 43. H.

Property.

'Twas agreed by the Juſtices, That if a Frenchman inhabit in England ; and after War is proclaimed betwixt England and France, none may take his goods, becauſe that he was here before : but if a Frenchman comes here after the War proclaimed, be it by his own good will, or by Tempeſt ; or if he yeilds, and renders himſelf, or ſtands to his defence, every one may arreſt him, and take his goods : and by this he hath a propertie in them, and the King ſhall not have them : and ſo 'twas put in ure the ſame year, betwixt the Engliſh and

U U   Scotch ;

Scotch; and the King himſelf bought divers priſoners and goods the ſame year when *Bullen* was
conquered of his proper ſubjects. 36. *H.* 8. *B.
Propertie*, and *proprietate probanda.* 38. the end.

Who ſhall have property in an eſtray, See Tit.
Eſtray.

Quare Impedit.

Contra P. 36.
H. 8. B. Quare
imped. 2. the
end. by Bromley
and Hales
Serjeants.
See Coke upon
Lit.

BY *Whorewood* the King's Attorney, clearly; If
two joynt Tenants are, the one preſents ſole,
and his Clerk inducted, the other is out of poſſeſſion,
35. *H.* 8. *B. quare imped.* 52. the end.

Quare imped. by *Mark Ogle*, againſt *Harriſon*,
Clerk incumbent; who was in by the preſentation
of the King: and therefore the Writ was brought
againſt him ſoly: and pending the Writ of *quare
imped.* the Plaintiff dyed after the ſix months paſt,
who had but *prox preſentationem* by grant, his exe-
14. H. 8. 3. by
Fitz James.
cutors brought another *quare imped.* by journies
accounts, intending to have ſaved the matter by the
journies. And by the Juſtices of the Common
Bench, where the Plaintiff dies, the Executors ſhall
not have a Writ by journies accounts. (and *B.* ſeems
See Coke Rep.
caſe of Journies
accounts.
that where the Plaintiff dies, none can have another
writ by journies accounts. But *contra* in ſome caſes
where the Defendant dies having the writ. (*B.
Journeies accounts.* 23; *Quare imped.* 58.) And
note by *B.* where the Grantee *de prox. preſentatione*
brings a *Quare impedit* as before, and dies, after the
ſix moneths paſt pending the Writ, and the Executors bring another *Quare imped.* by *Jernies*
accounts, and take a General Writ, and count how
that

that the grant was made to the Teſtator, and he brought a *Quare imped.* and dyed, and that they brought this Writ, and for that reaſon *pertinet ad ipſos preſentare,* and the Defendant *ipſos impedit,* and then this imports that this is of a diſturbance made to themſelvs after the 6 months paſt, & then the Writ lies not; for all ought to have been compriſed in the Writ, and count ſpecially and demand a writ to the Biſhop upon the preſentation, and writ of the Teſtator, & *quia non ideo male;* and nothing thereof comes in the caſe aforeſaid, betwixt *Mark Ogle,* and *Harriſton,* by B. 4. E. 6. B. *Quare imped.* 160.

Que eſtate, whoſe eſtate, &c.

'Tis ſaid for Law, That if a man recovers land againſt *I. S.* or diſſeiſes *I. S.* he may plead that he hath his eſtate, and yet he is in the *Poſt,* 31. H. 8. B. *que eſtate.* 48. [39. H. 6. 24. by Nedham.]

Que eſtate in another perſon of the Tenancy without ſhewing how, not ſo in Seigniory. See Tit. *Avowrie.*

'Twas agreed that a *Que eſtate* ſhall not be allowed in one who is mean in the conveyance; as to ſay that *A.* was ſeiſed in Fee, and Feoffed *B.* whoſe eſtate *C.* hath, who Infeoffed the Defendant; for the *que eſtate* ſhall be allowed onely in the Defendant or Tenant himſelf, *S.* whoſe eſtate the Tenant hath, 1. E. 6. B. *Que eſtate.* 49. [H. 2. E. 6. in banco regis accord. 37. H. 6. 32. by Davers.]

Note that 'twas agreed by the Juſtices, That a man cannot convey an intereſt by a *Que eſtate,* of a particular eſtate, as Tail for life or for years, without ſhewing how he hath this eſtate, be it of the part of the Plaintiff, or Defendant, 7. E. 6. B. *que eſtate.* 31.

Quinziſme.

Quinzisme.

'Twas agreed in the Exchequer, That Cities & Boroughs shall pay at Tenths, and Uplands at Fifteens, 34. *H.* 8. *B. quinzisme, &c.* 8.

Note by Exposition of those of the Exchequer, That Tax and Tallage is no other but Tenth, Fifteen, or other Subsidie granted by Parliament. And the Fifteen is of the Layitie, and the Tenth is of the Clergy, and is to be Levyed of their Land. And the Tenth and the Fifteen of the Layity, is of their goods : *S. decimam partem bonorum in Civitatibus & Burg. Et quinsesimam partem bonorum* of the Layity in *patria*, which was Levyed in ancient time upon their goods. *S.* of the beasts upon their lands, which was very troublesom. But now 'tis levyed *Secundum rat. terrarum suarum* by verges of Land, & other quantities ; so that now all know their certainty in every Town and Countrey throughout the Realm. But 'tis yet Levyed in some places upon their goods : but in most places upon their Lands, which was granted by the Barons. 34. *H.* 8. *B. quinzisme.* 9.

Quo minus.

8. H. 5. Fitz. Ley 66.

'Twas said for Law, that a man shall not wage his Law in a *quo minus*, 35. *H.* 8. *B. Ley.* 102. *quo minus.* 5. the ends.

Rationabill

Rationabili Parte, &c.

'TWAS faid for Law, That the Writ *de Rationabili parte bonorum* is by the Common Law; and that it hath been often put in ure, as a Common Law, and never demurred to: therefore B. feems that 'tis the Common Law. 31. *H.* 8. *B. Rationabili parte.* 6. the end.

F. N. B. 122.
L. Magna Chart. ca. 18.
Raft. det. to the King 2.

Recognizance.

Agreed for clear Law in the Chancery; if a man acknowledge a Statute ftaple, and after infeoffs the Recognifee, & he makes a Feoffment over, now the Land is difcharged; for the Feoffee is but a ftranger. But if the Cognifor repurchafes the Land, it fhall be put in Execution, and yet 'twas once difcharged. *Time. E.* 6. *B. Recognizance.* 9. the end.

See 36. *H.* 8. Tit. Stat. marchant.

5. *H.* 7. 25. by Townfend.

Note, that it did appear by fearch of the Records of the Common Bench, that the Juftices of the Bench may take and Record Recognizance, as well out of Term, as within Term; and as well in any County of *England,* as at *Weftminfter.* 4. *M.* 1. *B. Recognizance.* 20.

Note, that the King himfelf cannot take a Recognizance; for he cannot be Judge himfelf, but ought to have a Judge under him to take it. And none can take a Recognizance, but a Juftice of Record, or by Commiffion: as the Juftices of the two Benches, Juftice of Peace, and the like: for a Confervator of the Peace, which is by the cuftom of the Realm, cannot take

Lecture 8.

take ſurety of the Peace by Recognizance, but by obligation; the ſame Law of a Conſtable. *Lecture.* B. *Recognizance.* 14.

Record.

19. E. 4. 9.
See 21. H. 7. 9.
A man ſhall not plead a Record, except it be in the ſame Court where the Record remains; without ſhewing the Record exemplified *ſub magno ſigillo Angliæ*, if it be denied: for it ought to come into the Chancery by *Cerciorare*, and there to be exemplified *ſub magno ſigillo*; for if it be exemplified *ſub ſigillo de*
See 11. H. 7. 2.
by Fairfax.
communi banco, Scaccario, or the like, theſe are but evidence to a Jury. 22. *H.* 8. *B. Record.* 65.

'Tis ſaid that he that pleads a recovery in a writ of right in a court baron in barre of an Aſſiſe before the Juſtice of Aſſiſe, he ought to ſhew it exemplified *ſub ſigillo cancell.* otherwiſe 'tis no plea. But of a Record in the common bench, he may vouch it there, and have day to bring it in; the ſame law by *B.* of any other court of Record. Yet otherwiſe in a court baron, for there 'tis a recovery, but no Record, for 'tis not a court of Record. *Tims. H.* 8. *B. Record.* 66. the end.

1. H. 7. 20.
Contra. Com.
265.
Note that in the King's bench they have divers preſidents, that in a writ of error upon a fine, the Record itſelf ſhall be certified, ſo that no *plures proclam.* ſhall be made, for if nothing be removed but a Tranſcript, they may proceed in the common bench notwithſtanding that, and if it be reverſed, this makes an end of all: but if it be affirmed, then the Record
44. E. 3. 37.
by Knivet.
ſhall be ſent into the common bench by *Mittimus* to be proclaimed and ingroſſed. 4. *M.* 1. *B. Record.* 49.

Recovery

Recovery in value.

Recovery againſt huſband and wife by writ of entry in the Poſt where the wife is tenant in taile, and they vouch over, and ſo the demandant recovers againſt the huſband and wife, and they over in value, this ſhall binde the taile and the heir of the wife. 23. *H.* 8. *B..Recovery in value.* 27.

See 25. H. 8. after.

Where a writ of entry in the Poſt is againſt tenant for terme of life to bind the fee ſimple, he ought to pray in aide of him in reverſion, and then they to vouch upon the joynder, &c. And ſuch recovery with voucher is uſed for to dock the taile in ancient demeſne upon a writ of right, and voucher over; and this of freehold there. Yet *B.* doubts of ſuch recovery upon a plaint there of land of baſe tenure, for this cannot be warranted. *Ideo quære.* 23. *H.* 8. *B. Recovery in value.* 27. *the middle.*

See 24. H. 8. Tit. Entre congeable.

Note, that 'twas taken, if my tenant for life vouches a ſtranger, who enters into the warranty, and cannot barre the demandant, by which the demandant recovers, and the tenant over in value, that this land recovered in value ſhall not go to me in reverſion after the death of the tenant for life, nor the reverſion of the land recovered in value, ſhall not be in me in the life of tenant for life, and ſo 'tis holden at this day. 25. *H.* 8. *B. Recovery in value.* 33.

See 27. H. 8. after. 5. E. 4. 2. contra by Haydon. See 25. H. 8. after.

Note, by ſome, where a writ of entry in the Poſt is brought againſt a huſband and wife, where the wife is tenant in taile, and they vouch over and ſo the demandant recovers againſt the huſband and wife, and they over in value; if the wife tenant in taile dyes, and the huſband ſurvives, this ſhall not bind the iſſue in taile, for the recompence ſhall go to the

See 23. H. 8. before.

the furvivor, and then it fhall not bind the iffue in taile. Yet *B.* feems that this opinion is not law, for the recompence fhall go, as the firft land which was recovered fhould go. And voucher by hufband and wife fhall be intended for the intereft of the wife. 25. *H.* 8. *B. Recovery in value.* 27. the end.

See 25. H. 8. before.

See 25. H. 8. before.

Tenant for life, the remainder over, or tenant in taile the remainder over, is impleaded by a writ of entry in the Poft, and he vouches a ftranger, the demandant recovers againft the tenant, and the tenant over in value, this fhall bind him in remainder by *Mountague Juft.* and others, for the recompence fhall go to him in remainder. But yet in the cafe of the Lord *Zouch* and *Stowell* in the Chancery, the law was determined otherwife by all the Juftices. *B.* feems the reafon, becaufe that when he vouches a ftranger, the recompence fhall not go to him in remainder ; contrary, if he vouches the donor or his heir who is privy. But after this day many put in ure to bind the remainder. 27. *H.* 8. *B. Recovery in value.* 28.

N. B. 148.

Recovery againft Feoffees feifed to ufe in tailes. See *Tit. Feoffements to ufes.*

'Tis held, that where tenant for life is, the remainder over in tail, or for life and the tenant for life is impleaded, and vouches him in remainder who vouches over one who hath title of Formedon, and fo the recovery paffes by voucher, there the iffue of him who hath title of *Formedon* may bring his *Formedon,* and recover againft the tenant for life, for the recompence fuppofed fhall not go to the tenant for life, and therefore he may recover ; for his anceftor warranted but the remainder, and not the eftate for terme of life, and therefore the tenant for life cannot bind him by the recovery, for he did not warrant to
him.

him. And therefore in ſuch caſe the ſure way is to make the tenant for life to pray in aide of him in remainder, and they to joyn and vouch him who hath title of *Formedon*, and ſo to paſſe the recovery, for there the recompence ſhall go to both. 30. *H. 8. B. Recovery in value.* 30. See 24. H. 8. Tit. Entre congeable.

'Twas agreed that if tenant in taile the reverſion to the King, ſuffers a recovery, this ſhall bind him and his iſſue, but not the King by the common law. See now the Statute thereof that it ſhall not bind the iſſue. 33. *H. 8. B. Recovery in value.* 31. *Taile.* 41. *the end.* See 32. H. 8. Tit. Diſcontinuance de poſſeſſion.

Relation.

Where an office found for the King ſhall relate, where not. See *Tit. Intruſion.*

Of the Relation of an Act of Parliament. See *Tit. Parliament.*

Note, that the attainder of Treaſon by Act of Parliament, ſhall not have elder relation then to the firſt day of the Parliament, except it be by ſpeciall words that he ſhall forfeit his lands that he had ſuch a day and after. 35. *H. 8. B. Relation.* 43.

'Tis held for good Law, that by attainder of felony by verdict, a man ſhall forfeit all his lands that he had the day of his felony done or ever after, for this ſhall have relation to the Act, *contra* upon an attainder by outlawry. For *B.* ſeems there that he ſhall not forfeit but thoſe which he had, the time of the outlawry pronounced, or after, for outlawry hath not relation, as a verdict hath. *Time. H. 8. B. Relation.* 42. *the end.* 30. H. 6. 5. Perk. 6. C. St. 192. A.

30. H. 6. 5. & St. 192. A. Contra. Perk. 6. B. See Coke upon Lit.

Relation of an Inrolment. See *Tit. Faitz inrol.*

x x *Releaſes.*

Releaſes.

Huſband and wife purchaſe in fee, and after they leaſe for years by Indenture, and after the huſband releaſes to the leſſee and his heirs, this is no diſcontinuance, and yet this gives a freehold to the leſſee during the life of the huſband ; *Per plures,* without doubt. 29. *H.* 8. *B. Releaſes.* 81.

See Lit. Sect. 508. 509. accord.

G. Chancery was poſſeſſed of an Indenture, and loſt it, and *I. S.* found it, to whom the ſaid *G. C.* releaſed all actions and demands, and after the ſaid *I. S.* gave the ſame Indenture to *John Tiſon,* and after the ſaid *G. C.* brought an action of detinue againſt the ſaid *J. T.* who pleaded that the ſaid *J. S.* found the Indenture, and that the ſaid *G. C.* releaſed to the ſaid *J. S.* all actions and demandes, and after the ſaid *J. S.* gave the ſaid Indenture to the ſaid *J. T.* Judgment if action. And 'twas agreed in the common Bench, the caſe being of land demanded *ibidem,* that this is a good barre, and that the releaſe of all demandes ſhall exclude

6. H. 7. 15.

the party of ſeiſure of the thing and of his entry into the land, and of the property of the chattell which he had before. And it was moved in the King's bench, and they were of the ſame opinion, and ſaid that the reaſon is, becauſe that entry in land, and ſeiſure of goods are demandes in Law. 34. *H.* 8. *B. Releaſes.* 90.

Relief.

See Tit. *Debt.*

Remainder.

Remainder.
See Tit. Difcent.

Remitter.

No Remitter againſt an Act of Parliament. See *Tit. Parliament.*

Note a *Per curiam*, if Tenant in Taile makes a Feoffement to his uſe in Fee before the ſtatute of uſes made, 27. *H.* 8. and dyes before the ſaid Statute, his heir within age, and after the Statute is made before the full age of the heir, by which the heir is in poſſeſſion by the Statute, he ſhall not be remitted by it. Contrary of a diſcent after the Statute, for this ſhall be a remitter, 34. *H.* 8. *B. Remitter.* 49. See 29. H. 8. Tit. Parliament. 2. M. 1. Com. 114. See Dier.

If a man hath a Title of entry, and not a right of entry, as by eſcheat mortmaine, aſſent by a woman to a raviſher, and the like, and takes an eſtate of the terretenant, he ſhall not be remitted, for he hath but a Title. (And a man cannot be remitted, but in reſpect of a right before, as where a man is diſſeiſed and takes an eſtate of the diſſeiſor, he is remitted, for he had a right of entry before.) And the ſame Law where a man decaies his Tenements, or converts Land from tillage into paſture againſt the Statute, and makes an eſtate for life to his Lord, he ſhall have no other eſtate : for he had but a Title of entry, and not a right of entry. *Quære*, for *Non adjudicatur.* 34. *H.* 8. *B. remitter.* 50. See Coke upon Lit. 4. H. 7. ca. 19.

Where a Deviſe ſhall take away a diſcent, and will not remit. See Tit. Deviſe.

Repleder.

Repleder.

Repleder.

P. 7. E. 4. 1.
accord.

'Twas in ufe in the King's bench, though that the Jury be ready to pafs there, if there be a Jeofail aparent in the Record, the inqueft fhall be difcharged, 35. *H.* 8. *B. repleder.* 54.

Refcous.

See Tit. Diftrefs.

Refervations.

46. E. 3. 22.
Fenk. accord.
See 14. H. 8.
by Brudnel.

If a man Leafes his mannor except the wood, and underwood, by this the foile of the wood, is excepted by *Baldwine*, Chief Juftice of the Common-Bench: *Fitz.* Juftice, and *Knightly*, and *Mart* Serjeants: contrary, *Spilman*, and *W. Conigs'* Juft. 33. *H.* 8. *B. Refervations.* 39.

Reftitution.

See 32. H. 8.
Tit. Denizen &
Coke upon Lit.

A man is attainted of Treafon, the King may reftore the Heir to the Land by his Patent of Grant, but he cannot make the heir to be heir of blood, nor to be reftored to it without Parliament: for this is in prejudice of others. 3. E. 6. *B. Reftitution.* 37.

Reftore al primer aЙion.
Reftored to the firft aЙion.

See Tit. Judge-
ment. See Coke
upon Lit.

If a man enters where his entry is not lawful, as the heir in Tail after difcontinuance, or the heir of

a

a Woman, or the Woman herſelf after diſcontinuance, & the other upon whom he enters recovers againſt him, there they, S. the heir in Tail, or the woman, or her heir, is reſtor'd to their firſt action of *Formedon*, or, *Cui in vita*.   Yet, if ſuch who enters where his entry is not lawfull, makes a Feoffment, and the other upon whom he entered, recovers : now the firſt action is not reſtored to the iſſue in Tail, nor to the Woman, nor to her heir, by reaſon of the Feoffment, which extincts right and action.   But if he which ſo enters, makes a Feoffment upon condition, and for the condition broken, re-enters before that he upon whom he entered hath recovered : and then he recovers after the re-entry made by the condition, there he which made the Feoffment upon condition, is reſtored to his firſt action : for the entry by the Condition, extincts his Feoffment, 23. *H. 8. B. Reſtore al primer action.* 5.

9. H. 7. 25.
Fineaux accord.
& Thor. 41. E.
3. 18.

Retorne de avers.
Retorn of beaſts.

Note by the opinion of the Court, That if a man be nonſuited in a Replevin, and a retorn is awarded : and the Plaintiff brings a Writ of ſecond deliverance, and ſuffers it to be diſcontinued, retorn irreplegible ſhall be awarded, as well as if the Plaintiff had been *non ſuited* in the Writ of ſecond deliverance. 17. *H. 8. B. Retorne de avers.* 37. *Second deliverance.* 15.

19. H. 8. 11. 6.
& 7. E. 6. com.
82.

Revivings.
See *Tit. Extinguiſhments.*

Riot,

Riot, Rout, and unlawful Assembly.

Note, that Riot is where three or more do an unlawfull act in Deed, and execute it, as to beat a man,
enter upon poßeßion, or the like : unlawfull Aßem-
blie is, where a man aßembles people to do an unlawfull act, and doth not ·do it, nor execute it in
deed. And Rout is, where many aßemble themßelves
for their own quarrel; this is a Rout, and againßt
law, though it be not executed : as inhabitants of a
Town for to break down a hedge, wall, or the like,
to have Common there or to beat a man who hath
done to them Common dißpleaßure, or the like. *Lecture. B. Riots.* 5.

Sanctuary.

See Tit. Corone.

Saver default, Saving default.
See Tit. Judgement.

Scire facias.

Of a thing Executory ; a man ßhall have Execu-
tion for ever by *ßcire facias.* See *Tit. Execution.*
Where Debt lies, and where a *ßcire facias.* See
Tit. Debt.
Where a *ßcire facias* upon a Recognißance ßhall be
brought ? See *Tit. Lieu'.*

Second

Second Deliverance.

See Tit. Retorn de avers.

Seiſin.

If a man holds of the King, and holds other Land of another Lord, and dies, his heir within age, who intrudes at his full age, and pays the rent to the other Lord, this is a good Seiſin, and ſhall bind him after he hath ſued livery : for the Seigniory was not ſuſpended by the poſſeſſion of the King, but onely the diſtreſs : for after Livery, the other Lord may diſtrain for the arrearages due before, *per optim. opinionem tunc.* See now the Statute thereof, That the officers of the King ſhall render yearly the rent to the Lord, and the heir ſhall not be charged with it by diſtreſs after upon livery ſued, as he was at Common Law. 34. *H.* 8. *B. Seiſin,* 48.

13. H. 7. 15.

33. H. 6. 35. by Davers. St. 9. 26. H. 8. 8. by Norw. 2. & 3. E. 6. ca. 8.

Several precipe.

'Twas agreed that a man may have Debt and Detinue by one and the ſame Writ by ſeveral Precipe, the one ſhall be *Debet,* the other *Detinet, Tim. H.* 8. *B. ſeveral precipe.* 5. the end.

11. H. 6.

Several Tenancie.

In an Aſſiſe, ſeveral Tenancy is no plea : and the ſame Law in other actions where no land is demanded in certain. 24. *H.* 8. *B. ſeveral Tenancy.* 18.

30. Aſſ. 14.

Statute

Statute Merchant.

'Twas ſaid for Law, That if a man ſues Execution upon a Statute Merchant, or Statute ſtaple, and part of the Land is extended *nomine omnium terrarum*, which is retorned according, and the party accepts it, he ſhall never have an Extent, nor re-extent of the reſt.

26. H. 8. 7. by Fitz. ſee 33. H. 8. after.

And that upon a *Nihil* retorned upon a *Teſtatum eſt*, he may have Proces in another County : for there the judgement ſhal be *quod habeat executionem de terris quouſque ſumma Levetur.*

Yet *B.* ſeems otherwiſe of ſuch retorn of Goods. 29. *H. 8. B. Statute Merchant.* 40.

Note if a Statute ſtaple be extended, and ſo remains by ſeven years without *Deliberate* made, yet he may have a *Deliberate* at the end of 7. years, but he who hath the land delivered to him by liberate upon a Statute cannot make a ſurrender conditional to the conuſor, & enter for the condition broken, after the time of the extent incurred ; as land of 10*l.* per an. is delivered in execution for 40*l.* this may incurre in 4. years, there the Conuſee by ſuch condition, cannot enter after the four years incurred, for he ought to take the profits upon his Extent preſently.

15. E. 4. 5. Brian accord. 7. H. 7. 12. accord. by the Reporter. See 29. H. 8. before 4. E. 6. Com. 61.

And he ſhal not hold over his time *niſi in ſpeciali caſu*, as where the Land is ſurrounded with water, ſudden tempeſt, or the like. And the judgement ſhall be *Quod teneat terram ut liberum tenementum ſuum quouſque denarii leventur.* 33. *H. 8. B. Statute Merchant.* 41.

'Tis ſaid for Law, That if the Conuſor upon a Statute Staple hath a Reverſion, and grants it over, and after the Tenant for life dies, this Land ſhall not be be put in execution: for the Reverfion was never extendable in the hands of the Conufor. 33. *H.* 8. *B. ftatute Merchant.* 44. the end.

Note, by * *Bromley, Hales,* and *Portman* Juftices, and *Rich,* who was firft Chancellor of *England, &* *Apprenticius Curiam* That if the Conufee purchafes parcel of the Land after the Statute acknowledged or Recognifed, this is no difcharge of the Statute againft the Conufor himfelf. But the Feoffees of the Conufor of other Parcels, fhall be thereof difcharged. But if the Conufee hath the Land delivered in Execution, and purchafes parcel of the land of the Conufor, this is a difcharge of the intire Statute. 36. *H.* 8. *B. Statute Merchant.* 42.

'Twas faid for Law, that if the Conufee upon a Statute ftaple dies, and his executors fue execution in the name of the Teftator, as if he were in life, and the Sheriff takes the body in the name of the Teftator, *&c.* yet this is not execution for the executors, but they may after have execution in their own name ; for the firft execution in the name of him that was dead before the Tefte of the Writ, was void, and the body cannot remain to fatisfie him who was dead before. Nor the Sheriff cannot deliver the land nor goods to him who is dead, *juxta formam brevis.* And by *B.* in the book of Entries, the executors of the Conufee fhall have execution upon a Statute Merchant, without *Scire Facias,* and this upon furmife as it feems to him. And if the Conufor be retorned dead, yet execution fhall proceed of his Lands and Tenements without *Scire Fac'* againft his heir. And the extent and Liberate fhall be ferved immediatly. Yet by *B.* no remedy appears there for the goods of the Conufor, when the

conufor

Margin notes:
* 45. E. 3. 22.
by Finch. 13. H.
7. 22. by Keble.
fee Time E. 6.
Tit. Recogni-
fance.

11. H. 7. 4. 5.
E. 6. com. 72.

Liber intrac. fo.

conu*for* is dead, to have any execution of them. 36. *H. 8. B. Statute Merchant.* 43.

'Tis faid if a Writ of execution with *extendi facias* iffues upon a Statute Merchant, that the Writ ought to be retorned, and the land upon this delivered to the Conu*fee* by *Liberate Inde. Time H. 8. B. Statute Merchant.* 32. the end.

Super*fedeas.*

5. H. 7. 22. 4.
E. 6. Com. 49.
4. E. 6. Com.
49.

'Twas holden for Law, that in a writ of attaint a man fhall not have a Super*fedeas* for to difturb execution ; for the Verdi&t fhall be intended true untill 'tis reverfed, &c. And that the Regifter which gives a Super*fedeas* there, is not Law. Contrary upon a Writ of Error ; for it may be intended that Error is for the fuit of the Defendant, *&c.* 33. *H. 8. B. Super*fedeas. 24.

Sureties.

Where Sureties in *London* fhall remain after the a&tion removed ? *& econtra.* See *Tit. Procedendo.*

1. H. 7. 1. &
1. E. 3. 3.

Affirmatur pro lege, that Suretie of the Peace is difcharged by the death of the King, for 'tis to obferve the peace of that King, and when he is dead, 'tis not his peace. 1. *M.* 1. *B. Surety.* 20.

Surrender.

14. H. 8. 21.
Br. accord.

Tenant for term of life furrenders to him in reverfion out of the land to which he agrees, the freehold by this is in him prefently, and he is Tenant to the a&tion by *precipe quod reddat* without entry, but
he

he ſhall not have Treſpaſſ without Entry. 31. *H.* 8. *B. Surrender.* 50.

Where tail ſhall be extinct by ſurrender of Letters Patents, where not, ſee *Tit. Patents.*

Note in the Caſe of *Culpeper* 'twas ſaid that the King himſelf cannot record, or receive a ſurrender of land or Letters Patents, made to him *extra curiam,* but this ought to be before his Chancellor or other Juſtice to this authorized. 2. *E.* 6. *B. Surrender.* 53. the end.

If a man leaſes for years, the remainder over for years, and after the firſt Termor grants his intereſt to the Leſſor, this is no ſurrender by reaſon of the mean intereſt of the term in remainder. And a Termor makes his Leſſor his Executor and dies, this is no ſurrender, for he hath this to another uſe, *contra wherewood inde.* 2. *E.* 6. *B. Surrender.* 52. See Coke upon Litt. See 4. E. 6. Tit. Extinguiſhment.

Note, where a man leaſes land for term of years, the remainder over for life, the remainder over in fee, or reſerving the reverſion, there he in remainder for term of life, may ſurrender to him in reverſion, or to him in remainder in Fee, and the eſtate for term of years is no impediment, for though it cannot give the poſſeſſion of the land, yet it gives the poſſeſſion of the freehold which is in the thing which was ſurrendred. 3. *M.* 1. *B. Surrender.* 55. Perk. 115. H. See Coke upon Lit.

Suitor.

'Twas ſaid for Law in the Star-Chamber, betwixt *Brown* Juſtice, and *Lion* Grocer of *London*, that a Court Baron may be holden before two ſuitors, for the plurall number ſufficeſt. *Time. H.* 8. *B. Suit.* 17. See Tit. Court Baron, & Mannor.

Tail.

Tail.

RECOVERY upon voucher againſt Tenant in tail, is a bar by reaſon of the recompence in value. And a recovery by writ of entry in the poſt by ſingle voucher doth give but the eſtate which the tenant in tail hath in poſſeſſion *tempore recuperationis*, ſo that if it were in of another eſtate then the tail, there the tail is not bound againſt the heir. But the double voucher is to make the tenant in tail to diſcontinue, and to bring the writ of entry againſt the feoffee, and then the feoffee ſhall vouch the tenant in tail, and he ſhal vouch over, and ſo ſhal loſe ; and this ſhal binde all intereſts and tails that the vouchee had. 23. *H.* 8. *B. Tail.* 32.

Lit. 160. N. B. 1. 13. 13. H. 7. 24. by Townes. 10. H. 7. 8. Vaviſor accord. 2. M. 1. com. 110. N. B. 144. & 48. E. 3. 9. by Finch. contra. See Time H. 8. Tit. Formedon. Tenant in tail hath iſſue and aliens with warranty, and leaves aſſets, & dies, the iſſue cannot recover by *Formedon* ; for the warranty and aſſets is a barr : And if the iſſue aliens the aſſets, yet he ſhall not have a *Formedon*. But if he hath iſſue and dies, there the iſſue of the iſſue ſhal have a *Formedon*, becauſe that the aſſets is not diſcended to him. Yet 'tis ſaid that if the iſſue upon whom the warranty and aſſets diſcended brings a *Formedon* and is barred by judgement, and aliens the aſſets and dies, his iſſue ſhall not have a *Formedon*, becauſe that his father was barred by judgement. *B. Tail.* 33. And if the tenant in tail hath iſſue two ſons, by divers venters, and diſcontinues, and dies, and an *anceſtor collateral* of the eldeſt ſon releaſes with warranty, and dies without iſſue, and the eldeſt ſon dies

dies without iſſue, before any *Formedon* brought, the younger ſon may recover by *Formedon* ; for he is not heir to the warrantor, and his brother was not barred by judgement. Yet *B.* doubts thereof; for it ſeems to him that the diſcent of the *Collateral* warranty extinɑts the tail, But if the eldeſt had been barred by judgement, then clearly the younger is gon alſo. 24. *H. 8. B. Tail.* 33. *Formedon.* 18.

Tenant in tail, the reverſion to the King, ſuffers a recovery *quid operatur* by it. See *Tit. Diſcontinuance de poſſeſſion & Recovery in value.*

If the King gives lands in tail by his Letters Patents, and after the donee ſurrenders his letters patents to the K. the Tail by this is not extinɑ. 35. *H. 8. B. Tail.* 38. *See* 32. *H.* 8. *Tit.* Patents.

The King Tenant in Tail cannot diſcontinue by grant by Patent. See *Tit. Diſcontinuance de Poſſeſſion.*

Tenant at Will.

Note for Law, that there is no Tenant by ſufferance, but he that firſt enters by authority and lawfully, as where a man leaſes for years, or for term of anothers life, and holds over his term after the term expired, or after the death of *ceſtuy que vie.* And Tenant at will is, where a man leaſes his land to another at will ; for he who enters of his own head is a Diſſeiſor. *Time. H.* 8. *B. Tenant per copy,* 15. the end. *See* 22. *E.* 4. 38. by Huſſey.

Tenant by Copy.

Note, that 'twas ſaid for Law, that Tail may be of a Copyhold, and that a *Formedon* may ly of it in *Diſcender* by Proteſtation, in nature of a Writ of *Formedon* M. 26. H. 8. accord in Eſſex, & Fitzh. in the Dutchy Cham-

ber. Lit. 16. 4.
El. com. 233.
Weftm. 2. cap.
1. Raft. Tail. 1.
See Coke upon
Lit. & the 3.
Rep.

Formedon in *Difcender* at common Law, and good by all the Juftices, for though that a *Formedon* in *Difcender* was not given but by Statute; yet now this Writ lies at common Law, and it ſhall be intended that this hath been a cuſtome there *de tempore, &c.* and the Demandant ſhall recover by adviſe of all the Juftices, 15. *H.* 8. *B. Tenant per Copy.* 24.

Where a Stuard, or under-ſtuard may let by Copy, *& e contra,* See *Tit. Court baron.*

See Cook upon
Lit. and his
Rep.

Note, that if a man leaſes a Mannor for yeeres, in which are Copy-holds, and after a Copyholder dies, the termor of the Mannor grants the land by Copy for three lives, this is good; for the cuſtome through all *England* is, that the Lord, for the time being, may demiſe by Copy, &c. and this notwithſtanding that hee is but *durante bene placit.* or at Will. And 'tis held that ſuch Tenant of a Mannor cannot demiſe, reſerving leſſe rent then the ancient rent, but he ought to reſerve the ancient rent, or more, *quære of that.* *Tenant by ſufferance. ſee Tit. Tenant at Will.*

Tender.

See 4. M. 1.
contra. after.
Cooke upon Lit.
& Cluns caſe in
his Rep.

'Tis ſaid for Law, that upon a Leaſe for yeers, rendring rent with re-entry the Leſſee ought to bee ready all the day and make attendance to offer it; and it ſuffices for the Leſſor to come any time of the day, yet the entry is, that the one and the other attended the intire day, *quære inde.* 36. *H.* 8. *B. Conditions.* 192. *the end. Entre Congeabll.* 2. *the end,*

4. M. 1. Com.
172. 36. H. 8.
before cont.
6. H. 7. 3. ſee
Cooks 10
booke, Cluns
caſe.

Note that 'twas agreed in the Serjeants Caſe, that where a man leaſes Land for yeeres, rendring rent, and for default of payment a re-entry, it ſuffices for the Leſſee to tender the rent upon the Land, the laſt houre of the laſt day of the Moneth, if the money
may

may bee told in that time : And ſo it ſufficeth for the
Leſſor to demand it the ſame houre, 4. *M.* 1. *B. Tender.* 41.

If a man Leaſes for yeeres rendring rent at *Michael-
maſſe*, and other Covenants, if hee bee bound in an
obligation to pay the rent preciſely, there hee ſhall
ſeeke the Leſſor, but if hee be bound to perform the
Covenants, &c. The tender upon the land ſufficeth,
for there the payment is of the nature of the Rent
reſerved, *Contrary* in the firſt Caſe. 6. *E.* 6. *B. Tender.* 20.

Tenures.

What ſhall bee a Tenure, and what a Condition,
ſee *Tit. Conditions.*

What ſhall bee a Tenure *in Capite* of the King,
what not, ſee *Tit. Liverie.*

A man makes a Feoffment of the moytie of his
Land, the Leſſee ſhall hold of the Lord by the intyre
ſervices which the intire Land was holden before,
for the Statute of *Quia emptores terrarum, tenend.
pro particula*, holds not place here ; for a moytie is
not *particula :* the ſame Lawe of a third part, and
the like, which goes by the halfe and the whole ;
contrary of an acre or of two acres in certain : And
if a man holds two acres by a hauke, and makes a
Feoffement in Fee of one acre ; the Feoffee ſhall
hold it by a hauke, and the Feoffor ſhall hold the
acre by another hauke, 29. *H.* 8. *B. Tenures.* 64.

Reſtitution by Parliament revives a Seignory or
or Tenure which was extinct by attainder of Treaſon,
by Parliament, *See Tit. Extinguiſhment.*

See in the Exchequer 3. *E. R◦.* 2. 'twas found that
a man held of the King in Knight ſervice *in capite*,

ut

Perk. 129. D.
Weſtm. 3. ca. 2.
Raſt. Tenure. 4.

Fitz. 235. A.

22. E. 4. 36. by
Cateſby.

See Tit. Livery.

ut de honore fuo de Rayleghe, and 'twas taken no tenure *in capite*, but a tenure of the honour; and therefore

11. H. 7. 18. by Rede. his heir ſhall have *ouſter L'maine* of his otheŕ Lands, which ſhould not be if it had been *in capite*, for then the King ſhall have all in Ward by his Prerogative: yet otherwiſe 'tis if the Honour be annexed to the Crown; for then the Honour is *in capite*. And 11. *H. 7.* the Honour of *Rayleghe* was annexed to the Crown; therefore now 'tis *in capite*. And where the King gives Land to hold of him by fealty, and 2. *d. pro omnibus ſervitiis*, this is Socage *in capite*, for 'tis of the perſon of the King, otherwiſe if it were to hold *ut de manerio de R.* 33. *H.* 8. *B. Tenures.* 94.

Weſtm. 2. ca. 2. Raſt. Tenure. 4. 'Tis held, that if a man made a Feoffment of land before the Stat. of *Quia emptores terrarum* to hold of him, and to make ſuit to his Court; this is good if he hath a Court. But a man cannot commence a Court by tenure made, where he had not a Mannor before; for there the ſervices ſhould be holden of his **See 33. H. 8. Tit. Mannor.** perſon (*B. Tenures.* 34.) And a man cannot make a Mannor at this day, though that he gives Land in tayl to hold of him, and by ſuit of his Court; for he cannot make a Court; for a Court cannot be but by continuance. And ſo a Man may make a tenure, but no Mannor nor Court; for a Mannor and Court cannot be but by uſage had *de tempore cujus contrarium memoria hominum non exiſtit.*

Teſtament.

Teſtament by a *Feme* Covert of the aſſent of the huſband, See *Tit. Deviſe.*

22. E. 3. 16. B. Deviſe. 33. See 4. E. 6. Tit. Eſtates. A man deviſes his Land to *J. S.*; this ſhall be taken but for term of his life; but if he ſaith paying a 100*l.* to *W. N.* this ſhall be intended a Fee-ſimple:

ſimple: and if he doth not pay it in his life, yet if See 24. H. 8. Tit. Conditions. his Heir or Executor pay it, that ſuffiſes; *Quære* of his Aſſignee. 29. *H. 8. B. Teſtament.* 18.

If a man holds three ſeverall Mannors of three ſeverall Lords in Knight ſervice, and every of them of equall value; he cannot make his will of two of the Mannors, leaving the third Mannor to the Heir; See Cook upon Lit. but of two parts of every Mannor; for otherwiſe he ſhall prejudice the other two Lords. 35. *H. 8. B. Teſtament.* 19.

Note, by the Doctors of the Civill-Law, and Ser- 5. M. 1. Com. 185. jeants of the Common-Law; if a man makes his Teſtament, and names no Executors, this is no Teſtament; but yet 'tis a good Will of the Land in it, for thoſe are not Teſtamentary; but in the firſt where Executors want, yet the Legacies ſhall be paid. But if it appears that he made part of the Teſtament, and not the whole; there the Legacies ſhall not be paid. And where a man makes a Teſtament and Executors, and they refuſe, yet the Legacies ſhall be paid; for there is no default in the Teſtator; and the Teſtament ſhall be annexed to Letters of Adminiſtration. 37. *H. 8. B. Teſtament.* 20.

Note, for Law by the Chancellor of *England* and See Cook upon Lit. Juſtices, That if the Tenant who holds of the King in Knight ſervice *in capite*, gives all his Land to a Stranger, by act executed in his life, and dyes; yet the King ſhall have the third part in Ward, and ſhall have the Heir in Ward if he be within age: ·And if of full age, he ſhall have *primer ſeſin* of the third part, by vertue of that clauſe in the Stat: *Saving to the King Ward, Primer ſeſin, Livery,* and 32. H. 8. ca. 1. Raſt. Wills 2. the like, by which it appears that the intent of the act is, that the King ſhall have as much as if the

z z   Tenant

See H. 10. El. Tenant had made a will, and had dyed ſeized; yet by all, after that the King is ſerved of his duty of it, the gift is good to the Donee againſt the Heir. 2. *E. 6. B. Teſtament.* 24.

Note, that 'twas adjudged betwixt *Umpton* and *Hyde,* that the explanation of the Statute of Wills, is not to take effect only from the time of the explanation; but the firſt Stat: which is explained ſhall be ſo taken *ab initio:* So that the Wills of *Umpton, Gainesford* and others which are excepted in the explanation, ſhall be taken good by the Stat: of 32.

32. H. 8. ca. 1.
Raſt. Wills 2. *H.* 8. of Wills which was explained. 4. *M.* 1. *B. Teſtament.* 26.

Teſtmoignes, Witneſſes.

The age of Witneſſes in an *Ætate probanda,* is 42 years, *Lecture B. Teſtmoignes.* 30. the end.

Titles.

See Tit.
Pleadings. Note that a man ſhall make a good title in an Aſſize to ſay, that *J. N.* was ſeized in Fee to the uſe of *T. P.,* which *T. P.* infeoffed the Plaintiff, who was ſeized and diſſeized, &c. without ſhewing what perſon made the Feoffment to the uſe of *T. P.,* or how the uſe commenced. 36. *H.* 8. *B. Titles.* 61.

Travers of Office.

4. H. 7. 3. by
Keble. Stp. 63.
21. E. 4. 2. by
Noting. 'Tis ſaid for Law, that none can traverſe, except he makes title to the ſame land in the premiſſes, or cloſe of his traverſe. 22. *H.* 8. *B. Traverſe d' Office.* 48.

'Twas

'Twas found that *J. S.* dyed feized, by which *W. S.* his fon comes, and faith that the faid *J. S.* in his life was feized in Fee, and infeoffed *A. B.* in Fee, to the ufe of the faid *J. S.* and his Heirs, and dyed; and after by the Stat: of ufes 27. *H.* 8. he was feized in poffeffion without that that *J. S.* his father dyed feized *prout, &c.* and a good traverfe: And a Termor cannot traverfe an Office by the Common-Law, except it were found in the Office, and then he might have a *monftrans de droit*, and *oufter L'main* the King. 29. *H.* 8. *B. Travers d' Office.* 50.   *Stp. 62. See Cook upon Lit.*

Where a man fhall have a Petition, where traverfe. See *Tit. Petition.*

Where the King hath no other title but by falfe Office, there the party who can make title, may traverfe as well againft the King as againft the party, if the King had granted it over; but now this is helpt by Stat. 33. *H.* 8. *B. Travers d' office.* 51. the end.   *35. H. 6. 61. Laicon accord.*   *2. E. 6. ca. 8.*

Where a Tenure is found of the King *ut de Ducat: fuo Lancaftrie,* which in truth is falfe; yet this need not to be traverfed, for the King hath this Duchy as Duke, not as King; and a man fhall not be put to traverfe but where the Office is found for the King, *ut pro rege Angliæ,* for then he hath a prerogative, and as Duke none. 1. *E.* 6. *B. Travers d' Office.* 53.   *See Tit. Age.*

Non-fuit or relinquifhing of a traverfe is peremptory; *contra* of *Non-fuit* in a Petition; and the Judgement of traverfe is no other, *fed quod manus domini Regis amoveantur, et quod poffeffio reftituatur* to him that traverfed. *Lecture. B. Traverfe d' Office.* 54.   *4. H. 6. 13.*

Travers by, &c.

What thing ſhall be traverſable, what not, *See Tit. Iſſues joynes.*

Action for making falſe clothes in *Bartholomew-Fair*, contrary to the Stat. The other ſaith, that he made them well and truly at *D.* in the County of *F.* without that that he made them in *Bartholomew-Fair* in *L, prout, &c.* and a good Plea. 35. *H.* 8. B. *Travers by, &c.* 368.

See 4. E. 6. after.

If in Aſſize the Tenant Pleads that his Father was ſeized in Fee, and dyed by Proteſtation ſeized. 'Tis ſaid that the Plaintiff may make title by a ſtranger, without that that the father of the Tenant was ſeized in Fee, &c. 38. *H.* 8. B. *Travers by, &c.* 26. the end.

See Tit. Prerogative.

Information in the Chequer : the Defendant Pleads a Plea, and traverſes a materiall point in the information, upon which they are at iſſue ; there the King cannot waive this iſſue, as he may in other caſes where the King alone is party without an Informer *ut ſupra,* by the King's Attorney and others learned in the Law. 38. *H.* 8 B. *Travers by, &c.* 369.

Tender not traverſable in a Writ of intruſion, *maritagio non ſatisfac :* for the ſingle value, See *Tit. Forfeiture of marriage.*

Treſpas : The Defendant ſaid, that *J. N.* was ſeized in Fee, and leaſed to him for twenty one years, and gave colour ; the Plaintiff ſaid, that his father was ſeized and dyed ſeized, &c. and he entred and was ſeized untill the Treſpas, *abſ q' hoc*

See 38. H. 8. before : And Time E. 6. after.

quod dictus J. N. aliquid habuit tempore dimiſſionis, and a bad traverſe ; but he ſhall ſay without that that *J. N.* was ſeized in Fee *modo & forma prout,*

&c.

&c. in *Communi banco,* 4. *E.* 6. *B. Travers per.* 372.

Aſſize. The Tenant makes a barr by a Stranger *Caſus Cooks and Green.* and gives colour : the Plaintiff makes title by the ſame perſon by which the Defendant made his barr, *ſ :* that *J. S.* was ſeized and gave in tayl to his father, who infeoffed *W. N.* who infeoffed the Tenant, upon whom *A. B.* entred and infeoffed the grandfather of the Plaintiff, whoſe Heir he is in Fee, who dyed ſeized, and the Land diſcended to the Plaintiff, & ſo he was in in his Remitter, untill by the Defendant diſſeized : And in truth *A. B.* never entred, nor never infeoffed the Grandfather ; and yet 'twas held cleerly, that the Tenant in his barr to the title, cannot traverſe the Feoffment of *A. B.*, but ought to traverſe the dying ſeized of the grandfather of the Plaintiff which remitted him, for this binds the entry of the Tenant, and is the moſt notable thing in the title, 4. *E.* 6. *B. Travers per.* 154.

Treſpas. The Defendant ſaid that *J.* was ſeized, See 4. *E.* 6. and infeoffed him, and gave colour; The Plaintiff before. may ſay, that *H.* was ſeized and leaſed to *J.* at will who gave to the Defendant, and *R.* re-entered and infeoffed the Plaintiff; he ought to ſay, without that that *J.* was ſeized in Fee *modo & forma prout,* *&c. Time. E.* 6. *B. Travers per.* 217. the end.

Place not traverſable, See *Tit. Attaint,*

Treaſon.

A Chaplaine had affixed an ancient ſeal to a See St. 3. B. Patent of non-reſidence, made by himſelfe, of the part of the King, and was impriſoned in the Fleet for it : And 'twas holden miſpriſion, and no Treaſon,

ſon, by the Juſtices, and he eſcaped, and was not put to death; for 'twas ſaid, That becauſe he did not counterfeit the King's ſeale, but tooke an ancient ſeale, this is not Treaſon. 37. *H. 8. B. Treaſon. 3. the end. 5.*

Note, that in *January* this yeere, *H. Howard* Earle of *Surrey*, ſonne and Heir apparent of *Thomas* Duke of *Norfolke*, was attainted of high Treaſon, for joyning the Armes of *England* before the Conqueſt, and other Armes after to his owne Armes; and other pretences againſt the Prince; and hee was tryed by Knights and Gentlemen, and not by Lords; *nec per pares regni*, becauſe that hee was not Earle by Creation, but by Nativity as Heir apparent of a Duke, which is no dignity in Law, for if hee had beene of dignitie by creation, and Lord of Parliament, he ſhould be tryed by his Peeres. 38. *H. 8. B. Treaſon. 2.*

'Twas agreed that for miſpriſion of Treaſon, or if a man knowing counterfeit money, and imports it out of *Ireland* into *England*, and utters it in payment or the like, a man ſhall loſe his goods for ever, and the profits of his Land, for his life, and ſhall be impriſoned for term of life. 6. *E. 6. B. Treaſon.* 19. the end.

Note that it appeares by divers Records and Preſidents that theſe words (*compas or imagine the death of the King*) are large words, for he that maliciouſly deviſes how the King ſhall come to death, by words or otherwiſe, and doth an act to explain it or the like, this is Treaſon: And hee who intends to deprive the King, in this is intended the death of the King; *quære* of the depriving, for by *B.* a man may deprive and yet intend no death. And for this cauſe a Statute was thereof made, *Time H. 8. & E. 6.*

See 33. H. 8. Tit. Triall.

See 2. M. 1. after; and ſo 'twas adjudged, M. 4. M. 1.

St. 38. B.

See St. fo. 1. E. fo. 2. H. and fo. 6. A.

6. And the detayner of a Caftle, Fortreffe or the like, againft the King, is levying of warre againft him; all which words (levying of warre, and the others afore) are in the Statute of 25. *E.* 3. And adhering to the Enemies of the King, *ibm* : ayding and ftrengthening them: 1. *M.* 1. *B. Treafon.* 24.

1. E. 6. 12. Raft. Treafon 18.

'Twas agreed in Parliament that for mifprifion of Treafon, the Fine ufed to bee the forfeiture of all his goods, and the profits of all his Land for his life, and his body imprifoned *ad voluntatem Regis,* for mifprifion is finable. 2. *M.* 1. *B. Treafon.* 25. *the end.*

See 6. E. 6. before.

Note, that if an alien borne of a Countrey which is in amity and peace with this Realme, comes into the Realme with Englifh Traytors, and levies warre, this is Treafon in all; *contrary,* if the Country of the alien were in warre againft *England,* for then the alien may bee killed by Marfhall Lawe. 4. *M.* 1. *B. Treafon.* 32.

Trefpas.

Note, that in the Regifter amongft the Writs of Trefpas, there are many Writs of Trefpas, *quare vi & armis equum fuum apud D. inventum cepit & effugavit, &c.* And fo fee that if they be taken in a Common, or other land which is not to the owner of the beafts, yet he fhall have Trefpas *vi et armis,* but not *quare claufum fregit,* 3. *M.* 1. *B. Tenants.* 421.

34. H. 6. 28. 12. H. 8. 2. by Brook.

Tryall.

Peere of the Realme fhall bee tryed by his Peeres, if hee bee arraigned upon an Indictment; *contrary,*

if

10. E. 4. 6. by
Lit. St. 152. A.
See Tit. Corone,
and Treafon.
if he be arraigned upon an Appeale, for at the fuite of parties he fhall not be tryed by his Peeres : and fo was *Fines* Lord *Dacres* of the South this yeere, and hanged for Felony, for the death of a man who was found in his company at a hunting in *Suffex*. 33. *H.* 8. *B. Jurors.* 48. *the end, Tryalls.* 142.

12. H. 7. 18.
Fineux accord.
D. S. 14. 15. 6.
and 7. E. 6.
Com. 82. D. S.
20.
Note that in a Court Baron the tryall is by wager of Law, but they may bee by Jury *ex affenfu partium.* And the Maximes and generall Cuftomes of the Realme, which is the common-Law, fhall bee tryed by the Juftices : And the fame Law of expofitions of Statutes ; And by the Civill-Law, the Judges have the conftruction of Statutes like-wife : But particular Cuftomes fhall not bee tried but *per Patriam.* 33. *H.* 8. *B. Trialls.* 143.

See 2. M. 1.
Com. 117. &
27. H. 8. Tit.
Enqueft.
Note, that a Bifhop is a Peere of the Realme, and fhall bee tryed *per pares fuos* upon an arraign-ment of a Crime, and fo put in ufe ; therefore Knights fhall be of the Jury, and if not the Panel fhall be quafhed ; yet fee 27. *H.* 8. that the Bifhop of *Rochefter* was not tryed by his Peers. 2. *M.* 1. *B. Trials.* 142. *the end.*

Variance.

Quare Impedit upon a grant *de proxima prefenta-tione* granted to *I. N.* Gentleman, and in the writ brought by *I. N.* this word [Gentleman] is omitted, and the Defend'. demanded Oyer of the Deed, and had it, and the variance no matter ; for the action of 4. E. 3. 23. by
Finch. *quare Impedit* is founded upon the difturbance, and not upon the deed, as an action of Debt is founded upon the Obligation. 2. *E.* 6. *B. Variance.* 109.

Verdict.

Verdict.

Note, That the Court of Common Bench would not permit a Verdict at large in a writ of entry in nature of an assise : because 'twas a *Precipe quod reddat*, at which B. admires : for it seemeth to him that upon every general issue a Verdict at large may be given. 23. *H.* 8. *B.* Verdict. 85.

Special Verdict, where the issue is upon an *absque hoc.* See *Tit. Issues, Joynes.*

Contra in a Formedon. 16. E. 3. Fitz. Verdict. 21. 3. M. 1. Com. 92. 93. See Cokes Rep.

Villeinage.

If a Villein comes to an Executor, or to a Bishop, Parson or the like, in *jure Ecclesiæ*, and he purchases Land, the executor enters, he shall not have it *jure proprio*, but as Executor, and it shall be Assets. And if the Bishop, or the Parson enters, he shall not have it but in *jure Ecclesiæ*, because that they had not the villein in *jure proprio*, but in another right : contrary, if they had had the villein *jure proprio.* 33. *H.* 8. *B. Villeinage.* 46.

The King shall not have the villein of another in ward : and yet if there be an Ideot, he shall have the villein of the other who is so Ideot. *Quære.* And the King shall have the perquisite of a villein of another if he hath him as Ideot. *Lecture. B. Villeinage.* 71.

D. S. 92. 7. El. com. 292. See Coke upon Lit. 3. El. com. 235.

Voucher.

See *B. Tit. Voucher.* 84.

Usury.

Ufury.

Note that where a man for 100*l.* fels his Land upon condition, That if the Vendor or his heirs repaies the fumm *citra feftum Pafche*, or the like, *tunc. prox. futur.* that then he may re-enter, this is not ufury: for he may repay the day before, or any time before Eafter, and therefore he hath not any gain certain to receive any profits of the Land: and the fame Law where a defeifance, or Statute is made for the repayment *citra tale feftum: E. contra*, if the condition be that if the faid vendor repays fuch a day, a year, or two years after, this is ufury: for he is fure to have the Lands and the Rents, or Profits this year, or thefe two years. And fo where a Defeifance, or Statute is made for the repayment *ad tale feftum*, which is a year or two after. 29. *H.* 8. *B. Ufury.* 1.

See 29. H. 8. before.

If a man mortgages his land upon defeafance of repayment to re-enter, by which Indenture the Vendee Leafes the fame land to the Vendor for years, rendring rent: there if there be a condition in the leafe, that if the Vendor repaies the fumm before fuch a day, that then the Leafe fhall be void: this is not ufury. Otherwife if it be to repay fuch a day certain, a year, or more after. 31. *H.* 8. *B. Ufury.* 2.

Waife.

ft. 186. A.

'Twas agreed, if a man be purfued as a Felon, and he flees, and waives his own goods, they are forfeited, as if they had been goods ftolne. 37. *H.* 8. *B. Eftray.* 9.   *Wafte.*

Waſte.

'Twas ſaid for Law, That if a Termor commits Waſte, and makes Executors, and dies, the action of waſte is gone: for it doth not lie againſt his Executors but for waſte done by themſelves, and not for the waſte of the Teſtator: for 'tis a Common Treſpaſs, which is an action perſonal, and dies with the perſon. 23. *H.* 8. *B. Waſte.* 138. 46. E. 3. 31. B. Waſte 48. N. B. 38. Lit. accord. 10. E. 4. 1. See 4. E. 6. after.

Nontenure no plea in waſte. *See tit. Pleadings.*

'Twas agreed that Beech of the age of 20 years, nor under 20 years, cannot be cut by Tenant for term of years, or Term of life: for they are of the nature of Timber, and may be Timber, and by this way they ſhall never grow to be Timber. *Time. H.* 8. *B. Waſte.* 134.

Note by *Bromley* Chief Juſtice: If a man doth waſte in Hedge-rows that inviron a paſture, nothing ſhall be recovered but *locum vaſtatum*, S. the circuit of the Root, and not the whole paſture; and by him and *Hales*, Juſtice: the cutting of Beech of the age of ten or eight years is waſte, for they may be timber after. See Coke upon Lit. See Time H. 8. before. & 13. H. 7. 21. by Brian. 48. E. 3. 25. Finch accord. 10. H. 7. 215.

And that where there is a wood, in which grows nothing but underwood, the Termor cannot cut all. *Contra*, of underwood, where Beech, Aſh, and other principall Trees grow amongſt them; for there he may cut all the underwood.

And a Termor may take Beech, Aſhes, and the like, which are well ſeaſonable, which have been uſed to be felled every 20, or 16, 14, or 12 yeares. And by ſome at 26, 27, or 30 years if it be ſeiſonable wood, which is called *Silva cedua* 4. *E.* 6. *B. Waſte.* 136.

'Twas

See Coke upon
Lit.

'Twas holden by the Chief Juſtice, That the
racing of a new Frame, which was never covered, is
not waſte : but 'twas agreed, That if a houſe be
ruinous for default of any covering at the time of
the death of the Leſſor, and after the Tenant ſuffers
it to be more ruinous, that of this new Ruin the heir
ſhall have an action of Waſte : for this is waſte
which continues : for of the decay which came in the
time of the heir, the heir ſhall have an action of
Waſte : *è contra,* of that which was in the life of
his Father. 2. *M.* 1. *B. Waſte.* 117. the end.

Writ.

30. H. 6. 5.
ſee Dier.

'Twas in ure in debt againſt I. N. of C. Yeoman,
alias dictus I. N. of C. ſon and heir of *W. N.* and
charged him as heir, that the Writ abated, becauſe
that he charges him as heir, and he is not named
heir in the premiſes, but in the *alias dictus.*

So in Debt againſt I. N. of C. Yeoman, *alias
dictus* I. N. of C. Executor of the Teſtament of
W. P. and declares againſt him as Executor. 24.
H. 8. *B. Brief.* 418.

Prot. accord.
21. H. 6. 49.
34. H. 6. 8.
by Priſot cont.

Note by *Fitz.* and *Shelley* Juſtices, that if a man
pleads a plea which goes to the action of the Writ,
he may chuſe to conclude to the Writ, or to the
Action. 26. *H.* 8. *B. Brief.* 405. 492.

Where a writ brought in ſuch a name of Dignity,
which was loſt by intermarriage, ſhall abate. *See
Tit. Noſme.*

FINIS.

The Table.

Aſſets

Diff.

Done.

3 C   Executors.

Forfeiture

Extent

Leafe

Leafe for 300 or 400 years is Mortmain, 134.

Otherwife of a covenant for fo many years, 135.

99 or 100 years is not Mortmain, 135.

Mortmain, 135.

Defeifin and difcent takes not away the entry of the Lord for Mortmain, 135.

NONABILITIE.

Obligation for ufury, 135.

Conclufion, 135.

Nonfuit.

King nonfuited, 136.

Nonfuit upon demur, 136.

Nontenure a good plea in an attaint for a ftranger; contra for a privy, 136.

Where non tenure fhall be a good plea in attaint, where not, 136.

Entry in attaint after the laft continuance, 136.

Nofme.
Name.

Where a woman fhall lofe her name of dignity by marriage, 137.

Notice.

Notice of refignation fhall be given by the Ordinary, 137.

Office devant.

Where the king fhall not feife without Office, 137.

Tenant for life, the reverfion to the King dies, 138.

Full age fhal be expreffed, when, 138.

Office ought to be certain, 138.

Office findes dying feifed, but tenuram ignorant, 138.

Where an Office intitles the K. to the Seigniory, and Tenancie, 138.

Servitia ignorant, 138.

Melius inquirend, 138.

Foundation not obferved, 138.

Land which is a chattel fhall be by office, 138.

Where the King fhall feife without office, and where ècontra, 139.

Fees granted to him, who after is made Iuftice, 139.

Steward and after made Iuftice, 139.

The fame man made Bailey and Steward, 139.

Iuftice of the Forreft, and keeper of the Forreft, 139.

Parfon created a Bifhop, 139.

Forfeiture of office, 139.

Steward of a Forreft and Iuftice, 139.

Authority of the Iuftice of Forreft, 140.

Sheriff and Efcheator, 140.

Obligation.

A man bound to *B.* ad ufum *I.* who releafes; and good, 140.

Oyer of Records, &c.
See Tit. Monftrans de Faits.

Proclamation.

Explanation

CHISWICK PRESS:—PRINTED BY WHITTINGHAM AND WILKINS,
TOOKS COURT, CHANCERY LANE.